ST Paul

House

289 Highway

Newton 206

NJ NORTH

07860

LOYALTY FIRST

The Life and Times of Charles A. Willoughby,
MacArthur's Chief Intelligence Officer

DAVID A. FOY

CASEMATE
Philadelphia & Oxford

Published in the United States of America and Great Britain in 2023 by
CASEMATE PUBLISHERS
1950 Lawrence Road, Havertown, PA 19083, USA
and
The Old Music Hall, 106–108 Cowley Road, Oxford OX4 1JE, UK

Hardcover Edition: ISBN 978-1-63624-349-8
Digital Edition: ISBN 978-1-63624-350-4

A CIP record for this book is available from the British Library

Printed and bound in the United Kingdom by CPI Group (UK) Ltd, Croydon, CR0 4YY
Typeset in India by DiTech Publishing Services

For a complete list of Casemate titles, please contact:

CASEMATE PUBLISHERS (US)
Telephone (610) 853-9131
Fax (610) 853-9146
Email: casemate@casematepublishers.com
www.casematepublishers.com

CASEMATE PUBLISHERS (UK)
Telephone (0)1226 734350
Email: casemate-uk@casematepublishers.co.uk
www.casematepublishers.co.uk

To the men and women of the American intelligence
community, past, present and future.

Contents

Preface

While there have been several historical treatments of Major General Charles A. Willoughby, USA, since his passing in 1972, most focusing on his pivotal role during the Korean War, this is the first complete biography of the man MacArthur referred to as "my lovable Fascist." In the context of human history, the time which has elapsed since Willoughby's death is little more than a puff of smoke, too brief a period, perhaps, for true perspective. In any event, the seed from which this work sprang was planted years ago when my reading and research led me to Willoughby—a peripheral comment noted there had been no serious scholarly treatment of a man who, by all accounts, had a profound impact upon the development of Military Intelligence as a legitimate and significant discipline; to that end, my hope is this volume will partially fill that void. The breadth and depth of historical material available on his wartime service is much greater than the record of his non-military life prior to and following World War II, though the general date and place of his birth, combined with his colorful post-World War II career, ensured he would lead an interesting life.

The most important historical resource for a study of Willoughby's life, especially apart from the more-publicized aspects of his Army career, consists of his official papers, some of which he donated to Gettysburg College, Pennsylvania—his *alma mater*—and materials at the MacArthur Museum and Archives, Norfolk, Virginia. In particular, the author is indebted to Catherine Perry, Chris Ameduri, and Ron Couchman, Special Collections/Musselman Library, Gettysburg College; and to James Zobel, Archivist, MacArthur Museum and Archives, Norfolk, Virginia. All demonstrated the combination of helpfulness and subject matter expertise that ensure an historian's best friend will always be the collective librarians and archivists of the world.

Introduction

As military conflicts go, the Korean War is the red-headed stepchild of United States military history—it was historian Clay Blair who reminded us of that unfortunate fact when his book *The Forgotten War: America in Korea, 1950–1953* was published in 1987. Since that date, this oversight has been increasingly corrected, with a plethora of titles in the past three decades, which is commendable. The Korean War proved to be a crucible for the United States and its international allies; less than five years after the victorious conclusion of World War II, they were faced with a formidable challenge in an unfamiliar part of the world, dealing with an unknown enemy, while confronted with the routine military drawdown and focus on restoration of civilian life that usually comes with peace, but which makes a wartime footing so hard to resume.

It was the invasion of the Republic of Korea by their brothers to the north in June 1950 that prompted President Harry Truman to select a commander for the joint American/United Nations military effort on the Korean Peninsula. The choice seemed obvious—who better than the larger-than-life World War II Pacific Theater commander and victor, General Douglas MacArthur? As any competent commander realizes, his choice of staff officers can be critical in securing victory and, of all the staff functions necessary, intelligence had demonstrated its utility, even criticality, ever since the days of the American Revolution and the nation's first spymaster, General George Washington.

Ironically, despite the proven significance of intelligence as a staff function, the best and the brightest military officers, the "fast trackers" destined to wear stars, generally were not found within the military intelligence community, but rather in infantry, artillery, and related combat-arms specialties. Yet, not long after they first met, MacArthur knew he wanted the virtually unknown Charles A. Willoughby as his G-2 (Intelligence Officer). As fate would have it, the German-born Willoughby, with scant intelligence experience, and a raft of undesirable personal and professional traits that would affect his performance, would serve as MacArthur's G-2 for more than a decade, throughout World War II and the Korean War. Early in his career, Willoughby demonstrated a deep-seated desire to follow and serve powerful men known for their authoritarian leadership styles—most notably, Italy's Benito Mussolini, Spain's Francisco Franco, and, yes, Douglas MacArthur—with detrimental results, remaining consistently loyal, perhaps to a fault. This is his life story.

Bellmann

B, Loti = M, ss

Schleswig

Germany

CHAPTER ONE

Of Uncertain Origins: The Early Years of "Sir Charles"

Among the various questions that surround the life of Major General Charles A. Willoughby, perhaps none has been so persistent as that of his origins. Most accounts explain he was born with the last name of Tscheppe-Weidenbach ("willow brook" in German), and that he was allegedly of German birth; however, questions about his shadowy origins persist five decades after his death. The story Willoughby himself told was that he was the product of a German aristocratic father and an American mother, Emma Willoughby, from Baltimore, Maryland—a story which a leading historian writing recently characterized as "generally believed false." At other times, however, he stated that he was an orphan who didn't know his mother or father, his father was the American Consul in Heidelberg, he had three older brothers in the German Army, and his mother was either German or American. One writer has commented that, when Willoughby landed on American soil in 1910, he adopted "what he believed was a suitably aristocratic anglicized name." There is no documented evidence of aristocratic background and a childhood friend claimed both his parents were ethnic Germans. When journalist Frank Kluckhohn, from *The Reporter* magazine, asked Willoughby about this claim, "Sir Charles"—as U.S. Army Lieutenant General Robert Eichelberger dubbed Willoughby—replied he was an orphan who never knew his father and his official biography was that which he had provided to the Army and to *Who's Who in America*. According to ex-Office of Strategic Services officer Carleton West, Willoughby's name should have been pronounced with a "V" instead of a "W," which he thought fitting given Willoughby's authoritarian, arrogant Prussian nature. Even his physical appearance did nothing to remove the scent of aristocracy—"In appearance, his bulk reminded many of Hermann Goering, on whom he consciously modeled himself ... This toadying bully regarded himself as the living embodiment of the old Prussian military caste. During the dark months at the end of 1950 he was to wreak terrible damage upon the United Nations army in Korea," acidly observed one writer, who also noted Willoughby's "arrogance" and "lordly bearing in public" had earned him the moniker of "Sir Charles" early on in life.[1]

Writing in 1952, however, Kluckhohn noted that in the *Who's Who in America, 1950–1951* volume, Willoughby was reportedly the son of Freiherr T. von Tscheppe und Weidenbach and Emma von Tscheppe und Weidenbach, nee Willoughby, and that he was born in Heidelberg on March 8, 1892. The problem is there was only one birth recorded on that date in the Heidelberg registry and that child was Adolf August Weidenbach, listed as the son of ropemaker August Weidenbach and Emma, nee Langhauser. Nor does a standard German genealogical registry clear the fog any; according to the *Gothaisches Genealogisches Taschenbuch der Briefadeligen* (Gothic Genealogical Paperback of the Letter Nobles), General Franz Erich Theodor Tulff von Tschepe (one "p") und Weidenbach had no title of "Freiherr" (Baron) attached to his name and was not authorized by Kaiser Wilhelm II to use the surname "von Tschepe und Weidenbach" until 1913. Furthermore, of the general's five children, none were born in 1892.[2]

While consensus on his place and circumstances of birth remains elusive, there is more unanimity of comments concerning his personality, which was generally true to his presumed Prussian roots, though with a dramatic twist. A fellow officer quipped that "there's probably more of von Stroheim than von Rundstedt about him." One report had it that he always appeared in impeccably tailored uniforms, often sported a monocle, and was remembered by classmates at the U.S. Army Command and General Staff College as "one of the most gifted thespians" to ever play romantic leads in the drama club. He was fond of purple prose, later describing MacArthur's egress from Corregidor to Australia as a "dramatic breakthrough" and, in the self-aggrandizing description of a military history written while at Fort Benning, Georgia, as "monumental."[3]

Others were less kind, referring to him as "an unreliable character";[4] "interesting and highly controversial," with a "background shrouded in mystery"; and "swashbuckling" and "cocksure."[5] The author of a study of United Nations special operations during the Korean War described Willoughby as "MacArthur's most loyal supporter" but added more caustic comments—"imperious and difficult to deal with on even a good day," a man whose reputation "suffers with a rare uniformity of denigrations from virtually all who knew him at the time."[6] His other nicknames reportedly included "Baron von Willoughby," "Bonnie Prince Charles," and "Lord Willoughby."[7] Journalist and author John Gunther described Willoughby as "tall and stout as an ox, with what seems to be a square yard of decorations on his cask-like chest … a man of the world, gay, clever, irreverent."[8] Whatever his true origins, Willoughby emigrated to the United States in 1910, when he was 18, in the company of his parents, became a naturalized citizen, and adopted his mother's maiden name as his last name to celebrate his new beginning. A 1952 letter to Willoughby from a Mrs. Austin Prescott provides additional rationale for Willoughby's coming to the United States; she wrote, "You were young—and had received a great disappointment in having to give up your studies at the University." Given this apparent "financial crisis"—which translated to not enough money for the young "Sir Charles" to finish his degree program—Mrs. Prescott observed "there seemed to be nothing for you in that country [presumably Germany] where you could develop according to your ability." The information about the family's "financial crisis" was in a letter Austin (apparently Mr. Prescott) had received from a Mr. Diehl in Paris; Diehl apparently served with Austin in the Philippines and the arrangement struck was that Austin Prescott would "sponsor" him, and Willoughby's mother would sign the Army enlistment papers and the necessary citizenship application papers. Reportedly, all the necessary documents were signed at the U.S. Embassy in Paris on an unspecified date and Willoughby was bundled off to the United States, arriving in Plattsburgh, New York, with his entire fare paid; thus, whatever else Willoughby may have been, he apparently was not an immigrant. Writing the year after Willoughby's retirement, Mrs. Prescott wrote, "Knowing the struggle that it must have been to start anew in a strange country as an enlisted man—and 'make good' as you have done deserves more than the Drew Pearsons [a prominent journalist of the day and inveterate critic of Willoughby] can understand."[9]

It is not entirely clear whether he enlisted in the U.S. Army as "Adolf Charles Weidenbach" or as "Charles Andrew Willoughby"; however, he did serve with Company K, 5th U.S. Infantry from October 10, 1910 until October 9, 1913, as a private, corporal, and sergeant. Although now a non-commissioned officer, Willoughby nevertheless decided to enter Gettysburg Military College, in Pennsylvania, as a member of the senior class; his advanced placement was based on his supposed previous three years' worth of studies at the University of Heidelberg in Germany and the Sorbonne in Paris, France (though one biographical sketch claims there is no direct evidence he ever attended university in Germany and his claims about being educated in France were never thoroughly investigated). Willoughby graduated from Gettysburg in 1914 with a Bachelor of Arts degree in philology and modern languages, particularly French, Spanish, and German. In May of that year, he was commissioned as a major in the U.S. Army Officers' Volunteer Corps. He then began a graduate program at the University of Kansas, Lawrence, completing a Master of Arts degree, which allowed him to teach languages in 1915–16 at the Howe School for Girls, a private institution located in Howe, Indiana, and in the Modern Languages Department at Racine College in Wisconsin. However, in August 1916, now 24 years old, he left the Reserves to re-enter the U.S. Army as an infantry second lieutenant, under the name Adolf Charles Weidenbach. His first active-duty assignment, in December 1916, was with the 35th Infantry, performing border patrol duty near Nogales, Arizona. He was transferred to the 16th Infantry at Fort Bliss, Texas, and promoted to captain on June 30, 1917, the year the United States entered World War I—ironically fighting soldiers from his native land. In the course of his World War I service, which began in June 1917, Willoughby served with the 16th, 35th, 24th, and 65th Regiments, Infantry, First Division, American

Expeditionary Force. He served on the Mexican border and participated in the 1917–18 manhunt for bandit Pancho Villa. In 1918, he transferred to the air service, training in aviation, flying Nieuport and SPAD fighters and teaching Allied fliers, ultimately commanding the Aviation Instruction Center at Châteauroux, France. While serving as a pilot in France, Willoughby—who, according to fellow flier Eddie Rickenbacker and others, was still known as "Weidenbach"—served as the Executive Officer/Adjutant to the Commandant of the Aviation Training Center at Issoudun, France—Carl "Tooey" Spaatz, the future Commander of Strategic Air Forces in Europe during World War II.[10] Newspaperman C. L. Sulzberger noted the men of this unit—already disgruntled at having been assigned to an air unit with no aircraft—disliked both the personalities, as well as the names, of Spaatz and Weidenbach, whom they collectively referred to as "the Prussians," and that their French hosts were equally suspicious of the pair.

Later allegations that, during his days in France, he was intimately involved with Baroness Elyse Raymonde DeRoche—the first female pilot in the world, who died in a plane crash on July 18, 1919—cannot be substantiated, nor can a similarly tantalizing claim that Willoughby was recalled to Washington in 1917 to, ironically, answer charges made by Army Intelligence that he harbored pro-German sentiments.[11] Although it seems his contribution was from behind a desk rather than in the cockpit, between May and December 1918, "Captain C. A. Willoughby" was one of eight officers mentioned by name in a September 1918 article by Postmaster General Albert S. Burleson as contributing to the beginning of successful operations in the birth of the Aerial Mail Service, which had just been subordinated to the Post Office Department and which had begun the nation's first airmail delivery service, from Washington, D.C., to Garden City, New York.[12]

Following the Great War, in December 1918, Willoughby returned to his home branch, the Infantry, at Fort Benning, Georgia, where he took command of the demonstration machine-gun units in the nascent but soon legendary Infantry School. In October 1919, then-Captain Willoughby was reassigned to the 24th Infantry Division, stationed at Columbus, New Mexico, a unit composed of African-American troops. As his official bio sheet puts it, in a comment reflective of the era, "only officers of recognized disciplinary capacity, combined with great tact, are assigned command of Negro troops." Willoughby served as a company and battalion commander, and it was during his tenure there that Mexican bandit Pancho Villa raided the post. Willoughby then received orders for San Juan, Puerto Rico, where he served in a similar role in the 65th Infantry from February 1921 to May 1923. He next joined the Military Intelligence Division of the War Department for temporary duty, in preparation for assignment as a military attaché abroad. Besides his many other talents, Willoughby discovered his love of the military and his penchant for foreign languages made him an ideal candidate to serve in such a post. From 1923 to 1927, he served in this capacity for the American legations in Caracas,

Venezuela; Bogota, Colombia; and Quito, Ecuador.[13] It was also while working as an attaché that Willoughby met—and in May 1923, married in a ceremony in San Juan, Puerto Rico—Juana Manuela Rodriguez, described as a "Puerto Rican beauty." Less than two years later, the happy couple was blessed with their only child, Olga, on Christmas Eve, 1925.[14]

From his South American vantage point, then-Captain Willoughby surveyed the inter-war period and pondered the possibility of American troops having to fight "savage or semi-civilized foes" in counterinsurgency or contingency operations. In a military journal article discussing the French military presence in Morocco at the time, the imperious Willoughby wrote:

> With the spread of democratic doctrine, half civilized people have promptly taken advantage of the magic formula of self-determination and flaunt it with great effect. Every struggle becomes a struggle for "freedom"; every unwashed savage becomes a potential hero of a war for independence … From China to Mexico, the conception of government by the people, with the observance of certain outwardly republican forms, has repeatedly become a cloak for absolute anarchy, hopeless administrative management, or civil war.

Even at this early juncture, "Sir Charles" was already expressing—in very non-Wilsonian terms—the right-wing political tendencies that would come to the fore following World War II.[15]

It was during Willoughby's tenure as a military attaché in several countries in South America that he learned of the man who would be his "other" great hero—besides MacArthur, of course; that was Spain's dictator, Generalissimo Francisco Franco who, as historian David Halberstam noted, was neither an ally of, nor even a friend to, the United States during World War II. While serving as MacArthur's G-2, Willoughby began working on a biography of the generalissimo, never finished,[16] and in his 1939 work, *The Element of Maneuver in War*, Willoughby described Franco as a "great captain."[17]

Willoughby was equally taken with the first Fascist—Italian dictator Benito Mussolini. Lauding *Il Duce*, Willoughby wrote, "Historical judgment, freed from the emotional haze of the moment, will credit Mussolini with wiping out a memory of defeat by re-establishing the traditional military supremacy of the white race." As the post-World War II years would confirm, such sentiments were not the exception but rather the rule for Willoughby, who also defended Mussolini's 1935 conquest of Ethiopia and criticized the British abolition of slavery in South Africa in the early 1800s.[18] It was while serving as a military attaché in Ecuador that Willoughby received a decoration from Mussolini's government—the Order of Saints Maurizio and Lazzaro—for his assistance to the Italian Pan-American Flight while in Venezuela (1924) and to the Italian Military Mission in Ecuador (1925).[19]

It was also while serving as an attaché that Willoughby published his first book, *House of Bolivar*, a study of the Latin American soldier–statesman Simon Bolivar, a native of Caracas, Venezuela. The governments of Venezuela and Ecuador awarded him several military medals in recognition of his work as a diplomat. It was also during these years that Willoughby became a self-proclaimed military historian and intelligence officer, with only a moderate amount of experience in the former and next to none in the latter; yet he spent the "Roaring Twenties" as an instructor at various Army staff schools, where, as one observer put it, he "began building a brilliant reputation as a military historian and expert on military intelligence." In May 1927, he was transferred to Wyoming's Fort D. A. Russell (renamed Francis E. Warren Air Force Base in 1949), the same year the last cavalry units left the post, and, in September 1928, now promoted to major, traveled to Fort Benning to attend the Infantry School Advanced Course. Graduating in June 1929, he stayed at Fort Benning until August to finish writing *A History of the Infantry School*.[20]

In August 1929, he began the then-two-year course at the U.S. Army's Command and General Staff School (later the Command and General Staff College, CGSC), Fort Leavenworth, Kansas. During his stint there, one student in particular impressed him—future Army Chief of Staff and General, Maxwell Taylor—so much so that, as the librarian, Willoughby requested Taylor be assigned as his assistant, though Taylor managed to sidestep that move.[21]

Following his graduation in June 1931, Willoughby remained at the school as an instructor, teaching courses in military history and intelligence and serving as the editor of the *Command and General Staff School Quarterly*. In 1931, he completed his second book, *The Economic and Military Participation of the United States in the War 1917–1918*, referred to as a "monumental study" and translated into several foreign editions which "did much to orient the Latin-American countries towards the United States and acquaint them with its tremendous military industrial capacity." However, his emerging claim as an historian was somewhat sullied by his failure to come to any conclusions with regard to his topic, prompting one writer to note this lapse "reflects the fact he had not mastered the art of the historian." From July 1932 to May 1934, Willoughby served as the first editor in chief of *Military Review* magazine, published by CGSC, and continued instructing in military history and intelligence. In 1933, he entered a graduate program at the University of Kansas but did not complete it. In later years, the retired major general and septuagenarian would recall that some of his major accomplishments while editor of *Military Review* included adopting a new title for the publication, a new format, and the use of foreign students in the inclusion of summarized articles from foreign publications. The magazine's editor in 1972 noted Willoughby had had "an outstanding career as writer, lecturer, publisher, and editor."[22]

As Willoughby recalled in a 1971 interview with historian D. Clayton James, he first came to the notice of Army Chief of Staff General Douglas MacArthur when the latter made a 1935 visit to the school. MacArthur found Willoughby teaching a course on military history and was so entranced he stayed for the entirety of one of his lectures. As Willoughby remembered the events of almost four decades earlier, he said MacArthur told him later he had picked him as one of his staff officers based on the strength of that brief contact.[23]

Another source claims it was a column in the *Army–Navy Journal* in the early 1920s that brought Willoughby to the attention of MacArthur and the two may have corresponded during the mid-1920s. In any event, legend has it that MacArthur was very impressed by the junior officer when the two met face-to-face. In 1939, Willoughby was assigned to serve as the G-4 (Supply Officer) on the staff of General Grunert in Puerto Rico. MacArthur took over shortly before the United States entered the war and brought Willoughby over, initially as his chief of supply, but soon made him his Assistant Chief of Staff for Intelligence (ACSI), reportedly due to his "extensive intelligence experience." While the exact sequence of events resulting in Willoughby becoming MacArthur's G-2 is a bit murky, the biographer of Clare Booth Luce claims that, while Willoughby was on Grunert's staff, she was so impressed with Willoughby in private conversations with him that she suggested to MacArthur in Fall 1941 that he make him his G-2. By the time Willoughby arrived in the Philippines in 1940, specifically as a logistics officer, he was nevertheless recognized as the intelligence expert on MacArthur's staff, although everyone soon learned he had a more significant—albeit unwritten—job description, what David Halberstam referred to as the "amplifier of the MacArthur myth."[24] In his new role as intelligence chief, he would "repeatedly be a source of controversy, as well as insight, with regard to Japanese strengths and intentions."[25]

During their nearly fifteen years together on a daily basis, "Sir Charles" and Douglas MacArthur enjoyed a special and especially close relationship. On one occasion, MacArthur referred to then-colonel as his "versatile" G-2;[26] Willoughby, fond of colorful expressions, described MacArthur as "a fellow craftsman in a distinguished historical company of great commanders—Napoleon as well as Lee."[27]

Willoughby was often referred to as a "key figure" in MacArthur's inner circle, a member of the near-sacrosanct "Bataan Gang" who would stay with him until ordered off embattled Corregidor to the relative safety of Australia. A recent author has characterized the relationship between MacArthur and his intel chief in this cogent assessment: "No staff officer was ever more skilled in giving the great man [MacArthur] a bath in his own preconceptions than Charles Willoughby."[28] Described as "widely despised," Willoughby could be "intimidating, arrogant, and vindictive"; however, he was no fool—he spoke five languages, including Japanese, and clearly enjoyed the trust and confidence of his commander, no small accomplishment. As is often the case between individuals, those who think alike on a variety of topics are likely to get along well, and such was the case with MacArthur and Willoughby. As historian Alan Millet has pointed out, both disliked "Democrats, the British, most Asians, Washington agencies in general and the navy in particular, army officers who might be critical of [MacArthur's] infallible judgment, potentially unfriendly representatives of the press, civilian diplomats, and Communists, generally defined."[29]

MacArthur referred to Willoughby on occasion as "my lovable fascist" and he clearly was the only intelligence officer who mattered to the general. "Mac" wanted no dissenting voices, no alternative analysis—as far as he was concerned, the business of intelligence was to mesh analysis with what the commander had already decided to do, an attitude that would explain much of what transpired over the coming years.[30]

All of that was still to come in a relationship that would provide the weight and apparent credibility for Willoughby's career. Meanwhile, after graduating from the Army War College in Washington, D.C., in June 1936, the service's pinnacle course for those destined for senior positions, Willoughby began a four-year assignment as an instructor in the Infantry School at Fort Benning and was promoted to lieutenant colonel on June 1, 1938. The following year, he completed *The Element of Maneuver in War*, which traced the art of warfare throughout the 18th century. Willoughby's book became a CGSC textbook, despite Willoughby's prognostications in areas in which he had little or no expertise, notably economics, which detracted from the otherwise noteworthy accomplishment. For example, speaking of Japan, he wrote, "… it may well be acknowledged that under this heading Japan assumes the role of champion of the capitalistic and monetary economy." In broader terms, he also demonstrated his sycophantic nature in the volume, describing the German Chief of the General Staff during World War I, Count Alfred von Schlieffen, as "a superior mind—perhaps a genius."[31]

In February 1940, he served briefly in New York City as the initiator of the War Department's ambitious "Military Dictionary Project," which developed and published pocket-size foreign language dictionaries, which would be valuable during World War II. That June, Willoughby was ordered to Headquarters, Philippine Department, in Manila as the Assistant Chief of Staff (ACS), G-4, where he established a network of roads and ports on Bataan and Corregidor that would prove critical in short order. As Willoughby acclimated to Manila, he spent an increasing amount of time at the Spanish Club, an environment familiar to him from his days as a Latin American attaché. Club members were primarily Spaniards who retained their ties to the mother country rather than to the upstart Philippine Commonwealth. Not surprisingly, the same families who dominated the club controlled most of the wealth in the islands; dominating the business and banking industries in the Philippines, 80 percent of them were political reactionaries, supporters of Franco and the Falangists. In short order, Willoughby soon counted Andrés Soriano, the most influential member of the club and one of the richest men in the Philippines, as one of his closest friends. A close personal friend of Francisco Franco—who appointed him honorary consul general in Manila—Soriano was also a close personal friend of two other individuals in Willoughby's circle—General MacArthur and Major General Courtney Whitney, who was a promoter and lawyer in Manila prior to the war.[32]

In the days immediately preceding the Pearl Harbor attack, the sentiment in the Philippines was that war between Japan and the United States was imminent and that, in any such war, Franco would side with the Axis Powers. For Soriano and his fellow travelers in the Philippines, such a turn of events would undoubtedly result in the confiscation of their extensive land and other holdings in the islands. So, Soriano applied for Philippine naturalization, a request which—despite the objections of the Civil Liberties Union of the Philippines—was quickly and quietly granted. When the Japanese attack came, Soriano volunteered and was made a captain in the Filipino Army. Present at Bataan and Corregidor, he flew out of the Philippines with President Manuel Quezon shortly after MacArthur and Willoughby made their dramatic departure by PT (patrol torpedo) boat and aircraft. When the Philippine duo arrived in Washington, D.C., Quezon promptly appointed Soriano Secretary of Finance in the Philippine government-in-exile. A hue and cry rose from members of the U.S. Congress, who were flummoxed by the presence within an Allied government of a man who, just a few months prior, had been a leading fascist and an ally of the enemies of the United States. Calls for Soriano's resignation were blunted when MacArthur's headquarters in Australia invited the larger-than-life Filipino to join the general's staff as a colonel. Soriano accepted the gracious offer and was at MacArthur's side during his triumphant return to the Philippines, serving as one of two principal advisors on Philippine politics and business.[33]

It was, of course, in the Philippines that Willoughby fell under the considerable sway of MacArthur (then Chief of Staff of the Philippine Army), the individual who would shape his life more powerfully than any other. On November 12, 1941, MacArthur signed General Order No. 26: "By command of Lieutenant General MacArthur, Colonel Charles A. Willoughby (O-4615), General Staff Corps, is announced as Assistant Chief of Staff, G-2, United States Army Forces in the Far East." The Order was signed by Chief of Staff Brigadier General Sutherland. The formality of the act simply confirmed what everyone already knew—namely that, since 1940, Willoughby had been recognized as the intelligence expert on staff.[34]

The deteriorating diplomatic relations between Japan and the United States in the Pacific region prior to Pearl Harbor afforded Willoughby the opportunity to further practice the intelligence craft he sought to perfect and in which he could train others. As MacArthur's G-2, Willoughby had access to the *Magic* file of intercepts of Japanese Navy communications and concluded, in hindsight analysis, these intercepts by a competent intelligence officer with some tactical background would have led "instantly to the unmistakable conclusion that Pearl Harbor naval installations were a target for attack, with November 25th or 29th as the deadlines ..."[35] However, tempting conclusions about Willoughby's prescience as an intelligence officer should be tempered by his tendency, proven repeatedly over time, to minimize his flaws, especially with regard to intelligence analysis.

Following the December 7, 1941, Japanese attack on Pearl Harbor that brought the United States formally into World War II, Willoughby was at MacArthur's side as the Japanese assault reached the Philippine island of Corregidor. As a vaunted

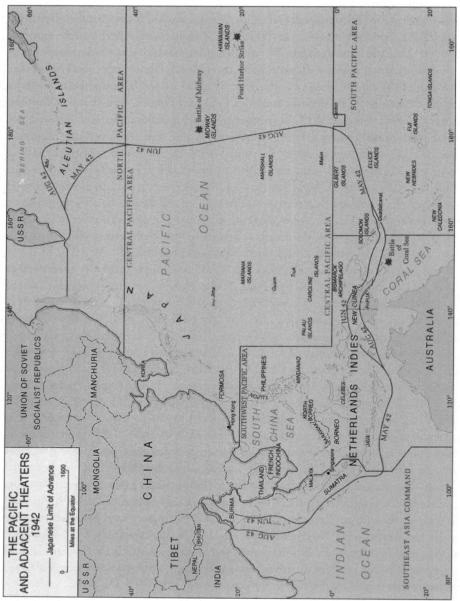

The Pacific and Adjacent Theaters, 1942. (U.S. Army Center of Military History)

"Bataan Gang" member—described by a pair of MacArthur biographers as "an exclusive group that resented and suspected 'outsiders',"[36] Willoughby was one of 13 staff officers and civilians evacuated from Corregidor on March 11, 1942, on PT boats 32, 34, and 35—MacArthur and his family departed on the leading vessel, PT-41.[37] Willoughby was aboard PT-35, which had missed the designated rendezvous point and did not reach Cagayan until March 13, causing more than a few anxious moments.[38] The voyage almost turned tragic when, in a thick fog, PT-32—convinced it was under attack by a Japanese destroyer—nearly fired a torpedo at PT-41. At the last second, an Army officer recognized the PT boat and called out "Hold fire!" When Willoughby later learned of the near-disaster, he commented, "It was close—a real 'squeaker.'"[39]

CHAPTER TWO

"Sir Charles" in the Pacific, 1942–45

On December 8, 1941, as the U.S. Pacific Fleet was assessing the damage wrought by the surprise attack on Pearl Harbor, Hawaii, the Japanese launched air strikes on the Philippines, destroying half of MacArthur's air assets, as well as ground assaults by the Japanese Fourteenth Army, which landed at Lingayen Gulf and quickly routed the inexperienced Filipino troops. Faced with the rapidly advancing Japanese juggernaut, MacArthur ordered a retreat to the Bataan Peninsula where, on February 22, 1942, he was ordered by President Franklin Roosevelt to leave the Philippines for Australia but purposely delayed his departure for two weeks; by early May, American forces in the Philippines had surrendered to the Japanese.[1] Willoughby the soldier personally engaged in combat during the fighting on Bataan and was awarded the Silver Star for "gallantry in action." His award citation read:

> For gallantry in action in the vicinity of Agloloma Bay, Bataan, Philippine Islands, on January 24, 1942. During an attack to expel an enemy landing party, Colonel Willoughby, who was engaged in a reconnaissance of the general area, voluntarily joined in the attack when he learned that the company commander had been wounded and that the company was without an officer. This gallant officer assisted in reorganizing stragglers, and in the face of heavy enemy small arms fire and mortar fire, demonstrated courage and leadership in proceeding through heavy jungle terrain to a position within twenty yards of the enemy line. After the initial attack, Colonel Willoughby disregarded enemy snipers in administering first aid to a wounded officer and assisted him to the rear. The example of the courage and leadership displayed by this staff officer was a significant factor in the ultimate success of the attack.

This level of commendation for an intelligence/staff officer vice a field commander is noteworthy. Also of note is that the Filipino unit involved was the Philippine Constabulary Battalion, which held a defensive sector on the China Coast, and was commanded by Colonel M. Castaneda, a former pupil of Willoughby's at the Infantry School.[2]

Although MacArthur would live to fight another day, thanks to the intervention of the president, he was clearly unhappy about the circumstances. Those who observed MacArthur at his headquarters in Brisbane, Australia, in June 1942 described him as "tired and depressed" and even sympathetic correspondent and Corregidor

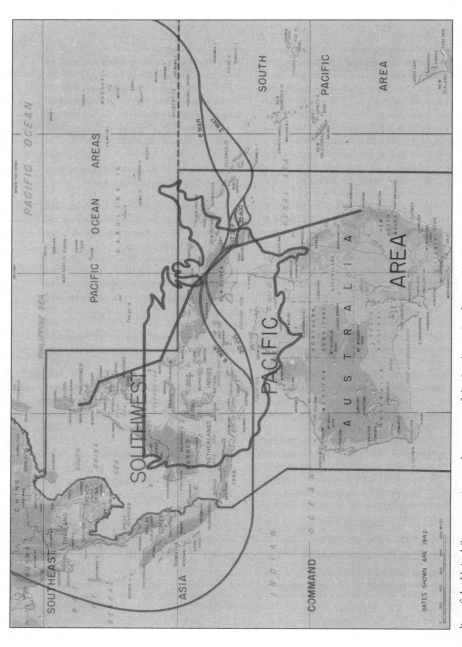

The outline of the United States superimposed on a map of the Southwest Pacific Area (SWPA), to reiterate Willoughby's characterization of the conflict as a "war of distances." (Plate 12, *Reports of General MacArthur: The Campaigns of MacArthur in the Pacific*, Volume 1)

veteran Clark Lee admitted that "Mac was hard to get along with in those early Australia days."[3]

In light of the ultimate outcome, nearly four long years distant in early 1942, it is easy to forget the unique geography of World War II in the Pacific Theater—while other theaters during the war were also of considerable size, no other involved such long distances over water from the very beginning, a fact that posed an endless series of logistical problems. It was nearly four thousand miles from Melbourne, Australia, to Manila, capital of the Philippines, 3,900 from Pearl Harbor to Tokyo. As Willoughby once noted, the war in the Pacific Theater was truly "the War of Distances." As newly arrived officers at MacArthur's headquarters in Melbourne could attest, they were immediately presented with a wall-size map of the Southwest Pacific, with a map of the 48 states imposed on it, all to drive home the harsh geographic reality. Willoughby often referred to logistical difficulties in the Southwest Pacific as "something tremendous" and also stressed the extended lines of communication with which they all had to contend. As the ranking intelligence officer, "Sir Charles" no doubt also felt compelled to point out that "the entire route was by water at a time when the Japanese Navy was undefeated and roaming the Pacific almost at will."[4]

MacArthur enjoyed a reputation in the Philippines only slightly lower than that of a god, a spirit mimicked by his newly appointed intelligence chief. Willoughby once described MacArthur's arrival in the Philippines in these fawning words: "Constantly on the front line—at times well ahead of it—his sheer physical endurance and his reckless exposure of himself excited the native population and even his own forces to a pitch of effort that became the dismay of the enemy."[5] Such sycophancy would follow Willoughby into, and beyond, the Korean War. And, in somewhat more measured terms, MacArthur returned the favor; he once described his staff in the Philippines as "unsurpassed in excellence," consisting of such "outstanding figures" as "Willoughby in Intelligence."[6] But others have argued MacArthur's adoring subordinates served him poorly. Roosevelt biographer Eric Larrabee critically noted, "General MacArthur was ill-served by his admirers, who enveloped him in a cloud of exaggerated claims that have to be dispelled before anything like reality is visible."[7]

To hear the *Gettysburg College Bulletin* tell the story, Willoughby also made quite an impression in the Philippines not long after his arrival. Midway through the war, the paper described in overblown terms how well the German native had adapted to the Islands: "His sureness and adaptability to varied situations made General MacArthur raise him to assistant chief-of-intelligence *(sic)* before the war broke out."[8] Still possessed of a thick Teutonic accent, even after three decades in the United States, the man known to some subordinates as "the Prussian drillmaster" or "Sir Charles" was already described by others as a "tough professional, skilled in his trade,"[9] a part of MacArthur's "competent HQ staff" in July 1941.[10] However, in 2016, historian Arthur Herman commented that Willoughby "would repeatedly be a source of controversy, as well as insight, with regard to Japanese strengths and intentions."[11] He was apparently disliked almost as much as Chief of Staff Lieutenant General Richard K. Sutherland, "which was saying a lot," in the opinion of one writer, who described Willoughby as "pompous, overbearing, arrogant, big and strong, called 'Sir Charles' behind his back. The real problem, however, was that Willoughby frequently colored his analyses with unsupported opinions, contradictions, and idle speculation."[12]

And "Sir Charles" made a less than auspicious impression, both initial and lingering, upon fellow officers, most notably Sutherland, who had a "cordial dislike" for him and who, on several occasions, openly stated he would relieve him of his duties as the Assistant Chief of Staff G-2 at Headquarters Southwest Pacific Area (SWPA). Brigadier General Elliott R. Thorpe—Willoughby's counterpart Assistant Chief of Staff G-2 at U.S. Army Forces in the Far East (a strictly American command, as opposed to the multinational SWPA)—noted he could always tell when Willoughby and Sutherland had crossed swords; Willoughby would be shorn of one duty or another which then became Thorpe's responsibility. Thorpe would later write, "I think this officer's [Willoughby] talents were completely summed up by another general of the MacArthur staff who said, 'Willoughby has the best hindsight of any intelligence officer in the army.'"[13] Others concurred in that caustic assessment. "Willoughby's affectations," wrote one historian, "including his polished, Prussian-like manners, continued to irritate many on the staff. His inconsistent and sometimes wildly off-the-mark intelligence estimates irritated them more, although MacArthur never seemed to lose faith in the man who was, above all, dedicated to MacArthur officially and personally."[14]

Despite the strident criticisms, in April 1942, MacArthur announced "Sir Charles" had been appointed G-2, ACSI, General Headquarters, Southwest Pacific Area; on June 20, Willoughby was promoted to brigadier general (temporary). It was at this juncture he began to realize the scope of his new responsibilities; in addition to his own weak intelligence background, collecting intelligence in the Pacific Theater had its own challenges, and there was essentially no foundation for such an effort, leaving him to essentially begin from scratch.[15]

But, always a quick learner, Willoughby began making intelligence preparations for the anticipated Japanese assault, whenever it might come. He began working collaboratively with a Captain (later Colonel) Joseph R. McMicking, the scion of a wealthy Spanish–Filipino family. Born in Manila, well-educated, and well-traveled throughout the islands, with numerous contacts, McMicking became the youngest and only Filipino on MacArthur's staff. He had left the Philippines with MacArthur on March 12, 1942, to help set up the South West Pacific Command in Australia. Prior to the move to Corregidor, he and Willoughby were working on a plan for select communications workers to go underground and form clandestine nets should the Japanese attack. He had an important role in the organization of the Philippine resistance network and developed detailed procedures for guerrilla currency exchange. He would accompany MacArthur on his return to the Philippines on October 20, 1944, as part of the landing on the island of Leyte.[16]

As the Japanese advanced on Manila, American and Filipino troops were compelled to retreat to Corregidor, where Willoughby, serving as Assistant Chief of Staff, Headquarters, Southwest Pacific Area, shared an office with Chief of Staff Sutherland and others.[17]

Willoughby was among those who, in January 1942, had advised MacArthur that Philippine President Manuel Quezon was too ill to move from Corregidor to the United States.[18] MacArthur and Quezon had a very special relationship, born of the former's love of the Philippines and the latter's near deification of the general. For years since the war, there had been ugly rumors about the president of the besieged Philippine Islands bestowing an embarrassingly lavish gift on MacArthur, and others, that seemed particularly offensive given the shortage of everything else at the time. In 1978, MacArthur biographer Carol Petillo found the incriminating letter, formally known as "Special Executive Order from President Quezon," aka Executive Order No. 1, which awarded MacArthur $500,000 for his service to the Philippine Military Mission, as well as $75,000 to Richard Sutherland and lesser amounts to several others. Oddly enough, this award did not make the pages of Willoughby's *magnum opus*, *MacArthur, 1941–1951*, and there is no indication he received any monetary award as part of this bequeath.[19]

On one notable occasion, Willoughby was dispatched on a mission of critical importance to MacArthur, one which directly involved Quezon. In February 1942, MacArthur learned President Roosevelt would be making a radio speech telling of the thousands of aircraft on their way to war … in Europe. MacArthur correctly assumed that not only would Quezon hear the news but that he would be incensed when he heard the reporting. He thus dispatched Colonel Willoughby to go to Quezon and somehow placate him. When Willoughby walked to the Filipino president's tent, located on a slope near the Malinta Tunnel on Corregidor, Willoughby found him in his wheelchair, angrily listening to Roosevelt's speech. At the end of his speech, Quezon unleased a Spanish-language tirade at Willoughby, which translated to:

> For thirty years I have worked and hoped for my people. Now they burn and die for a flag that could not protect them. I cannot stand this constant reference to Europe. I am here and my people are here under the heels of a conqueror. Where are the planes that they boast of? America writhes in anguish at the fate of a distant cousin, Europe, while a daughter, the Philippines, is being raped in the backroom.

Willoughby calmed the exasperated Quezon down until he could meet with MacArthur later that day. Aware of Quezon's ill health and always planning ahead, in March 1942, MacArthur appointed a wealthy, influential Filipino friend of Quezon's, Manuel y Acuna Roxas, MacArthur's and Quezon's choice of successor, a reserve brigadier general on Willoughby's G-2 staff. MacArthur's intention was to retain Roxas as a source of Filipino political intelligence, a fact known to very few, but including Willoughby, who commented to an accomplice, "Roxas has been our man [in Manila] all the time." Only conflicting loyalties among Japanese overlords in the Philippines at the time saved him from summary execution.[20]

As both MacArthur and Willoughby demonstrated, apparently the more time one spent in the Pacific, the less events elsewhere in the world were of concern.[21] In 1943, Willoughby commented to Lieutenant Colonel Gerald Wilkinson, a British liaison officer who reported directly to Prime Minister Winston Churchill, that the Allied strategy should be to stop fighting in Europe and "let Nazism mellow and encourage the Germans and the Russians to kill each other off." As shocking as such a statement might seem, these words only reflected, predictably, the views of MacArthur, that the "main enemy" was Japan, not Germany. To reiterate the point, when distinguished poet and playwright Robert Sherwood arrived at MacArthur's headquarters in the Philippines with news of General Omar Bradley's troops taking the Ludendorff Bridge at Remagen, Germany, on March 7, 1945, Willoughby sourly remarked, "We don't give a god damn out here for anything that happens in Europe." In relating this incident to President Roosevelt, Sherwood characterized it as "unmistakable evidence of an acute persecution complex at work."[22]

Willoughby was expecting a Japanese attack on the Philippines in June 1942—not December 8, 1941—though he did add that "it might come sooner." It is possible, though unproven, Willoughby had adjusted his prediction of when the Japanese might attack, aware MacArthur did not want the Japanese to move until he was ready for them. However, two biographers of MacArthur assess that "Otherwise, Willoughby predicted with great accuracy the Japanese strategy and tactics for the invasion." The fact he was wildly off in his prognostication of the timing of the Japanese assault "simply means that he was in a numerous and distinguished company which included nearly every American official from Roosevelt down."[23]

In confronting the Imperial Japanese Army in combat, American commanders faced a formidable challenge, and what would prove to be a painful education, for various reasons. Perhaps most critically, they faced a dearth of information on a foe they apparently never expected to face, an opponent on whom there was very little order-of-battle information in 1942. Similarly, largely due to the inter-service rivalries that would lessen during the war, though never disappear, there was no means of sharing intelligence between the various theaters of war. Thus, information on Japanese combat techniques from the China–Burma–India Theater might never reach the South West Pacific Theater, and vice-versa, negating the potential value of any "lessons learned" from having encountered them in combat previously.[24]

As their Allied opponents soon discovered, the heart-and-soul of the Imperial Japanese Army was its infantry arm—a peasant army accustomed to hard phys- ical labor, characterized by a high level of endurance and a heightened sense of self-discipline. The service was dedicated to the proposition that competently led and properly motivated troops could best a more numerous, technically superior foe. Such Western-bred military concepts as initiative and the importance of "lessons learned" were repressed, leading, ironically, to a condescending view of Western forces in general, including those of the United Kingdom and the United States in particular. Stealth and deception were hallmarks of the emperor's soldiers, who would sometimes set off fireworks to confuse the foe. A former member of the American military attaché's staff in Tokyo attested to "the superb offensive spirit which permeates all of the armed forces of the Empire" and assessed that perhaps American troops needed "spiritual training" like the Japanese, in order to develop a more aggressive spirit, the sort of mentality reflected in the following extract, from a captured Japanese diary:

> I am glad to participate in this great mission as a Japanese. I am sure that the dawn of greater East Asia is near. Morale is high and my belief in ultimate victory is firm. I shall never give in until the enemy is destroyed. [Our] country is God's country and I am son of God, hence I shall fear nobody. I shall smilingly undertake this mission. Long live the Emperor.

It was, of course, the basic task of G-2, Army Intelligence, to research its foes and assess its combat capabilities but there proved to be no effective means to disseminate whatever intelligence was gleaned to War Department policy makers, limiting the value of such to tactical and operational levels, if that, rather than to the strategic, war-winning level. The unfortunate result was that the War Department entered World War II with a very skewed picture of Japanese combat capabilities, leaving America to fight an unfamiliar opponent.[25]

Colonel Alison Ind, who would be a critical part of Willoughby's emerging intelligence system in the SWPA, believed Willoughby deserved credit for the foundational work he had to do in order to serve MacArthur's intelligence needs. As Ind put it, "Willoughby, who had been told to 'land on your feet running,' gave every appearance of having done so in his tremendous efforts to overcome the dearth of intelligence information. In rapid order he planned and secured approvals for half-a-dozen projects that were to be of great importance," such as the Allied Geographical Section and Allied Translator and Interpreter Service (ATIS). Ind continued, "He created and instilled efficiency into organizations for processing the strategic information that came from all over the Allied world as well as the meager bits and pieces that came from the immediate tactical front." When Ind reported to Willoughby at the bank building located at 121 Collins Street, Melbourne, the latter immediately handed Ind a sheaf of Top Secret files from the Australian Commander-in-Chief, General Thomas Blamey. The Australian, a conventional, old-school soldier, had no interest in dealing with such tawdry documents as reports from saboteurs, secret agents, Coastwatchers, commandos, and those of such ilk.[26]

Even in the days preceding American entry into World War II, MacArthur and Willoughby were of one mind when it came to the involvement—usually viewed as "interference"—of non-U.S. Army entities in the South West Pacific Theater; in short, both were opposed to such "help." Journalist Douglas Waller stated it is "undeniable" that MacArthur was "constitutionally incapable of working jointly with almost everybody" and that he "demanded total control of every outfit in his theater." It is little wonder, then, that Willoughby mimicked MacArthur's professional dislike for a former brother-in-arms, Major General William J. Donovan, better known as "Wild Bill." MacArthur and Donovan had both served in the 42nd "Rainbow" Division during World War I—MacArthur as Chief of Staff and Donovan as Commander of the "Fighting 69th" Infantry Regiment. Though both received multiple awards for their service, it was Donovan who received the Medal of Honor, a slight which some argue loomed large in the relationship, but which others minimize. Donovan had major plans in mind for the Coordinator of Information (COI), which dated to late 1941, and its successor, the Office of Strategic Services (OSS), which stood up in June 1942. However, "Wild Bill" faced powerful critics in the War and Navy Departments who saw no need for an organization such as OSS. Three weeks prior to the Pearl Harbor attack, journalist and COI employee Edgar Ausell Mowrer had met MacArthur to brief him on COI capabilities; MacArthur "saw no reason for the creation of a new intelligence service under Donovan." He had changed his tune by December 28, all but begging for COI materials to counteract the effects of Japanese propaganda on his forces, then besieged on Bataan and Corregidor. The office responded, with materials broadcast over the 12 radio stations still in American/Filipino hands.[27]

Not opposed to Donovan on a personal level, Willoughby, along with his deputy, Colonel R. F. Merle-Smith, simply believed there was nothing the OSS could do in the Pacific Theater that G-2 couldn't do better. Willoughby's professional disagreements with Donovan may also have been a reflection of the former's crossing swords in 1942–43 with General George Veazey Strong, a West Point graduate and law professor at the Academy, who was the head of Military Intelligence in Washington, D.C., at the time. Strong was also the keeper of such intelligence crown jewels as the *Magic* intercepts in the Pacific and the *Ultra* signals intercepts of German coded military transmissions. One author has described Strong at the time as "the most powerful intelligence figure in Washington."[28] As one historian has noted, "The imperious and conventional warfare-minded Pacific commander, General Douglas MacArthur, simply banned the OSS from his domain." Part of the bone of contention between Willoughby and Donovan was the former's presumption OSS would be carrying out "raids" in the Pacific Theater, indistinguishable from military operations—the proper domain of MacArthur and Willoughby.[29] Donovan biographer Corey Ford asserts Willoughby's ego played a role in the frayed OSS–FECOM (Far East Command) relationship as well, fearing cooperation with Donovan would detract from the attention paid to *his* intelligence unit. Others believed that, as a West Pointer and a stickler for the chain of command, MacArthur objected to the presence of a uniformed civilian in his theater acting independently and having the ear of powerful personalities in Washington.[30]

In the wake of increasing complaints that MacArthur and Willoughby were actively shutting OSS out of the SWPA, Willoughby responded that MacArthur could not wait for COI to send personnel to Australia "to get up and running." Ever defensive of his protective boss, Willoughby also stressed that difference in the war to the west and to the east. The war in Asia, as he pointed out, had been a shooting war from the outset, meaning MacArthur "had to improvise his intelligence from scratch with the Japanese breathing down his neck. He could not sit back and ransack libraries, even assuming the data were there."[31]

In early July 1942, Donovan made his initial proposal to the Joint Chiefs to establish an OSS network in Australia, an idea rejected out-of-hand by MacArthur and the Joint Intelligence Committee (JIC). A determined Donovan then attempted to use the "good offices" of Army Chief of Staff General George Marshall to pass to MacArthur a proposal to create an OSS Secret Intelligence Group in the Netherlands East Indies, supervised by Dr. Amry Vandenbosch. Within 48 hours, MacArthur replied that such a capability already existed within his headquarters and, if they needed assistance, they would request such from Vandenbosch. General Strong, dual-hatted as the Chairman of the JIC and Chief, War Department General Staff's Military Intelligence Division, backed MacArthur, adding the Joint Chiefs had delegated authority to theater commanders to determine what intelligence activities would occur in their respective theater. OSS personnel would spend the next two years trying to get their foot in the door of MacArthur's command.[32]

Eager to please his similarly-minded boss, and supremely confident of his own abilities as an intelligence officer, Willoughby set to work to create an intelligence structure that would secure Allied victory, albeit on his and his liege's own terms. As a consummate senior Army officer, Willoughby was dedicated to, as he put it, "strenuous efforts to maintain and defend basic staff principles, particularly the absolute centralization of intelligence and the operational control of GHQ intelligence agencies."[33]

A relative flurry of intelligence-related organization followed; in June 1942, MacArthur called in Willoughby—described as "shrewd, incisive, and demanding"—and tasked him with the creation of a large undercover warfare capability that would aid in the ultimate defeat of the Japanese. The Supreme Commander envisioned hundreds of spies operating behind Japanese lines, conducting acts of murder and sabotage in hit-and-run fashion, always keeping the enemy off-guard. A robust propaganda campaign would augment the direct-action element of MacArthur's plan. In hushed tones, Willoughby's Deputy G-2, Colonel Merle-Smith, delegated Willoughby's tasking to then-Captain Ind, who set the wheels in motion to create what was ultimately known as the Allied Intelligence Bureau (AIB), MacArthur's envisioned undercover warfare organization, which included a variety of intelligence and special operations groups. More specifically, the AIB was tasked with the clandestine collection of intelligence in enemy-held areas, usually by means of radio supplemented by couriers. It also had the challenging responsibility of coordinating and deconflicting the various activities of American, British, Dutch, and Australian intelligence units. In this sense, it directly contributed to Allied sabotage, espionage, irregular warfare operations, and the support of indigenous resistance movements. Its most well-known representatives were the Coastwatchers, the Australian creation of 1939 which set up observation posts along the coasts of New Guinea and the Solomons and used the local populace to report on Japanese air and naval movements.[34]

Created in July 1942 and commanded by Australian Brigadier C. G. Roberts, the AIB consisted of five sections—two functional and devoted to special operations, and three regional—the Northeast (i.e., eastern New Guinea and the surrounding islands), Netherlands East Indies, and the Philippines—devoted to intelligence. Roberts' two deputies were two Americans, the now-promoted Lieutenant Colonel Ind and Major Bob B. Glenn. In terms of subordination, Roberts answered to MacArthur's Chief of Staff, Sutherland, and to Willoughby, MacArthur's G-2. Predictably, such a polyglot organization contained headstrong individuals with specific ideas as to what the AIB should be doing; while many of the field leaders emphasized sabotage and espionage operations, Roberts and Willoughby were more focused on intelligence collection to help turn the tide on the battlefield. Over time, they decided to reorganize the disparate organization along geographic lines, with section leaders responsible for both sabotage/espionage operations and intelligence-collection duties. Sometimes referred to as "MacArthur's OSS," the AIB—which grew to a force of 3,000—served as a convenient excuse for keeping Donovan's OSS out of the theater. It also contributed to the ultimate Allied victory by killing or capturing some eight thousand Japanese, rescuing more than a thousand Allied personnel from behind enemy lines, and, most significantly, collecting valuable intelligence from its 264 long-range reconnaissance elements. For its accomplishments, the AIB suffered some 400 casualties during the war.[35]

The following month, Willoughby created the Allied Geographical Section (AGS), focused on collecting Pacific Theater geographical information, to establish a baseline for the largely unknown, uncharted, and expansive area. Ultimately, the AGS created 200,000 copies of 110 terrain studies, 62 terrain handbooks, and 101 special reports on various aspects of the geography of the Southwest Pacific. In August, he organized an Order of Battle Section, to conduct the all-important task of locating specific Japanese units and assessing their leadership, equipment, tactics, and most likely courses of action. And, on September 19, 1942, Willoughby replaced the Australian Combined Services Detailed Interrogation Centre in

Brisbane with the American-led ATIS, headed by fluent Japanese speaker Colonel Sidney F. Mashbir.[36]

Willoughby had met Mashbir during General Pershing's expedition targeting Pancho Villa, when the former was a young officer with the 1st Arizona Infantry. Impressed with Mashbir's ideas for translation work, Willoughby entrusted him with ATIS. The Service began modestly, with Mashbir, Major David Swift, eight Nisei linguists (adult children of Japanese immigrants to the United States), and three enlisted clerks.[37] Eventually, the unit would consist of 40 multi-lingual officers and men from the Australian, Canadian, and British armies, along with a smattering of White Russians, East Indies Netherlanders, and a handful of Americans. The mission of the unit was to "coordinate and expedite the translation of captured enemy documents and prompt collation and distribution of the results." Willoughby bemoaned his difficulties in finding the linguists he needed, reiterating an old complaint that "linguist requirements for the European theater of war could have been met without leaving the sidewalks of New York City, but there was a vastly different story in the Far East." The dearth of Japanese linguists was eventually alleviated by the contribution of both Australian and American bodies and ATIS, whose numbers included some four thousand Nisei, and which eventually interviewed over fourteen thousand prisoners and translated 20 million pages of enemy documents.[38]

Willoughby had also benefited from and generally recognized the value of signals intelligence (SIGINT). For example, not long after arriving in Australia, he was exposed to intercepted enemy radio traffic, which was analyzed in a small hut outside the gate at Fort McKinley, the Philippines, known as Station 6. However, there were often multi-day delays in getting the decrypted messages back to Willoughby, who routinely edited the information before passing it to the theater commander.[39]

A more mature and valuable SIGINT intercept capability was embodied in the Central Bureau (CB), a multi-national and joint cryptologic unit Willoughby established in 1942 to engage in code-breaking and that most ungentlemanly of pursuits, "reading the enemy's mail." Headed by Colonel Spencer B. Akin, a former U.S. Army Signal Corps officer in Panama, the CB collected communications intelligence gathered by four American radio intelligence companies and 10 similar British Commonwealth units. This element was among those ordered to Australia to escape the clutches of the Japanese as they swept over the Philippines. Once the unit arrived in Melbourne, the American element of the CB—the Army's 2nd Signal Company—was reinforced with the addition of the 837th Signal Service Detachment, to form the distinctly American element of the multi-national unit. MacArthur soon determined that intelligence based on intercepts of enemy traffic were of little value to him in his defense of the "Land Down Under," so its care and keeping originally fell to the land deputy, Australian General Blamey. The original intent behind the CB, which moved to Ascot Racetrack, five miles outside Brisbane in September 1942, was that it be a multi-national SIGINT analysis organization from the get-go, and so it remained, though Americans normally comprised half its strength. Manned by some one thousand personnel in 1943, it would soar to over four thousand before war's end. MacArthur's attitude toward the CB, which might have been characterized as *laissez-faire*, was powerfully altered by his concern about sloppy Australian operational security procedures, which prompted him to make Willoughby responsible for the CB, which he would be throughout the duration of the war. Under the watchful eye of Willoughby, the CB disseminated its collected and analyzed intelligence in the form of Special Intelligence Bulletins, which in the SWPA environment soon became known as "Willoughby Bulletins." However, distribution of the intelligence product was limited to MacArthur, his Chief of Staff General Sutherland, and the G-3; noticeably missing from the distribution list was MacArthur's air deputy and Fifth Air Force Commander, Major General George Kenney.[40]

While as a theater commander MacArthur may have had little use for the SIGINT emerging from the CB, others did. For example, in May 1943, Army Chief of Staff General George Marshall sent a letter to MacArthur outlining the standard policy on the use of the intercepted and decoded Japanese diplomatic messages, collectively known to the Allies as *Magic*. More resistant to outside influence than most, MacArthur viewed this letter as yet another example of Washington interference in SWPA SIGINT business and so did not respond to Marshall for two months. When he did deign to respond, he said such an idea violated the concept of military organization and that, given his druthers, he would just as soon not have such an entity in his theater. During a subsequent visit to Washington, D.C., MacArthur acceded to his boss's request, but insisted the SSOs (Signals Security Officers) be "under my control for administration and discipline." To the surprise of no one assigned to SWPA, both MacArthur and his senior staffers—no doubt including Willoughby—viewed SSOs from Washington with suspicion throughout the war. As one author noted, it would be "tempting to conclude that MacArthur's apparent dismissal of SIGINT from Washington lay in his egotism," though a more dispassionate conclusion would be that the theater commander already felt well served with his current intelligence capabilities.[41] His intelligence chief shared his boss's misgivings and did so over the course of the war. In 1945, Willoughby complained, "… the Melbourne station is under direct orders of Washington, is not bound by local responsibilities, forwards what they select, and when it suits them. The possibility of erroneous or incomplete selection is as evident now as it was in 1941."[42]

In the immediate aftermath of the European War, Willoughby, as MacArthur's right-hand intelligence man for the continuing Pacific conflict, had the opportunity to testify at the Pearl Harbor hearings concerning the extensive use by the British ally of the super-secret *Ultra* intercepts of German naval codes, which provided a tremendous advantage for the Allies during the war. However, Willoughby knew

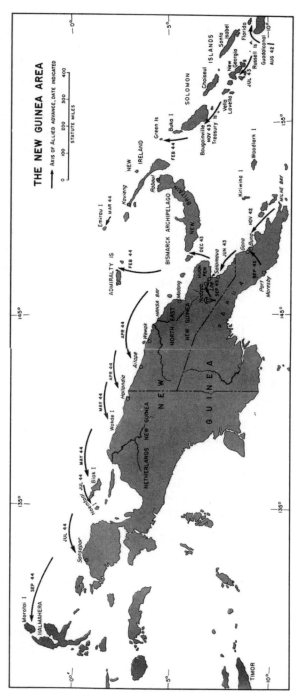

New Guinea, 1942–44. (U.S. Army Center of Military History)

full well his beloved U.S. Army was not being provided with much, if any, of this treasure. This gap was neatly filled as a result of the actions of Royal Air Force (RAF) officer Benjamin King, who had been transferred from the Bletchley Park headquarters of His Majesty's Government Code and Cypher School, where the clandestine decryption of the German signals intelligence occurred, to Washington. King arranged for American naval intelligence routinely passed to England to be repeated to him through the normal Army/RAF channels, allowing him to pass on critical information to his starved U.S. Army colleagues. In his testimony, Willoughby caustically noted that "in an otherwise meritorious desire for security (though every modern nation knows that cryptanalysis is going on) the Navy has shrouded the whole enterprise in mystery, excluding other services."[43]

But squabbles with the Navy were of long duration and not nearly as significant as the relentless move of the Japanese to the south. Planners in Tokyo set their sights on the tempting target of New Guinea, the world's second-largest island (after Greenland), and the front door to Australia. Predictably, Allied assumptions about the actual Japanese target within the sizable boundaries of New Guinea varied. Based on intercepts from Station HYPO, the Navy's codebreaking center at Pearl Harbor, Commander Edwin Layton, the intelligence chief for Commander in Chief, Pacific (CINCPAC) Admiral Chester Nimitz, read the decoded message traffic in late April 1942 and concluded the Japanese target was Port Moresby. Willoughby read the same messages as Layton but, based on the fact there were four Japanese carriers as part of the invasion force, concluded the target was either the northeastern coast of Australia or New Caledonia, a critical location in the "pipeline" connecting the west coast of the United States to Australia. On April 21, Willoughby sent a memo to the Chief of Staff, G-3, which stated:

> On the basis of reported increases of enemy naval forces in the Truk–Rabaul area in the latter part of next week, the strengthening of his air forces at Rabaul, Truk, Wake, and Jaluit, combined with one source of information (Kroner radio, April 15th, derived from "most secret" sources, dated April 11th, to the effect that THERE ARE INDICATIONS OF AN IMPENDING ATTACK ON PORT MORESBY FROM THE SOUTHEAST ON APRIL 21ST) [emphasis in the original] an assumption has been made that the enemy will strike at Port Moresby.

This document, which specifically identified five Japanese airfields within 500 miles that could support such an offensive, continued:

> If an attack is made in early May, (and the concentration of enemy naval forces tends to confirm this belief), the order of priority must be assumed to be, first, the North-East coast of Australia, second, New Caledonia, and last, Port Moresby.

The memo closed with five recommendations to prepare for the expected attack. By May 5, however, Willoughby had altered his assessment; a G-2 *Information Bulletin* issued that day, with the subject line "General review of probably enemy plans," listed probable enemy courses of action, in order from most likely to least likely:

1. Landing at Port Moresby … Probable date, May 5–10th. Estimated strength, one (1) Division
2. Air raids on the North Eastern coast of Australia by Carrier borne planes …
3. Attack on New Caledonia.[44]

Repeatedly thwarted, by November 1942 Japanese forces were resolutely determined to capture the strategic Allied base at Port Moresby, New Guinea, at the southwestern end of the forbidding, 13,000-foot peaks of the Owen Stanley Mountains. As Franklin D. Roosevelt biographer Eric Larrabee noted, "This was miserable country to fight in, a fact at first insufficiently appreciated at MacArthur's headquarters." Privy to *Ultra* intercepts, Willoughby had concluded in mid-summer 1942 that the Japanese were headed for the grassy airfields at Dobodura, 15 miles south of Buna, site of the pre-war center of government, or perhaps Milne Bay, and suggested that G-3 Lieutenant General Chamberlin begin aerial reconnaissance in those areas. Yet, just three days later, Willoughby reversed himself, decided an invasion was not likely, and that the new Japanese movements were intended to shore up present positions on New Guinea rather than establish new ones. By late 1942, Willoughby assessed as "very low" the ability of the Japanese to move their 8,000-man force, under General Horii at Buna–Gona, across the mountains. Willoughby believed instead the Japanese target was airfields and disputed the idea of any "overland movement in strength," in light of the rugged terrain. According to the official U.S. Army history of the campaign, Willoughby "conceded that the Japanese might go as far as the Gap [near the crest of the Owen Stanleys] in order to establish an outpost there, but held it extremely unlikely that they would go further in view of the fantastically difficult terrain beyond," an assessment he held fast to as late as mid-August. Thus, any threat to Port Moresby was either overblown or simply wrong. He confidently assured MacArthur there was no intelligence which indicated the Japanese ships massing off Rabaul were headed to Buna, an assurance which prompted Sutherland and Chamberlin to dismiss such a threat. In part due to the reassurances of his intelligence chief, MacArthur continued to mistakenly believe that Japanese strength on the only avenue down the Owen Stanley Range, the Kokoda Trail, was light and there was little prospect of their attacking Port Moresby. While Willoughby was proven wrong about enemy capabilities, he was spot-on concerning enemy logistics—Japanese troops were approximately 35 miles from their target when they ran out of rice.[45]

MacArthur had ordered all available forces from the Australian mainland to New Guinea and by mid-November they were ready to strike a blow at Japanese forces in the Buna–Gona area on the northeastern coast of Papua, New Guinea. Little thought had been given, however, to actually conducting jungle warfare; there was a shortage of the critical machetes and no insect repellent or waterproof containers.[46] Nevertheless, since Australian forces had earlier blocked the Japanese advance, and they and the Americans of the 32nd Infantry Division had pushed it back across the Owen Stanleys, division-level intelligence estimates were optimistic concerning MacArthur's November 1942 offensive. Although he initially assessed heavy fighting against sizable enemy forces lay ahead, which proved correct, Willoughby nevertheless characterized an Allied victory in the campaign as "practically assured."[47] Although Allied forces were able to overrun the Japanese base and numerous documents and a sophisticated radio were captured, MacArthur was displeased, having heard various reports that American troops were reluctant to fight. As MacArthur viewed the situation, if Japanese forces were feeble, as Willoughby indicated, the only reason the US/Allied offensive would not be gaining ground would be because of "bad leadership on the ground and poor soldier material." In the words of one writer, MacArthur had committed "an untrained and ill-equipped division" against Japanese regulars, and the Allied offensive had ultimately ground to a halt. On the evening of November 30, a predictably grim meeting was underway in MacArthur's headquarters in Port Moresby. Among the attendees was Willoughby, described by another participant in these words:

> Major General Charles Willoughby, MacArthur's intelligence officer, was also present … He was proud, aloof, and distant. His German background and his haughty attitude caused his contemporaries to compare him to a rigid, unfeeling Prussian officer. His greatest attribute was his intense loyalty to MacArthur, which has been cemented by service on Bataan. Willoughby could point out problems to his boss, but he also had no solutions now.[48]

At the recommendation of Chief of Staff General Sutherland, MacArthur summoned U.S. Marine Corps Lieutenant General Robert Eichelberger to take command of the stalled offensive; his terse command guidance to the marine was, "Take Buna or don't come back alive!" Known as the "Fireman of the Southwest Pacific," Eichelberger took Buna—arguably regarded by some as "the most controversial American battle of World War II"—in 32 days at the cost of only 124 American lives, the first of four occasions in which he would save MacArthur's bacon.[49]

In retrospect, some writers have charged that the intelligence provided to MacArthur in planning the Buna offensive was "faulty." Willoughby had assured MacArthur the Japanese garrison there consisted of 1,500 exhausted survivors of General Horii's rigorous overland march over the Kokoda Trail to within sight of Port Moresby. Just prior to the beginning of the operation, he had told MacArthur there was "little indication of an attempt to make a strong stand against the Allied advance." In reality, the Japanese garrison at Buna comprised 8,000 troops, including 2,500 fresh, well-trained and confident Japanese Army veterans of fighting in China and Malaysia. In the years since, Willoughby has been faulted for "grossly inaccurate" and incomplete reports on the actual conditions at Buna, though it should also be noted that most of the American troops deployed in the Buna campaign had received only five weeks of training prior to their baptism of fire. Furthermore, Willoughby's sources were limited to photo intelligence, incomplete order-of-battle data, fragmented ULTRA intercepts, and a smattering of information from Papuan natives and Allied patrols. One historian has assessed that Willoughby's "error was one of over-confidence that bred unfounded conclusions" and that MacArthur was "not inclined to questions Willoughby's flawed prognostications."[50]

And yet, there were certainly success stories; as luck would have it, both Willoughby and MacArthur, as well as the entire Allied war effort, benefitted tremendously from a specific body of translation accomplished by the former's brainchild, the ATIS. In February 1943, Japanese Army Lieutenant General Adachi, Commander, Eighteenth Army, decided to strengthen his forces at Lae, in New Guinea, using some 6,500 troops from the garrison at Rabaul, New Britain, the heart of Japanese Army and Navy power in the South Pacific. Allied signals intelligence personnel learned of Adachi's plans in mid-February; on February 22, Adachi ordered reinforcements to Lae in preparation for an offensive. Armed with this critical information, General Kenney, commander of Allied Air Forces in the Southwest Pacific, scrambled Fifth Air Force aircraft to intercept these troops in transit, as did the Royal Australian Air Force, intended to attack the convoy as it passed through the Bismarck Sea. The convoy consisted of eight transport vessels, ferrying nearly seven thousand troops, escorted by eight destroyers. Setting sail at midnight on February 28/March 1 from Rabaul Harbor, the convoy was spotted early on the morning on March 2 and was attacked repeatedly by a force of 28 B-17 bombers in the misnamed Battle of the Bismarck Sea (most of which actually occurred in Huon Gulf). Other American and Australian aircraft attacked the convoy mid-morning and, by nightfall, all the transports had been heavily damaged or were sinking and most of the assault troops were either dead, floundering in the water, or had been rescued by the surviving destroyers.[51]

Despite formally being an intelligence officer, and a senior one at that, Willoughby was still a soldier and a combat veteran, as he demonstrated on several occasions. By early 1943, he had already earned the Silver Star and the Distinguished Service Cross, which prompted the Gettysburg College Bulletin to once again brag about their short-duration favorite son: "Let it suffice to say that when the pressure was on, a Gettysburg man was not found wanting." The article went on to say that, since the escape from Bataan, Willoughby's actions had clearly demonstrated that "MacArthur made no mistake by placing him in a position of such importance."[52]

That "position of such importance" into which Willoughby had been thrust came in handy for a MacArthur-directed task in 1943, albeit not one connected to the war effort. In the summer of that year, MacArthur dispatched Sutherland, Kenney, and Willoughby—now sporting the single star of a brigadier general—to discuss a possible presidential campaign with Michigan Republican Senator Arthur Vandenburg. Hearing the praise heaped upon MacArthur by the trio, Vandenberg created an informal "MacArthur for President" campaign, led by newspaper publisher Frank Gannett, and former general and now Sears Roebuck chairman, Robert E. Wood. However, at the 1944 Republican convention in Chicago,

MacArthur received one vote compared to 1,056 for Thomas Dewey. Recognizing the delicacy of the situation, MacArthur eagerly sought to portray this opportunity as the "spontaneous draft" of an acknowledged war hero instead of the culmination of a pre-meditated campaign.[53]

Back at the front line, in late December 1943 and January 1944, Australian troops were advancing along the east coast of New Guinea, in an attempt to cut the critical Japanese supply line that ran through the area. When American troops landed across the planned Japanese withdrawal route, commander of the Japanese 20th Division, Lieutenant General Katagiri, decided to destroy the unit's cryptographic materials rather than drag them along as the unit retreated into the nearby mountains. But the combination of rain and the danger that Allied air forces would see a fire prompted the unattributed decision to simply place the materials in a steel trunk and bury it in a stream bed. However, an Australian Army sapper detected the trunk and dug it up, believing it to be a mine. An intelligence officer recognized the materials as codebooks and they were soon on their way to the CB in Brisbane, where the sodden pages were dried out and photographed. On February 4, 1944, CB codebreakers decrypted a 13-part message which summarized the decisions made at a conference of senior Japanese officers. Copies were quickly dispatched to Arlington Hall, Virginia—the headquarters of the Army's Signal Intelligence Service—which used the codebooks in March 1944 to increase the number of decrypted Japanese Army messages twentyfold. Such an intelligence coup enabled MacArthur to conduct subsequent operations with the advantage of enemy intelligence rather than second-guessing.[54] An historian of the SIGINT contributions to the Pacific war has characterized the operations of the CB as a "critical asset" in the recapture of New Guinea and the Philippines.[55]

However, it was not until the second week of March that ATIS was able to make its most significant contribution. Australian soldiers of the 47th Battalion on Goodenough Island, to the east of New Guinea, found a lifeboat from the *Teiyo Maru*, one of the Japanese troop transports, washed ashore. Inside the lifeboat they found large quantities of enemy documents, in sealed tins, which were quickly dispatched to SWPA headquarters in Brisbane. Officials discovered one of the captured documents was dated October 15, 1942, and was tantalizingly entitled "Register of Army Officers." Allied officials were stunned to discover that the three-volume, 2,700-page document provided a complete list of some forty thousand Japanese Army officers, along with their unit assignments. For Willoughby and MacArthur, who had had to subsist intelligence-wise on the rudimentary and largely useless data on the Japanese Army provided by the War Department, all of which dated to the pre-war period, the treasure trove proved to be an unspeakable gift. At this juncture, the critical documents were turned over for translation to ATIS, a unit under Willoughby's ultimate control. He kept personal control of the list for a time and established a separate section within the Headquarters for its exploitation. He then requested the best translator available and got him—U.S. Army Master Sergeant Taro Yoshihashi, who had lived in Japan for five years as a teen and who had then gone on to graduate from UCLA with a degree in Psychology. Yoshihashi arrived in Brisbane in early June 1943 and dug in, creating and maintaining an order-of-battle (OB) card file and an OB section. Yoshihashi, described as "one of the workhorses of intelligence in the theater for the rest of the war," became part of a team of 20 Nisei and Caucasian translators who worked on the material, non-stop, for weeks, translating every name and assignment on the list. The resulting publication, ATIS Publication No. 2, Alphabetical List of Japanese Army Officers, 683 pages in length, was printed as an emergency order by the Australian Government printer and released in May 1944, the first detailed, reliable study of the Japanese Army in more than two years. Willoughby praised the dedication of the ATIS translators and described their work as a "notable tour de force"; on another occasion, Willoughby referred to ATIS as "possibly the most important single intelligence agency of the war." This magnum opus was quickly dispatched to Allied intelligence units from Ceylon to Alaska and enabled ground order-of-battle analysts to break down every Japanese unit in detail, from army to corps to division to company. Though Willoughby could not take personal credit for this intelligence coup, the fact that it was the product of the unit he had created is certainly worth noting.[56] Willoughby also received credit from academia for his skillful use and appreciation of Japanese language translators during the Pacific war; the November/December 2000 issue of the Brown University Alumni Magazine, paying tribute to Lieutenant Colonel John Fugio Aiso, the first director of the school which trained all the Japanese-language specialists, noted Willoughby had credited these translators with saving "countless Allied lives and shortening the war by two years."[57]

***

Willoughby and his intelligence staffers also had the responsibility of apprising MacArthur of casualties—both Allied and Japanese—as a result of combat operations. In mid-March 1943, Willoughby dispatched a memo about enemy casualties in the Philippines and the Southwest Pacific Area since the Pearl Harbor attack. His memo broke out the range of casualty figures as follows:

Philippines	73,000–76,000
New Guinea	30,007–33,035
Coral Sea	1,161–1,183
Elsewhere S.W.P.A.	18,100–21,300
TOTAL	122,268–131,518

Approximately a month later, Willoughby's G-2 section released a "Summary Review of Enemy Losses in S.W.P.A., April 21, 1942–April 10, 1943," which included the comment, "The enormous scale of enemy effort on land, sea and air is recognizable in the record of enemy losses, in all categories, sustained by him in combat." This document concluded that, during that period, enemy casualties in the New Guinea area were 37,538; the comparable American casualty figure for the period, exclusive of Java and the Philippines was 4,319.[58] Whatever discrepancies played into such figures, it seemed clear the Japanese were suffering increasingly unsustainable losses in combat.

When MacArthur's staff, including Willoughby, arrived in the Philippines, they found, besides the Japanese, a vibrant guerrilla presence; a report Willoughby provided later identified 64 distinct groups operating independently of one another. One group was considered by some Allied observers as a natural ally—the "Hukbalajaps"—from the Filipino term "*Hukbong Bayan Laban sa Japon*," or "The People's Army to fight the Japs," more commonly known as the "Huks"—a peasant resistance group operating in central Luzon against the Japanese from 1942. Although the group itself claimed 100,000 members, independent observers assessed a truer figure was 2,000 to 5,000. Willoughby described the group in an intelligence assessment as "openly communistic," though he added that ordinary members were believed to be pro-American and that only the leaders were violent and anti-American in nature. He was also put off by his observation that the leaders' ambitions were "personal and political" and by the group's stated ambitions: to "propagate Communism in the Philippines; establish a communistic government in the Philippines when peace comes; fight and not surrender to or cooperate with U.S. forces when peace comes." Willoughby also pointed out with concern that the Japanese did not bother the Huks and that some reporting suggested they might actually be arming them. As a final word of warning, he reported the Huks might have been capturing or betraying Americans to the Japanese, hardly a ringing endorsement of their trustworthiness.[59] However, in the final analysis, neither MacArthur nor Willoughby had any use for the Huks. As a more palatable means of skinning the cat, Willoughby opted to instead appoint "trustworthy" Filipinos at the local level rather than support the left-leaning Huks.[60]

A student of U.S. Army special operations during World War II has observed that Willoughby—whom he described as "MacArthur's domineering intelligence chief"—had little use for Filipino guerrillas as of March 1943, save as sources of information. Even the fact of the existence of an active guerrilla group on the southern Japanese-occupied island of Mindanao, led by activated U.S. Army Reserve officer and civil engineer Wendell Fertig, did not change Willoughby's mind on the subject. Besides, Willoughby had assured MacArthur there was no possibility of effective armed resistance on Mindinao specifically or even in the Philippines in general. The G-2 was convinced that providing guerrillas with arms and ammunition was "a waste of resources." He was firmly of the opinion that if regular U.S. Army forces could not withstand the Japanese in the Philippines, no irregular force could do any better. The only purpose for guerrilla forces, in Willoughby's mind, was to provide intelligence and, once American forces returned to the Philippines in triumph, to fight as regular forces under the command of American officers.

However, Courtney Whitney, the former lawyer in Manila and the new director of the Philippine Regional Section (PRS) within MacArthur's intelligence staff, urged Willoughby to make more extensive and aggressive use of the guerrillas. Given Whitney's status as one of MacArthur's "inner circle" and the latter's emotional attachment to the guerrillas, the PRS ultimately became a near-autonomous element.[61] In a 1971 interview, Willoughby noted Whitney "had considerable influence on the General [MacArthur], which to us who had been with the General longer, was mysterious to us to this day."[62]

Willoughby also leveraged information he received from U.S. Navy and U.S. Army air forces' intelligence channels; each had its own communications intelligence networks and fed the information to the SWPA G-2. Given the predominance and seeming omnipresence of the Imperial Japanese Navy in the early days of the Pacific war, Willoughby benefited greatly from the Navy's take. The particular contribution of the Fifth Air Force to the G-2 consisted of aerial reconnaissance and photography, which especially enhanced the terrain studies so critical for planning ground campaigns. At a particular juncture in the Pacific war, the intelligence cooperation and collaboration between the Fifth Air Force and Willoughby's intelligence network provided an example of the latter's ability to "get it right" when it came to assessing enemy order-of-battle information. In February 1944, the Japanese occupied the Admiralty Islands, one of which was Los Negros, which Fifth Air Force commander General Kenney wanted to use as an airbase for the targeting of the huge Japanese base at Rabaul. Based on imagery from overflights, Brigadier General Ennis Whitehead, Fifth Air Force Deputy Commander, estimated there were 400 Japanese troops on the island. The 1st Cavalry Division estimated 4,900, and Willoughby, who based his estimate on enemy radio traffic, thought the correct figure was between 3,250 and 4,000. As the one with the final call, MacArthur went with the lower estimate and pegged an invasion date of February 29. When the Allies landed with 1,000 troops, they were surprised by the 4,000 Japanese of Colonel Ezaki Yoshio, hidden in the jungle, a figure that nearly matched Willoughby's OB-data-driven estimate. Although the Allies ultimately took Los Negros, the conquest took longer than anticipated and demonstrated the potential dangers of altering plans already in-train when contradicted by OB data.[63]

Thus, by the spring of 1944, Willoughby's G-2 staff had matured on its own and also developed a generally positive working relationship with allies and the other American military services.[64] This relationship proved especially valuable thanks to one of those serendipitous events that sometimes determines the victor in a battle, or even a war. In April 1944, Willoughby was involved in the processing and exploitation of a key Japanese war plan that unexpectedly fell into Allied hands, known as the "Z Plan." This plan was the last throw of the dice for the Imperial Japanese Navy, whose Combined Fleet commander in chief Admiral Mineichi Koga had replaced Admiral Isoroku Yamamoto after the latter's plane had been shot down by American fighters in April 1943, an ambush resulting from a communications intercept. The "Z Plan" document itself dated from August 25, 1943, and detailed Japanese naval defensive plans against Allied attacks on Japan's possessions in the South Pacific. More significantly, the plan outlined the strategy for a decisive, winner-take-all naval showdown. After American aircraft attacked Japanese fleet headquarters at Truk in the Caroline Islands in February 1944, Koga boarded his then-flagship, *Musashi*, and sailed to Palau, in the western Carolines, 1,500 miles from Truk, from which location he would set the "Z Plan" into motion.[65]

Koga continued to refine the plan, issuing a final draft version of Combined Fleet Secret Operations Order No. 73 to the fleet on March 8, 1944, which committed virtually all remaining Japanese naval power to one final battle. On March 28–29, Koga learned the American fleet was heading toward the Palau Islands and decided to move his command ashore. His chief of staff, Rear Admiral Shigeru Fukudome, was given charge of the leather pouch containing the red leather-bound "Z Plan." As American forces drew closer, Koga decided to withdraw to Davao, 600 miles to the west. On the night of March 31, 1944, Koga boarded a flying boat headed for Davao; for security reasons, Fukudome and 14 staff officers followed in a second flying boat. A third aircraft left early on the morning of April 1, carrying communications and clerical staff, with top-secret codes aboard—the only aircraft of the trio that would actually arrive in Davao. Koga's aircraft ran into an immense tropical storm front and crashed into the Pacific, with the loss of all aboard. When Fukudome feared the exhausted pilot of his aircraft was about to crash, he grabbed the controls, but the plane lost control and crashed into the water. It caught fire and an injured Fukudome hung onto a seat cushion to save his life; around him were 12 other survivors, and 12 bodies. As Fukudome watched the plane settle into the water, he assumed the "Z Plan" document aboard was safely lost. He soon became a prisoner of Filipino guerrillas, who tended his wounds.[66]

Meanwhile, Japanese authorities had launched a massive aerial search for the two downed aircraft, as well as "important documents" that might have drifted ashore. Their concern was well founded, as the "Z Plan" document was actually intact, inside a box found by several locals, who took the soaked documents inside and dried them out, then buried the box. Fukudome and his fellow captives had been turned over to the Cebu Area Command, a guerrilla organization consisting of several thousand Americans and Filipinos commanded by U.S. Army Lieutenant Colonel James M. Cushing, who had been a mining engineer in the Philippines prior to the war. When officials in Tokyo grew increasingly concerned over the disappearance of Admiral Koga and the sensitive documents, they dispatched a message stating Koga and his staff were missing and that the Navy was investigating, a message intercepted and decoded by American authorities in Washington, though it would be a while before MacArthur and his staffers became aware of the situation. To escape the clutches of the relentless Japanese searchers, the guerrillas dispatched the attention-getting red portfolio of military secrets to Cushing, likely on or about April 8. Cushing had learned two days prior that he would soon be receiving prisoners of war and passed that information via radio, asking for orders concerning the prisoners. Colonel Courtney Whitney of AIB reiterated they must be treated in accordance with the laws of land warfare and offered assistance in relocating them to another island if necessary.[67]

As Japanese troops approached Cushing's camp the following day, he sent a message—including their names and ranks, as reported—to SWPA to notify his headquarters about the prisoners and how they came to be his temporary guests. The fact that a Japanese general was within the group (though intentionally misidentified as "General Furomei") caused excitement in Brisbane, where seniors decided the captives had to be gotten off Cebu as quickly as possible. Headquarters arranged with the U.S. Seventh Fleet at Fremantle to have a submarine standing by, ready for a special mission. Commanding a group of only 25 and facing an enemy force of 500, Cushing and a group of guerrillas then fled his camp, with the prisoners in tow, learning later that day the Japanese had not only taken Filipino hostages to force the return of the prisoners but had also begun executing them. Cushing ultimately negotiated a truce of sorts with the commander of the Cebu City-based Japanese pursuit force, Lieutenant Colonel Seiti Ohnisi: if the Japanese would cease executing captives, Cushing would turn over the general, the three other officers, and the six sailors to the Japanese on the morning of April 10.[68]

With the prisoners off his hands, Cushing turned his attentions to the intelligence treasure trove he had inherited. The fact the documents were in a red leather-embossed portfolio likely meant they were of considerable intelligence value. Cushing decided to roll up the documents and place them in empty mortar shells for safekeeping, notifying SWPA he had the documents on April 13. When his message was received at headquarters the following day, Whitney informed Willoughby the documents would be arriving on a late May supply run by the submarine USS *Narwhal,* unless Willoughby wanted them sooner, which he did. Willoughby ordered Whitney to get the documents to Brisbane as soon as possible. Cushing entrusted two former American prisoners of war, Russ Snell and Jimmy Dyer, with the mortar shells, for delivery to Cushing's superior, Lieutenant Colonel Edwin Andrews, whose headquarters was on southern Negros, the fourth largest island in the Philippines. After nearly a two-week trek through the jungle, Snell and Dyer turned over the mortar shells with the all-important documents inside to Andrews. So certain were the Japanese the documents were still on Cebu that they offered a reward of 50,000 Philippine pesos (approximately US$25,000) for their return.[69]

Although more Japanese documents were available, Willoughby was unwilling to wait for *Narwhal* to complete its refit, instead recommending to Whitney the documents be picked up immediately, without tipping their hand as to what they really had. Willoughby advised of the documents, "avoid blowing up their importance any more than is absolutely necessary to ensure security, to minimize the danger of the enemy acquiring knowledge that we have actually recovered them. The value of the documents may well largely depend upon our ability to keep such information from the enemy." Whitney and Sutherland decided a special pickup was needed and asked the Navy for the nearest submarine. Thus, at 11:30 p.m. on May 7, 1944, USS *Crevalle*, patrolling off the northern coast of Borneo, received top-secret orders to proceed north to the eastern portion of the Sulu Sea, prepared to conduct a special mission on May 11. The captain was instructed to take aboard a collection of documents and 25 personnel. Traveling on the surface for speed, *Crevalle*, which actually took 41 personnel aboard, arrived in Brisbane on May 19, having been depth-charged twice during the mission. To mask the true intent of the mission, the cover story was that the submarine had been dispatched to evacuate American refugees.[70]

Thankfully, as Whitney examined the documents, he discovered they were in plain text, rather than in code, and were clearly significant. On May 21, Whitney sent the documents to Willoughby, who passed them to Colonel Mashbir and his ATIS translators. They quickly identified one document as copy six of 550 copies of "Secret Combined Fleet Order No. 73," issued on March 8, 1944, from the Japanese flagship *Musashi*, signed by the since-deceased Admiral Koga. Even the preamble made excited reading:

> The Combined Fleet is for the time being directing its main operations to the Pacific Area where, in the event of an attack by an enemy Fleet Occupation Force, it will bring to bear the combined maximum strength of all our forces to meet and destroy the enemy and to maintain our hold on vital areas.
>
> These operations will be called "Z Operations."

On May 22, Willoughby was excited to read the translation and directed Mashbir to mimeograph by hand 20 copies of the related 22-page top-secret manual, entitled "Guiding Plan of Z Operations." The first of the 20 copies went to Army Chief of Staff Marshall, the second to MacArthur. A copy also went to Commander Edward Layton, Admiral Chester Nimitz's Fleet Intelligence Officer, at the Joint Intelligence Center of the Pacific at Pearl Harbor. Getting copies to Nimitz/Layton required an Army bomber flying 5,000 miles in 48 hours, with refueling stops along the way, to deliver the critical document. As Layton pored over the documents, the bottom line of the Japanese plan was to wage an all-out, last-ditch defense against the open secret of the American attack plan targeting the Mariana Islands. This American attack plan, known as Operation *Forager*, involved 535 ships (including 15 carriers and 900 aircraft) and 127,571 troops, making it the largest amphibious operation in the Pacific Theater to date. It began with an American airstrike on Saipan on June 15 and culminated in the "Marianas Turkey Shoot" on June 19–20, in the Philippine Sea west of the Marianas, in which the Japanese suffered the loss of 476 aircraft, a loss they could ill afford. Eventually, a second batch of captured Japanese documents

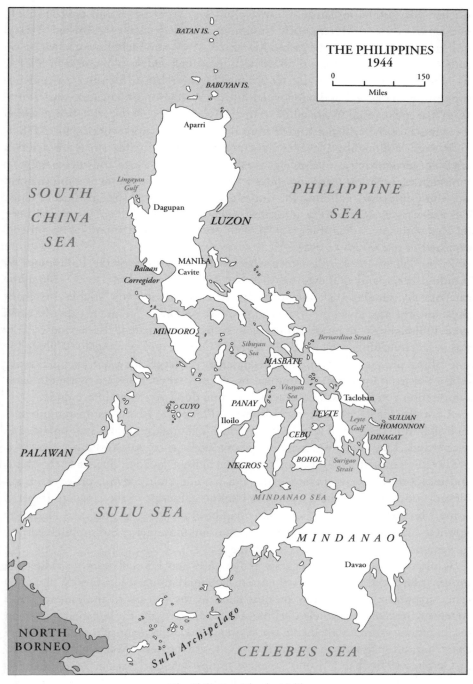

The Philippine Islands, 1944.

reached MacArthur in Australia, two volumes of typewritten and penciled radio messages, decoded and translated. This group of messages largely consisted of naval unit traffic from the end of 1943 to March 29, 1944, and included information on code changes, data most useful to the CB, the Allied codebreaking unit in SWPA. In July 1944, Willoughby and ATIS chief Mashbir began focusing on evidence supporting charges of, and anticipated future prosecution of, Japanese war crimes. With that end in mind, Willoughby set up the War Crimes Investigation Board, which drew much of the evidence it used from the Nisei translators working for ATIS.[71]

Though Willoughby played only a peripheral role in this story, he deserves credit for recognizing a true intelligence diamond-in-the-rough and encouraging its thorough exploitation, ensuring those who most needed to know the information were duly informed, fulfilling the duties expected of a wartime intelligence chief. On February 1, 1945, ATIS informed Willoughby the "Z Plan" story had been released to the press, describing it as "probably one of the most important documents captured in the SWPA to date."[72]

In the fall of 1944, Allied forces began the reconquest of the Philippines by invading the island of Leyte on October 20. Some 10 days later, Willoughby categorically stated it was unlikely the Japanese would send any "sizable" merchant ships into the area given the American presence on Leyte. Yet, at virtually the same time Willoughby's prognostications were being disseminated, the Japanese Army was in fact unloading some 11,000 soldiers at Ormoc, on Leyte. Again, Willoughby was falling prey to that most understandable, yet tragic, flaw for an intelligence officer—mirror imaging: presuming the enemy, when provided with the same information you have, will do exactly the same thing you would have done.[73]

A sample intelligence document from the Philippine Islands campaign provides an insight into the typical intelligence product Willoughby and his staff provided to MacArthur. The "Daily Summary of Enemy Intelligence" for November 12, 1944, predictably covered a number of topics, including: Japanese logistics; the status and location of enemy aircraft; barge and landing craft activity; prisoner of war interrogations (such as the 21-year-old Filipino conscript to the Japanese Imperial Army who had surrendered because he had been routinely slapped and kicked by Japanese Army non-commissioned officers); troop movements and supplies; convoy movements; and ground/air/naval sightings.[74]

While the above sample suggests Willoughby and his staff were providing the information necessary for MacArthur to make sound military decisions, Willoughby came up wanting again a few months later, in the run-up to the January 1945 American invasion of Luzon in the Philippine Islands. Again, the bugaboo concerned his inaccurate estimates of enemy troop strength. Despite controlling three distinct collection and analysis entities—ATIS, the CB, and the AIB—Willoughby estimated in October 1944 that 121,000 Japanese troops defended Luzon, an estimate he continued to raise throughout November and December, finally assessing there were 172,400 Imperial Army troops awaiting combat with American forces. In reality, the Japanese Fourteenth Army commander, General Yamashita Tomoyuki, had more than 275,000 troops at the ready. Although a number of these soldiers were insufficiently trained and poorly equipped, having just been transformed into combat troops, he led a force that was "far stronger than General Willoughby … had estimated." Willoughby's estimate was off by nearly 50 percent, a staggering miscalculation. In sharp contrast was the more accurate enemy estimate of 234,500 provided by Willoughby's Sixth Army counterpart, Colonel Horton White, described as "a quiet and good-natured staff officer, unlike Willoughby," who was characterized as "talented and intelligent," but egotistical and resentful of "any interference in his domain." Command Historian of the U.S. Army Intelligence and Security Command Michael Bigelow has referred to Willoughby's resentment as "the Achilles' heel of the SWPA intelligence structure." Assessing Willoughby as a G-2, Bigelow noted he was "always either impressively correct or hopelessly incorrect. Unfortunately, he was hopelessly incorrect during the Luzon campaign." Bigelow also raises the question if Willoughby deliberately skewed the intelligence picture out of loyalty to MacArthur, whom he knew harbored an obsessive desire to return to the Philippines in victory. Bigelow concludes that while White "put seemingly discordant pieces of information together into a coherent whole, Willoughby did not. Willoughby's failure caused inaccurate and fragmented estimates. Lacking flexibility, Willoughby never acknowledged that his original enemy strength estimate was too low. Therefore, he consistently underestimated the Japanese strength." It is significant the discrepancy between the estimates of Willoughby and White was due to *interpretation* of data, rather than different data. Willoughby had counted only larger units, rather than including unattached and service troops, missing over 230 Imperial Army units in the process, while White had included the additional troops in his estimate. Willoughby also wrongly assumed Yamashita was intent upon a campaign of maneuver (he was not, instead planning a defense in depth) and assessed as late as January 15, 1945, that the Japanese would not defend the Philippine capital of Manila, on Luzon; in actuality, the Japanese desperately fought for the city, resulting in a month-long, house-to-house battle which cost the lives of over 100,000 Filipinos.[75]

In his Order of the Day for January 22, 1943, MacArthur cited a number of senior officers for their conduct during the New Guinea campaign, among them "BG Willoughby"—each of the cited officers received the Distinguished Service Cross (DSC) for serving with "devotion and gallantry." His particular award citation read: "For extraordinary heroism in action in New Guinea, during the Papuan Campaign, July 23, 1942 to January 8, 1943. As Assistant Chief of Staff, G-2, Southwest Pacific Area, Brigadier General Willoughby displayed extraordinary courage, marked efficiency and precise execution of operations during the Papuan Campaign."[76] The following year, he received the Distinguished Service Medal (DSM). In the words of the citation, Willoughby had been "charged with the particularly complex and difficult task of organizing and coordinating intelligence activities in the theater," a reference to Willoughby's initiative to stand up a bona fide intelligence service in the SWPA during the war. His award particularly highlighted his demonstrated skills as an Intelligence Officer:

> … his assessment of enemy strengths and intentions was conspicuously accurate, and data were assembled upon which sound plans of attack could be based. General Willoughby, by his noteworthy achievement as an organizer and by his penetrating analysis of the military situation, made an invaluable contribution to the success of military operations in the Southwest Pacific Area.[77]

In February 1944, Willoughby and his staff completed an intelligence assessment on the Japanese stronghold at Hollandia, New Guinea; although the Japanese had some 42,000 troops on the island, the G-2 and his analysts assessed only 3,000 of these were in the immediate vicinity of Hollandia. According to *Ultra* intercepts, there were 8,647 Japanese ground troops at Hollandia, plus 7,650 air troops, though Willoughby assessed they were mostly service personnel, with only one combat maneuver battalion represented. The actual enemy figure was closer to 16,000, though Willoughby was correct about the number of combat troops available. In light of these figures, he suggested to MacArthur that he launch an amphibious landing at Hollandia, sidestepping the enemy stronghold in the Madang–Hansa Bay area. Swayed by his G-2, MacArthur directed his staff to begin planning for an amphibious assault there, to occur in April 1944. The following month, MacArthur tasked Willoughby—then described as MacArthur's "king-sized intelligence chief"—with reporting to him personally any references to "Hollandia" in Japanese radio intercepts. Throughout March and April, Willoughby supplied his commander with information on Japanese troop dispositions in New Guinea; although there was evidence the Japanese were reinforcing their units in the Hollandia area, Willoughby assessed these were likely base defense and support units, rather than first-line combat forces, and the greatest threat to the amphibious assault would come from Japanese air power.[78] Willoughby also recommended the use of subterfuge to convince the Japanese that Allied forces were intent upon an invasion in the Madang–Hansa Bay area—rubber boats were left on beaches in the area, to persuade the Japanese pre-invasion beach intelligence operations were underway, and B-25 bombers were ordered to conduct distracting bombing missions in the vicinity.[79]

On April 22, MacArthur launched his amphibious assault at Hollandia, achieving a tactical surprise, and had a clear victory within just four days, thanks in large measure to the intelligence provided him by Willoughby and his G-2 staff. They had identified a weak point in the Japanese lines and, in response to Willoughby's concerns about Japanese aerial attacks, MacArthur had waged a bomber strike against Hollandia's airfields, negating that threat. Similarly, in response to Willoughby's assessment of Japanese troop strength, MacArthur plussed up his ground forces in preparation for the assault. The results of the operation had demonstrated the value of accurate and timely intelligence, gathered from a variety of sources; as one historian has noted, "the allies achieved victory at Hollandia using intelligence from every source."[80]

Willoughby had alerted MacArthur that there were 11,000 Japanese troops at Hollandia, which he believed included one Japanese naval infantry regiment and two veteran infantry regiments; in reality, the majority proved to be the poorly trained Japanese service troops that Willoughby had assessed. "Willoughby's information, as usual, was very inaccurate," noted one historian. In the conquest of Hollandia, General Eichelberger's I Corps troops killed 3,000 Japanese troops—the total number Willoughby claimed were there—plus captured 611 and determined that 7,000 more had fled into the jungle.[81]

But Willoughby and MacArthur were not just busy fighting the Japanese; there were other foes to address, most notably in the form of OSS. A prominent attempt to insert OSS into the SWPA occurred in January 1943, in the person of Joseph R. Hayden, a professor of Political Science at the University of Michigan and the world's foremost expert on Philippine political affairs. He had known MacArthur since the 1930s and had served as vice-governor in Manila. Just completing an OSS assignment in China, Hayden was dispatched by Donovan to plead the OSS case in person. Hayden extended Donovan's greetings, described MacArthur as "cordial and receptive," and indicated Donovan would be agreeable to having OSS personnel under MacArthur's command, a persistent sticking point in earlier negotiations. MacArthur, however, rejected the offer out-of-hand, perhaps because Willoughby and Merle-Smith, among other staffers, persuaded MacArthur OSS was not needed in the theater. However, Hayden remained on MacArthur's staff until the end of the war and continued to aid the command. For example, he realized GHQ had no specific order-of-battle information on the soon-to-be invaded Philippine Islands, especially information on potential landing beaches, local foodstuffs, the transportation network, and the general Philippine economic and political landscape. As Hayden knew, his erudite colleagues in the OSS Research and Analysis Branch in Washington could put their hands on the necessary information; MacArthur's planners truly appreciated the critical information, especially that derived from OSS interviews of American businessmen in the Philippines. The information provided was deemed so valuable by MacArthur and Willoughby that the latter personally flew to Washington to meet with Branch Director Dr. William D. Langer and requested 20 of his best men to work on the task at MacArthur's headquarters. Initial hopes for cooperation were dashed, however, when Willoughby made clear that, with regard to the OSS personnel, the service would have to "give them up completely and MacArthur would take them over," a proposal rejected by Donovan. While some level of grudging collaboration would continue into 1945, there would be no further advances during the war.[82]

But, on April 2, 1944, Donovan paid his former comrade-in-arms a visit, hoping a personal visit would secure permission for OSS to operate more fully in the SWPA.

Though welcomed aboard MacArthur's command ship off Hollandia, Donovan was subjected to pointed discussions, with MacArthur willing to only use OSS personnel attached to his staff and to use frogmen from the OSS Maritime Unit but unwilling to accept OSS Morale Operations personnel for his Psychological Warfare Branch in Australia. As it had been from the beginning, the rub was in who would control the OSS personnel, the OSS Director or the theater commander and, as he usually did, MacArthur had his way, in sharp contrast to the conduct of combat operations in the other wartime theaters. Thus, OSS would be shut out of the Pacific Theater throughout the war.[83]

The Pacific war would provide additional examples of Willoughby's intelligence acuity, or lack thereof. In late Spring 1944, as part of the preparations for his much-anticipated return to the Philippines, MacArthur set his sights on the island of Biak, in western New Guinea, as the next logical place to confront the Japanese. Willoughby had concerns, however, that the small American naval footprint in the area could be defeated by a larger Japanese naval contingent nearby. Two weeks prior to the May 27 assault, Willoughby provided G-2 comments on the possibility of Japanese naval involvement and responsive Allied air countermeasures. He advised MacArthur:

> G-2 Comment: The Allied Air Force must be capable of providing air cover for the Allied Invasion Force as it proceeds to Biak and, providing flying conditions are average, can probably be depended upon to turn back any Japanese surface forces before they arrive in a position to attack the Allied Forces. However, if adverse weather conditions were to develop [underlining in the original], thereby hampering the Allied air operations, then our surface forces might possibly be left to rely solely on the naval strength available for defense. There is also the possibility that the enemy may attempt a carrier plane strike against our Wake and/or Hollandia airdromes, just before he attempts to engage our surface units. Such attack could cripple our air offensive striking power in that area ... Our operation should again, if possible, be timed to coincide or be near a proposed Allied fleet action.
>
> Recommendation: To postpone the occupation of Biak to coincide with CINCPAC sortie into the Marianas or delay it to bring it near that target date, in order to confuse the enemy and divert his attention from our own operation.[84]

Such a balanced intelligence assessment meets or surpasses the expectation of most commanders regarding their intelligence needs and assessment of most likely enemy courses of action and is commendable.

Less commendable was Willoughby's lack of precision when it came to estimating the strength of the opposing enemy, a critical skill for any order-of-battle analyst, especially a G-2 advising a theater commander. In this regard, as part of the intelligence preparation for the assault on Biak, Willoughby estimated 4,380 Japanese defenders; the actual number was over eleven thousand, many of whom were dug into nearly impenetrable caves. One student of the campaign there concluded Willoughby also "had forgotten the tenacity and ferocity with which the Japanese infantry could conduct a defense," though in a May 22 intelligence summary, he assessed it was "probable that it [Biak] will be defended very strongly." As developments would soon make clear, the Japanese commander, Colonel Naoyuki Kuzume, had had five months to prepare defenses and was "a soldier of the highest caliber and a tactician commanding respect." In this instance, Willoughby's inaccurate assessment was partially responsible for heavy American casualties and the delay of MacArthur's offensive, though, as noted above, Willoughby had argued against the attack or at least its delay, fearing the small U.S. Navy contingent nearby might be defeated by a potentially larger Japanese naval force. As several historians have noted, Willoughby would take pains to cover up this erroneous estimate and the tactical consequences of such in his future writings.[85]

Critics of Willoughby also point to his estimate of enemy strength in the October 20, 1944, assault on Leyte in the Philippines. Described by one observer as "MacArthur's ever-inaccurate Intelligence Officer," Willoughby estimated the Japanese garrison there at 21,000 troops, while in reality there were 35,000. This pattern repeated itself in the January 9, 1945, assault at Lingayen Gulf, as General Walter Krueger and his Sixth Army began the invasion of Luzon. On this occasion, Willoughby estimated total Japanese forces at 150,000; the actual figure was 275,000. Of greater import was Willoughby's failure to determine their commander was General Tomoyuki Yamashita, the near-legendary "Tiger of Malaysia." Not only could MacArthur have benefitted from knowing such information, but identifying such a significant opposite number is again the responsibility of an intelligence officer.[86] In a startling statement at the time, MacArthur candidly told a briefing officer, "I want to give you my idea of intelligence officers. There are only three great ones in the history of warfare—and mine isn't one of them."[87]

Ironically, in view of his later assessment of North Korean and Chinese troops, Willoughby had high praise for the troops of the Empire of the Rising Sun. On one occasion, he described the Japanese soldier as "a well-trained, well-disciplined, first-class fighting man who lives cheaply."[88]

Although MacArthur had made his much-publicized return to the Philippine island of Leyte in October 1944, it was January 1945 before American forces made an amphibious landing on the main island of Luzon. In mid-October, Willoughby estimated 121,000 Japanese defended Luzon, a number he continued to increase throughout November and December. Encouraged by a SIGINT estimate on December 1, of at least 153,500 defenders, Willoughby increased his estimate to 172,400, still far short of the 275,000 troops General Tomoyuki had. Despite the fact these troops were new to combat, undertrained and underequipped, they constituted what one historian has referred to as a "respectable force," and "one that was far stronger than General Willoughby … had estimated." In response to such flawed analysis, two intelligence co-authors described Willoughby and Whitney in these terms: "Like good court jesters, they fed their king's humor. Rational operational planning received secondary attention. They also continued the bad habit they had exhibited in the SW Pacific, which was to underestimate Japanese opposition and confuse press releases with the truth." Willoughby also misread the intentions of the enemy commander, expecting him to wage a battle of maneuver when Yamashita instead planned a defense in depth, in order to tie down as many American troops as possible.[89]

The invasion armada consisted of 1,000 ships, 3,000 landing craft, and 280,000 troops, with MacArthur using the cruiser USS *Boise* as his command ship. Despite vicious attacks by Japanese *kamikaze* suicide pilots and numerous American casualties, by nightfall on January 7, 50,000 men and their equipment were firmly ashore, occupying a beachhead that in some areas was 8 miles deep. On January 9, Willoughby was conferring with Lieutenant Colonel Russ Volckmann, who had arrived on horseback and brought with him an intelligence treasure trove—a thick stack of detailed sketches of the Japanese defenses along and south of Lingayen Gulf. This valuable cache of ground order-of-battle information was the result of many days of dangerous work by local bands of guerrillas.[90]

Even as brutal as the fighting was in the Pacific Theater, by early 1945 American authorities were already planning for the invasion of the Japanese Home Islands, in what was known as Operation *Downfall*, a virtually American affair which would consist of two assaults beginning in November 1945. This massive offensive was expected to involve more than 40 percent of those still in uniform in 1945—1.5 million in the two assaults, with three million in reserve. In April, Willoughby sent MacArthur an estimate that the Japanese would mount a no-holds-barred defense of Kyushu, the southernmost of the Home Islands, the target of 14 American divisions of soldiers and marines in Operation *Olympic*.[91] Intercepted messages detailing the movement of Japanese vessels prompted an intelligence assessment that some 30,000 to 60,000 troops were being moved to the island as of that date. Other intercepts discussed the mining of harbors and coastal areas by the Japanese, the movement of *kamikaze* aircraft to Kyushu, and the movement of specific combat units from such locations as Manchuria and the Kuril Islands. A late April assessment by MacArthur's intelligence staff concluded, "It is apparent [the Japanese] now consider invasion certain if not imminent." By early-to-mid May, the Military Intelligence Service (MIS) estimated there were 246,000 Japanese forces on Kyushu and that, by November 1, there would be an additional 100,000 ground troops awaiting American forces. By mid-June, based on additional intercepted messages, the MIS estimated there were now 300,000 troops on Kyushu, a figure provided to President Truman only two days prior to his June 18 meeting with his senior military advisors to discuss planning for the invasion. The focus of this meeting was to "reopen the question of whether or not to proceed with plans and preparations with Olympic ... a campaign that was certain to take a large price in American lives and treasure." President Truman's personal representative on the Joint Chiefs of Staff (JCS), Admiral William Leahy, indicated that, among other items, the commander in chief wanted "an estimate of the time required and an estimate of the losses in killed and wounded that will result from an invasion of Japan proper." Leahy, who estimated there would be 250,000 killed or wounded on Kyushu alone, explained to his JCS colleagues that President Truman's intention was to "make his decision on the campaign with the purpose of economizing to the maximum extent possible in the loss of American lives." Thus, it was important for Leahy and Army Chief of Staff General Marshall, in communication with MacArthur, to understand the metric being used for casualty estimates. In concert with their Medical Corps brethren, MacArthur's G-2 personnel assessed the casualties incurred on Okinawa would be the best overall model for future projection. But the G-1 (personnel) estimate of 50,800 seemed too optimistic and was not convincingly presented to Leahy, who suspected President Harry Truman would be dissatisfied with such an off-the-cuff assessment. The formula the G-2 analysts used was that "two to two and a half Japanese divisions [could] extract ... approximately 40,000 American casualties on land. Willoughby, who estimated that total American casualties by the fall of 1946 would be one million men, nevertheless supported the G-2 formula and stated that "This [ratio] affords a completely authentic yardstick to forecast what it would have taken in losses had we gone in shooting."[92]

That same day, Marshall had confidently predicted that, at a certain point, Japanese reinforcements headed for Kyushu would stop; however, the continued intercept and evaluation of Japanese military message traffic made abundantly clear that such a halt had not occurred. The resulting alarm over the possible implications emerged clearly in a July 29, 1945, paper circulated by Willoughby, portions of which read:

> The rate and probable continuity of Japanese reinforcements into the Kyushu area are changing that tactical and strategic situation sharply ... There is a strong likelihood that additional major units will enter the area before target date; we are engaged in a race against time by which the ratio of attack effort vis-à-vis defense capacity is perilously balanced.

This report also noted the six enemy divisions originally predicted as a defensive force—as well as three or four more expected post-invasion that had "since made their appearance and the end is not in sight." Nor did MacArthur's analysts yet know of the 10th and 11th divisions on Kyushu and the evidence that at least two more were heading that way. The American intelligence assessment that 60 percent of the defensive forces were in southern Kyushu also confirmed the Japanese had correctly surmised the planned invasion site. Once the communications intelligence (COMINT) information concerning the defenders was deciphered and analyzed, it became clear there were some 14 divisions on Kyushu, nearly twice the original estimate, and that nine of these were deployed to the southern part of the island. Meanwhile, the estimated total of Japanese defenders continued to climb, to 549,000, and, ultimately, to a staggering 600,000.[93]

MacArthur fully realized the implications of this COMINT-derived information for Operation *Olympic*; if true, resulting squeamishness might alter or even cancel the offensive, both equally distasteful to MacArthur. As historian Doug MacEachin noted, "MacArthur's practice was to not allow intelligence to interfere with his aims" and when it did, the theater commander was critical of Willoughby's estimates. In the case of *Olympic*, MacEachin concluded, "His [MacArthur's] denigration of the reported buildup on Kyushu directly contradicted the performance record of his G-2 under Willoughby." In this instance, post-war information would clearly show there were indeed 14 Japanese combat divisions on Kyushu and COMINT had identified every one of them. Furthermore, Japanese documents obtained after the war showed that, when the MIS was estimating 600,000 troops on Kyushu, there were actually 900,000 assigned to its defense, supported by an estimated 6,000 to 7,000 aircraft.[94]

From an intelligence vantage point, such an operation would obviously require a sizable contingent of Japanese linguists. Thus, in the spring of that year, Willoughby requested 1,106 of them from the Military Intelligence Language School (MILS) at Fort Snelling, Minnesota. In April, however, Colonel Mashbir, the head of ATIS, advised Willoughby he needed 4,000 additional Nisei translators to support the planned invasion. The ever-excitable Willoughby responded, "Well, I'm not going to stand for any such God-damned thing as that!" Mashbir, no shrinking violet himself, roared back at his superior officer, "Well, General, I don't give a damn whether you do or not. Frankly, if we don't have these linguists, somebody is going to be tried by court-martial and I'm going to be God-damned sure it isn't me!" Mashbir ultimately did not get his 4,000 linguists, but 1,073 MILS graduates were dispatched to U.S. Army forces in the Pacific Theater between May and July 1945.[95]

And it wasn't just translators that Intelligence was expected to provide when it came to planning for the long-awaited invasion of the Japanese Home Islands. Kyushu had been heavily photographed and mapped, but there were few prisoners of war who could provide detailed information on the defenses of the island, where the number of Japanese troops had increased from 150,000 to 600,000 in the first six months of 1945. On July 29, Willoughby noted "If this development is not checked it may grow to a point where we attack on a ratio of one-to-one which is not a recipe for victory."[96]

CHAPTER THREE

Victory and the Occupation of Japan

Willoughby was doubtless among the minority, certainly among men in uniform, when it came to criticizing President Truman's use of the atomic bomb in August 1945, though not out of any due concern for the suffering of the Japanese. He made the point that Japan was on the verge of collapse and was seeking to negotiate. "There was then no reason to use the Atom bomb," he commented, "and give the show away that we had perfected the most revolutionary weapon in modern history. MacArthur was not consulted; he was merely presented with a *fait accompli*."[1] Why the commander in chief should feel compelled to justify his strategic decisions to a subordinate commander was never addressed by Willoughby.

The use of the atomic bomb made the sobering, in-depth invasion plans for the Japanese Home Islands mercifully unnecessary. As the Pacific war neared its end, American military planners had drawn up Operation *Blacklist* to determine troop dispositions for the immediate post-war period. According to this planning document, the Eighth Army would occupy Tokyo and northern Honshu, with the Sixth Army and III Amphibious Corps occupying the south; the Tenth Army would be deployed to Okinawa, minus XXIV Corps, which would be dispatched to the former Japanese possession, Korea. As the details of this operation were announced, there was marked concern the Japanese might lure them into the country only to slaughter them or kill their leaders. As Willoughby noted, "the enormous initial military risks of landing with token forces on the Japanese mainland, into a colossal armed camp ... All possible landing areas, in the event of American armed landing, were completely organized by the Japanese Army and each of these had the potentiality of another Okinawa." He predicted 700,000 casualties if American forces had been compelled to invade the Japanese Home Islands.[2]

Willoughby became deeply involved in preparations for this post-war administration. On August 12, just three days after the atomic bomb was dropped on Nagasaki, Willoughby wrote a memo to the commander in chief (MacArthur), Deputy Chief of Staff, and G-3 offering some of his personnel to deal with a specific aspect of the occupation:

1. In view of the manifold problems arising in the occupation of Japan and its completely alien characteristics in language, political, and social institutions, your attention is invited to the considerable facilities and expert knowledge presently contained in T.I.S. (Translator and Interpreter Service).
2. Selected individual interpreters (40) are already slated for direct attachment to the principal staff sections of G.H.Q.
3. In addition, ... specialized knowledge is available, for research and consultation, in the Research Section of T.I.S.; the officers concerned and listed below have lived or served in Japan, attached to the U.S. Embassy, as language students, M.I.D., etc., etc.

Willoughby's memo included the names of 21 officers available and thoughtfully even included a draft of the letter-directive to effect such a change, should it be approved:

> The Chief of Staff has designated the Assistant Chief of Staff, G-2 and the Military Intelligence Section, General Staff, G.H.Q., A.F.P.A.C., as his representative to co-ordinate and supervise [sic] general contacts with the Japanese Army and the maintenance of a uniform policy of procedure and protocol ...[3]

On August 27, 1945, several days prior to the signing of the Japanese surrender aboard USS *Missouri* in Tokyo Bay, Willoughby drafted a memo to the Far East Command General Headquarters Chief of Staff, Major General Sutherland, pointing out what he believed were flaws in an aspect of the post-war planning. Reiterating a theme popular with both Willoughby and MacArthur, the former charged that several of the annexes to two Operational Instructions were clearly modeled on Supreme Headquarters Allied Expeditionary Forces (i.e., European Theater) documents but that the situation in the Far East was obviously different. As the G-2 pointed out, "... the German occupation involved the complete dissolution of a hostile Government and its ideology; Japanese occupation involves its complete maintenance and the use of a specific ideology, the Shinto basis of secular government ... It is essential that a revision of phraseology and intent of these Annexes be undertaken at once ..." As any good staff officer memo does, this one concluded with "Recommendations":

> a. That G-2 Section and its Japanese specialist group be utilized to the fullest extent as a research and reference agency.
> b. That G-2 Section is particularly fitted by background, training and documentation, to act, as the Chief of Staff's representative ... and that it formally charged as such ...[4]

The bombing of Hiroshima and Nagasaki in early August 1945 made such grim prognostications moot, turning thoughts to the mechanics of surrender. When the time came for the formal ceremony, MacArthur apparently decided it would be unseemly for the Far Eastern Commander to personally be involved in such a trivial administrative task as accepting the Japanese surrender; after all, he considered himself Hirohito's successor and believed the Japanese people viewed him the same way. To the surprise of virtually no one, MacArthur opted to have Willoughby, Assistant Chief of Staff, G-2—along with Sutherland, Dick Marshall, Chamberlin, and others—do the honors representing the Supreme Commander Allied Powers

(SCAP) and to negotiate the how and when of the entry of American forces into Japan. Willoughby had formed an advisory committee of experts on Japan to aid MacArthur and his other staffers. Thus, when the Japanese surrender delegation of 16, led by Lieutenant General Torashiro Kawabe, arrived on board an American Army transport at Nichols Field near Manila on August 19, onlookers were treated to the bizarre picture of the hulking Willoughby walking beside a group of diminutive Japanese officers and diplomats. The image of Willoughby reminded some of the physical and sometimes behavioral similarities with another senior military officer—former *Luftwaffe Reichsmarshall* Hermann Goering. Accompanying Willoughby was Lieutenant Colonel Mashbir, several Caucasian interpreters, and two Nisei officers—Second Lieutenants Thomas T. Imada and George Kenichi Kayano. Watching the gathering crowd of Filipinos, some of whom were starting to pick up rocks to throw at the hated Japanese, Willoughby ushered the delegates into waiting cars for the ride into Manila proper. During the ride, Willoughby queried General Kawabe what language he preferred for the surrender proceedings; to Willoughby's utter delight, Kawabe replied "German" and the two former foes were soon chatting amiably. Just as the Japanese delegation was about to board its return flight to the island of Ie Shima, however, Rear Admiral Yokoyama, the senior Japanese naval delegate, handed Willoughby a request to MacArthur for "special consideration in the enforcement of the occupation, to the traditional veneration of the Japanese for their shrines and ancestral tombs, and the privacy of their homes."[5]

***

Although MacArthur's dominance in post-war Japan went largely unchallenged, a deep divide between his SCAP subordinates continued to percolate just below the surface. The basic divide was personality driven and resulted in a feud between the Government Section (GS), headed by Brigadier General Whitney—described as a "good lawyer" but "a politician, not a soldier"[6]—and the Counterintelligence Section (CS), headed by Willoughby. Whitney, a conservative Republican, personal friend of MacArthur, and "Bataan Gang" member (like Willoughby), was skeptical of democratization efforts in post-war Japan and left running that program to a more "New Deal"-supporter subordinate. Despite the personal rancor between Willoughby and other MacArthur subordinates, in this instance Willoughby and Whitney shared a common viewpoint—namely, that the democratization of Japan was a bad idea that likely wouldn't work anyway.[7] The third key individual to serve MacArthur during this period was his Chief of Staff, Major General Edward "Ned" Almond, who would cross swords repeatedly with Willoughby during the Korean War.[8] Historian D. Clayton James described Almond as a:

... high grade professional who went through all the service schools on his way to an almost irresistible career ... He was a Southerner with all the charm that you typically think of a Southerner as having ... When Almond was chief of staff in Tokyo, he asked for and obtained the command of the X Corps, which played an important, if not brilliant, role on the east coast of Korea.[9]

Further compounding the situation was an organizational change made by MacArthur—as the war wound down and the prospect of a post-war occupation of Japan became likely, the headquarters elements of USAFFE (United States Army Forces in the Far East) and SWPA were combined, at least in part—specifically, the G-1 (Personnel), G-3 (Admin), and G-4 (Logistics and Supply) sections came together. However, MacArthur purposely kept the G-2 sections segregated, with Willoughby's focused on combat intelligence and Elliott Thorpe's designated the Counter-Intelligence and Civil Intelligence Section. In Thorpe's assessment, this organizational construct and peacetime meant Willoughby had little to do, save "meet distinguished visitors, write history, and conduct a personal note-writing battle with the heads of almost all the other staff sections in the Dai Ichi building [SCAP headquarters]. The war correspondents enjoyed this no end."[10] In 1946, Thorpe requested Stateside reassignment, which allowed Willoughby to gain control of his former section, making him "more powerful than ever," according to one historian.[11]

The writing of history also fell within the scope of Willoughby's expansive responsibilities, an effort that was an intentional holdover from the war years. In 1943, MacArthur's G-3 element began the routine but important task of documenting the course of World War II in the Pacific Theater, intended to be a three- or four-volume history predictably lauding the many and towering accomplishments of MacArthur himself. However, the monumental task was reassigned to the G-2 in the fall of 1946 by order of MacArthur, who was displeased by the lack of progress on this *magnum opus*. To the surprise of no one who knew Willoughby, even in passing, he took on the task with what one writer has described as "his usual flair for the dramatic." The G-2 not only assigned most of his staff to the project, but also added a new group of sources—a group of fifteen or more former Japanese admirals, generals, and colonels to attest to the greatness of MacArthur in engineering their defeat. The burgeoning staff took over an entire floor of the Nippon Yusen Kaisha building—one of the largest in Tokyo and named for the leading Japanese steamship line, Nippon Yusen Kaisha, whose offices used to be there—where they worked in secret. Everyone working on the project had to destroy their notes once finished with them and had to sign for any materials taken out of the building. At the printing plant, the manuscript was treated as a classified document and, after each press run, the waste paper was collected and burned.[12]

When the 3,000-page tome was finally completed, in late 1950, it had been distilled into three volumes—*Campaigns of MacArthur in the Pacific*, *Japanese Operations Against MacArthur*, and *MacArthur in Japan: Military Phases* (though these titles would be changed prior to publication, to take the spotlight off MacArthur). It was the second volume into which Willoughby poured his heart and soul; the idea for *Japanese Operations Against MacArthur* had been his originally and he had hired the requisite Japanese specialists to help him. He intended this volume to be the pinnacle of his writing prowess and, indeed, those who were privy to the page proofs were impressed, especially with the high-quality maps and the approximately two dozen color plates, many of which were from commissioned paintings done by prominent Japanese artists. Up until late 1949, progress reports were being sent to the Pentagon, albeit sporadically; however, after that date, they ceased entirely. According to staff working on the project, the reason was simple: the Pentagon had reserved the right to review and edit the work which, given it was intended as MacArthur's personal memoirs, was clearly unacceptable. Upon completion in late 1950, four sets of proofs were set aside; they would be packed in MacArthur's personal baggage and shipped back to the States several months later when MacArthur bid farewell to Tokyo. All other copies were ordered destroyed. Interestingly, when Willoughby was asked about the history in late 1952, he denied such a work had ever existed, insisting the only histories his G-2 staff had written were some dozen monographs on various aspects of the Pacific war, all of which had been sent to Washington and were in daily use. Efforts by the Department of the Army's Office of Military History to acquire a "master set" of the three volumes proved fruitless and spokesmen from that office indicated they had never seen them, lending an appropriate air of mystery to the self-proclaimed greatest work of the enigmatic Willoughby.[13]

In a bizarre twist, the ultimate fate of these volumes would become a prolonged mystery, the solving of which owed virtually nothing to the two men who should have known the most about the subject, Willoughby and MacArthur. Two of the historians who were involved in the research and writing of these volumes shared their confusion with the general public in 1952. Jerome Forrest and Clark Kawakami referred to this "labor of love" as "The Great MacArthur Historical Project," a name MacArthur would have likely approved of. The two historians described the project as:

> ... the compilation of an exhaustive but so far unpublished record of the activities of MacArthur's command between 1941 and 1948 ... Probably the most remarkable thing about this episode was General Willoughby's denial of any knowledge of an operation that had, according to all reliable reports, consumed much of the time and effort of a substantial part of his own G-2 staff for four years and resulted in some millions of words of printed text.[14]

As archival records noted, the volumes and all the supporting materials were stored in a staggering 30 footlockers—10 for Volume 1, 15 for Volume II, five for the Volume I supplement [which ultimately became Volume III], and one supplementary locker for all the photographic references for these volumes. To aid in quick identification, the Volume I footlockers had blue markings, Volume II red, and the supplement, green. Since the supplementary locker was relevant to all three volumes, it was logically marked in blue, red, and green.[15]

Forrest and Kawakami explained that, in 1946, the G-2 Historical Division, GHQ, Tokyo, began, at MacArthur's direction and under Willoughby's supervision, "a fully documented, exhaustive, and definitive history of the Second World War in the Southwest Pacific." As they remembered, the volumes were completed, in page-proof form, by the end of 1950, ready for the printing press. However, according to Japanese press reports at the time, only five sets had been run off, that the plates and the proof copies had been destroyed, and that all five sets and notes "were taken back to the United States by General Willoughby after the dismissal of General MacArthur." While Willoughby's office was in the Dai Ichi building, along with MacArthur's, the Historical Division's offices were five blocks away, in the NYK building. At the height of its activity, the Historical Division had some 100 employees who, while they did have other projects, were primarily working on the soon-to-be-missing volumes. As completed, the volumes were entitled "Allied Operations in the Southwest Pacific" (Volume I); "Japanese Operations Against MacArthur" (Volume II); "Occupation of Japan: Military Phase" (Volume III), a total of some 1,200 pages. Of the three volumes, the most valuable—at least to historians, though controversial to the general public—was Volume II, as Willoughby took the bold step of allowing the vanquished to tell their own story, sometimes with greater accuracy than the official American versions of such events as the Battle of the Bismarck Sea in March 1943. The "vanquished," who were recruited for this effort, were the more than fifteen senior Japanese Army and Navy officers who had both the placement and access to compile the history. No doubt galling to American personnel in the office was that they were required to address the ex-officers by their former rank and salute them accordingly. An American editorial staff of 12 (at its height) oversaw the writings of the Japanese officers; predictably, Willoughby had the final say in the case of disputes and always took the American side. Journalists from *The Reporter* asked Pentagon officials about the three MIA volumes, pointing out the volumes were official United States Government (USG) property and wondering why they were not turned over, or even made available, to the Army or any other government agency. Pentagon officials confirmed they had never received the volumes and agreed they were certainly USG property.[16]

Neither in this series, nor in the General Intelligence Series, also on the Pacific war, did Willoughby acknowledge his "numerous errors in estimation in the Pacific context." The source of this charge commented, in understated fashion, that "this is hardly commendable in a military officer, who as a leader of soldiers, is required by his profession to function by the concept of honor."[17]

MacArthur also tasked Willoughby with overseeing the writing of a wartime history of intelligence operations specifically. The request for such a series had come from the War Department in 1947 and MacArthur discussed the development of the series in a foreword he penned from Tokyo on September 30, 1950. MacArthur wrote, "General Willoughby who has been on my staff continuously since 1941, has produced a series of monographs, dealing with the many facets of operational intelligence, on the level of an overseas theater of war … This series, developed in addition to other duties, is of monumental scope; it aggregates 11 volumes of text and 15 volumes of documentary appendices, with a total of 6,004 pages and 1,509 plates, maps and illustrations; it embodies wartime experience and wartime techniques that proved entirely adequate to my requirements in campaigns." In the foreword, MacArthur also gushed about his G-2. Speaking of Willoughby, he wrote:

> [He] was charged with the particularly complex and difficult task of organizing and coordinating intelligence activities in the theater. Speedily and with brilliant resourcefulness he planned and put into action necessary agencies for providing the command with reliable and comprehensive information concerning the terrain, the native inhabitants, enemy installations, dispositions, and movements in a vast and inaccessible area ... his assessment of enemy strengths and intentions was conspicuously accurate, and data were meanwhile assembled upon which sound plans of attack could be based. General Willoughby, by this noteworthy achievements as an organizer and by his penetrating analysis of the military situation, made an invaluable contribution to the success of military operations in the Southwest Pacific Area ...

Unlike the mysterious three volumes on Southwest Pacific Area (SWPA) operations during the war, these monographs were directly and routinely sent to the Department of the Army.[18]

In October 1945, Willoughby named Colonel Frederick Munson as chief of the Historical Investigation Section; Munson had been the military attaché in Tokyo in 1941 and would play a critical role in the collection and exploitation of Japanese military records in the immediate post-war years, a task that would occupy the attentions of Willoughby and MacArthur as well. In the fall of 1946, Willoughby supervised two major historical efforts led by University of Maryland history professor Gordon W. Prange (a name familiar to generations of Pearl Harbor scholars). Prange, on a leave of absence, was commissioned to write a history of MacArthur's SWPA operations on the one hand and also to exercise oversight of the Japanese side of the story, written by former Japanese Army and Navy officers.[19] In a controversial move, Willoughby recruited these former officers at their old imperial ranks, based on a remarkable assessment the United States would need a Japanese ally in the inevitable war against the Soviet Union.[20]

The perceived mollycoddling of the recent enemy seemed even more troubling thanks to Willoughby's involvement with a former Japanese general accused of war crimes against American military personnel. Recently declassified records and uncovered archival materials have divulged Willoughby's connection with former commander of the Japanese Thirteenth Army, Sadamu Shimomura, who, shortly after taking command of the unit, personally signed the execution orders for three of the captured "Doolittle Raiders." Despite his involvement, Shimomura became Japan's war minister near the end of World War II and, following the surrender, worked with American authorities to demobilize the Japanese Army. In December 1945, investigators requested Shimomura's arrest, but MacArthur's staff refused, arguing he was too valuable an asset in the reconstruction of Japan. On January 11, 1946, prosecutors formally requested his arrest, only to be denied again by the SCAP's staffers, who replied that the case would be approached from an "international standpoint," an allusion to Shimomura's perceived importance. Shimomura was finally arrested and interned in Tokyo's Sugamo Prison in early February 1946, as MacArthur's staffers tried to elicit statements from witnesses to exonerate the former army commander. It was at this juncture that Willoughby weighed in, writing "As the final decision for the execution of the fliers had been made by Imperial General Headquarters, Tokyo on 10 October [1942], the signature of the Commanding General Thirteenth Army on the execution order was simply a matter of formality." When all was said and done, MacArthur's subordinates were so successful in delaying the legal process that prosecutors ran out of time to try Shimomura. As a September 1946 memo put it, "The War Crimes mission in China is about to close. Further action by this Headquarters with respect to the trial of General Shimomura is no longer possible. Accordingly, this Headquarters is not disposed to take any further action in the case." Willoughby arranged for Shimomura's secret release and for the expunging of his name from all prison records. A driver took Shimomura home on March 14, 1947, shortly before officials sent him to "a quiet place for a few months." Later, Shimomura was elected to the Japanese parliament before dying in a 1968 traffic accident at the age of 80.[21]

Before the challenging work of administering post-war Japan began, Willoughby paid a return visit to the States in January 1946. At each stop along the way—Hawaii, San Francisco, New York—he spoke to the press, singing the praises of the Nisei and their contributions to the war effort. "The nature of Nisei service," explained Willoughby, "from an intelligence point of view, represented the greatest single contribution to the Pacific war ... Their loyalty was never questioned ... They did their job quietly, and with great efficiency ... I have been employing several thousand Nisei since 1942, and feel morally obligated to report on them."[22]

As many military veterans can attest, rank afforded in wartime is often downgraded in peacetime and such was Willoughby's experience as well. On June 12, 1946, Willoughby's military rank was "readjusted," according to the euphemistic language in the War Department Special Orders. In typically straight-forward fashion, the orders announced to Willoughby "the termination of your temporary appointment as Major General, Army of the United States" and his reversion to the rank of brigadier general, with a date of rank of June 20, 1942.[23]

***

Praise for the accomplishments of Nisei soldiers during the war made even more irritating the perceived Communist conspiracies at home, abroad, and even within MacArthur's staff that he saw, prompting him to provide the Counterintelligence Corps (CIC) with tremendous latitude. The CIC spied on American citizens and curried favor with former Japanese secret police and military members. Even peaceful activity by Japanese labor unions came in for censure. Referring to such activity as "Communist agitation," Willoughby, after 1948, and with MacArthur's blessing, ratcheted up his burgeoning anti-leftist campaign, focusing his harsh light on the spy ring led by double-agent Richard Sorge, a German Communist posted to Shanghai in early 1930 and who later ran a successful Russian spy network in Tokyo during the war. Also a part of the Sorge ring was a female GRU (Soviet military intelligence agency) agent known as "Sonia," who, in about 1930, became acquainted with co-conspirator Agnes Smedley, who began as Sorge's assistant and eventually "progressed" to being his mistress (The Sorge spy ring, and Agnes Smedley in particular, would occupy a special place in Willoughby's heart for years to come). Sorge had gained the trust of the Nazi Ambassador to Japan, served as the embassy's press attaché, and began feeding a sizable amount of intelligence—though virtually ignored by Joseph Stalin—to Moscow concerning the war plans of the Rome–Berlin–Tokyo Axis. Early on the morning of October 23, 1941, the German Ambassador in Tokyo, Major General Eugen Ott, sent a top-secret telegram to Berlin, informing the Foreign Office that Dr. Richard Sorge—who had been part of the German colony in Tokyo since 1933—along with German national Max Klausen, had been arrested by Japanese police on October 17 and charged with espionage. Before his 1944 execution by the Japanese, Sorge acknowledged Smedley's assistance in a written confession.[24]

With both an interest in, and some responsibility for, counterespionage in post-war Japan, Willoughby played a key role in publicizing the Sorge espionage case. In September 1945, the Military Intelligence branch of the American post-war administration in Japan was established and the following month freed 500 Japanese political prisoners, among them eight individuals integral to the Sorge case. As Willoughby recalled, it was "an excited Japanese official who advised me that the release list of political prisoners contained foreign espionage agents, the remnants of the Sorge espionage ring—in particular, one Max Klausen." At Willoughby's expressed direction, Lieutenant Colonel T. P. Davis of the Civil Intelligence Service (CIS) was ordered to compile a report on the case. This report was forwarded to Washington in early 1946. Convinced the Sorge case was merely the tip of the iceberg in terms of a Soviet worldwide espionage network, Willoughby also directed CIS historian Dr. H. T. Noble to redraft the Davis report and send it to Washington in December 1947, with a recommendation to use it as "instructional material in view of the apprehensions aroused by the Canadian espionage case" (a reference to the 1945 defection of Soviet cipher clerk Igor Gouzenko, assigned to the Soviet Embassy in Ottawa). Willoughby was reluctant to release any of this material to the press, since it involved sensitive information on the inner workings of the espionage ring, although the Japanese press was already on the story. In June 1948, the War Department cabled Willoughby that the State Department wanted to release the Sorge material at the request of Walter Bedell Smith, the U.S. Ambassador to Russia, in order to refute Soviet charges of espionage activity by American staffers in Moscow. Willoughby and the War Department wrangled over this issue for the remainder of the year until the former ultimately welcomed the fact of the inevitable publicity on the case. A summary was cleared by the War Department and released to the press in Tokyo on February 10, 1949. That same month, Willoughby published *Report of the Sorge Case,* which he claimed "electrified Japanese opinion, and transformed the whole issue" by implicating Ito Ritsu, a member of the Politburo of the Japanese Communist Party. Willoughby indicated Ritsu, who represented the political entity already approved by American authorities as the legitimate political organization in post-war Japan, had betrayed Sorge and fellow conspirators to the Japanese police.[25]

So significant was this case to Willoughby that he wrote a book on it—*Sorge, Soviet Master Spy.* According to a review of the book, it was based on an original report written by Sorge and was compiled from Japanese court records and other materials the author would have had access to, though perhaps indirect and unauthorized. The reviewer, however, dismissed the intelligence officer's tome, charging that he had "distorted the historical significance of the case by highlighting it as one episode in a conspiracy extending to the United States," a charge certainly in keeping with Willoughby's opinions and stated beliefs. Other reviewers castigated it for being "poorly-organized, containing interpretations that reflected Willoughby's political values, and drawing conclusions with less care than is paid to the fact of the case itself. The reader will do best by relying on Deakin and Storry" (a reference to the "far superior" work, *The Case of Richard Sorge).*[26]

Willoughby assiduously fed his incriminating research material to the infamous House Un-American Activities Committee in the late 1940s and early 1950s. Aware of the need to practice at home what was being preached abroad, MacArthur gave Willoughby permission in 1948 to purge from the SCAP ranks "New Deal liberals" and Jews—often considered one and the same by MacArthur and Willoughby.[27]

In October 1947, Willoughby also sent a report to the FBI on his discovery. Although the larger-than-life Bureau Director J. Edgar Hoover found Willoughby's report flawed, the U.S. Army nevertheless used it to accuse American Agnes Smedley of complicity in the Sorge spy ring, only to withdraw its charges a week later. In July 1948, Willoughby wrote the Army Chief of Staff given the possibility of libel cases being filed as a result of the charges and disclosures. After pointing out that if anyone were to be sued, it would have to be either the State Department or the Military Intelligence Division (MID), Department of the Army (DA), Willoughby offered his suggestion as to how to proceed with the bombshell case:

> In view of the "cold war" now being waged, we should not withhold material of this sort especially as the Tokyo correspondents have been increasingly alert. It is now a matter of "timing." I suggest that we give the Military Intelligence Division, Department of the Army, a "break" and release the story before some local hack-writer snoop exploits our hundreds of manhours of patient research.

He listed the individuals exposed, in descending order of significance—Agnes Smedley, Guenther Stein, Ticho L. Lilliestrom, Joseph Newman, Eugene H. Dooman, and British Military Attaché General Francis S. Piggott. Willoughby reiterated that Smedley and Stein had already been reported to MID, DA, and the FBI as "security risks to the United States." He added:

> They are now "molders of public opinion." That is how the public is poisoned and misled. The publication of this story will help to undo these traitors and Soviet stooges … My guess is, that when the facts become known, they will carefully abstain from libel suits. At this point, it should be noted that no individual may sue the United States Government without its consent. This includes actions for libel.

Stung by the criticism and unfortunate turn of events, Willoughby devoted much of 1949 to uncovering ties between Smedley and the Sorge ring, which he then turned over to the House Un-American Activities Committee in 1951. Subsequent information clearly implicated Smedley—who had conveniently died on May 6, 1950, precluding a libel suit—meaning that, despite some missteps, Willoughby had indeed helped uncover a spy, the clear mark of success for a counterintelligence/intelligence officer.[28] Comintern (the abbreviated title for the Communist International organization) documents have since clearly implicated Smedley in the ring's operations in China, as well as in her affair with Sorge.[29] Fascinated, Willoughby turned his research on the case into *Shanghai Conspiracy*, a detailed account of Communist espionage activity in Japan during the war and which included several references to American Communists.[30]

Bad as Communists in Washington, D.C., or in the Army as a whole were, even worse of course were known or suspected leftists within Far East Command itself, a topic to which Willoughby devoted specific attention. In late January 1947, he wrote a memo on the subject of "Foreign Elements Employed in General Headquarters." On the basis of investigation and detailed statistics, he discovered there was "an unusually large percentage of leftist-inclined personnel among individuals with Russian or Russian-satellite backgrounds." Specifically, of the 3,877 civilian employees within the General Headquarters, 199 were either first-generation Russians or from Russian satellites, or were either naturalized United States citizens born in Russia or in satellite nations. Forty percent of the 199 were of Russian background, which meant 60 percent came from Russian satellites; of that 40 percent, 16 percent were naturalized United States citizens. More disturbing was the G-2's conclusion that "a comparatively large number of leftist personnel … now occupy exceedingly responsible positions in this Headquarters, where they are able to exercise a direct influence in matters of policy making …"[31]

Two months later, Willoughby expressed some of his misgivings in a special report provided to the chief of staff. He informed his immediate superior that he had discovered 11 cases to varying degrees of leftist penetration into GHQ "through the medium of regularly employed War Department civilian personnel." He wrote:

A review of the cases indicates an increasing tendency toward leftist penetration into GHQ. This constitutes a direct menace to the security of the United States and to the progress of the occupational program in Japan and its ultimate reputation ... At the same time, the presence of these leftist personnel in responsible positions in GHQ constitutes a serious threat to the security of classified information. It is known that some of these individuals associate with leftist newspaper correspondents in Tokyo, and on at least two occasions there have been known information leaks.[32]

In a case of "mission creep," Willoughby found himself dealing with another topic that seems quite alien to the duties generally associated with an intelligence officer—namely, police matters, another of the issues on which he and Whitney disagreed. Allied occupation authorities were intent upon removing the pre-war police state in Japan, so onerous that the police dictated when and even how citizens would clean their homes. As a means to that end, on December 26, 1947, the Ministry of Home Affairs Abolition Law was implemented, ushering in a period of reform for the Japanese police system. Willoughby was involved in this endeavor by virtue of his position as the head of the Public Safety Division (PSD) and, in that guise, approved an increase of 48 percent in the size of the Japanese police force when the population had increased only 20 percent. In answer to the inevitable question of "why," he said the end of the undesirable pre-war police practices had reduced the efficiency of the force, necessitating more officers to do the work. It is also interesting to note, in regard to other criticisms concerning his selective use of information, that Willoughby and PSD chief Colonel Harry S. Pulliam, ensured they did *not* report a rising crime rate, despite a rising population and a bevy of new laws. Japanese observers were generally critical of Willoughby's skewed findings, especially once they discovered he had included neither economic crimes (a category in which the increase was the most significant) nor misdemeanors.[33]

On February 22, 1947, Willoughby and Pulliam forwarded a police reform plan to the Japanese Government, which then was pressured to recommend it to MacArthur. The rub was that this plan ran counter to the decentralized administration General Whitney and his Government Section sought for Japan. Wrangling between the two Bataan veterans continued, until Whitney became so adamant on the point that MacArthur finally ordered Willoughby to accept Whitney's counterproposal. Instead of a single, nationally unified police force with 118 local forces, Whitney's plan called for 1,605 small police forces, each independent and financially autonomous. This proposal became the Police Law, effective December 17, 1947. In the face of mounting criticism, however, especially concerning the use of private subsidies to support the police forces (which Willoughby warned against), the plan put forward by Willoughby and Pulliam was revived. In July 1950, MacArthur called for a National Police Reserve (NPR) of 75,000 officers (later increased to 110,000) under the personal control of the prime minister. Separate from the regular police, NPR officers would be equipped with American weapons and would receive American military-style training. Although both Japanese and American officials were very careful not to refer to the NPR as a military force, in May 1951, MacArthur, appearing before a Senate special investigating committee, noted the NPR "could readily be converted into excellent ground troops." By the end of February 1953, it had become obvious a decentralized police force was costly, inefficient, and—because it provided no room for advancement—lowered morale; the Whitney proposal had been completely repudiated.[34]

During his post-war years in Japan, Willoughby also cut his teeth on a little-appreciated ally of counterintelligence, psychological operations (psyops), experience which would come in handy in just a few years' time. In 1947, MacArthur stood up a small Psychological Warfare Branch (PWB) in the Far East Command (FECOM) G-2 in Tokyo. To head the PWB, Willoughby selected retired U.S. Army Colonel Woodall Greene, who fleshed out his staff with other World War II psyops veterans. The day after President Truman announced American troops would be heading to Korea to support the UN offensive, the PWB had already designed, printed, and airdropped the first propaganda leaflets over enemy troops. By December 1950, the unit was 35 strong and by the summer of 1951, 55 strong, comprised primarily of civilians and select military personnel on loan. Soon renamed the Psychological Warfare Section (PWS), it was eventually subordinated to the G-3 (Operations).[35]

In the immediate post-war years, Willoughby was displeased with the emerging intelligence structure and looked on the successors of the Office of Strategic Services (OSS) with increasing envy, given his view that he was compelled to operate on a shoestring. In 1946, he whined, "Here I am losing money and personnel because of Washington orders. You people in CIG [the CIA's predecessor, the Central Intelligence Group] have all this money and personnel; why can't I get some of both from you?"[36]

In January 1947, Willoughby came to terms with Director of Central Intelligence (DCI) Hoyt Vandenberg, whereby Major James Kellis and a communications officer—both from the CIG—established a CIA–FECOM liaison unit in Seoul with XXIV Corps, with appropriate organizational camouflage.[37] Outwardly cooperative with the fledgling CIA, Willoughby proved to be less so in reality and early on his intentions to control the CIA in-theater became obvious. "He was unable to accept any newcomers or competitors …," one historian assessed. "He seemed to like to remind CIA that his wartime clandestine and covert operations were of such high quality that they outshone OSS and therefore his 'surveillance' of current and coming operations in and from Japan was necessary as long as the occupation lasted."[38] In a private letter to fellow Japanese war veteran and friend General Albert Wedemeyer, Willoughby described CIA officers as "complete newcomers … working under various thin covers," complained they were "not in business long enough," or, worst of all, were "left-overs from OSS." He observed, "They are out here in our area. I have given them moral support and urge co-operative joint operations; we are of course years ahead of the game. I did not need OSS during the war and expect to operate without the CIA. They have nothing to offer in the past or at this time."[39]

There were, however, brief bursts of cooperation between Willoughby and his CIA "colleagues"—in April 1948, a Soviet cutter arrived in the Japanese port of Nemuro, on the island of Hokkaido. The cutter's commander, Captain Andreyev, and his crew requested asylum; however, the next morning authorities discovered a suicide note allegedly written by Andreyev, and no captain. CIA's Office of Special Operations (OSO) had faked his suicide and spirited him away, with no notification to FECOM. Subsequently, a Soviet patrol boat captured a Japanese fishing vessel that had strayed into Soviet waters, towing it to the Kuril islands, where the crew was interrogated and released. On May 11, 1949, a very-much-alive Captain Andreyev was transferred from FECOM G-2 custody to CIA Tokyo; the Agency promptly placed him in a safe house outside Japan.[40]

Eager to enlist the Japanese as allies in the international fight against the "Red menace," Willoughby was among a group of individuals who sought to rebuild the Japanese military following the war—a predictably volatile topic. To this end, Willoughby closely collaborated with General Seizo Arisue with the goal of consolidating the sharpest minds on the Japanese General Staff into an "historical research" team while also functioning as a covert intelligence organization operating within the confines, and protection, of Willoughby's G-2 section of FECOM Headquarters. To assist in this endeavor, Willoughby also kept track of Japanese veterans through the records of the Demobilization Bureau.[41]

As MacArthur's G-2 in post-war Japan, Willoughby was also called upon to develop expertise in another area of military intelligence, namely, counterintelligence. The issue at hand was Japanese expatriates released from Soviet prisoner-of-war camps, 95,000 of whom were "probably Communists sent back by Soviet authorities to form the nucleus of a Japanese Communist Party," according to one source.[42] Tasked with investigating these Japanese repatriates, Willoughby brought more enthusiasm to the task than knowledge or skill, but created a new Civil Intelligence Section within the framework of the Supreme Commander for the Allied powers and tasked the 441st Counter Intelligence Corps (CIC) to collect information on subversive activity by these individuals. As a result of Willoughby's on-the-job training as a counterintelligence officer, he concluded that Herbert Norman—who represented Canada's Ministry of External Affairs and who was attached to the CIC unit within the U.S. Army Office of General Headquarters in Tokyo—might be a Communist or Soviet agent. Willoughby was able to remove him from his position within four months and, while debate about Norman's complicity continues, a 1986 book (*No Sense of Evil*) by James Barros argues a strong case for Norman's guilt.[43]

Surprisingly, the fall of Nationalist China to the Communists in 1949 seemed to elicit little outward reaction from MacArthur or Willoughby, despite their common attitude toward leftists. However, although MacArthur was openly supportive of

Chiang Kai-Shek, he privately assessed the latter's unpopularity, both at home and abroad, made the defense of Taiwan challenging. Thus, in late 1949, MacArthur began efforts to oust his ally-of-sorts from power. In that vein, Willoughby visited Taiwan to broach the idea of an "officer from General MacArthur's staff" as a "special advisor." In early 1950, Willoughby further promised to create a spy network in China and to assist in an anti-Communist guerilla campaign following the fall of the Nationalist government.[44] During a visit to Tokyo, Britain's High Commissioner in Southeast Asia, Malcolm MacDonald, asked about Willoughby's assessment of the *Kuomintang*, the Nationalist Army of Chiang Kai-Shek. The SCAP G-2 responded that he included Taiwan in "the line of vital American defense," likely a parroting of MacArthur's assessment. When the press asked Willoughby about the possibility Japanese had been smuggled to Taiwan to assist the *Kuomintang*, he admitted that some had probably come in that way, but such an infiltration could not be avoided given the limited numbers of police in post-war Japan.[45]

***

Though it occurred during the post-war period, Willoughby's involvement in the uncovering of a new and ugly chapter in the history of World War II in the Pacific Theater would not come to light for many years. In 2005, a Japanese researcher working in the U.S. National Archives discovered two critical documents. In that year, Kanegawa University professor Keiichi Tsuneishi, an expert on chemical and biological weapons, uncovered two declassified documents in the Archives. One of the formerly "top secret" documents was a report dated July 17, 1947, on biological warfare written for the Far Eastern Commission's Chief of Staff—the author of the report was then-Brigadier General Charles Willoughby. The other document was a letter dated July 22, 1947, written by Willoughby to Major General S. J. Chamberlin, Director of Intelligence, U.S. War Department General Staff, to urge the continued use of confidential and unrestricted funds to collect such intelligence. Both documents brought to public light the barbaric crimes of the Japanese Army's infamous Unit 731, which conducted biological warfare experiments on the unsuspecting Chinese populace during World War II from its headquarters in the suburbs of Harbin in northeastern China's Heilongjiang Province. Reportedly, some three thousand died in these medical experiments, notably including an unknown number of American prisoners of war later in the conflict. In these documents, Willoughby characterized the value of his unit's investigations reflected in these reports, indicating the collected information "will have the greatest value in future development of the U.S. BW [bacteriological warfare] program." Indeed, the Pentagon was so taken with the potential value of this information in a widely expected showdown with the Russians that officials granted these Japanese immunity from prosecution in return for their laboratory records. On December 12, 1947, the Pentagon acknowledged Willoughby's "wholehearted cooperation" in this endeavor, which consisted of examination of the "human pathological material." The reports also further discussed Unit 731—created by the Japanese Army in 1936 and intended to be used against the Soviet Union—noting assigned personnel created a variety of biological weapons using plague, anthrax, and other bacteria and conducted numerous human experiments during the war, resulting in injuries and deaths of tens of thousands of Chinese, among others.[46]

Meanwhile, Willoughby—the consummate letter writer, with a wide and impressive group of correspondents—gave all appearances of being gainfully employed in post-war Japan. On October 21, 1948, he wrote former President Herbert Hoover, "Incidentally, intelligence continues under Occupation, perhaps intensified and here again, we operate on our own quite nicely and economically and without benefit of C.I.A." He expanded further on his views of the then two-year-old intelligence community "whiz kid" in a letter to Major General Harry H. Vaughn, the military aide to President Truman, on June 7, 1949:

> As regards intelligence in war, they seem to be making a terrific fuss over CIA recently? I do not quite understand this? CIA is the foster child of Donovan's war-time OSS? As an old SWPA member you may recall that OSS has never operated in the whole Pacific; they were neither required nor needed. We take pride in having operated on our own military resource, behind the Jap lines, from the Solomons to Singapore, from Bali to the Philippines. We sank Jap transports in Singapore under the nose of the Southern Fleet and operated an underground in the P.I. [Philippine Islands] with daily radio reports on everything from airfields in Negros, to the daily guest list in the Manila Hotel; of course, no one ever asked our opinion, in legislation, on CIA, but the record is there ...[47]

***

During the post-war years, Willoughby continued to faithfully reflect MacArthur's unwillingness to entertain observers of his business. On one occasion, the Joint Staff's Joint Security Control entity asked MacArthur three times for permission to send two of its officers to the theater to determine the success of American deception operations during World War II. Despite the persistence of the Joint Staff, they never received such permission, prompting one student of the topic to opine, "One is inclined to see in this the hand of MacArthur's intelligence chief, Major General Charles A. Willoughby; temperamental and explosive, Willoughby was near-paranoid about any outside interference in his domain"—again, mimicking his boss's hostility to having his actions second-guessed.[48] Influential State Department officer George Kennan detected much the same sentiment, noting that "Washington did not loom very large on the horizons of that highly self-centered occupational command."[49]

Willoughby was never one to suffer fools gladly and an incident in Japan provided additional grist for the mill for his critics. The proximate cause of the row appeared to be the unwillingness of Columbia Broadcasting System correspondent William Costello to blithely accept the information dispensed by MacArthur's staffers concerning true conditions in post-war Japan. Lauded by his home office, Costello was vilified by FECOM; he began hearing MacArthur was "distressed" by his cavalier actions and a friend called him and casually mentioned he should watch his step because counterintelligence agents had turned over his old "Communist card" from California to the G-2. Having never been either a Communist or a Californian, Costello responded in kind, openly sharing his negative opinion of Willoughby with anyone who would listen. The disagreement came to a head in the spring and summer of 1948, when MacArthur's Chief of Staff General Ned Almond repeated the baseless charge that Costello was a Communist. Knowing Willoughby had staffers who monitored all outgoing press cables, Costello wired his home office that he had traced the slander to its source and was preparing to take action. The cockfight came to an end a few weeks later when Willoughby's secretary called and invited Costello to a no-holds-barred stag dinner hosted by the G-2 himself.[50]

***

Willoughby's ever-expanding portfolio of duties broadened to include politics, actually a specific subset of that broad category. Given the overweening presence Douglas MacArthur was during the war, it was not surprising that, at the urging of influential friends and colleagues, he sought to secure the Republican presidential nomination, in both 1944 and 1948. Willoughby, of course, was involved in both such campaigns, along with his lover at the time, the larger-than-life Clare Booth Luce, described as the "vivacious and talented wife" of Henry Luce. Willoughby served as the "clandestine knight errant" between MacArthur on the one hand and a group of moderate Republicans, led by Senator Arthur Vandenberg, on the other; Vandenberg hoped to quietly coalesce a group around MacArthur and make him a viable candidate. However, there was disquieting news on that front; as Vandenberg told MacArthur supporter and Sears Roebuck chairman Robert Wood, "veterans returning from the South Pacific are not enthusiastic about our friend," meaning MacArthur.[51] When MacArthur fared poorly in the 1948 open primary in his official home state of Wisconsin, it was clear he was not really presidential timber. Besides, as Willoughby noted in an August 1944 comment, MacArthur had no real interest in politics; rather, he claimed he was interested in "the soldier's profession."[52]

Willoughby reflected the near paranoia of his boss in the latter's belief the primary mission of the CIA in the Far East was to furnish information to MacArthur's enemies in Washington. MacArthur's continuing uncooperativeness, combined with CIA complaints, prompted President Truman to directly order him to allow the CIA to operate *sans* harassment within FECOM. The general complied, albeit reluctantly, and staff members soon came to understand that "The Boss" would be displeased by any other collaboration aside from that through "official channels"—meaning, MacArthur, Willoughby, or someone designated by Willoughby.[53]

Willoughby's hostility towards OSS in the theater carried over to its CIA successor as well. His relations with Office of Policy Coordination chief George E. Aurell were strained, despite Aurell's positive stance with MacArthur. The former Consul of Yokohama, born and raised in Kobe, Japan, Aurell was an SWPA veteran (a Nisei team chief), a history which endeared him to MacArthur's staff. However, it was his colleague Hans Tofte who arrived in Japan in mid-1950 to organize covert action operations. Despite John Singlaub's assessment that Tofte was "a really brilliant, suave and sociable guy with an extensive Asian background," Willoughby allegedly threatened to throw the CIA out of the Far East all together, a marked *lack* of cooperation. Tofte, however, made of sterner stuff, ignored the threats of the FECOM G-2, who apparently was unable to back up his threats. Tofte defiantly established six stations in Japan, the major one at Atsugi Naval Air Station, and worked with the Air Force Office of Special Investigation to set up a network of agents in North Korea to aid downed American pilots.[54]

Just two months before the North Korean invasion of the South, MacArthur, Chief of Staff General Almond, Willoughby, and CIA Office of Policy Coordination chief Frank Wisner had a joint conference in which they hammered out an initially-promising agreement, though it ultimately proved ineffectual. In a letter to CIA Headquarters, Wisner reported that:

> [Willoughby] had willingly obstructed OSO operations in Northeast Asia, including Korea. He refused to accept the letter or the spirit … and chose to ignore the contents of the letter from the Director of Intelligence, Department of the Army, dated 1 April 1949, which set forth the approval and legal position of CIA in the Far East Command as interpreted by the Department of the Army.[55]

The testiness of Willoughby was also on display shortly after the occupation of Japan began. One evening, American military policemen (MP) raided Tokyo's Hotel Marunuchi, looking for black marketers. They made the unfortunate error of disturbing Willoughby and his guests, who included the stranded Italian Fascist ambassador to Japan and his staffers. Since Willoughby previously had received an award from Mussolini's government, he took a dim view of the law enforcement raid. Furious, he gave the MPs "a good piece of his mind."[56]

Like his boss, Willoughby had a deep aversion to the press, which returned the favor. Given his "stature, his German accent, and his arrogance," he came to be viewed as "an exotic and sinister presence in a flawed command," in the words of one observer. When a movie producer in post-war Japan blamed the coming of the war on the influence of the financial cliques, collectively known as the *zaibatsu*, and the emperor, Willoughby blocked a showing of the film, with the producer—in true Hollywood fashion—claiming he had been browbeaten and roughed up by "professional killers." Willoughby took seriously the mission of intimidating reporters hostile to MacArthur or otherwise deemed "subversive" and continued to hammer the theme that all criticisms of the American occupation of post-war Japan were unjustified. When the *Nippon Times* was about to publish an editorial mildly critical of the occupation, Willoughby and two MPs physically stopped the presses to prevent publication of the offending editorial.[57]

Willoughby and MacArthur's ally in keeping the press at bay was Brigadier General LeGrande A. "Pick" Diller, MacArthur's aide-de-camp and press relations advisor; he became known to the press as "Killer" for his killing of many of their potential stories in advance. Both Diller and Willoughby viewed all criticism of the occupation as a direct reflection on MacArthur and thus did all they could to keep bad news from the press, a direct holdover from attitudes and actions in the SWPA during World War II. "Any mention of high casualties," noted one author, "was carefully censored and in some cases victory was proclaimed days in advance."[58] The course of events in the next few years would ensure Willoughby's battle with the media would not only continue, but heat up considerably.

CHAPTER FOUR

The Korean War: The Curtain Rises

Korea's geographic isolation from the rest of world came to an abrupt end in the 19th century, when Westerners discovered the peninsula, increasingly referred to by the descriptive phrase coined by American author and astronomer Percival Lowell—the founder of Arizona's Lowell Observatory—as "The Land of the Morning Calm." Most Westerners assumed, however, that Korea was little more than a vassal state of China. And it proved to be Japan that better understood the Confucian "father–son" relationship[1] and sought to make the strategic region a part of the Japanese empire. In 1910, Japan had annexed the peninsula and transformed it into a semi-industrialized Japanese colony. Among the changes imposed was a highly structured educational system, which in turn took many of the brightest Korean males and made Japanese Army officers of them. By the 1941 Pearl Harbor attack, Japan had quelled repeated attempts at rebellion by the Koreans and made the peninsula an important military base within the Japanese Empire.[2]

Korea came to full attention of the international community after more than three decades of exploitation by the Japanese. In 1943, President Franklin D. Roosevelt, British Prime Minister Winston Churchill, and Chinese Premier Chiang Kai-Shek stated in the Cairo Declaration that year their collective intention that "Korea shall become free and independent"; however, at the February 1945 Yalta Conference, Roosevelt told Soviet Premier Joseph Stalin he did not think the Korean people would be ready for independence for two to three decades. Shortly after the Japanese surrender in September, Roosevelt's successor, Harry Truman, proposed the Soviets accept the Japanese surrender north of the 38th Parallel and the Americans that of the Japanese south of that artificial demarcation line. This promise was renewed at the Potsdam Conference of 1945 and acceded to by the Soviet Union, after Korea's entry into the war against Japan in August 1945. At that juncture, not only did Korean dreams of independence end abruptly but the agreement also "turned a homogeneous people into implacable enemies."[3]

The gradual shift of the "north" and "south" Korea into the Soviet and American spheres of influence, respectively, highlighted the stark differences in the geographic and economic distinctiveness of each region. The Soviet zone to the north was rich in natural resources and provided the bulk of the manufactured goods needed in the south; it also had the only petroleum processing and cement plants, and its Japanese-built hydroelectric plants were among the best in the world. Thus, the south was dependent upon the north for its electric power but had a primarily agricultural economy and two-thirds of the peninsula's population of 30 million.[4]

American strategic planners realized the potential importance of the peninsula—the Japanese surrender had left the Soviet Union the dominant presence in the region and American leaders were unwilling to stand idly by as the Soviets merely replaced the Japanese as overlords. Thus, a joint committee of State, War, and Navy officials began planning for an American role in the post-war occupation of Korea. They directed two young colonels—one of them future Secretary of State Dean Rusk—to begin the requisite planning. Consulting a National Geographic map of the unfamiliar peninsula, they concluded that, since the 38th Parallel neatly divided it, the notional bifurcation would serve as an acceptable line of demarcation between the Soviet and American occupation zones. Such a division would divide the peninsula roughly into two countries of somewhat equal proportions, with the capital city of Seoul, more than half the population, and most of the agricultural land and light industry to the south of that geographic feature. Much to the amazement of American officials, the Soviets agreed, which was fortunate, since the United States could not have stopped them at the time had they chosen to simply continue driving south.[5]

As time passed, however, it became increasingly clear that, left to its own devices, Korea would fall entirely under Soviet control—the Soviets quickly closed their border with the south, largely ending transit into and out of the North. In short order, Korea became a prize in the post-war war of ideas between East and West; in July 1946, President Truman described the peninsula as "an ideological battleground on which our entire success in Asia depends." In September 1947, the United States, over Soviet objections, referred the future of Korea to the United Nations General Assembly, which directed national elections be held followed by independence and the departure of all foreign troops in the country. But the election proved to be a farce, with the results tainted by the opposition of Russia and North Korea to the UN mandate and by the non-participation of leftists in South Korea. The election of Dr. Synghman Rhee in July 1948, the South Korean Republic's first elected leader, was characterized by a ruthlessness that resembled a dictatorship more than a democracy. Rhee, 75 years old in 1948, was American educated, an ardent patriot, and a dedicated anti-Communist but also a "feisty aristocrat" not in touch with his own people, thanks in some measure to his marriage to an Austrian. In the North, the People's Democratic Republic of Korea (DPRK) was announced in September, with Soviet-backed strongman Kim Il Sung as premier. Premier Kim was a combat veteran of the Chinese Civil War and one of the few Koreans who adopted both Chinese and Soviet Communism. Soviet troops left North Korea in 1948—the United

States would like to have matched the Soviet move, but the general opinion that the South Korean Army was still largely untrained and poorly-equipped persuaded the United States to keep some of its troops there for a time. The last American troops left South Korea in June 1949, leaving only the 500-man contingent known as the U.S. Military Advisory Group to the Republic of Korea (KMAG), with the unenviable and increasingly impossible mission of turning the South Korean Army into a modern fighting force.[6]

On March 22, 1949, the National Security Council issued its report to the president, known as NSC 8/2. Council members had considered three possible courses of action for the United States in Korea and recommended to the president he adopt the middle one—namely, that the United States would support the Republic of Korea (ROK) in drawing down the number of American soldiers and amount of equipment in Korea while simultaneously minimizing the potential of Communist domination once the United States left the peninsula. Quoting the Joint Chiefs, NSC 8/2 stated unequivocally, "The U.S. has little strategic interest in maintaining its present troops and bases in Korea." While certainly true at that time, there were already disquieting rumblings concerning the potential for conflict on the peninsula. On April 13, 1949, U.S. Secretary of State Dean Acheson dispatched a note to the American Mission in Korea. It referred to a source in the Far East, "who has an excellent reputation for accurate reporting," who said he expected "serious trouble in Korea within a 60-day period" and that the Democratic Republic would take the initiative in any such development."[7] While such a prognostication proved premature and partially incorrect, it was nevertheless noteworthy.

As head of state, President Rhee had asked as early as April 1949 if the United States would regard an invasion across the 38th Parallel by the North as an attack upon the American people and if such should occur, could South Korea count on full-fledged American military assistance. He had to wait until January 12, 1950, for his answer when, during a luncheon address to the National Press Club, Secretary of State Dean Acheson gave a major American foreign policy speech. Acheson discussed the concept of a "defensive perimeter" that ran from the Aleutian Islands to Japan, to the Ryukus, and then to the Philippines. Areas within that designated perimeter were considered of strategic significance to the United States and would be defended under all circumstances. President Rhee could not miss the fact that Korea lay *outside* that defensive perimeter and thus the ROK could not count on full-fledged military support from the United States should North Korea seek to unify the peninsula by force. Acheson specifically noted no one could guarantee external areas against attack and, should the populace face such an eventuality, they were expected to wage their own resistance efforts until the matter could be brought to the United Nations.[8]

As 1949 progressed, there continued to be debate between State Department personnel in Washington and in Korea about the prospects for conflict on the peninsula, and especially concerns South Korea might be the instigator of such. On June 11, 1949, U.S. Ambassador to South Korea John Muccio wrote to Dean Acheson that "it is the settled view of this Mission that no general invasion of North Korea is contemplated or is capable of being developed at this time … it is the considered view of this Mission that neither South Korea nor North Korea … is likely in the foreseeable future to assume the risks associated with a deliberate all-out invasion." Muccio did add that "recent reports from North Korea suggest that North Korean military preparations are being appreciably intensified," though there was no "substantial" (emphasis in the original) stockpiling of military equipment and supplies. He also confirmed the tit-for-tat cross-border raids between the two Koreas that were so well known to State Department and military personnel familiar with the theater. "As has been reported from time to time," wrote Muccio, "incidents continue to occur daily along the 38th Parallel. Most of these incidents are of a minor character and possess no real significance … No doubt, the future will see a continuation, if not an acceleration, of these border incidents." In a June 27 memo, the Joint Chiefs reiterated their earlier point about the peninsula in American strategic planning when they tersely noted, "Korea is of little strategic value to the United States and … any commitment to United States use of military force in Korea would be ill-advised and impracticable in view of the potentialities of the over-all [sic] world situation and of our heavy international obligations as compared with our current military strength." Three days later, the last GI in the Korean occupation force departed the peninsula.[9]

In the wake of the creation of the North and South Korean states, the U.S. Army in Korea took advantage of the smoldering animosity between countrymen to engage in a focused intelligence collection effort. Landowners, Christians, and other "privileged" Koreans were increasingly embittered by the oppressive Communist regime becoming established in P'yŏngyang; many of these individuals fled southward, preferring to live in what had been the American zone of occupation, now the Republic of Korea. These restive Koreans, described by one author as paramilitary "youth associations," resorted to conducting terrorist operations in the North and South alike—on March 1, 1946, such a group had attempted to assassinate DPRK leader Kim Il Sung in P'yŏngyang. During the occupation period that preceded the creation of the two Koreas, the U.S. Army used these groups to gather intelligence in the Soviet zone and, in 1949, a year after the creation of South Korea, Willoughby was ordered by MacArthur to create a secret intelligence office in Seoul, which became known as the Korean Liaison Office (KLO). The mission of the KLO was two-fold—to monitor the movement of troops in the North and Communist guerillas active in the South, although it was also to gather intelligence on China and the USSR. The KLO recruited Korean peasants, provided them with a modicum of training, and then airdropped them behind enemy lines to collect information and provide reports. It also set up Tactical Liaison Offices at division-level units to recruit Koreans as line crossers to gather clandestine human intelligence (HUMINT). The haphazard, slap-dash nature of the enterprise generally resulted in high numbers of casualties and little intelligence of value. The establishment of the KLO ended the roving gangs of paramilitaries, with some joining the ranks of the South Korean Army or police, and with others joining the KLO. An early recruit to the KLO's ranks was Wonsan native activist Choe Kyu-bong, who had made a name for himself as a member of the right-wing White Shirt Society in Seoul; following a stint with U.S. Army Counterintelligence, he cast his lot with the KLO. Choe was justifiably proud of the accomplishments of the KLO, though he lamented the fact their numerous and accurate reports on P'yŏngyang's war preparations went unheeded in both Tokyo and Washington.[10]

Commanded by Major Lawrence J. Abbott, the entire KLO office consisted of only two commissioned officers, one warrant officer, and two enlisted clerks. Though the Far East Commander's area of influence did not include Korea, Willoughby nevertheless considered it "essential" to maintain this group on the peninsula. By the date of the North Korean invasion of the South, the KLO had 16 operatives deployed in North Korea, compared with only four for the young CIA. On the plus side, KLO was prolific in terms of providing reports—a total of 1,195, with 417 of those submitted in the six months prior to the invasion. Willoughby recalled that KLO reporting topics generally included: pre-invasion preparations; the stand-up of new military units; military unit movements; the training, preparation, and development of the North Korean Air Force; and Soviet and Chinese assistance to the North Korean People's Army (NKPA). However, the consensus opinion was that KLO's reporting focus was too narrow to be valuable and the unit had no means of collecting critical strategic warning information. Serious concerns about source credibility also limited the value of the reporting. Of 59 reports submitted between January and June 1950, only 13 were from sources described as "fairly reliable." The fact the entire network dissolved in the wake of the invasion seems to confirm initial concerns many KLO sources had been doubled and were working for North Korea. Nor were KLO reports highly regarded in either Tokyo or Washington—historian D. Clayton James suggested three reasons for this situation: 1) MacArthur and Willoughby's hostile and arrogant attitude toward the CIA and State intelligence collection efforts in the Far East; 2) the fact that Korea was the responsibility of KMAG; and 3) the fact that Willoughby had previously discounted KLO warnings of impending attacks which did not occur.[11]

The KLO was certainly not the only intelligence asset the United States had in Korea at the time to assess North Korean military might and most likely courses of action. The pre-existing Army intelligence unit, KMAG—commanded by U.S. Army Brigadier General Lynn Roberts but described by one historian as an "intelligence vacuum" with no inherent collection capability[12]—had been around since April 1950 and was staffed with U.S. Army officers working alongside their

South Korean counterparts. However, the intelligence section consisted of only six personnel, who produced a hard copy, weekly intelligence summary beginning in April 1950; reports were described as "short," the sourcing "vague," and the emphasis as almost entirely tactical in nature.[13] Roberts' charge was to train the newly created Army of the Republic of Korea, a force which ultimately grew to 100,000 men, equipped with American weapons (albeit largely obsolete ones, so as not to encourage Rhee to re-unite the peninsula by force). But the American and ROK forces were also focused on intelligence collection targeting North Korean units. In that endeavor, however, MacArthur and Willoughby alike were especially vexed by the fact KMAG was assigned to the State Department rather than to MacArthur's Far East Command (FECOM) in Japan, which meant that potentially critical tactical- and operational-level intelligence collected by KMAG was delivered to Washington directly, bypassing Tokyo completely. Additionally, the United States could rely upon a steady stream of reporting from its military attachés and political analysts assigned to the Embassy in Seoul. As later historian James Schnabel—who reported to the FECOM G-2 in November 1949—has since pointed out, these military attaché groups consisted of Army, Navy, and Air Force personnel, as well as State Department diplomatic and political specialists "whose sole business was to gauge the trend of events." And it was not as though these organizations proved ineffective; rather, they detected such pre-attack indicators as civilians north of the border being displaced by soldiers, the forward massing of supplies and military equipment, and the by-now-routine border skirmishes, which occurred with such great regularity that U.S. Secretary of Defense Louis A. Johnson referred to them as "Sunday morning excursions." And yet, even the buildup just prior to June 25—and the 1,200 warnings dispatched to Washington by FECOM between June 1949 and June 1950—did not strike anyone viewing the scene as unusual.[14] On December 30, 1949, Willoughby forwarded reports to Washington indicating North Korean intentions to invade South Korea in March or April 1950, but caveated that report with his personal observation that such an invasion at that time was "unlikely."[15]

It was also in late 1949 that Willoughby learned there were hundreds of native South Koreans who were training at the Kangdon Police School in the North, the DPRK's primary guerrilla training center. Once these guerrillas had completed their training, they were directed to return to their own houses and farms in South Korea, working quietly by day but arming themselves from secret weapons caches at night and terrorizing their countrymen by setting fires and shooting bystanders. At one point, Willoughby estimated 60 percent of Kim Il Sung's entire guerrilla force was living in the ROK. Willoughby sent a report to Major General Alexander Bolling, the Army's intelligence chief in Washington, claiming many of these guerrillas were entering the South by boat. "The South Korean Navy," Willoughby reported, "is of little value in stopping these infiltrators because ROK patrol boats allow the [guerrillas'] boats to pass in return for bribes." By the end of 1949, Willoughby claimed to have 16 spies operating inside North Korea, though the KLO often questioned the reliability and the skills of these recruits.[16]

In addition to counterintelligence activity, Willoughby also became involved in psychological warfare in the early days of the conflict, at the behest of his commander. Shortly after MacArthur was formally named the commander of all United Nations forces in Korea, he ordered Willoughby to establish a classified organization known as the Joint Services Operation (JSO). The idea was to combine American, Japanese, and Korean intelligence and counterintelligence organizations into a single entity and to manage the covert operations of these disparate pieces. To head the JSO, Willoughby selected an illustrious armored corps officer from World War II, Major General Holmes E. Dager. Among other missions MacArthur envisioned for the unit, he wanted the JSO to insert spies and saboteurs into North Korea and behind enemy lines in the South; conduct commando raids; create and operate escape-and-evasion networks to rescue downed pilots; recruit South Koreans as guerrillas and create a small fleet to insert them into the theater; and wage a psyops campaign involving newspapers, broadcasts, and the use of loudspeakers.[17]

On a larger scale, in mid-February 1950, Secretary of State Acheson's favored Far East source ominously noted that:

> ... in North Korea military preparations have been intensified; liaison between the North Korean army and the Chinese Communists in Manchuria has been constant; military equipment reportedly has funneled across the Yalu River; defense measures have been stepped up, including the founding of plans to move the capital from Pyongyang nearer Manchuria; and the railroad from the 38th Parallel north to Pyongyang has been ripped up.

He added that the "feeling-out" process continued, with "frequent minor forays by both sides into the 'target range' neighborhood of the 38th Parallel—no longer guarded by American troops."[18] In February 1950, two reports from KMAG pegged the seemingly inevitable invasion of South Korea by the North for May, another for June, yet on March 25, 1950, the FECOM G-2 postulated war was unlikely before the end of the summer and that lesser forms of conflict would predominate during the interim. As Willoughby put it, "The most probable course of North Korean action this spring and summer is furtherance of attempts to overthrow the South Korean government by creation of chaotic conditions in the ROK through guerrillas and psychological warfare."[19]

In a series of oral history interviews conducted in 1971, Ambassador Muccio elaborated on his thoughts in the spring of 1950 concerning the situation in Korea. He recalled, "our intelligence reported the arrival of certain military hardware, Yaks [Soviet fighters], and a few Ilyushins [Soviet bombers], a few tanks. Also the return of two elements of North Koreans that had been with the Chinese Communists returned as units. That part of our intelligence was good." He noted, however, the challenge of reading the Korean tea leaves, "particularly from the north, during the whole period from the end of '47 until the spring of 1950 … We knew of the military buildup in the north, but it was hard to determine whether this was additional posturing or whether they actually had some action in mind, and if so just what. That's where the uncertainty was." He also noted that "as far as happenings along the border, we had better intelligence than old man Rhee had, because we had advisory personnel with each Korean military unit along the front."[20]

In the spring of 1950, Willoughby's intelligence staff had warned of potential North Korean offensive action, but Willoughby had drawn incorrect conclusions from the information. As official Army historian James Schnabel has pointed out, the uptick in North Korean troop levels that spring was dismissed as simply the latest round of troop rotations which had been occurring since 1947, with Willoughby attempting to gloss over this most basic error in intelligence estimation.[21] However, when Schnabel reported to G-2 in late 1949, he was briefed that the predominant intelligence assessment was that North Korea would attack and conquer the South the following summer. As he recalled, "the fact seemed to be accepted as regrettable but inevitable."[22]

On May 12, Soviet Ambassador to North Korea T. F. Shtykov was told by Kim Il Sung that he had ordered his military staff to prepare for military operations against the South to begin in June. Although ROK Defense Minister Shin Sung-Mo described the threat of invasion as "imminent," Willoughby rejected such assessments out of hand, dismissing Shin's figures as "greatly exaggerated." Despite such a rebuke, the May 23 G-2 Intelligence Summary felt compelled to admit, "Outbreak of hostilities may occur at anytime in Korea."[23]

***

As many of the planners of and participants in the new war would discover, certainly in stark military terms, the Korean Peninsula was "a terrible place for a modern army to fight a war." Korea was a now-bifurcated nation of mountains and hills separated by valleys filled with rice paddies. Most roads were only wide enough for one-way traffic, single file, and most bridges would not support military trucks, much less tanks and artillery. Airfields were limited in both capacity and capability and the rail facilities were inadequate for the needs of wartime military logistics. Surrounded by water on three sides, the peninsula was subjected to high temperatures and humidity levels in the summer, when 90-degree readings at night and above 100 degrees during the day were not uncommon. What few maps there were of the region in 1950 tended to be Japanese maps from the 1920s–30s, containing many mistranslations and misplaced contour lines.[24] A lack of critical linguistic skills would plague UN forces until late in the war and, at least in part, because the U.S. Army had assessed that Korean terrain was unsuited for armored warfare, ROK forces had never been supplied with the tanks and anti-tank weapons they would need to stop the oncoming columns of Soviet-supplied

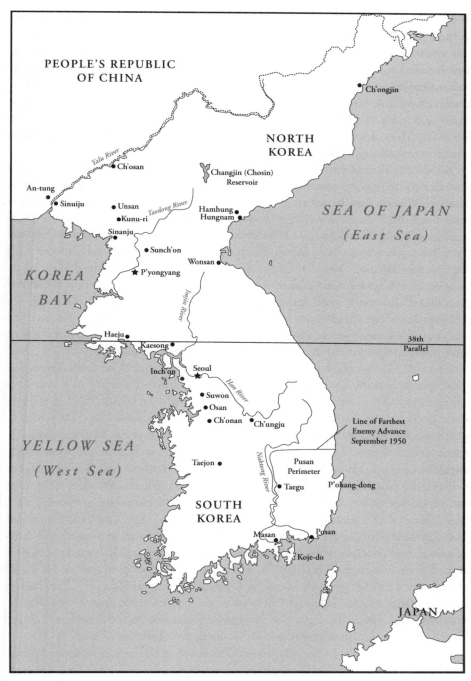

The Korean Peninsula, 1950.

T-34 tanks. As South Korean and American troops in particular would discover, to their peril, the current-generation bazooka anti-tank weapon deployed in Korea was ineffective—better weapons were available, but, for reasons of "economics and inertia," had not been supplied to troops in-theater.[25] Yet, in Willoughby's correspondence of the period is a letter by a Korean War veteran which attests to the accuracy and value of 20 to 30 studies of Korean beaches from former Japanese Army and Navy High Command personnel who had lived and fought in the area for years. Thus, apparently not all the extant information about the topography was either outdated or useless.[26]

When the Korean War broke out, the American military in general and the American intelligence community in particular was, in the words of historian Michael Warner, "no better than mediocre." There were, he admits, "pockets of innovation and excellence, but the overall picture was bleak." The intelligence lessons of World War II had not been learned and cutbacks and reorganization were the predictable watchwords in the aftermath of victory. "At the start of the Cold War," writes Warner, "the United States and its allies were half-blind with regard to Soviet and Communist Chinese intentions and capabilities." As time would tell, even those "intentions and capabilities" were often poorly understood, if at all. The fact that American Intelligence improved during the early days of the Korean War was "because events simply compelled it"; in that sense, he posits, "Korea was an important catalyst for the evolution of the intelligence community."[27]

On paper, Willoughby had 2,500 intelligence personnel at his beck and call in 1950, but those soldiers were largely dedicated to the duties of an army of occupation, which meant they were in Japan, not Korea. His largest single intelligence element at the beginning of the Korean War was the 441st Counterintelligence Detachment, which was focused on the detection and deterrence of subversive Japanese elements. A Military Intelligence Service company supported the 441st but had only two Korean linguists assigned—Youn P. Kim and Richard Chun, both of whom were assigned to the Army Language School at Monterey, California. Kim hailed from California, the son of Korean immigrants, while "Dick" Chun had grown up in Hawaii. Both were World War II veterans hired by the Army Security Agency (ASA) because of their knowledge of Japanese; however, in June 1950, neither possessed a security clearance. Furthermore, while ASA Pacific had two companies, with two detachments in the Far East, the signals intelligence agency operated from fixed sites and it would be October 1950 before ASA could deploy tactical units to Korea.[28] "The country [United States] found that in the field of intel," wrote a U.S. Army historian, "as in almost everything else, 5 years of peacetime neglect and limited budgets had left American forces less than well-equipped to meet the challenge of war."[29]

In a 2014 U.S. Army Command and General Staff College monograph, Major Charles Azotea, who studied Willoughby's shortcomings as a G-2 in Korea, observed the latter's intelligence collection requirements "hinted at an impressive array of collection assets and a fully manned and integrated staff, but this was not reality." Willoughby was "not well-liked, nor was he considered a competent intelligence officer. Egotistical and resentful of those who intervened in his domain, Willoughby's intelligence assessments proved significantly correct or incorrect due to this subjective evaluation of the available data."[30] Historian Bruce Riedel described Willoughby as a "self-styled admirer of the general [MacArthur]" and noted he would later write a biography of MacArthur that ran to over one thousand pages. Just as significantly, he had inculcated MacArthur's strong preference for no outside interference in running the intelligence show in Korea where, ironically, MacArthur never spent the night, preferring his more pleasant accommodations in Japan to the inhospitable Korean peninsula.[31]

The personal relationship between MacArthur and Willoughby was not only key to the way in which the Korean conflict unfolded but also to the way in which intelligence concerning current and projected enemy activity was used (or ignored). Alexis Johnson, the State Department's Deputy Director for Northeast Asian Affairs, wrote "Mac and the headquarters looked upon everybody outside of the immediate coterie as an enemy or a potential enemy, and this included his own commanders." In Johnson's estimation, this was precisely the reason Willoughby was of such great value to MacArthur; by 1950, Willoughby had been fiercely loyal to MacArthur for nearly a decade.[32] In short, MacArthur paid no attention to Korea, which lay beyond his bounded area of responsibility, which left Willoughby free to carry on the intelligence war as he saw fit.[33]

In terms of subjectivity, a key to understanding the toxic relationship between Willoughby and the rest of what was becoming the American intelligence community—such as it was in the late 1940s—was the attitude he and MacArthur shared towards the CIA. Based on its own network of sources, the Agency had, in February 1948, begun penning analytic reports, the bottom line of all of which could be succinctly stated—namely, the Soviet Union directly controlled all North Korean military and political planning—and all other decisions emanated from this crucial observation. As far as the CIA was concerned, North Korea was a Soviet satellite, period, and in the July 16, 1948, *Weekly Summary,* Agency analysts referred to North Korea as a Soviet "puppet" regime. As one author concluded, this bore-sighted belief in a Soviet-directed monolith of Communist regimes worldwide was *the* dominant belief within military and political leadership in Washington, D.C., at the time. In its heart of hearts, the Agency was fairly convinced Stalin was unlikely to give the DPRK the go-ahead for an invasion of the South, at least any time in the foreseeable future. Furthermore, in terms of the worldwide threats to the United States in 1950, the USSR was clearly the major threat, followed by a post-revolutionary China, and then, possibly, Korea, at least in terms of an intelligence target, an order of priorities even FECOM supported. Despite credible warnings and intelligence to the contrary, Washington was shocked by the North Korean invasion because, after all, it was really Moscow calling the shots and they wouldn't risk nuclear war over Korea, would they?[34]

It was that very perception and its general acceptance within the Washington policy community that was reflected in a June 19, 1950, CIA paper on DPRK military capabilities. This paper categorically stated that "the DPRK is a firmly controlled Soviet satellite that exercises no independent initiative and depends entirely on the support of the USSR for existence." It assessed the DPRK on its own likely did not have the military capability to defeat the ROK without Soviet or Chinese assistance; since such a decision would mean global, likely thermonuclear, war, there would be no such assistance and no invasion of the South by the North. The State Department agreed with this assessment, as did the military intelligence entities of the Army, Navy, and Air Force. This attitude in Washington was shared by MacArthur and his subordinates in Tokyo, which prompted them to ignore the pre-war indicators so familiar to order-of-battle analysts. Willoughby later claimed he reported "often and accurately" on the Korean situation in the months preceding the outbreak of war and repeated the oft uttered and valid, though self-exonerating, statement that Korea was the responsibility of the Korea Military Advisory Group, not FECOM. Referring to the mistaken belief North Korea would not seek to reunify the peninsula, historian P. K. Rose noted this:

> ... strong and perhaps arrogantly held belief ... did not weaken even in the face of DPRK military successes against U.S. troops in the summer of 1950. By then it had become an article of faith within the FEC [Far East Command], personally testified to by MacArthur, that no Asian troops could stand up to American military might without being annihilated. This attitude ... resulted in the second strategic blunder—the surprise Chinese intervention in the war.[35]

The June 1950 invasion came as less of a surprise for the small CIA footprint on the ground in Korea. In 1949, reporting from Field Research Unit/FECOM cited increasing numbers of cross-border clashes and, by May 1950, the chief of FRU/FECOM was convinced "something was afoot just north of the 38th Parallel." But despite the missed prognosis, in retrospect, some authors have pointed out that the CIA did as well as most other Asia-watchers in terms of making a call. As one writer concluded, "The CIA, contrary to subsequent general opinion, did a fairly good job in predicting a looming North Korean threat, if not the actual invasion (which would be expecting quite a lot)." It is also worth noting that two Office of Special Operations (OSO) agents in North Korea provided forecasts, on June 16 and 19, 1950, that the North Korean invasion was set for, according to one, June 22, and the other, June 25.[36] The initial inability of CIA and FECOM to "work and play well with others" negatively impacted the situation; "The bitter petty bureaucratic infighting between Willoughby and the CIA," wrote the editors of a study on clandestine warfare in Asia, "only served to hamper the effectiveness of the U.S. intelligence effort in the Far East." These editors also cited the "severely fragmented and poorly coordinated" HUMINT collection program in the Far East, which they also blamed on "the infighting between Willoughby's FECOM G-2 staff and the CIA."[37]

After years of provocations by both the DPRK and the ROK, a series of border incidents heightened tensions between the two neighbors on the peninsula and, at 4:00 am local time (3:00 pm the same day in Washington, D.C.) on Sunday, June 25, 1950, with the sanction of the Soviet Union and the support of the People's Republic of China (PRC), North Korea invaded South Korea. The attackers comprised at least seven, and possibly 10, divisions, many of whom were Chinese and Soviet veterans of World War II, supported by artillery and approximately 150 T-34 tanks. Although the Republic of Korea (ROK) Army numbered 98,000 men, it was an incompletely trained and minimally equipped force, with no tanks and only 89 howitzers, supplemented only by the 500-man KMAG contingent. Muccio later recalled, almost with relief, that "Fortunately, when the clash came, it was very clear-cut ... that it was definitely overt Communist aggression." Predictably, Muccio suddenly became a very busy man:

> The morning of the 25th of June, I got a call from my deputy [Everett Francis] Drumright, just about 8 o'clock, telling me that in the past hour KMAG headquarters had been receiving reports from the several units along the front of an onslaught across the 38th Parallel. (We had so many reports of that kind in the two years prior that it was hard to determine if these were just forays across the 38th Parallel or whether it was something beyond that.)

Muccio informed Washington of the latest developments via the use of secure one-time pads and inserted at the end of each sentence the direction "Repeat CINCFE," ensuring MacArthur's headquarters in Tokyo was being kept aware of activities. These messages could only be decrypted at Foggy Bottom (State Department headquarters), though he recalled Willoughby sought to break them down while on the move, leading to delayed transmission of the information.[38]

So certain was MacArthur that war would not come that he, "with a well-deserved reputation for ignoring any input from above or below that did not accord with his strongly held convictions," as one study observed, had neglected to ensure American occupation forces in Japan were trained for combat operations, so when he learned within hours of the attack, he was understandably stunned. And yet, recovery came quickly and, somewhat ironically, initial post-attack reports were encouraging. MacArthur's headquarters sent a summary to Joint Chiefs of Staff G-2 in Washington, assessing that five ROK divisions were engaged in combat with three North Korean divisions; however, the reality was that it was *seven* fresh, full-strength divisions versus four depleted South Korean divisions. The North Korean attack was described as "serious in strength and strategic intent." In a subsequent telephone conversation with Willoughby, the latter admitted he was concerned about two NKPA divisions nearing an important road junction at Uijongbu and the fact that 40 tanks were

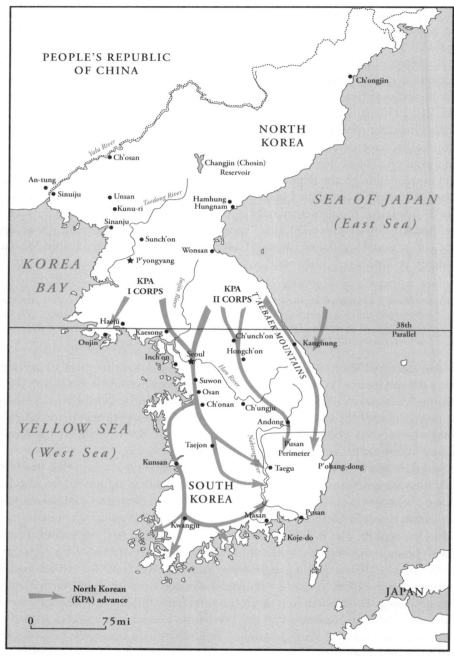

North Korean avenues of approach into South Korea, June–August 1950.

reportedly within five kilometers of the city. However, the G-2 retained his rosy viewpoint—the ROK troops were staging an orderly retreat, civilian morale was described as good, and the government of President Syngman Rhee was "standing firm and maintaining internal order." Nevertheless, this unfortunate turn of events proved a shock to both the U.S. Embassy staff in Seoul and Willoughby; both parties had assessed a North Korean invasion of the South was unlikely and the North Koreans were more inclined to use guerilla and psychological warfare rather than resorting to force of arms. In stark order-of-battle terms, the conflict was a mismatch from the outset. North Korea brought 135,000 well-trained troops, Russian T-34 tanks (considered by many military analysts as the best tank of World War II), an ample supply of artillery, and 200 Russian-built fighters and bombers to the fight; in contrast, the Republic of Korea could muster only 98,000 troops (eight infantry divisions and one armored cavalry regiment and only four divisions at full strength), had no tanks, no anti-tank weapons, and no artillery greater than 105-millimeter pieces. The ROK Army had some two dozen armored cars and less than half that number of halftracks and the Air Force had only 22 serviceable aircraft, with 10 of those trainers. One-third of its military vehicles were inoperable, and the Army only had a six-day ammunition supply. Predictably, North Korean forces routed their southern relatives, and four strong armored columns drove south toward the capital of Seoul.[39]

For several months prior to the invasion, there were what one writer has described as "palpable indicators" a North Korean invasion of the South was more than just a remote possibility. Back on December 8, 1949, the Plans and Operations Section, General Staff, Department of the Army, had asked FECOM, "What are the prospects with regard to time and probability, of a mutually supported Chinese Communist–Korean Communist attempt to take over the Korean Peninsula?" In response, Willoughby's G-2 section replied such could happen only at the direction of, and in agreement with, the USSR; that conditions for such would be favorable in April or May 1950; and that the conclusion of the civil war in the PRC enabled the freeing up and dispatching of men and materiel to Korea, which would increase the danger to the ROK.[40]

By January 1950, he had advanced his assessed timetable for the North Koreans, assessing that their leadership had firmly set the invasion date for March or April. On February 19, 1950, he dutifully passed on—but gave no credence to—two agents' reports, one saying that the North Koreans would attack in March, the other in June. By March 10, with no North Korean invasion, Willoughby re-examined the tea leaves and fixed June as the target date. On April 12, the interagency Watch Committee convened to consider the assessment of Willoughby's analysts that "the North Korean People's Army will invade South Korea in June of 1950." This more-focused assessment did not, however, prompt the Armed Forces Security Agency to shift its emphasis to monitoring the signals intelligence traffic that likely would have provided the most credible and timely indication of such activity. Furthermore, Willoughby's warnings, echoed by KMAG, fell on deaf ears in Washington, where the widely accepted position was such an invasion could only be approved by the Soviet Union, an unthinkable act by the Soviets, since it would be considered as prelude to a declaration of war. Although he clearly acknowledged the prospects of a North Korean invasion of the South in advance, Willoughby did not deem such an action of strategic significance and his reports were not taken seriously, either in Tokyo or Washington. In reality, Washington was more concerned about events in Indochina, which seemed ripe for Communist takeover. It also did not help that Willoughby's intelligence reports were deemed to be of "generally poor quality," making it more likely this proved-to-be accurate assessment was ignored by the Watch Committee.[41] As Secretary of State Dean Acheson testified before Congress, after the war:

> ... all these agencies [FECOM, CIA, Department of the Army, State Department] were in agreement that the possibility for an attack on the Korean Republic existed at that time, but they were all in agreement that its launching in the summer of 1950 did not appear imminent.[42]

As MacArthur's intelligence chief in Tokyo, Willoughby's primary product was the *Daily Intelligence Summary* (DIS), a document that usually ran some 40 pages in length and focused on the entire Far East. Each day's product included detailed accounts of the day's fighting in Korea, political material on nations in the FECOM region (including Japan and China), and order-of-battle annexes.[43] However, readers of these products likened the quality and the content of each edition to "the babble of old women in the marketplace," rife with rumor, speculation, grousings, and accompanied by minimal to no verification of the reported information. Yet, clearer heads would notice in retrospect from a careful reading of even these summaries in early-to-mid 1950 that a North Korean assault upon the South was certainly possible, if not probable. In the craft of ground order-of-battle analysis, intelligence officers search for various "indicators" to more accurately predict the enemy's most likely courses of action—in Spring 1950, the clearest indicator of a pending attack was the fact North Korean tanks were massed in forward areas, a bellwether indicator to a competent intelligence analyst. In late May 1950, an informant also provided an extraordinarily detailed report on the formation of a new NKPA tank brigade, composed of some 180 light/medium tanks, 10,000 men, and support equipment. In a telling commentary, this critical information was pooh-poohed by Willoughby and his staffers, who blithely characterized the move as "not ... economically or militarily practicable." When, just 30 days later, these same tanks would be smashing through the ROK's defenses, it was certainly fortunate for the NKPA that they were unaware they were accomplishing what their opponent had already deemed impossible for them. In early 1950, the G-2 had ignored another classic pre-attack indicator—the displacement of families living within two miles of the 38th Parallel, explained away at the time as a natural reaction to escape the admittedly numerous land mines planted by North Korea.[44]

It is a truism that an intelligence assessment can only be as good as the quality of the sources providing the information that, when subjected to analysis, becomes usable intelligence. In this regard, Willoughby predictably, albeit unfortunately, was getting much of the information he used to compile the DIS from the American military and from diplomats on Formosa, sources which themselves relied heavily on data from tainted information from Chinese Nationalist sources. In fairness to Willoughby, some of the DIS editions contained a statement to the effect that some of the Taiwan-based reporting was "open to question." Readers familiar with the DIS also pointed out that Willoughby's daily product was notorious for including diametrically-opposed conclusions, often on the same page.[45] While researching *MacArthur, 1941–1951*, Willoughby demurred from responsibility for detecting possible enemy courses of action when he wrote, "Military-political research dealing with the intentions of a foreign nation fell normally into State Department or C.I.A. channels."[46]

The infant intelligence agency was one entity that bore the brunt of Truman's wrath, castigated for failing to foresee the North Korean invasion. Director of Central Intelligence Admiral Roscoe Hillenkoetter appropriately responded to these charges by reminding Truman the Agency had few assets in either Korea or Japan because MacArthur had specifically excluded them from operating in the theater, preferring the information he received from his G-2, Willoughby. Although MacArthur had relented enough in May 1950 to allow a modest Agency presence in Japan, the selected personnel were not due to arrive in theater until July, which meant the CIA was also forced to rely upon the Teutonic intel chief. Despite those arrangements in train, however, Hillenkoetter found himself appearing before the Senate Appropriations Committee on June 26, the day following the invasion. Not known for his reticence, Admiral Hillenkoetter testified the Agency had specifically warned the president, the secretary of state, and the secretary of defense on June 19 that North Korean forces were on the verge of invading the South; he added that he had no idea why the information did not prompt some action in response. Two cabinet officials promptly denied Hillenkoetter's charges, noting that while the CIA had indeed sent an intelligence estimate on the unfolding situation to State, Defense, and the White House—actually on June 14—they said the estimate assessed that North Korea was *capable* of invading South Korea at any time and capturing Seoul within 10–12 days but provided no indication North Korea *intended* to take such action.[47]

In his memoirs, Eighth Army Commander Lieutenant General Matthew Ridgway made reference to the CIA report to FECOM—which Ridgway says was dated June 19—and its mention of "extensive troop movements north of the 38th Parallel" as well as the movement of ammunition to the forward areas, the evacuation of civilians from these areas, and the suspension of civilian rail freight, all classic order-of-battle pre-attack indicators. He observed, "How anyone could have read this report and not anticipated an attack is hard to fathom." He added the report apparently sparked no action on the part of the G-2 at Headquarters in Tokyo—namely, Willoughby—and was instead passed on to Washington with no indication of urgency. Stung by such charges, Headquarters later responded it had "forwarded all the facts" to Washington and could not be held responsible for the lack of any subsequent action. It is possible it was this report to which Hillenkoetter was referring in his Congressional testimony. Willloughby consistently claimed he reported "often and accurately" on the situation in Korea in the months preceding the invasion and noted besides that Korea was the responsibility of KMAG rather than FECOM. In response, an historian of the conflict concluded Willoughby's staff simply dismissed any indications of imminent attack, and characterized his information as "unreliable," based on "dribbles of second- and third-hand information from low-level defectors, refugees, and the few Western diplomats stationed in P'yŏngyang.

However, in describing the chaotic retreat of the South Korean forces in the wake of invasion by their brethren to the north, Willoughby provided an account that is subject to question—one historian has described it as "fictionalized." Willoughby wrote that the road on the way to Suwon was "clogged with retreating, panting columns of men interspersed with ambulances filled with the groaning, broken men, the sky resonant with shrieking missiles of death and everywhere the stench and misery and utter desolation of a stricken battlefield." In addition to a torrent of purple prose worthy of a budding but unaccomplished author, Willoughby was criticized for his reference to "roads clogged with ambulances," difficult to envision since ambulances were virtually non-existent in Korea at that time.[48]

Intelligence historian Matthew Aid has described the North Korean invasion of the South as arguably one of the worst American intelligence disasters in the 20th century, Pearl Harbor the other. He observed the two events have interesting parallels—both attacks occurred early on a Sunday morning, the United States was caught largely by surprise in both cases, and there was, in his estimation, significant intelligence available that should have served as a warning and impetus for action.[49]

An undated but clearly contemporary document, possibly written by recruited University of Maryland historian Gordon Prange, explained how it was not an intelligence failure that resulted in the South Korean collapse and the rapid retreat southward:

> 1 Failure to prepare for and meet the attack upon the Republic of South Korea by the army of North Korea cannot be laid at the door of intelligence agencies. Information concerning the build-up of North Korean army forces and offensive equipment and the threat therefrom was gathered from various sources and forwarded to Washington continually over a period of six months prior to the outbreak of full-scale fighting on 25 June ... It was not the lack of

intelligence data concerning North Korean offensive operations that led to the early disastrous situation in Korea but rather the inadequacy of counter-measures prepared to meet just such an attack as intelligence warned of that has aroused criticism of the work of the armed forces in that area ...

The primary cause of the criticism being levelled at intelligence agencies stems from the initial failure of the supposedly well trained and prepared ROK forces to stem the tide of invasion.[50]

***

When the invasion occurred, the U.S. Army had sizable numbers of troops in theater—but not on the Korean Peninsula. On January 1, 1950, the U.S. Army had a grand total of 573 members in Korea—compared to 96,175 in Japan—and only 485 on July 1, figures which increased to 48,268 by July 30.[51] Furthermore, those few troops available and quickly rushed into combat were woefully unprepared; as one historical study assessed, "it is difficult to overstate the shock of the first encounter between U.S. and North Korean forces." The soldiers of the 24th Infantry Division, for example, had few anti-tank weapons at their disposal and those few they had proved inadequate to penetrate the thick armor of the North Korean T-34s. The paltry number of maps they had were outdated and inaccurate. There seemed to be no strategy behind their deployment, aside from plugging the gap with bodies, and their World War II-vintage commanders seemed "paralyzed by fear and indecision that in some cases bordered on cowardice." To say the least, the U.S. Army had seen better days.[52]

Historian D. Clayton James also identifies Willoughby and MacArthur, ironically, as two other weaknesses plaguing the U.S. Army in mid-1950.

> MacArthur's staff shielded the Far East commander from evidence suggesting the Eighth Army's progress toward combat readiness was not impressive and he was quite shocked by the troops' poor performances early in the Korean War ... MacArthur seldom visited or inspected military units and installations but relied instead on information fed to him by his trusted staff leaders ... Sadly, his trust in Willoughby was so deep by then that MacArthur's intelligence data came almost solely from his G-2, and Willoughby could be quite selective and sometimes erroneous in what he provided his commander ... It was as if MacArthur existed in Tokyo in a cocoon, perhaps of his own choosing but possibly created by his sycophantic staff section chiefs. The price he would pay for such insularity would be tragically high.[53]

Interestingly, just a few days prior to the invasion, the CIA had reported classic pre-attack indicators, including the replacement of North Korean frontier guards with Army members, the evacuation of civilians from the frontier zone, and the fast-paced movement forward of munitions, fuel, and various stores. This information, obtained at great risk by Korean agents, was sent to Tokyo, for the attention of Willoughby's intelligence analysts. However, instead of commenting on the information and providing the expected additions and evaluation of the data, Willoughby forwarded the information to Washington, indicating it was "routine" in nature. Furthermore, Willoughby's sweeping aside of the Korean human intelligence information was mentally mirrored in Washington, where Lieutenant General Ridgway—soon to be commanding the ground forces in Korea but then still at the Pentagon—wrote about this incident many years later, noting "Our national mind was made up to liquidate this embarrassing military commitment and we closed our ears to the clashing of arms that sounded along the border as our last troops were taking ship for home."[54]

In the U.S. Embassy in Seoul, Ambassador Muccio was also concerned about the situation, based on the reports he was receiving. In a June 23 message, he wrote:

> Considerable movement of NKSF [North Korean Special Forces] units, tanks, trucks, landing craft and equipment North 38 parallel being reported. No large concentration any given area.
>
> Comment: Significance movements cannot be judged this time. Possibly movements in preparation maneuvers and training projects similar those carried out Spring of 1947 and 1948. KA intelligence agencies taking special immediate steps determine significance these movements.[55]

On the evening of June 25, the United Nations Security Council hastily convened, unanimously (minus the Soviet delegate, who had walked out back in January) passing a resolution condemning the invasion and calling on North Korea to withdraw its forces to the 38th Parallel. Two days later, the UN Security Council passed an American-sponsored resolution to provide aid to South Korea and to restore the *status quo ante bellum*. President Truman, unwilling to wait on a declaration of war from Congress, ordered American troops to Korea as part of an optimistically-named UN "police action." For his theater commander, he chose the Supreme Commander of the Allied Forces in the Pacific, General MacArthur, whose headquarters was in Tokyo. When MacArthur took command of all UN forces on July 7, Truman directed him to conduct a "limited" war—by which the president meant a war limited to the Korean Peninsula. However, the Supreme Commander adamantly believed there could be nothing "limited" about combating Communism—today Seoul, tomorrow San Francisco. MacArthur first dispatched three U.S. Army divisions from Japan to South Korea, a force designated the Eighth Army; however, this element was, in the words of one historian, "understrength, undertrained, and under-equipped" and was able to do little to stem the North Korean offensive. One of Willoughby's initial roles with the invasion was as a member of the Far East Command Target Selection Committee which, for six weeks (until superseded by Far East Air Force's Target Committee) chose targets for American aerial bombardment in support of its South Korean ally; Willoughby suggested the best use of the United States Air Force's B-29 bomber force might be in an interdiction campaign waged north of the 38th Parallel. However, such plans were rapidly overcome by events: Seoul fell on June 30, Inchon on July 3, Suwon the next day, and Taejon on July 20. By September, the ROK forces and the U.S. Eighth Army had been driven far to the south, clinging to the southeast corner of the peninsula in an area which came to be known as the Pusan Perimeter. British and U.S. Marine Corps support prevented UN forces from being run out of Korea entirely.[56]

Even with a war now on, Willoughby remained ... Willoughby. In late July 1950, when Major General John Church, the newly appointed commander of the soon-to-be-decimated 24th Infantry Division (ID), sent frantic pleas to FECOM for air support in his defense against the North Korean 6th Division, Willoughby characterized them as "unofficial" and demanded confirmation. Since CIA personnel were nominally assigned to the 24th ID, Willoughby decided that, in the future, all Agency messages from Korea would have to go through the Joint Special Operations Branch of FECOM, in an approved format, regardless of resulting delays. Similarly, on June 30, 1950—just five days after the North Korean invasion—Willoughby ordered his office to take charge of the FRU/FECOM/OSO teams throughout Korea, to which the FRU/FECOM commander replied he would remain under CIA control short of any orders to the contrary from Washington.[57]

Much as they had done in June 1950, Willoughby's cadre of intelligence analysts saw lots of trees in the late summer and early fall of 1950 but missed the forest almost entirely. They did point out, however, in July that Chinese troops could march 40 miles per day for successive days and that "without materially weakening their control of the China mainland, the Chinese Communists are believed capable of redeploying a considerable force of regular troops for the assistance of the North Koreans ... The employment of Chinese Communist troops can possibly be expected should Mao Tse Tung [sic] believe the situation favorable for decisive action."[58] Willoughby was quick to point out, however, that "The Embassy in Seoul maintained military attaché groups—Army, Navy, and Air, as well as their own diplomatic and political specialists whose sole business was to gauge the trend of events."[59]

Of the missed Chinese pre-attack indicators, one of the most significant was the late summer shift of ground force units from the southern and central provinces of China into Manchuria, which bordered the People's Democratic Republic. In the FECOM's DIS of July 6, 1950, Willoughby's analysts assessed there were 189,000 Chinese Communist Forces (CCF) in Manchuria—115,000 regulars, the rest militia troops—as well as 176,000 regulars in North China. By August, the figure had been elevated to 246,000 regulars in Manchuria and by September 21 to the alarming figure of 450,000. Willoughby and his analysts were able to explain away the sudden increase, however, by noting the return to garrison of the 4th Field Army, considered the CCF's best formation, following combat operations against Chinese Nationalist forces. In none of the calculations resulting in these enemy troop strength estimates did Willoughby consider the possibility these buildups could be preparation for war. An independent U.S. Air Force intelligence memo of September 8 estimated sizable elements of the 100,000 combat veterans of the 4th Field Army were deployed along the Korean border and were prepared for "rapid commitment" into Korea. As Joseph Goulden pointed out in his book, *Korea: The Untold Story of the War*, compounding the flawed analysis was the recurring inability of the FECOM G-2 to clearly distinguish between Chinese troops *per se* and North Korean troops serving with the CCF.[60]

Yet the decision to cross the 38th Parallel was Harry Truman's; throughout July, his advisors, convinced victory in Korea was inevitable, seriously debated the question of whether or not to forcibly reunite the peninsula once the DPRK military had been unceremoniously run out of the South. By late July, UN military commanders, skittish until their defensive lines had been firmed up, had been won over, and within two weeks the commander in chief directed the changed war plans. Notably, the military operations he approved on September 1 included actions to minimize the chances of Chinese intervention, actions ignored by Willoughby and MacArthur.[61] The August 27 DIS noted that, according to a "usually reliable Chinese Nationalist source," the USSR had "allegedly ordered the Chinese Communists to have 200,000 troops ready to support North Korea." The Summary also surmised that General Lin Piao, commander of the 4th Field Army, would be appointed commander of all the Chinese Communist forces supporting their brethren in the DPRK. These 200,000 troops were subordinate to the North China Special Army Group.[62]

Though it took several months to do so, the KLO ultimately proved its mettle, specifically in the run-up to the key amphibious assault at Inchon in September. Working under U.S. Navy Lieutenant Eugene F. Clark, a veteran of the G-2's Geographic Branch, KLO operatives labored alongside members of Willoughby's clandestine Z Unit, as well as members of the U.S. Army, U.S. Navy, and CIA for several weeks prior to the assault. As part of Operation *Trudy Jackson*, they gathered intelligence data on mines, tides, water depths, and enemy fortifications that made the landing at Inchon possible. Twenty-two agents, mostly South Korean partisans, reported information on some 90 targets, a process Willoughby described as "a check against other sources—a routine and time honored intelligence precaution."[63] On D-Day minus 1, Choe Kyu-Bong and several others conducted an armed assault against the lighthouse on Palmido, an island at the mouth of Inchon harbor; despite being shot twice, Choe managed to locate a critical piece of equipment that finally enabled the team to turn on the lighthouse lamp at midnight, as planned. MacArthur's assault force saw the light and observed the American flag flying from the lighthouse at dawn. For his part in the operation, Choe was invited to an audience with MacArthur aboard the latter's flagship, USS *Mount McKinley*, and was presented with the flag that had flown over the lighthouse.[64]

The intelligence pre-planning for the amphibious assault at Inchon provided another example of Willoughby's pettiness when he did not get his way. The subject of his displeasure on this occasion was Lieutenant Colonel William W. Quinn, a member of MacArthur's staff who was selected to be in charge of intelligence planning for the attack. As one authority put it, "His intelligence preparation for the invasion was thorough and accurate and significantly contributed to one of the most daring and successful amphibious landings in history." In the wake of the offensive,

Lieutenant General Almond had selected Quinn as the G-2 for X Corps, prompting the rift with Willoughby. As Quinn himself assessed after-the-fact, Willoughby's nose was out of joint because he didn't get to put one of his protégés in the coveted position. Exacerbating the situation was the fact Quinn was an OSS/Strategic Services Unit veteran, tasked with preserving the organizations' intelligence capabilities until a permanent civilian intelligence entity could be stood up—which of course meant Willoughby was "not predisposed" to trust him. Quinn was also aware Willoughby had tried to have him fired for producing sub-standard intelligence reports from a combat field headquarters, though author Peter Knight denies any malicious intent by Willoughby in so doing.[65]

The Inchon amphibious assault was just the sort of tactical and operational surprise which had served MacArthur so well in the past, a bold offensive by the 70,000 men of X Corps at Inchon, halfway up the western coast of South Korea. However, not all who were aware of the operation, codenamed *Chromite*, took it as a sign of MacArthur's tactical brilliance. Speaking of the Inchon landing, Department of State Asian expert John Melby commented, "It was a spectacular fluke and it worked. There was no stopping MacArthur after that!" Even Willoughby referred to Mac's decision as "gambling" as UN forces entered what he called "the hornet's nest." Fluke or not, the North Korean troops were stunned by such an audacious move and rapidly and chaotically retreated, beset by X Corps moving to the east and Eighth Army moving north, having broken out of the Pusan Perimeter. By September 26, both segments of American troops had linked up near Osan, and Seoul was recaptured the following day. After facing near collapse only a few months prior, UN forces now had 125,000 North Korean soldiers "in the bag" and the People's Army was in full retreat. Yet this happy circumstance prompted a strategic question: now what? The original UN declaration called only for the restoration of South Korea and its borders, thwarting the presumption of the American military that the next logical step would be continuation of the offensive across the 38th Parallel until the People's Army was soundly defeated and Korea could be reunited under a democratic government. Furthermore, the protesting Soviet delegate had returned to the UN and would certainly veto any extension of the conflict into his subordinate's territory.[66] On September 29, the day South Korean head of state Syngman Rhee returned to Seoul, Secretary of Defense George Marshall, after conferring with the Joint Chiefs, told MacArthur, "We want you to feel unhampered tactically and strategically to proceed north of the 38th Parallel."[67]

MacArthur, meanwhile, had flown back to Tokyo, history once again having affirmed the righteousness of his decision making. He returned, as historian Max Hastings put it, "mantled in his own serene sense of destiny fulfilled, imbued with an aura of invincibility that awed even his nation's leaders. He was confident that the war for Korea had been won, and that his armies were victorious. Now it was just a matter of cleaning up."[68]

No doubt swayed by the intelligence support rendered to the Inchon assault, MacArthur was also clearly pleased by the performance of Willoughby as his G-2 and of his staff. As the Supreme Commander Allied Powers, ensconced in his headquarters in Tokyo, pontificated on September 30, 1950:

> ... the recent Korean War, calling for the exhausting employment of every resource of this command, under initially critical tactical and strategic conditions, found the intelligence services, in collective employment, swinging into action with remarkable speed and efficiency, to render the same precise and valuable service, as in the campaigns of the Southwest Pacific Area.[69]

A more generous assessment characterizes the intelligence support for the Inchon landing as "outstanding," noting that intelligence analysts had determined the proposed landing site was practicable and the defenses were manned by second-rate troops.[70]

One author views Operation *Chromite* as yet another indication of how MacArthur rewarded sycophants and excoriated critics; those who remained loyal to his "vision" were favored, those who opposed it were soon shunned, due to the abiding perception of disloyalty.[71]

Other observers were less laudatory of Willoughby's exploits. While noting the FECOM G-2 "covered Asia like a vacuum cleaner," one historian observed the G-2 collectively spent its time collecting "minutia, unconfirmed reports, and wild guesses," activities which left precious little time for actual *analysis* of the collected information. In an indirect dig at Willoughby, this observer concluded much of the fault lay in "a lack of competent leadership." Fifty-eight years old in 1950, Willoughby had been a member of MacArthur's "palace guard" since 1941 and had endeared himself to his boss by, among other talents, writing the "baroque communiques" MacArthur favored. Several of Willoughby's colleagues claimed he spent as much time ghostwriting as doing intelligence work. "Willoughby was the ideal man to be Mac's G-2," penned one writer. "He knew exactly what Mac wanted to hear and he told him exactly that, and no more." The two men also shared a marked aversion to any non-traditional intelligence collection means—in other words, to anything *not* from a prisoner-of-war interrogation, from an attaché, or acquired by means of document exploitation; the Supreme Commander and his chief lieutenant had particular disdain for, and distrust of, human spies, an attitude which goes a long way towards explaining their collective animosity towards the OSS during World War II and its successor, the Central Intelligence Agency.[72] A specific pre-war incident demonstrated this bias. In late May 1950, when the North Korean informant provided an "extraordinarily detailed report" to the FECOM G-2 on the new North Korean tank brigade (180 tanks, supporting equipment and 10,000 personnel), Willoughby dismissed the numbers as "excessive" and openly expressed doubts the North Korean People's Army would ever form so large a tank unit. Given the G-2's dismissal of the information, it was never passed to Seoul.[73]

In the pitched intellectual and operational battle that divided the CIA and Army Intelligence, supporters of Willoughby and MacArthur could point to the fact that, on June 25, 1950, the CIA had four agents in North Korea, Willoughby, 16; from June 25 to September 25, the CIA had 15 operatives behind enemy lines, compared to Willoughby's 65. Not surprisingly, Willoughby's operatives also turned in more reports than CIA agents, overlooking the hard fact of intelligence that more reports does not necessarily lead to more credible information or result in better intelligence. In a December 1950 article, Scripps-Howard staff writer Jim Lucas, a defender of Willoughby, stated he had little use for the CIA's cloak-and-dagger methods and that, even after Willoughby provided CIA operatives with office and warehouse space, the nascent foreign intelligence agency still refused to cooperate.[74] The journalist brothers Joseph and Stewart Alsop, in an article provocatively entitled, "Who Failed?", highlighted MacArthur's lingering dislike for, and distrust of, the CIA, beginning in the Southwest Pacific during World War II and extending through the Korean War. The Far East Commander shared information with the Langley contingent only grudgingly, even though they were still under Willoughby's operational control. At the time, MacArthur even acknowledged the value of the intelligence gathered by the CIA in the overall success of the Inchon amphibious landing, but in the aftermath of that operation, the situation returned to "normal." An Air Force officer who has researched the development of clandestine CIA operations in Korea observed, "MacArthur had never made secret his intense, long-standing objections to the presence of an independent intelligence organization within the boundaries of 'his' command."[75]

Predictably, CIA officers on-scene had a different view of the relationship. Carleton Swift, the Agency's Korea Desk Chief, commented:

> As the Communists took over more and more territory, we sold our intelligence product to General [Charles] Willoughby and General [Douglas] MacArthur, and they wanted to receive it. And to do so we established a liaison office, and sent a regular Army colonel assigned to OSS, Robert Delaney, who had been the deputy of the OSS operation in Burma (Detachment 201). We passed our information to the Willoughby command there.[76]

Furthermore, Director of Central Intelligence Hillenkoetter and Willoughby continued a productive personal correspondence, despite the static between their respective entities. On July 7, 1950, the director sent Willoughby a letter thanking him for the Agency's recent receipt of "Terrain Study No. 4, South Central Siberia." Hillenkoetter described the product as "a beautifully assembled job, and one which contains much information of real value on an area whose outlines are increasingly hard to discern through the curtain which our late Allies, and present antagonists, have erected."[77]

And on rare occasions, Willoughby responded in kind—on July 17, 1950, he made a complimentary reference to the CIA, writing Hillenkoetter that FECOM enjoyed "good, fast communications" through the FRU, the CIA entity assigned to MacArthur's command. Similarly, a September 24 CIA mission involved personal coordination with Willoughby, with positive results; a Soviet-origin agent was airdropped from a B-26 bomber into the region just south of the Soviet port of Vladivostok. For "plausible deniability" purposes, the crew was Japanese. Willoughby neither protested nor interfered in this CIA operation.[78]

And yet, it was the vilified CIA that, in the early months following the North Korean invasion, began referring to the potential for Chinese intervention, in addition to stressing Soviet control of the DPRK. On June 30, 1950, CIA Intelligence Memorandum 301, *Estimate of Soviet Intentions and Capabilities for Military Aggression*, stated the Soviets had "large numbers of Chinese troops" which could be introduced anytime into the Korean theater, radically changing the strategic, operational, and tactical picture for the United States. This message was reiterated in the July 8 CIA Intelligence Memorandum 302, which credited the Soviet Union with the Korean invasion and warned the Soviets could use Chinese troops should the DPRK offensive lag (which happened by early July). That same day, Chinese Foreign Minister Zhou Enlai convened a national security meeting, focused on strengthening the Korean–Chinese border area; one of the decisions reached at that meeting was to move the most experienced unit of the People's Liberation Army (PLA), the 4th Field Army, to the border by the end of July. The CIA *Weekly Summary* dated July 28 estimated 40,000 to 50,000 ethnic Korean soldiers from PLA units could be used to supplement DPRK forces; however, this warning of potential tactical significance was counterbalanced—as it would be throughout November 1950—by the unshakable assessment that Chinese *actions* would be directed solely by Russian *directions*. In late July, at the behest of the CIA, U.S. Marine Corps Lieutenant Colonel Vincent R. "Dutch" Kramer began training irregular troops for intelligence collection missions behind enemy lines. Among the tantalizing tidbits uncovered was Chinese communication in late July which confirmed elements of a Chinese Field Army—the 4th, as was discovered later—had moved to Manchuria and that its commander, the semi-legendary Lin Piao, would lead the Chinese intervention in Korea.[79]

By early August, Mao had concluded American intervention in the Korean conflict spelled likely defeat for his North Korean protégés, a potential result that augured poorly for the People's Republic and which called for a specific response. On August 4, the PRC leader categorically stated that if the United States won in Korea, it would threaten China, which meant China, more for its own national sovereignty reasons than loyalty to a Communist monolith, had to intervene to help North Korea. By late that month, Zhou En-lai was lodging written protests with the United Nations concerning American air raids just north of the Yalu River, simultaneously with the strengthening of Chinese forces in the southern border areas of Manchuria. FECOM analysts assessed there were some 246,000 PLA and

374,000 militia troops in Manchuria, near the Korean border. Such developments prompted the CIA, in its September 8 Intelligence Memorandum 324, *Probability of Direct Chinese Communist Intervention in Korea*, to assess that the Chinese were already providing covert assistance to its DPRK junior partner including, in some cases, replacements for combat troops. Even at this relatively late juncture, however, this assessment, the most strident prior to the Chinese assault on American and allied forces in late November, still stressed that *overt* involvement by PLA soldiers would require explicit Soviet approval, given the generally accepted view that such would mean worldwide war.[80]

By mid-September, U.S. Marines were steadily pushing DPRK forces to the north, prompting Chinese officials to conclude DPRK forces faced not only defeat but possibly destruction. On the 17th, a delegation of senior Chinese intelligence and logistics officers arrived in North Korea—not only to study the tactical situation first-hand, but also, and more ominously, to make the necessary preparations prior to Chinese military intervention. Meanwhile, Chinese diplomatic personnel sent notices to international middlemen expressing their extreme concerns about a potential American occupation of North Korea. In late September, the acting PLA chief of staff told the Indian Ambassador in Peking that China "would never allow U.S. forces to reach Chinese territory." The Indian Foreign Minister passed this warning to the U.S. Ambassador in New Delhi, while in Washington, the British Ambassador passed the same dark message to the U.S. State Department. In case there was any doubt concerning Chinese intentions, a September 22 public announcement by the Chinese Foreign Ministry seemed to remove such: "We clearly affirm that we will always stand on the side of the Korean people ... and resolutely oppose the criminal acts of American imperialist aggression against Korea and their intrigues for expanding the war." Meanwhile, intercepted communications revealed the movement of massive numbers of PLA troops from southern and central China toward the joint border with North Korea.[81]

In late September 1950, Willoughby met in Tokyo with Lieutenant General James M. "Jumping Jim" Gavin, the legendary officer who had commanded the "Screaming Eagles" of the 82nd Airborne Division during World War II. Gavin, then head of the Weapons System Evaluation Group in the Pentagon, was concerned about the modern hardstands and revetments he had recently witnessed at Kimpo airfield—far beyond the pale of anything the tiny North Korean Air Force could need or even want. In Gavin's mind, "Either the North Koreans were wasting their time, which seemed unlikely, or a first class air power was about to intervene in the war." Based on that observation, Gavin tried to persuade Willoughby that the PRC was on the verge of intervening on the Korean Peninsula. Willoughby was unimpressed, noting that if such was the intention of Chairman Mao, he would have done so as soon as the Marines had landed at Inchon, roughly two weeks prior.[82] Gavin replied that the speed with which the Inchon amphibious landing occurred meant they hadn't yet had time to respond, "but if they do plan an intervention, the preparation of Kimpo is a sure indication that this is what they are going to do, and when they are ready, they will come in." Willoughby was still not impressed by Gavin's argument and replied, "The Chinese would never cross the Yalu and march into the peninsula …" Willoughby assured Gavin he "had his own sources. He <u>knew</u>" [emphasis in the original].[83]

At this juncture, and bypassing the Security Council, the government took advantage of tantalizingly close victory and authorized MacArthur to deliver the *coup de gras* to the People's Army in North Korea—under certain strict conditions. First, he was to suspend military operations should either Russian or Chinese forces threaten; his forces were not to cross either the Soviet or Manchurian borders; only Korean forces were to engage in combat along the Soviet and Manchurian borders; and he was forbidden from using air or naval power against Soviet or Manchurian territory. On October 2, with American/UN forces driving northward, Mao Zedong cabled Stalin to inform him China would intervene and to ask the USSR for military assistance; on October 5, the Central Committee of the Chinese Communist Party officially decided to intervene on the Korean peninsula. On the 9th, the Eighth Army crossed the 38th Parallel and, for the next week, the People's Army conducted a stiff defense. However, they then broke contact and fled north, with the 1st Cavalry and 24th Infantry divisions in hot pursuit.[84] That same day, the Joint Chiefs directed MacArthur that:

> … in the event of open or covert employment anywhere in Korea of major Chinese Communist units, without prior announcement, you should continue the action as long as, in your judgment, action by forces now under your control offers a reasonable chance of success. In any case, you will obtain authorization from Washington prior to taking any military actions against objectives in Chinese territory.[85]

It was at this point that Truman, wanting to confer with his Supreme Commander prior to proceeding with the offensive, summoned MacArthur to meet him at Wake Island on October 15. With MacArthur was his intelligence chief, Willoughby. MacArthur assured the commander in chief that all resistance in Korea would end by November, which would permit the withdrawal of the Eighth Army to Japan by Christmas, leaving X Corps as a temporary occupation force. MacArthur also reassured the president that "FECOM's own intelligence organization under his trusted aide, Major General Charles Willoughby, was more than sufficient to meet American requirements … Any political or military intelligence President Truman might need, they could supply." When Truman pointedly asked, "What are the chances for Chinese or Soviet interference?", MacArthur dismissed the possibility as a "remote contingency" and answered:

> Very little. Had they interfered in the first or second month it would have been decisive. We are no longer fearful of their intervention. We no longer stand with hat in hand. The Chinese

have 300,000 men in Manchuria. Of these probably not more than 100,000 to 125,000 are distributed along the Yalu River. Only 50,000 to 60,000 can be gotten across the Yalu River. They have no air force. Now that we have bases for our Air Force in Korea, if the Chinese tried to get down to Pyongyang there would be the greatest slaughter.[86]

Despite MacArthur's reassurances, by the time he was meeting with President Truman, an estimated 120,000 Chinese troops were deployed inside North Korea.[87]

MacArthur added that, should Russia intervene, the professionalism of their air force would likely mean they would "bomb the Chinese as often as they bomb us." Apparently, the president liked what he heard; his comment at the time was, "I've never had a more satisfactory conference since I've been President." Truman might have had a different reaction had he known that, as he was speaking to his Far East Commander, elements of the Chinese 4th Field Army were actually crossing the Yalu and disappearing into the hills of North Korea.[88] The CIA assessment was similar to MacArthur's assurances. In a top-secret memo of October 12, Agency analysts had reported to Truman, "While full-scale Chinese Communist intervention in Korea may be regarded as a continuing possibility, a consideration of all known factors leads to the conclusion that barring a Soviet decision for global war, such action is not probable in 1950. During this period, intervention will probably be confined to continued covert assistance to the North Koreans."[89]

Willoughby's recollections of the critical meeting were somewhat different. He recalled:

> The item of Chinese intervention was brought up almost casually. Truman and his advisors had known from intelligence reports for some time that a build-up of Chinese forces in Manchuria was a *fait accompli* ... To determine if the Red hordes were on the move or not, by day or night, was made impossible by Truman's own *suicidal orders* [emphasis added] that kept our planes twenty miles south of the river border. It was the general consensus of all present that Red China had no intention of intervening.

Willoughby added that when MacArthur was asked about the prospects of Chinese intervention, the latter replied that the answer could only be "speculative" and pointed out neither State nor CIA, "to whom a field commander must look for guidance as to a foreign nation's intention to move from peace to war," had reported any evidence of intent by the Peiping government to intervene with major forces. Willoughby too expressed his clear understanding that "military-political research dealing with the intentions of a foreign nation normally was handled by the State Department or the CIA." Furthermore, MacArthur's own local intelligence sources (which he regarded as unsurpassed anywhere) reported heavy concentrations near the Yalu border in Manchuria whose movements were indeterminate. Finally, MacArthur's own military estimate was that "with our largely unopposed air forces, with their atomic potential capable of destroying at will bases of attack and lines of supply north as well as south of the Yalu, no Chinese military commander would have dared hazard the commitment of large forces upon the Korean peninsula. The risk of their utter destruction would be too great."[90]

***

On October 19, the North Korean capital of P'yŏngyang fell to ROK forces and, six days later, the American X Corps made a second amphibious landing, this time at Wonsan, on North Korea's eastern coast. Although the American troops discovered the waters were heavily mined, the fact the Chinese waged an initial assault and then seemingly disappeared, and the fact the city had fallen to South Korean troops two weeks prior, ensured there were no casualties. At this juncture, the field of those who agreed with Secretary of State Dean Acheson, that Chinese intervention in Korea was "unlikely," was an assessment shared by a crowd of influential American seniors, including President Truman, the Joint Chiefs of Staff, members of the National Security Council, CIA Director Lieutenant General Walter Bedell Smith, most congressmen, and the general public.[91] After all, as FECOM officials viewed the situation in late 1950, the Chinese had too much to lose to risk intervention; their potential defeat in the field would endanger the hard-won revolution, would lessen China's chance for a much-desired seat in the United Nations, and tangling with American and UN forces on the peninsula risked heavy casualties, especially given the acknowledged lack of Soviet air and naval support.[92]

However, as UN forces continued their inexorable march northward, there were growing concerns of the dangers of encroaching on perceived, or actual, Chinese territory. Great Britain proposed the creation of a buffer zone south of the Yalu River, a touch of Talleyrand that prompted MacArthur to acidly remark that such a proposal "finds its historic precedent in the action taken at Munich on 29 September 1938." On October 24, fearing the diplomats would undo with the stroke of a pen what had taken the soldiers months and lives to win, MacArthur instructed his senior commanders to "use any and all ground forces as necessary, to secure all of North Korea." MacArthur fended off the Joint Chiefs' questions and when they requested that he issue a statement ensuring the safety of the critical Suiho hydroelectric plant in North Korea, he refused, saying he could not prove it was not being used to support arms production. The connection in the public mind of MacArthur to World War II victories and the successful Inchon landings, paired with his optimistic prophecy concerning the imminent end of the Korean War, undoubtedly saved him from what might otherwise have been a very public sacking in October 1950. But events during the following month would come as a rude awakening for MacArthur and his G-2.[93]

CHAPTER FIVE

"A Period of Miscalculations"

As the fall of 1950 neared and Washington continued to debate whether or not United Nations forces should enter North Korea, the indicators that Mao was set on intervention began to accumulate. On August 31, Willoughby estimated there were 246,000 Chinese soldiers just across the Sino–Korean border in Manchuria, organized into nine armies of 37 divisions total; 80,000 of these troops were assessed to be in Antung, on the north bank of the Yalu River. He also counted into the mix the estimated 374,000 Militia Security Forces in Manchuria. The September 27 *Daily Intelligence Summary* (DIS) from Willoughby's staff noted that, according to a Chinese Nationalist report from Manchuria, Chinese Communist forces on the Korean border "show indications of moving south into Korea." Nevertheless, on the same day, the Joint Chiefs of Staff authorized MacArthur to cross the 38th Parallel in order to conduct decisive combat operations. His orders included the clear direction to report any contact with either Soviet or Chinese troops "as a matter of urgency."[1] On the 30th, G-2 assessed the Chinese Communists (CHICOM) would provide 250,000 troops for Korea and that the first group would arrive in September, the rest in October, a prognostication that proved correct. A week later, the DIS noted, somewhat after-the-fact, that "the potential exists for Chinese Communist forces to openly intervene in the Korean War if UN forces cross the 38th Parallel."[2]

As several observers within Far East Command (FECOM) pointed out, with a certain degree of logic, there were sound reasons why the Chinese would not intervene in the Korean imbroglio. First, were they to suffer defeat at the hands of United Nations forces on the battlefield, it could seriously endanger their recently fought revolution. Second, intervention could seriously jeopardize a key Chinese foreign policy goal, entry into the United Nations. Finally, acknowledging the recognized Chinese weakness in aircraft and ships, CHICOM forces could face heavy casualties without the reassuring umbrella of Soviet air and naval power. Yet, as early as October 2, Chinese Premier Chou En-lai had explicitly told the Indian Ambassador that if UN forces crossed the 38th Parallel, China would intervene; Truman dismissed the premier's words as a clumsy attempt to blackmail the United Nations.[3]

Despite concerning logistics and supply problems, the Eighth Army offensive rolled northward into North Korea, buoyed by Willoughby's assessment the North Korean People's Army (NKPA) was now reduced to some twenty thousand effectives and was withdrawing in poor order. Interestingly, the CIA assessment was that the NKPA still had 132,000 troops, 80,000 of whom were engaged in combat. It would take the intervention of the Chinese People's Army to compel Willoughby's staff to alter their estimate of NKPA strength to 11 divisions and over one hundred thousand troops. But, for the moment, MacArthur's presumption the war was all but over ruled the day.[4]

On October 2, the United Nations Command issued its Ops Plan, which essentially was MacArthur's plan, described by Willoughby as "the classical one made famous by von Moltke"—in other words, "action by separated forces off the enemy's axis of movement."[5] This ops plan, which directed the deployment of Major General Almond's X Corps to the east coast, with Major General Walton H. Walker's Eighth Army to the west was not technically flawed, given the current tactical situation—unless the Chinese intervened. However, whatever misgivings there were became irrelevant given the unwillingness of anyone to challenge the Commander in Chief United Nations Command on the point. The fact that the Taebaek mountain range, a daunting 7,000-feet high, separated Almond's and Walker's commands was of little concern given the offensive to date and the widely assumed near-cessation of hostilities.[6] The following day, UN Command intelligence staff reported some indications of the presence of 20 Chinese Communist Forces (CCF) divisions in North Korea and assessed they had been there since September 10. It also cautioned that while the alerting statements of Chou En-lai about the threat of Chinese intervention were obviously propaganda, "they cannot be fully ignored since they emit from presumably responsible leaders in the Chinese and North Korean governments. The enemy retains a potential of reinforcements by CCF troops."[7]

It was also early in what proved to be the critical month of October that Admiral Arleigh Burke, Deputy Chief of Staff to Commander, U.S. Naval Forces, Far East, approached his Japanese counterpart, Admiral Kichisaburo Nomura, a man experienced in dealings with the Chinese, concerning the threat of potential Chinese intervention in Korea. Nomura's response was that the situation was "most serious," an assessment Burke promptly took to Willoughby; however, the G-2 rejected the assessment out of hand, commenting that Nomura had no special sources and was thus merely guessing.[8]

On October 7, Willoughby's DIS included an entry in which an unnamed American officer had been interrogated by three Soviet counterparts, who told him that if UN forces crossed the 38th Parallel, "New Communist forces would enter the war in support of North Korea." In fairness to Willoughby, his early October daily intelligence estimates "consistently gave high priority to the possibility of 'Reinforcement by Soviet Satellite China.'" Also, his October 14 assessment concluded, with what one author has characterized as "commendable accuracy," there were then nine Chinese armies (38 divisions) in Manchuria; of these 38 divisions, some 24 were deployed along the Yalu, especially in the area near Antung. Despite such statements and conclusions, however, the FECOM G-2 remained ultimately unconvinced; Willoughby's analysis during the period October 8–14 characterized as "inconclusive" any evidence of Chinese troops in North Korea and Zhou en-Lai's statements as "probably in the category of diplomatic blackmail." Mimicking the lead of their Army colleague, the CIA's National Intelligence Estimate (NIE) for October 12 summarily declared with regard to Chinese intervention that "the most favorable time for intervention in Korea has passed."[9] Mao's warnings of mid-October should have served as the trigger for MacArthur to report to Washington; however, Willoughby's dismissal of the warnings provided MacArthur with the erstwhile rationale to continue his offensive. Besides, MacArthur could point out he hadn't yet had contact with the enemy, a statement in accordance with the letter of the law though likely not in the spirit intended by the Joint Chiefs.[10] As one historian noted, "In embarrassed hindsight, intelligence analysts came to recognize that the major warnings they dismissed as 'diplomatic blackmail' were exactly what they purported to be: a clear statement of the course of action China intended to follow if American troops crossed the 38th Parallel."[11]

On October 15, Willoughby and MacArthur flew to Wake Island to meet with Truman and his advisors concerning the emerging situation in Korea. Also present for the meeting were Commander in Chief Pacific Fleet Admiral Arthur W. Radford; Ambassador Muccio; Secretary of the Army Frank Pace; battalion commander Colonel Archelaus L. Hamblen, Jr.; Ambassador at Large Phillip C. Jessup; Assistant Secretary of State Dean Rusk; and statesman Averell Harriman. Serving as the amanuensis for the conference was General Omar Bradley, Chairman, Joint Chiefs of Staff. In a cover memo to MacArthur accompanying the detailed notes he took during the conference, General Bradley wrote, "The conference, I feel, was most satisfactory and profitable—all of us from here got a great deal out of it."[12]

While a fairly routine meeting between a theater commander and the commander in chief in wartime, and one in which a number of disparate topics were discussed, the meeting took on a larger-than-life significance due to statements MacArthur made, particularly to the answer he provided to one particular question posed by President Truman. When the conversation turned to the operational level military situation, MacArthur explained:

> It is my hope to be able to withdraw the Eighth Army to Japan by Christmas. That will leave the X Corps ... After elections are held I expect to pull out all occupying troops. Korea should have about two divisions with our equipment, supplemented by a small but competent Air Force and also by a small but competent Navy. If we do that, it will not only secure Korea but it will be a tremendous deterrent to the Chinese Communists moving south. This is a threat that cannot be laughed off.

But it was a simple question from President Truman to MacArthur that has prompted recriminations ever since:

> THE PRESIDENT: What are the chances for Chinese or Soviet interference?
>
> GENERAL MACARTHUR: Very little ... My intelligence has established that there are some twenty-five to thirty thousand Chinese in that area [in the path of the Eighth Army's advance north of P'yŏngyang], but not more than that could have crossed the Yalu *or my intelligence would know about it.* [emphasis added]

MacArthur expanded on that statement, noting that should the Chinese foolishly intervene, there would be "the greatest slaughter" due to overwhelming allied airpower. Overall, he certainly minimized, if not dismissed all together, Chinese intervention in the Korean War. He explained the Soviet threat was completely different, but it was his words about the People's Republic of China that would be remembered. Ironically, in light of what was to come, the conversation turned to other topics and there was no further discussion of the Chinese threat during the conference.[13]

Aware his boss would brook no interference with his strategic plan to push to the Yalu, Willoughby was reticent to offer any analysis that would question the wisdom of that strategy and thus his earlier assessments were lowered in significance. He was no doubt feeling the heat from Washington to conclude the war, especially in light of recent UN victories in the field—and now he was in the presence of that "heat." Ambassador Muccio recalled MacArthur admitted there were already Chinese troops in North Korea but minimized their significance. Such a statement reflects the assessment of one author who noted that one of the problems of the intelligence provided prior to the Chinese invasion was that it generally got only as far as the G-2, with only "confirmed" intelligence being forwarded to FECOM. "Overall," wrote this historian, "Far East Command generally received outdated, often misinterpreted, incomplete intelligence reports from its subordinate units." The unfortunate result was that MacArthur and his key staff officers were often making decisions based on faulty intelligence.[14]

Five days after the conference concluded, MacArthur's Headquarters issued "Ops Plan 202," the plan for the disposition of UN occupation troops throughout North Korea. Such optimism accurately reflected the widely held belief—in Washington as well as Tokyo—that the war in Korea was virtually over and that the primary concern of the Joint Chiefs was getting the troops back to Europe to deal with the rising "Red Menace" of Soviet Russia. Equally reflective of this general euphoria was that, on October 22, Walker's Eighth Army requested that six ammunition ships on their way to Korea be sent *back* to the United States, as their cargo would not be needed. Similarly, on the 25th, Major General Lawrence B. "Dutch" Keiser, Commander, 2nd Infantry Division, told his officers he had received orders to redeploy Stateside—by Christmas. As one historian concluded, the actions of both

MacArthur and Willoughby produced "second order effects" which hamstrung the ability of UN forces to successfully meet the Chinese onslaught.[15]

However, just three days after MacArthur had smoothed the ruffled feathers of his commander in chief regarding the likelihood of Chinese intervention in Korea, Willoughby and FECOM air commander Lieutenant General George Stratemeyer received a shocking aerial reconnaissance report. On the 18th, American reconnaissance planes flying along the Yalu River spotted an estimated 75–100 unidentified aircraft at a Chinese airfield near Antung, in Manchuria, just north of the Democratic People's Republic. This startling revelation made a mockery of the rosy picture MacArthur—fed by Willoughby and his analysts—had provided to President Truman; if true, this information seemed a clear and foreboding indication of Chinese tactical and operational intentions. Predictably, a reconnaissance flight was ordered over the same area the following day, which showed nothing. The sizable numbers of aircraft clearly there the previous day were gone, all of them, providing Willoughby and—by extension, MacArthur—a welcome reprieve. Willoughby chalked up the initial report to either a Chinese long-distance training mission or to saber-rattling by Chou En-lai. Stratemeyer came to the same conclusion, though with a different twist; he posited that the aircraft were Russian fighters, were there on October 18 only as a show of force, and would never have allowed American reconnaissance to observe them had they actually been intended for operational use.[16]

On the night of October 19, the same day P'yŏngyang fell to American forces, units of the People's Liberation Army's (PLA) Thirteenth Army Group began crossing the Yalu River into North Korea, a tactical move that took American intelligence "completely by surprise." Moving only at night to avoid detection, and strictly observing radio silence, four PLA armies—the 38th, 39th, 40th, and 42nd—plus three artillery divisions and an anti-aircraft gun regiment, a force of 260,000 men total—secretly crossed the Yalu at seven crossing points. That same day, General Peng Dehuai, the commander of the Chinese People's Volunteers, along with a small staff contingent, set up his headquarters in a mineshaft outside the village of Taeyudong, northeast of the town of Onjong. The Thirteenth Army Group staff crossed the boundary river two days later.[17]

The next day, Willoughby penned these words for the DIS: "Organized resistance on any large scale has ceased to be an enemy capability. Indications are that the North Korean military and political headquarters [staff] may have fled into Manchuria." He did, however, add that his intelligence officers assessed that the enemy could still be capable of "small-scale delaying actions." Turning to the likelihood of Chinese intervention, he wrote, "The decision, however, is not within the purview of local intelligence; it will be based on the high-level readiness of the Kremlin to go to war through utilizing the CC-Manchuria on orders." FECOM Deputy Chief of Staff Rear Admiral Arleigh Burke, however, had been discussing events with his own analysts in mid-October and disagreed with Willoughby's oddly worded assessment, and told

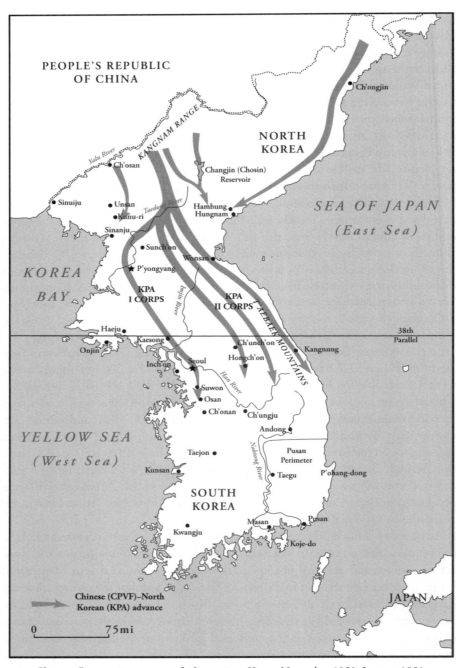

PEOPLE'S REPUBLIC
OF CHINA

Ch'ongjin

KANGNAM RANGE

Yalu River

Ch'osan

Changjin (Chosin)
Reservoir

NORTH
KOREA

SEA OF JAPAN
(East Sea)

Sinuiju

Unsan

Kunu-ri

Taedong River

Sinanju

Hamhung
Hungnam

Sunch'on

Wonsan

KOREA
BAY

P'yongyang

Imjin River

KPA
I CORPS

KPA
II CORPS

T'AEBAEK MOUNTAINS

Haeju

Kaesong

Onjin

Inch'on

Seoul

Suwon

Osan

Ch'onan

Han River

Ch'unch'on

Hongch'on

Kangnung

38th
Parallel

Ch'ungju

Andong

YELLOW SEA
(West Sea)

Taejon

Naktong River

Kunsan

Pusan
Perimeter

Taegu

P'ohang-dong

SOUTH
KOREA

Kwangju

Masan

Pusan

Koje-do

JAPAN

Chinese (CPVF)–North
Korean (KPA) advance

0   75mi

Chinese Communist avenues of advance into Korea, November 1950–January 1951.

him so. One of Burke's analysts had concluded, "It looks to us like the Chinese are in North Korea." Not one to back down from a challenge, Willoughby brought in *his* analysts to review the material which, not surprisingly, reaffirmed their earlier assessment, meaning it continued to be the exact opposite of what Burke's analysts had concluded. Willoughby reiterated the correctness of his initial assessment by adding, "I don't think they're in there either and I don't think they'll come in." A few days later, U.S. Navy analysts again concluded the Chinese were in North Korea; based on this renewed conclusion, Burke again approached Willoughby but found the G-2 unconvinced. Rebuffed, Burke shared his analysts' assessments with his boss, Admiral C. Turner Joy, and informed him that he planned to retain one of every five transports that came in with supplies so he would have some means to evacuate American forces in case of emergency. Both Admiral Joy and U.S. Navy seniors agreed with Burke's proposal and, over the next several weeks, Burke reserved some 90 transports for the evacuation he feared might be necessary.[18]

For his part, Willoughby admitted in October there were indeed large Chinese armies in Manchuria, which could doubtless cross the Yalu River and decisively engage UN forces on the peninsula. However, he advised MacArthur that the Chinese would take this action *only* if Soviet leader Joseph Stalin authorized it. Despite Willoughby's disagreement, he relented enough to authorize an intelligence fact-finding mission. He sent Lieutenant Eugene Clark USN—who had won a Silver Star for his recon/intel work in advance of the successful amphibious landing at Inchon the previous month—to take 150 South Korean guerilla fighters in five powerboats, travel up the Yellow Sea coast to the northernmost island of the Korean Peninsula, and look for evidence of the Chinese. When they reached the Yalu River in late October, they discovered large numbers of Chinese troops crossing the river into North Korea. Clark immediately transmitted this information by radio to FECOM in Tokyo, where it was promptly ignored.[19]

On the diplomatic front, as well, there were indicators of looming Chinese intervention in Korea. India's Ambassador to China, K. M. Pannikar, continued to provide reports of the increasing Chinese concern over the UN intervention in Korea, but doubts about his credibility stopped the ears of his intended audience. The CIA assessed the Indian report as a "plant," intended to influence American and British foreign policy. On October 4, the day following Chou En-Lai's threat to intervene, as related to Pannikar, the latter's warning was also discounted by former admiral and U.S. Ambassador to Moscow Alan Goodrich Kirk. Two days later, the CIA dismissed Chou's saber-rattling statement as a "bluff."[20]

Meanwhile, various sources had noted the movement of the Chinese 4th Army into Manchuria in mid-summer; the British Consulate in Mukden confirmed these reports and added that, as of mid-August, elite PLA units—with a sizable Korean contingent—were vigorously training in the area. British authorities in London, more concerned than their brethren across the pond in Washington about the prospect of Chinese intervention, tried in mid-October to urge Washington to stop its offensive just north of the 38th Parallel, but it was already too late. His Majesty's Government had to settle for MacArthur's being "firmly discouraged" from driving UN forces north of the Manchurian border; nor was it any more successful with its own—in Tokyo, Air Vice-Marshal Bouchier telegraphed his headquarters that the UN offensive was "on course and in sight of victory."[21]

As of mid-October 1950, United Nations Command (UNC) intelligence had positively identified 24 Chinese divisions deployed near the Yalu River, and 14 more lurking somewhere in Manchuria, an assessment which meant the total number of Chinese troops outnumbered those of the UNC.[22] Willoughby's intelligence summary for October 20 assessed that 400,000 Chinese soldiers in border crossing areas in Manchuria had been alerted. Ironically, it was that same day that FECOM issued Ops Plan 202, which described post-war plans for Korea, including the departure of one U.S. Army division for Europe as early as December.[23] This figure was not out of sync with the estimates of various intelligence services at that point, which pegged the total number of CCF soldiers deployed in Korea at 450,000; presciently, their assessment included the observation that the committed forces included the 4th Field Army and elements of the 3rd Field Army, reputed to be some of the best Chinese field units. Yet, when MacArthur met with President Truman at Wake Island mid-month, the figure he used as an estimate of committed Chinese forces in Korea was 300,000, certainly on the low end of the scale but not inconsistent with the figure the CIA was using and numbers already known by Truman.[24]

On October 25, the Republic of Korea's (ROK) 1st Division was heavily counterattacked, but in the course of the fighting had the dubious honor of capturing the first Chinese prisoner of war, at Unsan. During his initial interrogation, Private Chung San Shien, claimed he was a *Chinese* soldier, part of a much larger effort, and added that he and his comrades had been sent to Korea to "prevent a U.S. invasion of China." Quickly flown to P'yŏngyang, Chung convinced interrogators he could only be Chinese, since he was unable to speak either Korean or Japanese. Much better clothed than the normal North Korean captive, Private Chung mentioned, almost in passing, the "tens of thousands" of Chinese troops in the nearby mountains. In further interrogations, he stated his unit had marched from Antung (Andong), Manchuria, and had crossed into North Korea on the night of October 19, on a recently built wooden bridge. A Chinese officer had instructed the troops not to speak if captured but should they be compelled to speak, to do so in Korean. To heighten the subterfuge, these troops were also wearing North Korean uniforms, which Private Chung thoughtfully noted had just been issued on October 5. Most ominously, this same Chinese officer had claimed, so the prisoner stated, there were *600,000* Chinese troops on the way, intending "to defeat the U.S. Army." While information from a POW is always suspect, this young private had no reason to lie;

yet, even in the face of what seemed to be significant evidence that American troops were engaged in combat with forces other than those of North Korea, Willoughby refused to be swayed and dismissed the fight at Unsan as "unimportant." Although I Corps staff immediately sent this interrogation information to Eighth Army Headquarters and then on to FECOM G-2, Willoughby responded by saying the prisoner was likely a Korean resident of China, hence the apparent confusion, and promptly discounted the threat. To arrive at this mistaken conclusion, Willoughby had to ignore two key pieces of evidence: first, the interrogators assessed Private Chung as "fairly reliable"; second, he had fully answered no less than four pages of questions which detailed how he had entered the Chinese Nationalist Army in 1949, was captured by the Communists in February 1950, transferred to the 40th People's Army, and was ultimately sent to Manchuria. Mimicking the mindset of his boss, Eighth Army G-2 James C. (Clint) Tarkenton—the 34-year-old lieutenant colonel whom Willoughby had personally selected for the job, passing over more experienced, older officers[25]—concluded on October 26 there were "no indications of open intervention" by CHICOM forces; while technically correct *at that particular moment*, Tarkenton's assessment completely discounted Chung's information. The pair of American intelligence officers apparently were also baffled "for several weeks" by bogus Chinese unit identifications from prisoners of war, who indicated they had been supplied with such information in advance to sow confusion among their captors. During this same combat action, Major General Paik Sun Yup, 1st ROK Division commander, engaged at Unsan, informed the American I Corps commander that, as of October 27, he was facing "many, many Chinese." Paik's conclusion was based in part on the answer he received when he queried a prisoner, identified as Chinese, "Are there many of you here?" He replied, "Many, many."[26] The conclusions reached by Willoughby about the prisoner seemed intended to minimize the significance of the capture but also implied he didn't know who he was, what nationality he was, what unit he was with, or how many other soldiers were in his unit. As Korean War historian David Halberstam concluded, "It was a judgment that would have pleased the Chinese high command—it was exactly what they wanted the Americans to think."[27]

However, the conclusions reached by Willoughby and Tarkenton were not universally embraced. One such critic was Lieutenant Colonel Bill Train, Eighth Army Plans Officer, assigned to the G-3 (Operations) but pressed into the G-2 due to a personnel shortage at the time. With regard to what he had witnessed, Train was convinced a fully fledged Chinese invasion was underway and disaster was about to befall the Eighth Army. As he commented, "It was Mac's command, not a U.S. Army command, and if you crossed Willoughby it was not just a ticket out of there, it was probably a ticket straight out of your career," which explains why a number of staffers fell into line with Willoughby's pronouncements. Train and his G-3 boss, Colonel John Dabney, were also disturbed by the way in which the senior intelligence officers he was temporarily assisting dismissed the same compelling, even convincing, evidence he saw. When Train saw the estimates for the number of Chinese troops the Eighth Army was facing forwarded to Washington, the only conclusion he could draw was that they didn't *want* any better information. The pair of G-3 officers were incredulous that whenever evidence of a serious Chinese troop presence was presented, Willoughby's staffers minimized it.[28]

Willoughby's DIS for October 28 assessed:

> It can be assumed then, that all regular CCF ground forces now in Manchuria are available and could be employed in the Korean War. It is important to note that the bulk of these forces are now in position along the Yalu River at numerous crossing sites. Should the decision be made to launch a counter-offensive against the U.N., these 29 divisions, representing two-thirds of the total forces known to be in Manchuria, are immediately available …[29]

This is well short of a full-blown warning. Furthermore, despite breaking events at the front, the DIS still blithely observed that CCF troops "have no significant experience in combat operations against a major power" and added that their training was handicapped by a lack of standard combat equipment and a shortage of ammunition stocks.[30] Furthermore, the disbelief, both at the Eighth Army as well as Supreme Headquarters in Tokyo, that the Chinese could have surreptitiously deployed sizable numbers of troops into Korea without being detected prompted American intelligence officers to search for a more rational explanation: since it was undeniable by early November that Chinese ground forces were indeed engaged in Korea, American authorities explained simply that small numbers of Chinese troops had indeed reinforced their North Korean allies, though no one seemed quite sure why. One interrogator assessed the Chinese were helping a neighbor monitor their joint fence, as it were, another concluded they had been dispatched to protect key power plants along the Yalu River from falling into UN hands.[31] Despite the dismissive statements of Willoughby and others concerning Chinese combat capabilities, however, in reality CCF soldiers and their officers displayed effective battlefield tactics, employing deception, such as using code names for their respective units, to make them appear smaller than they actually were. Additionally, they moved only at night—Korean War veteran and combat historian Roy Appleman noted units would begin moving at 7:00 pm and march until 3:00 am—and maintained excellent camouflage during the day, hiding from view every man, animal, and piece of equipment. On the rare occasion when Chinese units had to march during the day, they were ordered to remain motionless anytime aircraft passed overhead; officers were empowered to immediately shoot any soldier who disobeyed.[32]

The only development as surprising as the swiftness and severity of the Chinese offensive was the abruptness with which it ended. Allied observers concluded the Chinese were battered and needed to withdraw and refit; in reality, they had withdrawn because they had achieved their tactical and operational goals, including luring the Eighth Army northward to trap it far from its supply lines and to isolate it near the Chinese border. They had learned a great deal about the largely unknown American forces, though the reverse was *not* the case, aided powerfully by an admitted racial prejudice and a general ignorance of Mao Zedong's strategic ideas. UNC would relearn this painful and tragic lesson many times over the next three years, becoming all too familiar with the enemy's expert use of terrain, deception, infiltration, and—perhaps most prophetic of all—the use of overwhelming numbers of troops in close quarters, essentially negating superior Western firepower, logistics, and technology.[33] But the attacker had paid a heavy price for his offensive and the Chinese participation in the Korean conflict would cost China both in manpower and in funds. In part due to the unusually cold weather during the winter of 1950–51, Chinese casualties were alarmingly high, at least by Western standards. For example, during the approximately two-week period between November 27 and December 12, 1950, the 9th Army alone suffered 45,000 KIAs. As one CHICOM soldier later recalled, they often had to sleep out in the open, without blankets, in temperatures of -30° Centigrade; under such brutal conditions, digits froze solid and fell off at a touch.[34]

Regrettably, these first encounters did nothing to alter the analytic picture portrayed of Chinese involvement in Korea. On October 24, General Walker noted, "Everything is going just fine," with no inkling that within 48 hours his ROK 6th Division would be decimated by elements of the Chinese 40th Field Army.[35] The next day, Willoughby released his Eighth Report to the United Nations, for the period October 15–31 and concluded, "There is no positive evidence that Chinese Communist units, as such, have entered Korea," a statement an historian writing some fifteen years later summarily dismissed as "one of the most egregiously wrong strategic intelligence estimates in history." The October 28 DIS breezily noted, "It would appear that the auspicious time for intervention has long since passed," despite the fact that same day Willoughby's staffers informed him of the interrogation of the first CCF prisoner three days prior. To come to such a conclusion meant ignoring the mauling suffered by the ROK 1st Division only three days prior, the information provided by Chinese prisoners during interrogation, and what deployed units characterized as vastly improved tactical capabilities on the part of the enemy. In reality, as policy makers in both Washington and Tokyo read the words of Willoughby, there were in reality at least four CHICOM armies already inside North Korea; at least three of these—the 38th, 39th, and 40th Armies, all subordinate to the Thirteenth Army Group—were deployed west of the Taebak range, within the Eighth Army's area of responsibility. Furthermore, these three CHICOM armies were reinforced by elements of the 1st Motorized Artillery Division, two regiments of the 2nd Motorized Artillery Division, and a cavalry regiment. Nor were these the only CHICOM troops committed into North Korea at this early date—the 42nd Army was deployed in the hills surrounding the Changjin (Chosin) Reservoir, in General Almond's X Corps area. Within the next week, the 50th and 66th Armies, as well as the 8th Artillery Division and a motor transport regiment, would cross from Antung, Manchuria to Sinuiju, North Korea, to join their countrymen. One student of the Korean War has assessed that, as of October 31, 1950, nearly two hundred thousand Chinese troops had been committed to North Korea, some of whom had crossed the Yalu into North Korea prior to October 15. On the 30th, Willoughby's curiosity had compelled him to fly from Tokyo to X Corps Headquarters to interview Chinese captives; after personally interviewing 16 CCF prisoners, he assessed them as "stragglers," not subordinate to any Chinese military unit. In his report the next day to Deputy Chief of Staff for Intelligence Major General Bolling, he acknowledged that UN forces had 28 CHICOM prisoners of war in hand and admitted these captives had been bagged by both the Eighth Army and X Corps, suggesting Chinese intervention over a broad geographic area. Yet, he cited only one interrogation report which, not surprisingly, supported his preconceived notions. In this report, Willoughby concluded that "only token forces from the Fortieth Army HQ and from each of its divisions entered Korea on 20 October."[36]

***

On the night of October 31, the 8th Cavalry Regiment was deployed near the North Korean city of Unsan, site of an old American gold-mine concession, 65 miles south of the Manchurian border. At Regimental Headquarters that night, Sgt. "Pappy" Miller brought in a local farmer who told an amazing tale—he claimed thousands of Chinese Communist (CHICOM) soldiers were waiting in the hills north of Unsan. However, no one at the headquarters considered the farmer a credible source of tactical intelligence and thus dismissed his fanciful account out of hand. Just two nights later, two CHICOM divisions mauled the 8th Cavalry Regiment in a nighttime battle which placed the Eighth Army on the defensive for the first time since September. As a knowledgeable observer noted in retrospect, this event was the first opportunity for MacArthur and Willoughby to assess, correctly, that China had entered the Korean War and done so decisively.[37]

That same night, soldiers from Almond's X Corps captured 18 Chinese near Chanjin and the Chosin Reservoir, troops ultimately identified as members of the PLA's 370th Regiment, 124th CCF Division, 42nd CCF Corps—their captors could not help but notice that, although they had not eaten in three days, they had new winter clothing. Upon hearing this information, Willoughby was certain enough of the report to inform the Joint Chiefs of Staff.[38]

Also worrisome was the fact that, on November 1, a flight of Fifth Air Force fighters had engaged six to nine enemy jet aircraft, damaging one, then watched helplessly as another escaped—*north* of the Yalu River. Again, Willoughby dismissed a significant intelligence indicator, preferring to believe instead an earlier report which assessed that a lack of Chinese air and naval support would limit their involvement in any combat that might occur. Such reasoning by Willoughby was a complete discounting of the situation from the very perspective that should be most familiar to an intelligence officer—that of the enemy. His myopia in ignoring the Chinese perspective on the developing situation was a direct reflection of his flawed analysis and of the Western mirror imaging that would serve the American/UN offensive so poorly in Korea. A CIA report provided to President Truman that same day reflected the thinking of the FECOM G-2—it estimated there were 15–20,000 Chinese troops in Korea, while Willoughby admitted there could be up to 16,500 committed to battle.[39]

That same day, the British 27th Brigade reported a skirmish with Chinese troops near the Ch'ongch'on River in which they suffered six killed and five wounded. One of the British soldiers, Lieutenant Colin Mitchell, noted, "They were unlike any enemy I had seen before. They wore thick padded clothing, which made them look like little Michelin men. I turned one body over with my foot, and saw that he wore a peaked cap with a red star badge. These soldiers were Chinese."[40]

During the week of October 25–November 1, South Korean forces captured more Chinese soldiers. For example, on the 26th, Second Lieutenant George Hong, 164th Military Intelligence (MI) Service Detachment, interrogated Private Chung San Syng, the day after he had been captured by ROK forces near Unsan. The prisoner indicated there were between 50,000 and 60,000 Chinese 40th Army troops in Korea. He also claimed to have seen 20 up-gunned T-34/85 tanks crossing the Yalu into North Korea on the 15th. Later that night, Chung said his unit had crossed from Antung, Manchuria, into Sinuiju, North Korea, using a wooden bridge. He also confirmed his namesake fellow prisoner's story about the PLA issuing the troops North Korean uniforms, and added they always moved at night to avoid American airpower.[41]

The interrogation of CCF prisoners illustrated another obstacle in terms of providing coherent intelligence analysis in late 1950—namely, the American military's shortage of capable Mandarin Chinese linguists who could combine a detailed knowledge of military terminology, equipment, and tactics with a near-fluency in the primary Chinese dialect. In November 1950, FECOM G-2 requested that the G-1 (Personnel) requisition 30 Mandarin Chinese linguists from the U.S. Army, "against possible future need." However, by December only nine had been received, none of whom were deemed qualified. A simultaneous attempt to secure the translation services of ethnic Japanese Chinese-speakers proved equally dissatisfying. As late as June 1951, of the 75 Mandarin linguists who had arrived at FECOM, only 16 were actually capable of translation duties. By March 1951, 75 fluent Mandarin-speaking Formosan nationals had been received at FECOM, too late to help Willoughby divine Chinese strategic intentions in Korea.[42]

As the number of skirmishes grew, so too did the numbers of "clearly Chinese" prisoners of war; according to one report concerning a group of captives, they "looked Chinese, spoke Chinese, and understood neither Korean nor Japanese." Eighth Army officials dutifully forwarded this information to Tokyo, but FECOM officials dismissed these reports out of hand, pointing out that since this information came from interrogation reports, the information was "unconfirmed and thereby unaccepted." As late as October 27, Willoughby still spoke of Chinese intervention as "potential." He also asserted that most CCF troops had had no combat experience—apparently, the two-decade-long civil war with the Nationalists didn't count, nor did engagements with Japanese troops during World War II—and characterized the People's Republic as a major power whose military training was handicapped by a lack of standard equipment and ammunition. Two days later, he wrote there was still "no indication of open intervention on the part of Chinese Communist forces."[43]

As the children of America took to the streets to trick-or-treat that Halloween of 1950, Willoughby edged ever so slightly toward considering the possibility the Chinese might be more involved in North Korea than he had first thought. On October 31, Willoughby cited earlier warnings he had received—though not believed—about Chinese intervention, but even then was only willing to admit that "greater credence must be given" to reports indicating the CCF had intervened in a big way in the Democratic People's Republic.[44] That same day, Willoughby debriefed a North Korean–Manchurian border agent, an opportunity that left the G-2 "apparently grateful," to the extent he sent to the Operation *Aviary* unit that sponsored the agent 10 scarce SCR-300 infantry radio transceivers as a "thank you" gift. However, even the information provided by the agent was insufficient to convince Willoughby of the Chinese intervention in force.[45]

Meanwhile, on November 1, the CIA provided President Truman with its assessment of the current situation on the Korean Peninsula. Since MacArthur and Willoughby had gone to great lengths to determine just how much rope the Agency could have in Korea, this document—not surprisingly—largely reflected Willoughby's way of thinking. CIA analysts had estimated there were then an estimated 15,000 to 20,000 Chinese troops in Korea—by comparison, Willoughby's own assessment was there might be "up to 16,500" troops in the country with about 516,000 regulars and 274,000 irregulars in Manchuria. But the assessment's bottom line was that the "CIA does not believe that the appearance of these Chinese Communist soldiers indicates that the Chinese Communists intend to intervene directly or openly in the Korean War."[46]

On November 2, the analytic wranglings going on within the United States' fold were abruptly interrupted by a Chinese radio broadcast, which essentially acknowledged the reality of their military intervention in North Korea. The spokesman characterized the CCF as "a Volunteer Corps for the Protection of the Hydroelectric Zone," a reference to Chinese concerns about the dams and power complexes along the Yalu, which supplied electricity to Chinese troops in the vicinity.

This helpful nugget from the enemy confused Willoughby more than it helped him, however. Nevertheless, he reported this information to Washington, accompanied by this ominous statement:

> Should the high-level decision for full intervention be made by the Chinese Communists, they could promptly commit twenty-nine of their forty-four divisions presently employed along the Yalu and support a major attack with up to 150 aircraft.[47]

The DIS for that day acknowledged the recent capture of numerous Chinese soldiers but added the blithe and almost-detached comment that:

> Recent captures of soldiers of Chinese nationality and information obtained from their interrogation together with the increased resistance being encountered by advancing United Nations forces removed the problem of Chinese intervention from the realm of the academic and turned it into a serious proximate threat.[48]

Indeed it did. Such information caused angst in Washington, D.C., especially in the State Department, though not enough to come to the correct conclusion. Rumors of Chinese intervention that had reached Foggy Bottom prompted the dismissive retort, speaking of the Chinese, "There is not the slightest chance that they can become involved in Korea; their problems are so enormous that it's not possible that they can do it for years." Fortunately for them, the Chinese were clearly unaware of this "truth."[49]

On November 3, the increasingly concerned Joint Chiefs of Staff asked MacArthur for an appraisal of the situation on the ground. In his reply the next day, MacArthur was still unwilling to admit full Chinese intervention or just how critical the situation truly was. He assessed it was impossible to characterize the nature of the enemy intervention—a truly disturbing observation by a ground forces commander, at any echelon—but that it clearly did not represent a full-blown intervention. Instead, MacArthur viewed the Chinese entry into North Korea as an example of "covert action" to serve ultimately diplomatic purposes—hence, the use of "volunteers." The unexpected outcome, from the Chinese perspective, MacArthur explained away by characterizing the intervention as a "misstep" on their part, in that they expected to meet only ROK troops in combat, not those of the American/ UN forces. That same day, MacArthur provided updated Chinese troop strength figures to Washington and to the United Nations—he reported there were some 868,000 Chinese troops in Manchuria—with no mention of any in North Korea. MacArthur later noted that either Washington or UN officials could have stopped his northward reconnaissance-in-force at any time, but "each preferred the opiate of wishful thinking, the myopic resignation of the ostrich." Overall, the message of MacArthur's report was a reassuring one, intended to smooth the ruffled feathers of the senior American service chiefs.[50]

On November 5, MacArthur sent a Special Report to the UN Security Council, based on the interrogation of 35 captured Chinese soldiers confirming what was becoming clear to UN forces, namely, that it was indeed elements of at least the 38th, 39th, and 40th Field Armies that were committed against UN forces in Korea. MacArthur also assessed there were some 40,000 to 60,000 CCF troops in Korea, getting closer to an accurate estimate but still far short of the 200,000 Chinese troops representing some fifteen armies which were already south of the Yalu.[51] The DIS for the day took a somewhat rosier view: "Regarding the Chinese intention to launch a large-scale counter-offensive, the enemy certainly has the potential, particularly in ground forces, and is in a position to exercise this capability at any time and without warning."[52]

However, a week later—November 8—the CIA released its NIE, which drove the first wedge between the FECOM G-2 and the spy agency. This NIE—the collaborative product of State, Army, Navy, and Air Force information and cooperation—assessed there were 30,000 to 40,000 Chinese troops already in Korea, with an estimated 700,000 more in Manchuria. Refuting Willoughby's assertion that the opportunity for the Chinese to intervene militarily had passed, the CIA raised the ugly possibility that the Chinese had the inherent power to not only change the nature of the conflict in Korea, but to change it significantly. Specifically, Agency analysts warned the Chinese could take full advantage of the challenging terrain and the brutal weather conditions "to expose them [the United Nations' forces] to attrition" and advised that "the Chinese Communists thus far retain full freedom of action with respect to Korea." Predictably, however, this grimmer assessment prompted neither MacArthur nor Willoughby to even postpone or alter, much less cancel, the planned offensive, now only a fortnight off.[53]

That same night, 7th ID soldiers, deployed on the eastern flank of X Corps, engaged an estimated Chinese battalion and killed at least fifty of the enemy before the latter withdrew. By then, all major units of Almond's X Corps, save the 3rd Infantry Division, deployed near Wonsan, had already encountered the PLA in strength. Furthermore, by that date, the Eighth Army had 10 Chinese prisoners in the bag, whom they had identified as belonging to the 119th and 120th divisions of the 40th Army and the 117th Division of the 39th Army—three different divisions from two separate Chinese army groups, both committed to combat in Korea. Thus, by October 30, or shortly thereafter, the two ranking field commanders in Korea, Walker and Almond, located hundreds of miles apart, had encountered significant numbers of troops confirmed as Chinese regulars. But even among those who accepted the Chinese presence in Korea, there were disputes about the actual numbers of CHICOM troops committed—for example, the CIA's October 30 *Daily Korea Summary* specifically denied the Chinese units above, identified by the Eighth Army, had been committed to the peninsula.[54]

By the end of the first week in November, Willoughby should have been able to sort and evaluate the disparate pieces of information he had to compile a fairly accurate Chinese order-of-battle picture and correctly assess that the PRC had entered the

Korean War in a big way. And indeed, in the second week of November, he estimated there were 100,000 Communist troops in Korea, total—30–40,000 North Koreans and 60–70,000 Chinese "volunteers." As became clear later, at that point there were actually about three hundred thousand Chinese in Korea and, rather than volunteers, they were in reality organized divisions and army groups belonging to Lin Pao's 4th Field Army and Chen Yi's 3rd Field Army. When several American commanders questioned Willoughby's figures, the latter reiterated his firmly held opinion that there were only Chinese "volunteers" in Korea. In potential defense of Willoughby, some order-of-battle analysts familiar with Chinese military nomenclature have pointed out he may have been fooled by the Chinese trick of using terms such as "unit" and "battalion" to disguise what were in reality full armies and divisions. Thus, the 55th "unit" was actually the 39th Army and the "1st Battalion, 55th Unit" was actually the 115th Division of the 39th Army. Even granting that concession, however, it is hard to exonerate Willoughby with this explanation, given his position dictated he know his enemy well enough to be aware of this historic deception. Yet, he continued to report divisions as battalions, despite conflicting information from units actually in contact. Interestingly, some Chinese prisoners evidently forgot the ruse, leading to initially confused UN interrogators, who ultimately unraveled the misdirection.[55]

However, by November 5, Willoughby did assess that the CCF had the capability of "launching an attack at any time" and, two days later, the DIS academically observed that "in the somewhat limited contact with UN forces to date, the Chinese Communist soldier has shown himself to be a capable, well-disciplined fighter."[56] Five days later, Willoughby's assessment had flip-flopped, now warning that the Chinese were likely to wage an "all out" attack on UN forces. He was especially wary of a major Chinese build-up in the Changjin–Pujon Reservoir area, which he warned could threaten Almond's X Corps and coastal areas in northeastern Korea. "It is believed," he wrote, "that this enemy concentration even now may be capable of seizing the initiative and launching offensive operations." He thought likely a Chinese attack to the south, in order to cut UN forces then deployed to the north and east of Hungnam.[57] Although these latter two assessments were clearly closer to the mark and have been used by some writers to blame MacArthur for the ultimate debacle, instead of Willoughby, they do not profoundly alter the nature of the intelligence support Willoughby provided to his commander. As Haynes has noted, Willoughby had correctly assessed that the Chinese were massing troops in Manchuria and was willing to acknowledge Chinese troops might have been committed to Korea as early as mid-October; however, he stubbornly refused to attribute to Mao Zedong the strategic intent already provided to the international diplomatic community, the average CHICOM soldier, and many in between. Most telling, though, was his failure to convince MacArthur of the strategic nature of the Chinese threat.[58]

The presumption that such apparent confirmations of Chinese entry into the war would cause shockwaves in Washington, D.C., was soon disproven. The first naysayers were at the U.S. Department of State, and it was not as though Willoughby and MacArthur were alone in their firmly held belief the Chinese would not intervene. No less a figure than General Carl A. Spaatz, USAF (Ret.), was quoted in a November 13, 1950, *Newsweek* article as being a skeptic as well. As Spaatz commented,

> ... it is difficult to believe that the Chinese will commit their forces in major strength unless guaranteed at least the support of the Soviet Russian air force. And if it is true that Soviet Russia does not want to enter the conflict at this time, then the Korean war should be liquidated within a few months ... Russia's conduct in the Korean affair has indicated up to now that it is not willing to risk its air force in the Korean conflict.[59]

An assortment of facts, half-facts, and assumptions led MacArthur, Willoughby, and FECOM to the hasty and presumptuous conclusion neither the Soviet Union nor the People's Republic of China were likely to intervene should UN forces cross the Yalu River. The CIA, sequestered by Willoughby, had mirrored his conclusion that neither Communist nation would intervene. Adding to the seemingly compelling evidence at the time was the fact there had been no response, either diplomatic or military, to the U.S. Air Force strafing of a Soviet airfield on October 8 or to UNC reconnaissance flights near Siberia.[60]

Furthermore, over all the plans and actions of North Korea and its Chinese ally loomed the ever-present figure of MacArthur. No assessment of the prospects of Chinese intervention in the fall of 1950 is complete without realizing that, in the United States, and especially the U.S. Army of 1950, the word of the World War II hero carried tremendous weight. Not surprisingly, once he stated categorically that the Chinese would not invade in any sizable numbers, all differing assessments were quietly shelved; to dispute the word of the man who embodied the United States' presence in the Far East for decades was unthinkable. As historian John Finnegan wrote, "MacArthur was in no mood to be deprived of triumph by the mere specter of a Chinese Army." Looking back, General Ridgway concurred with that assessment, noting that, like General Custer at the 1876 battle at Little Bighorn, MacArthur "had neither eyes nor ears for information that might deter him from the swift attainment of his objective—the destruction of the last remnants of the North Korean People's Army and the pacification of the entire peninsula."[61]

Thus, despite the CCF attacks at Unsan and against X Corps, MacArthur and Willoughby insisted the Chinese would not invade in force and as late as November 6 listed Chinese troop strength in Korea as only 34,500—the actual figure was over three hundred thousand, organized into 30 divisions.[62] Following the Chinese intervention, MacArthur claimed he did not have enough reliable information upon which to make an informed decision. He remarked, "No intelligence system in the world could have surmounted such handicaps [specifically, being forbidden to cross the Yalu River to conduct aerial reconnaissance missions, and a lack of political intelligence concerning China] to determine to any substantial degree enemy strength, movements and intentions." His claim was backed up by the comments of

Chairman of the Joint Chiefs General Bradley, who added, "We had the intelligence that they were concentrating in Manchuria ... We had the information that they had the capability [to intervene]." Bradley quickly added they did not know they *would* intervene.[63] Yet, despite the claimed lack of such information, on November 17, MacArthur optimistically predicted a 10-day campaign to clear the rest of Korea of enemy forces, after which would come a repatriation of Chinese prisoners and the withdrawal of the Eighth Army to Japan, which one writer described as an "example of wishful thinking ... encouraged by faulty intelligence."[64]

And yet, in November, UN forces on the Korean Peninsula—despite their first encounter with tough CCF forces—were generally stable or licking their wounds. The North Korean Army had been soundly beaten, the Eighth Army was manning a solid defensive line along the Ch'ongch'on River and, in the northeast, X Corps forces were fresh and the 1st Marine Division in particular was at full strength. The weary troops freezing their way northward looked forward to crossing the Yalu in victory and, as their leaders had told them, being "home by Christmas."[65]

In November, State Department Director of Policy Planning Paul Nitze observed there was actually a five-week gap between when Chinese troops might have begun filtering into Korea and the date of the actual assault along the Ch'ongch'on River. During this hiatus, MacArthur's messages back to Washington assured the decision makers that all was well. However, analysts at Foggy Bottom were concluding just the opposite. When news of the actual Chinese invasion reached the capital, Roger Tubby, the White House Assistant Press Secretary, characterized the reaction of the White House as "surprise." Even as late as November 20—only four days before the kickoff of MacArthur's planned offensive—U.S. Embassy staffers in Seoul, as well as CIA analysts, assessed that, unless they suddenly picked up the pace from the previous two weeks, the Chinese were likely fighting a delaying action rather than undertaking an all-out intervention.[66] The reality of the actual situation on the ground was slow to dawn on the nation's capital and its stewards; Washington simply refused to believe the Chinese were in the Korean War full-tilt, in large part because they saw no advantage in their doing so, not the first or last time American officials, in suits and uniforms alike, would be misled by the persistent bugaboo of mirror imaging. Not surprisingly, then, the war made little impact on the American home front—as one historian has put it, "The war brushed lightly on America." Not so in China, where, as soon as early November, slogans began to appear on the walls of buildings: "Resist America, Aid Korea, Preserve Our Homes, Defend the Nation." Propaganda messages were announced around the clock and inspirational meetings were convened to whip up a fervor of national defense sentiment. As the messages reiterated, no quarter would be asked or given until the "imperialist aggressors" were ousted or destroyed by the "Chinese Peoples Volunteers."[67]

Willoughby has been described as "a man dedicated to the proposition that there were no Chinese in Korea" and they were not going to intervene, at least not in numbers large enough to be decisive. As far as he was concerned, the G-2's job was "first and foremost to prove that the commander was always right." The alternative was too painful to even contemplate: should the Chinese actually intervene in Korea, Washington might start paying actual *attention* to what was going on in FECOM and might "interfere" with MacArthur's much-trumpeted plan to drive to the Yalu River. Such an eventuality was definitely not what MacArthur wanted; rather, what he wanted "was *what Willoughby always made come true* [emphasis added] in his intel estimates."[68]

One of the items in Willoughby's personal papers is an illuminating forerunner to a spreadsheet which records the CCF units by date of identification between October 25 and December 25, with the key date of November 25 as the pivot point. Per this record, as of October 25, there were no CCF in North Korea; as of October 30, there was one unit—the 120th Division, 40th Corps. By November 5, the count was up to four, with five others enumerated as of November 10 and five additional units collectively as of November 15 and 20. Predictably, after the full-fledged engagement between the Eighth Army and CCF on November 25, the pace of enemy unit identification picked up accordingly, with 20 distinct units identified as of November 30. This same document concluded that, as of December 27, there were 277,173 CCF in North Korea, supplemented by 350,000 countrymen (from the 1st, 3rd, and 4th Field Armies) on the Yalu River border, and 65,000 troops of the North China Special Army Group in Manchuria, for a grand total of 692,173 Chinese Communist soldiers arrayed against the UN forces on the peninsula.[69]

The clearer picture emerging of the extent and size of the Chinese intervention was in direct response to the taking of additional CCF prisoners. For example, an ROK 1st Division captive taken early on the morning of November 25, approximately two miles south of Taechon, North Korea, proved a lucrative catch. CCF Captain Lui Ping Chang—identified as the Operations Officer, 590th Regiment, 197th Division, 66th Field Artillery—had deserted to his southern countrymen. He helpfully provided the total strength of the 66th Field Army as 26,660 men or, put another way, 600 troops per battalion, 2,000 per regiment, and 6,600 per division, the level of detail that is so satisfying to enemy order-of-battle analysts. The deserter also provided a description of the unit's weapons, its complete order-of-battle, and the location of the parent Thirteenth Army Group.[70]

Little wonder that, on December 5, Lieutenant Colonel James H. Polk, one of MacArthur's junior intelligence officers, wrote his wife from Tokyo, "this time he gambled it a little too hard and really pressed his luck a bit too far and the whole house fell in on him … He just didn't believe that the whole CCF would be thrown against him. I really admire him in defeat but it sorta looks like the end of an era."[71] Following up on that theme, Polk, who would later become a four-star general, later commented, "We had the dope but old CAW [Willoughby] bowed to the superior wisdom of his beloved boss and didn't fight him as a good staff officer should. But he is getting his lumps …"[72]

CHAPTER SIX

The Dragon Sharpens its Claws

From the standpoint of late 1950, North Korean Premier Kim Il Sung, Chinese Premier Mao Zedong, and Russian leader Joseph Stalin had been collaborating for more than a year, cooperating in actions that had brought war to the Korean Peninsula. The Chinese had just emerged victorious from a civil war that had plunged the People's Republic of China (PRC) into chaos from 1945 to 1949, with Mao having proclaimed victory in October 1949. At the close of the conflict, the Chinese Communists had 2,017,000 men under arms, with another two million reserves, with many of these troops deployed along the Korean border.[1] Initially, however, the hostility present between the Democratic People's Republic of Korea (DPRK) and the Republic of Korea (ROK) appeared to be, as one Chinese authority put it, "first and foremost Kim Il Sung's war." China was not directly involved in the North Korean war plans for the reunification of the peninsula—rather, the DPRK looked to the Russian bear for any such support. Nevertheless, in late 1949, Mao, at Kim Il Sung's request, sent between 30,000 to 40,000 People's Liberation Army (PLA) troops of Korean ethnicity back to North Korea and, by early 1950, some twenty-three thousand others had returned "home."[2]

In April 1950, an envoy of Kim Il Sung met with Mao in Beijing to discuss the situation in Korea. Mao opined it was unrealistic to attack South Korea in the near future—not only was the international situation "unfavorable," but the Chinese Communist Party (CCP) was still considerably distracted by the ongoing civil war with Chiang Kai-Shek and the Nationalists. Mao ultimately recommended the DPRK wait until post-Chinese unification before dealing with the problem of Korea. Stung by the Chinese rebuff, Kim made a secret visit to Moscow later in April and received approval from Stalin to launch an attack on South Korea on June 25. In mid-May, a triumphant Kim returned to Beijing and told Mao the DPRK had the blessing of Stalin to carry out the attack. Mao noted he did not believe the United States would intervene and promised to commit one army to the Chinese–Korean border if the ROK compelled the Japanese to intervene on their side. Kim then boasted to Mao he could dispatch South Korea in a matter of two to three months. In early July,

Chinese officials dispatched a North Korean Chinese Embassy observation team led by Chai Chengwen to observe the war's progress. Worried about American intervention, on July 7 Chinese officials opted to create the Northeast Frontier Army (NFA), later known as the Chinese People's Volunteers (CPV), headed by General Deng Hua. Thus, by the end of July, there were already CPV units along the border with North Korea and by early August there were more than two hundred fifty thousand Chinese troops deployed along the northern banks of the Yalu.[3]

The specter of combat on the Korean peninsula also powerfully altered the previous American stance on the island of Formosa (Taiwan), which had become the home-in-exile of Chinese Nationalist leader Chiang Kai-Shek following the 1949 Communist victory in the mainland civil war. Convinced Formosa's ultimate fall to the Communists was inevitable, the Truman administration had announced on January 5, 1950, that the United States would not "provide military aid or advice to Chinese forces on Formosa" or "pursue a course which will lead to involvement in the civil conflict in China." However, the invasion of the ROK by the DPRK on June 25, and the prospect of proliferating warfare, radically changed the equation and convinced American leaders the best course of action would be to "neutralize" Formosa. Thus, when Truman announced on June 27 that he had ordered American forces to Korea, he added he had also ordered the Seventh Fleet to the area "to prevent any attack on Formosa" and advised the Chinese Nationalist government on the island to "cease all air and sea operations against the mainland." Such policy statements prompted leaders in Formosa to hope their island home could still be the base from which to ultimately regain power on the mainland. But in some foreign countries, the reaction was very different; for example, in Britain and India, both of which had recognized the People's Republic of China, the news seemed to indicate continued American support for the unreliable Chinese Nationalists.[4]

Nor were international concerns allayed when MacArthur made a surprise one-day visit to Formosa on the last day of July for mutually cordial discussions with Chiang Kai-Shek. MacArthur referred to his brief jaunt as "a short reconnaissance of the potential of its defense against possible attack." As he was leaving the island on August 1, MacArthur turned to Chiang and confidently said, "Keep your chin up, we're going to win." He announced that, as a result of the talks, arrangements had been made "for effective coordination" between American and Chinese Nationalist forces in the defense of Formosa, "the better to meet any attack which a hostile force might be foolish enough to attempt. Such an attack would, in my opinion, stand little chance of success." He added that the generalissimo's "indomitable determination to resist Communist domination ... parallels the common interest and purpose of Americans." The following day, Chiang Kai-Shek noted the foundation had been laid for "a joint defense of Formosa and for Sino–American military cooperation." He added, "Now that we can again work closely together with our old comrade-in-arms, Gen. MacArthur, I am sure not only will our determination in the struggle for this

PLATES

Captain C. A. Willoughby in his Air Corps Cadet uniform, 1918. (Wikipedia)

The brothers of *Phi Delta Gamma* fraternity at war—then-Brigadier General Willoughby, Lieutenant General Robert L. Eichelberger, and Brigadier General Clovis Byers. Photo taken in Brisbane, Australia, 1943. (PH00006036, MMA, Norfolk, VA)

Composite photo of all those who left Corregidor/Bataan by PT boat with General MacArthur and family on March 11, 1942. Willoughby is in the first column, third photo down. (PH00010413, MMA, Norfolk, VA)

Sketch of Brigadier General Willoughby by Bill Lines, a copy of the original by McClelland Barclay, 1943–44. (PH00030139, MMA, Norfolk, VA)

Major General Willoughby with General Kawabe and members of the 16-person Japanese surrender negotiation team, Manila City Hall, Philippines, August 19, 1945. (PH00010965, MMA, Norfolk, VA)

Artist caricature of Willoughby, Korean War. (Illustration by Rick Meyerowitz, used with permission)

October 14, 1952

A 1952 caricature of Willoughby (mistakenly wearing the rank of lieutenant general, a rank he never achieved) working during the post-war U.S. occupation of Japan with Japanese researchers on the history of World War II in the South Pacific. (MMA, Norfolk, VA)

Independence Day ceremony in Tokyo, Japan, 1948. Left to right: Major General Myron Cramer, International Military Tribunal for the Far East (IMTFE); Vice Admiral Russell Berkey, Seventh Fleet; Major General William Beiderlinden, Assistant Chief of Staff, G1, Far East Command; Major General Joseph Swing, 11th Airborne Division and Willoughby, who appears to be in on the joke. (PH00010935, MMA, Norfolk, VA)

A dour-looking Willoughby, wearing the Order of Nassau, a civilian and military Dutch order of chivalry dating to 1892. Willoughby received the award in April 1949, but the photo likely dates to the period 1949–51. (Boria photo, MMA, Norfolk, VA)

Signed 1949 official photo of Willoughby as the Assistant Chief of Staff for Intelligence, G2, Far East Command. (PH00020370, RG-12: Collection of Photographs, MMA, Norfolk, VA)

General MacArthur and his entourage leave for the Wake Island conference with President Truman, October 14, 1950. Facing the camera, left to right: Colonel Sidney Huff; General MacArthur; Brigadier General Courtney Whitney; Admiral C. Turner Joy, U.S. Navy; Major General Willoughby; and Brigadier General Edmund K. Wright. The aircraft in the background is MacArthur's personal transport, the Lockheed VC-121A Constellation "Bataan." (PH00011691, MMA, Norfolk, VA)

...age from Japanese-language U.S. Army ...ychological Operations leaflet, circa ...048. Willoughby is on the top row, on ...e left. (SGM Herbert A. Friedman, used ...th permission)

Willoughby explaining the need for an American "Foreign Legion," circa 1951. (MMA, Norfolk, VA)

General Matthew B. Ridgway bids farewell to Major General Willoughby, late May 1951. Ridgway, who has just presented Willoughby with the Distinguished Service Medal for his Korean War service, would be a staunch defender of Willoughby in the post-war years. (Matthew B. Ridgway Papers, U.S. Army Military History Institute, Carlisle, PA)

Photo of Willoughby from final issue of the *Daily Intelligence Summary* prior to his return to the United States and retirement, 1951. (Special Collections, Musselman Library, Gettysburg College, PA)

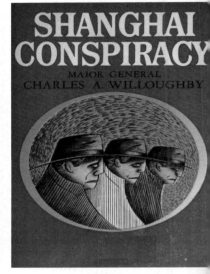

Cover illustration for *Shanghai Conspiracy*, Willoughby's exposé on Communist espionage activity in Japan during World War II. The book also included references to U.S. communists. (MMA, Norfolk, VA)

WPA Reunion and MacArthur birthday celebration, Waldorf Astoria Hotel, New York City, 1960. Willoughby and MacArthur are shaking hands, with former president Herbert Hoover in the background. (PH00024574, MMA, Norfolk, VA)

Illustration from June 1964 edition of *Christian Crusade*, published by Billy James Hargis. Willoughby served as a representative of the organization. (MMA, Norfolk, VA)

Grave marker for MG Charles A. Willoughby, who died in 1972, and his second wife, Marie Antoinette de Becker, Section 1, Grave 552-D, Arlington National Cemetery. (www.arlingtoncemetery.mil, used with permission)

common cause be strengthened, but the peoples of all Asia will be aroused to fight Communist aggression and they will be convinced that democracy and freedom will ultimately triumph." Two days later, a jubilant General Chou Chih-jou, Nationalist China's Chief of Staff, rejoiced as six American F-80 Shooting Star jet fighters landed from the Philippines. In train with that delivery came Major General Howard M. Turner, Thirteenth Air Force commander, also from the Philippines, and from Tokyo, Brigadier General Alonzo P. Fox, Far East Command Deputy Chief of Staff. Turner and Fox announced their collective mission was to make a more detailed survey of defenses on Formosa, speed up American aid, and establish a liaison staff. There was also talk of a Nationalist armed forces training program under American supervision.[5]

Such statements by the generalissimo and MacArthur created widespread angst among those who dismissed the Nationalist Government as a viable ally and who believed the reinstallation of the Kuomintang regime would thwart efforts to encourage anti-Communist movements throughout Asia. MacArthur was of course aware of the immediate criticism of his spur-of-the-moment trip and responded, in a statement intended for a speech before the Veterans of Foreign Wars. "Nothing could be more fallacious than the threadbare argument by those who advocate appeasement and defeatism in the Pacific that if we defend Formosa, we alienate continental Asia … The geographic location of Formosa is such that in the hand of a power unfriendly to the United States it constitutes an enemy salient in the very center" of the American defense perimeter in the Western Pacific. MacArthur's words were in sharp contrast to the expressed policy statements by the Truman administration and were countermanded by the president, but not before they reached the ears of the press.[6] Such pronouncements by a theater commander in direct contradiction to those of the commander in chief would help explain MacArthur's ultimate fate.

Chinese military leaders were of two minds on the prospect of intervening in Korea and facing down American and UN forces. Some were reluctant to take on such a fight, such as senior PLA commander General Lin Biao, who resigned rather than take command of Chinese forces in the future conflict. Other PLA leaders realized they would be engaging in combat with a technologically superior, modern military force, compared to their own admittedly more primitive forces. By the same token, however, the prospect of having an "imperialist" army on their doorstep was at least equally displeasing and the thought of having Manchuria, China's industrial heartland, only a border away from American presence and influence, was unconscionable. It was, of course, Chairman Mao who ultimately decided China must intervene. After all, he reasoned, his soldiers were veterans, with years of experience fighting Chinese revolutionaries and the Japanese, they knew the terrain intimately, they had not been intimidated in the least by American fighting prowess early in the Korean War, and the PLA could field five million men, a figure the UN forces could not hope to match.[7]

This MacArthur visit appears to have been the last straw for Mao, who decided China must come to the aid of its North Korean brethren, lest the United States grow even more arrogant and pose a threat to China. On August 5, a spokesman for Mao and the Central Military Commission (CMC) directed Deng Hua to be ready to enter Korea by the end of the month. Less than three weeks later, on August 23, CMC intelligence elements assessed American troop landings behind Kim's troops were likely and that an amphibious assault focused on Inchon was *most* likely. Informed of these tactical and operational assessments, Mao then directed the NFA to prepare for war, to advise both Kim and Stalin of the latest assessed American war plans, and to have the PLA General Staff and Foreign Ministry monitor the battlefield situation. In an August 31 report to Beijing, Deng Hua identified the two most likely enemy courses of action, one of which was to land a small force behind the North Korean forces and attack simultaneously from both front and rear.[8] The Chinese also used diplomatic and related channels to telegraph their thoughts and intentions—as early as August 16, a Communist Party publication entitled *World Culture* noted American actions in Korea constituted a threat to Chinese security and the PRC would not allow Korea to become dominated by "imperialist" powers. A few days later, Premier Chou En-lai sent a telegram to the United Nations which conveyed the same message.[9]

A 2004 PhD dissertation posited that Mao's ultimate decision was virtually inevitable, a veritable Greek tragedy, and the natural unfolding of Mao's "American strategy," which one historian assesses was already fully developed as early as late 1944 and accepted by mid-1945 as the CCP's official position concerning the United States. Chinese policy makers assessed, logically, that American strategic interests would best be represented by a pro-American government in China—given the weak state of the CCP at the end of World War II, a coalition government based on the American multi-party political system seemed a likely solution. However, it soon became obvious, at least to Mao, that a clash between the CCP and the Guomindang was brewing, whereupon the United States felt compelled to stand with the latter and against the former. The specific impetus for Chinese intervention, according to this author, was Truman's blockade of the Taiwan Straits and the crossing of the 38th Parallel and subsequent march to the Yalu River by UN forces in 1950.[10]

Chinese scholar Chen Jian has concluded Beijing's decision to enter the war was motivated by "concerns much more complicated than safeguarding the Chinese–Korean border." This decision was impelled much more, Chen posits, by Mao Zedong's desire for a "glorious victory" that would restore China to its ancient glory as the "Central Kingdom." He also wished to repay a debt of gratitude to North Korea, which had sent numerous troops to aid the Chinese Communists in their victory in the latter's civil war. Also motivating Mao was the increasingly strident demands of Joseph Stalin that China intervene to prevent American conquest of North Korea (to which end "the Man of Steel" promised Soviet air support).

Despite the misgivings of his advisors, Mao was able to wield his "wisdom and authority to persuade his comrades" that the prospect of American victory over the North could be a fatal blow to revolutionary nationalism in Asia. Chen states this latter reason alone made China's entry into the war virtually inevitable.[11]

As early as August 5, the Manchurian Border Force of the Chinese People's Army had been alerted to be ready for combat operations by the first week in September. Officers on the Chinese General Staff were watching the northward advance of UN forces with great interest and had correctly predicted the amphibious landings at Inchon on September 15. Two days later, the PRC's Military Affairs Committee ordered Chinese officers to Korea to "lay the groundwork for possible intervention." On September 25, PLA acting Chief of Staff Nie Rongzhen stated the People's Republic would have no option but to resist should the United States, as he put it, continued to "provoke" them.[12] This same day, during an informal dinner party in Peking, hosted by the Indian Ambassador to the PRC, Sardar K. M. Pannikar, PLA Chief of Staff General Nieh Jung-Chen told Pannikar in even tones that China did not intend to "sit back with folded hands and let the Americans come to their border." When an observer asked Nieh if he realized the full implication of his words, he responded, "We know what we are in for, but at all costs, American aggression has got to be stopped. The Americans can bomb us; they can destroy our industries, but *they cannot defeat us on land* [emphasis added]." Nieh continued, "They may even drop atom bombs on us. What then? They may kill a few million people. Without sacrifice, a nation's independence cannot be upheld … After all, China lives on the farms … What can atom bombs do there?"[13] Nieh's words reflected the sentiments of Premier Chou En-lai who, on September 30, blatantly declared, "The Chinese people will absolutely not tolerate foreign aggression, nor will they sit still watching their neighbor being savaged by imperialists."[14] In late September, Stalin broached with Beijing the idea of Kim Il Sung's setting up a government-in-exile in China.[15]

On October 1, North Korean Foreign Minister Pak Hon-yong passed to Chairman Mao a request for support troops from a troubled Kim Il Sung; that same evening, he made a personal plea to the Chinese Ambassador in P'yŏngyang, Ni Xiliang. From that date on, China actively began planning its intervention into Korea. Following a fiery anti-American speech that day, Chou summoned Ambassador Pannikar to the Ministry of Foreign Affairs and bluntly told him that if American troops crossed the 38th Parallel, China would enter the war. Despite this unequivocal warning, both Truman and MacArthur discounted it as nothing more than a propaganda ploy by Chou; furthermore, they discounted Pannikar as a credible witness, given his oft-observed Sinophilia.[16] Also dismissive of the threat of Chinese intervention was Secretary of State Acheson, who assessed any intention of Mao to take on the United States was "sheer madness" and that Pannikar's warning was the "mere vaporings of a panicky Pannikar." The frustrated Indian diplomat, later in 1950, wrote in his diary:

America has knowingly elected for war, with Britain following. The Chinese armies now concentrated on the Yalu will intervene decisively in the fight. Probably some of the Americans want that. They probably feel that this is an opportunity to have a show down with China. In any case, MacArthur's dream has come true. I only hope it does not turn into a nightmare.[17]

Initially, the Chinese leadership selected Marshal Lin Piao to head the "Chinese People's Volunteer Army"; however, he pled illness and Marshal Peng Teh-huai, a close personal friend of Mao's and former Deputy Commander of the People's Liberation Army (PLA), was chosen to replace Lin Piao. Marshal Peng immediate began establishing his headquarters in the city of Mukden (now Shenyang, in present-day Liaoning Province, some 420 miles northeast of Beijing).[18]

Having announced to his own colleagues that China must intervene, Mao cabled Stalin on October 2 to inform him Chinese troops would enter Korea on the 15th. In this cable, Mao expressed one particular concern—that Chinese troops might prove unable to destroy American forces in Korea, embroiling the PRC in a Sino–American armed quagmire that would likely damage China's economic reconstruction and further displease citizens ill at ease with the recent revolution. His colleagues opposed to intervention pointed out the military risks (including a direct attack on China), argued the PRC needed additional time to consolidate its political control and remove remaining Chinese Nationalist resistance, and pondered reliance on the perceived weak reed of Soviet assistance.[19]

Even at this juncture, however, Chou was anxious to avoid war with the United States. With that thought in mind, he summoned Ambassador Pannikar to his office at 1:00 am on October 3 and commissioned him to tell the world China wished to avoid war if at all possible. Not only were the memories of World War II and the Chinese Revolution of 1949 likely still very fresh in his mind, but he was also worried that, should the Korean War go badly for the United States, the post-war behemoth might resort to the use of nuclear weapons to turn the tide.[20] Yet, a week later, Chou fell back on his earlier rhetoric, warning that a "war of invasion" was a "serious menace" to Chinese security, another pointed warning largely dismissed by Seoul, Tokyo, New York, and Washington alike.[21] The strategy China ultimately decided to pursue should not have been surprising to anyone who had studied Mao's earlier campaigns—however, such numbers in the American military were very limited and certainly did not include either MacArthur or Willoughby.[22]

Meanwhile, a prolonged and rancorous debate was going on within the Chinese Politburo over whether or not to intervene militarily in Korea—most of the Chinese leadership was either adamantly opposed to intervention or at least advised waiting three to five years before engaging in such action. However, Mao—as well as Chou En-lai and Peng Dehaui—favored early intervention. As the head of state put it in an October 13, 1950, Politburo meeting, "All in all, we believe that we should enter the war and we must enter the war." Such a pronouncement is somewhat surprising considering senior leaders in Beijing—as well as in Washington—approached the situation in Korea by falling back on the comfortable explanation of the domino theory, i.e., that war in Korea would undoubtedly spread and have strategic consequences for both China and the United States.[23] It is worth noting, however, that the PLA had other pressing concerns at this juncture: the invasion of Tibet, planned for November; the consolidation of Communist power and authority in China itself; and tactical coordination with Viet Minh forces deployed along the French Indochina border.[24]

To appreciate the position faced by the Chinese leadership in the fall of 1950, it is worth remembering the historic relationship between China and Korea was essentially that of an older brother to a younger brother; since at least the 16th century, the path to invasions of China had increasingly traversed Korea. Furthermore, the two nations were also bound together by a common ideology characterized by authoritarian political rule.[25] North Korea and the PRC had also enjoyed "important and reciprocal" diplomatic relations since October 1949, and the northern provinces of North Korea has served as a staging area/sanctuary for PLA soldiers during the Chinese Civil War.[26]

Given Mao's stated resolve as of October 3 to bring China into the conflict, it is not surprising that, soon after his comments, he began to set the wheels in motion to intervene on the peninsula. On October 8, he dispatched Chou En-lai to Moscow to secure Russian cooperation for the invasion, particularly with regard to air cover. He also ordered Chinese forces to prepare to cross the Yalu River and engage the American troops now threatening P'yŏngyang, cabled his decision to intervene to Kim Il Sung, and formally named Peng Dehuai the commander of the Chinese "volunteers." As Peng departed, he was accompanied by several others, notably including Mao's son Anying, recruited to serve as a translator for the Soviet advisors.[27] Chou met with Stalin on October 11 at the latter's retreat in Sochi, where the Soviet leader agreed to provide weapons, tanks, and aircraft, but notably not air cover, as he did not want a direct confrontation with the United States. He stated that the Soviet Air Force needed more time before it could make such a commitment, though he compensated for that disappointment by pledging to provide weaponry to equip 20 Chinese divisions. In withdrawing the promise of air cover, Stalin promptly reneged on the promise he had made to the North Koreans back in July. Regardless, on October 13, the Chinese Politburo confirmed the decision to enter the Korean conflict—to provide what was dubbed "active support"—and the following day Stalin announced Russia would deploy air force units within the PRC, but only to protect coastal cities and would not, under any circumstances, enter Korea, either at that time or later. Both Stalin and Zhou expressed their confidence that Chinese troops could "manage the situation completely."[28] The consensus of senior Chinese military and political leaders was that their forces were to proceed "cautiously … avoiding a direct challenge to the United States." Rather, they were to focus their attacks on the South Korean forces. When all was said and done, Mao issued an order for intervention no later than October 18.[29]

The rapid advance of American forces and the increasing panic of the North Koreans prompted Mao to throw caution to the wind and order the entry into North Korea of the first CPV units late on October 19. As these units crossed the Yalu—with the advance units wearing North Korean uniforms—they practiced radio silence and light discipline, dousing the lights on their tactical vehicles in a harbinger of things to come. As military dictators playing general are wont to do, Mao took a hands-on approach during the early stages of the war, issuing numerous strategic and even tactical orders. Both on paper and in actual terms, the CPV "parent organization" of the PLA of November 1950 was a formidable force. The total number of soldiers in deployed field armies was between one and two million men, with an equal number in garrison, all of whom were supported by some five million militia. By November 15, the PLA had committed 250,000 soldiers to Korea, a figure markedly different from that of 70,000, Willoughby's initial estimate of enemy troop strength. Hidden in the deep recesses of southern Manchuria, the CPV soldiers—some two hundred thousand PLA soldiers from the Thirteenth Army Group, 4th Field Army—waited for the men of General Walker's Eighth Army. Initially committed to Korea in October, the Chinese troops had waged a successful offensive against American/UN forces between October 25 and November 5 and were confident of victory. Farther to the east, the Ninth Army Group had crossed the Yalu at Manpojin, able to cross on the still-standing bridges. As had their colleagues—both past and future—they expertly applied noise and light discipline in order to mask their crossing.[30]

As one authority has noted, the motivation behind Mao's ultimate decision to intervene was as complex as the mind that made the call. In his October 2 cable to Stalin, Mao justified his decision on the basis of Communist ideology—he felt "an internationalist duty to rescue the beleaguered Korean revolution and to help maintain revolutionary morale around the world in the face of a counteroffensive launched by American revolutionaries." He also, of course, had to be concerned with preventing an American invasion of China itself. Further, an American advance in Korea "would draw wavering countries and classes to the side of the United States, strengthen the resolve of revolutionaries at home and abroad, and encourage the United States to send troops to other points along China's borders." Zhou also did his part as cheerleader—in an October 24 address to the Chinese People's Consultative Congress, he fell back on a traditional figure of speech, Korea as the lips to China's teeth, to reiterate the strategic significance of the peninsula.[31]

The alliance between the DPRK and the PRC extended to military command-and-control as well. As of November 1, DPRK and PRC forces operated a combined headquarters staffed by both North Korean and Chinese officers. As head of state, Kim Il Sung was also Commander of the North Korean forces, stationed at Kanggye, hidden deep within the mountains of north-central Korea.

While DPRK strength on paper was more impressive, in reality North Korean forces in contact with UN elements in November were only two corps, consisting of five weak divisions and two under-strength brigades. The remaining DPRK troops were resting and refitting in north-central Korea, avoiding the advance of UN forces up the eastern and western coasts of the peninsula. The bulk of the enemy forces, however, consisted primarily of the 300,000 troops of the PLA who—as only later events would illustrate—had been in Korea since the last half of October.[32]

In early November, General Robert Ho Shai-lai, the Chinese Ambassador in Tokyo, called on MacArthur to inform him "the Chinese Regular Army had entered Korea, in great strength." Lending credence to the ambassador's words was the fact that he was a 1933 graduate of the Army's Command and General Staff College at Fort Leavenworth, Kansas, and very familiar with American military operations.[33]

Against this force was arrayed the UN forces—Eighth Army Headquarters, an ROK army headquarters, six corps headquarters (three each, U.S. and ROK), 18 divisions of roughly standard infantry strength (10 ROK, seven U.S. Army, and one U.S. Marine), three allied brigades, and a separate airborne regiment. The total combat ground forces were approximately four hundred twenty-five thousand troops, about one hundred seventy-eight thousand of which were American. Added to these forces were considerable naval and air force assets as well.[34]

Despite the sizable numbers of troops the Chinese could field, however, most Western observers were generally unimpressed by the combat capabilities of the Chinese People's Army. The PLA dated from 1927 and owed its birth to four individuals, the most prominent of whom was the Premier, Chou En-lai. Even though the PLA emerged the victor of what the Chinese referred to as the "Third Revolutionary Civil War," it was no modern army, even by 1949 standards; nevertheless, over the course of the civil war it had acquired a sizable amount of materiel, much of it from Nationalist troops who, ironically, had been supplied by the United States. Those individuals who were familiar with the Chinese military at the time—some of whom had trained the Chinese to fight the Japanese during World War II—regarded their troops as "poorly equipped, poorly led, and abysmally supplied." Described by one writer as "a peasant army" equipped with a hodge-podge of aging Japanese and American weapons, they were consistently short of artillery support and their standard means of tactical communications below division-level consisted of bugles and runners. The October 29, 1950, *FEC Intelligence Summary,* written in the wake of the first contact between Chinese and American/UN troops, stated matter-of-factly that "Chinese forces had little potential against a modern army."[35] While such comments are technically correct, they ignored several unconsidered but critical factors; namely, the revolutionary zeal of the Chinese troops, who had just emerged victorious in a civil war with the Nationalist forces of Chiang Kai-Shek—and the fact many of the officers of the Chinese People's Army had two decades of combat experience at this point. Furthermore, the Chinese commanders—who apparently knew their enemy better than did their American/UN counterparts—were determined to negate the well-known American technological advantage by fighting on their own terms, hence the major Chinese ambush waiting for UN troops along the Ch'ongch'on River.[36]

Colonel Paul Steinbeck, G-3 Comptroller in FECOM in mid-1952, included his observations concerning the average Chinese soldier in a 1985 oral history interview:

> The Chinese, the ones that I saw were mostly farm boys who hardly knew anything other than that they were soldiers. They were brought right off of the farms. I would judge that they made damned good soldiers because they could live on nothing really, and could survive. Actually, living as a soldier might have been a better situation for them than being at home trying to make a living.[37]

Other observers pointed out that, while the combat capabilities of the PLA were respected, the Chinese were faced with myriad logistical problems, especially shortages of food and ammunition. However, when Chinese soldiers crossed the Yalu to aid their North Korean ally, most of the "People's Volunteers" each carried 80 rounds of ammunition plus extra clips, four or five "potato masher" grenades, belts of machine-gun ammunition, a mortar shell or two, or TNT for satchel charges. In addition, they carried five days' worth of "emergency rations"—rice, tea, and salt. They impressed Korean and Chinese civilians to serve as porters for the heavier equipment. As one author assessed the situation, it was supply issues more than any other single factor that determined the pace of Chinese offensive operations once they intervened in North Korea.[38]

Still, for that day and locale, the Chinese Communist Forces could be a force to be reckoned with, as UN forces would soon discover. One writer has described the Chinese troops of 1950 as "tough, well-disciplined, and able ... to meet the demanding march schedules prescribed." Company and battalion commanders were trained to move their forces only under cover of darkness and they relied on North Korean guides, who knew the ground intimately, to guide them into Kim Il Sung's country. This same historian characterized Chinese forces overall as a "semi-literate peasant army, with a hardcore of experienced and dedicated veterans." The official U.S. Marine Corps history of the Korean War characterized the leathernecks' foe in these words:

> Although the Chinese Reds were represented by a peasant army, it was also a first-rate army when judged by its own tactical and strategic standards ... The Chinese coolie in the padded cotton uniform could do one thing better than any other soldier on earth: he could infiltrate around an enemy position in the darkness with unbelievable stealth ... It was not mass but deception and surprise which made the Chinese Red formidable.[39]

Even Willoughby, as part of his research into his monograph on MacArthur, admitted Chinese infantrymen were "excellent—hardy, well-trained, frugal, and could live on almost nothing. They were armed well." However, he was also dispassionate enough to observe that the Chinese Communist forces suffered from weaknesses in five critical areas—air, artillery support to ground units, anti-aircraft, supply, and signals communication.[40]

***

In the minds of a number of Western observers prognosticating on the chances of Chinese intervention, the stakes involved and the inherent weaknesses of the CPV/ PLA forces made such inadvisable. Thus, MacArthur and Willoughby were not the only ones observing events on the Korean Peninsula who had concluded the Chinese were unlikely to intervene. No less significant a figure than Secretary of the Army Frank Pace commented, "I do not believe at that time anybody seriously believed that the Red Chinese were going to enter the war."[41] Nor did such an unlikely action make sense to others in the American defense sector. A CIA estimate of October 12, sent directly to President Truman and assented to by the National Security Council, the Joint Chiefs of Staff, and the State Department, assessed that:

> The Chinese Communist ground forces, currently lacking requisite air and naval support, are capable of intervening effectively, but not necessarily decisively, in the Korean conflict. There are no convincing indications of an actual Chinese Communist intention to resort to full-scale intervention in Korea … while full-scale Chinese Communist intervention in Korea must be regarded as a continuing possibility, a consideration of all known factors leads to the conclusion that barring a Soviet decision for global war, such action is not probable in 1950.

MacArthur and Willoughby's arch-nemesis—the CIA—had raised the prospect of potential Chinese involvement in the conflict in Korea early on, though it had arrived at the same basic bottom line as FECOM analysts. As early as July 19, less than a month after the North Korean invasion, the Agency noted that:

> Chinese Communist troops can be brought into action covertly and, if necessary, openly … It is not yet clear whether the USSR will force the Chinese Communists to give open military support to the Korean operations or to start a new operation elsewhere in the area. The Peiping regime almost certainly would comply with a Soviet request for military action.

Several months later, on September 8, the Agency published an estimate entitled *Probability of Direct Chinese Communist Intervention in Korea*. In this document, analysts assessed there were some 400,000 Chinese troops either on or heading toward the Korean border yet concluded "it appears more probable that the Chinese Communist participation in the Korean conflict will be more indirect, although significant, and will be limited to integrating into the North Korean forces 'Manchurian volunteers,' perhaps including air units as well as ground forces." Twelve days later, CIA analysis grew more wary, noting "the concentration of Chinese Communist troops near the Korean border in Manchuria constitutes a powerful secondary reserve for the North Korean forces, which, if Moscow and Peiping should agree on it despite the attendant risks, could enter the battle and materially change its course at any time."[42]

On October 18, the CIA estimated there were between 40,000 and 60,000 "Chinese-trained Communist troops" already serving in the North Korean Army, but that the prospect for open Chinese intervention in Korea was "becoming less and less likely." In their *Review of the World Situation As It Relates to the Security of the United States* on the same day, CIA analysts blithely observed:

> The Soviet Korean venture, a laboratory test in the use of non-Soviet Communist forces to fight a local war of limited objectives, has ended in failure … the odds are that Communist China, like the USSR, will not openly intervene in North Korea … The time has passed when Chinese intervention would have turned the military tide toward a complete Communist victory in Korea … The Chinese Communists are unlikely to be willing to come to the assistance of the North Koreans at the risk of becoming involved in open hostilities with the U.S. and its UN allies.[43]

And on November 1, the Director of Central Intelligence, Walter Bedell Smith, sent a memo to President Truman on the subject of "Chinese Communist Intervention in Korea," which introduced notes of caution into the sanguine picture portrayed several months earlier:

> Fresh, newly-equipped North Korean troops have appeared in the Korean fighting, and it has been clearly established that Chinese Communist troops are also opposing UN forces. Present field estimates are that between 15,000 and 20,000 Chinese Communist troops organized in task force units are operating in North Korea while the parent units remain in Manchuria … This pattern of events and reports indicates that Communist China has decided, regardless of the increased risk of general war, to provide increased support and assistance to North Korean forces. Although the possibility cannot be excluded that the Chinese Communists, under Soviet direction, are committing themselves to full-scale intervention in Korea, their motivation at present appears to be to establish a limited '*cordon sanitaire*' south of the Yalu River, for the protection of a series of hydroelectric facilities on which the PRC relied for electricity.[44]

It is also interesting to note how the Chinese themselves characterized their intervention in Korea at the time; somewhat ironically for American observers, PRC sources likened it to the Marquis de Lafayette and French troops coming to the aid of the upstart American colonists in the 1770s, or the more recent intervention of the Abraham Lincoln Brigades in the Spanish Civil War.[45] In history, perspective often has an overweening significance.

CHAPTER SEVEN

"Don't Let a Bunch of Chinese Laundrymen Stop You!"

By October 29, 1950, there were 10 Chinese prisoners of war in United Nations Command custody; by November 2, the number was 55. Interrogators supported by lie detectors were able to identify the elements of some six Chinese Field Armies—the 38th, 39th, 40th, 42nd, 50th, and 66th, each with a minimum of three divisions of 10,000 men each. Thus, it was possible there were some 180,000 Chinese troops in Korea as of that date. Yet virtually no one among the Allied chain of command believed the Chinese could possibly hide 180,000 men without their being detected. Furthermore, the consensus opinion "of all American intelligence agencies" was that China would *not* enter the war.[1]

On October 31, Willoughby ordered First Lieutenant Bob Brewer to send him the principal agent from the Kanggye–Mampojin border area for an in-depth interrogation. As Brewer recalled, "The agent gave a rather complete picture of the Chinese units that had crossed the Mampojin Bridge into Korea during the month of October, including heavy weapons and hospital units, indicating that Chinese intentions were something more than border protection."[2] And yet, Willoughby's report to G-2 and the CIA's *Daily Korean Situation* update were nearly identical in language, leading to the suspicion one was merely feeding the other. In this report, Willoughby admitted there were 28 Chinese prisoners—interrogation identified these captives as from the 40th and 42nd Field Armies.[3] The next day, November 1, the new CIA chief, Walter Bedell Smith, penned his informed opinion to Truman that the Chinese deeply feared an invasion of Manchuria and sought to create a *cordon sanitaire* "regardless of the increased risk of general war."[4]

Until the very moment disaster befell them, Eighth Army Headquarters in P'yŏngyang could ascertain "no indications of open intervention on the part of Chinese Communist forces in Korea."[5] By late October/early November 1950, Willoughby estimated there were between 16,500 and 34,000 Chinese troops in Korea, a significant but not alarming number. Buoyed by the assessment from his G-2, and X Corps commander Ned Almond, MacArthur was equally unmoved by the numbers. His subsequent report to United Nations officials concluded "there is no such evidence that Chinese Communist units, as such, have entered Korea," an assessment later described as "excessively optimistic, if not delusional."[6]

Yet, with detachment sometimes clarity comes. Washington had grown increasingly concerned about the situation in Korea following the initial encounter with Chinese Communist forces at Unsan on November 1–2, especially when MacArthur voiced concerns of the imminent destruction of the forces under his command. Stunned, the Joint Chiefs of Staff demanded an explanation.[7]

As State Department's Paul Nitze pointed out, there was a five-week gap between the time Chinese forces began filtering into Korea and the date of their actual assault along the Ch'ongch'on River. Throughout this period, MacArthur continued to assure Washington all was well; ironically and simultaneously, State Department analysts were concluding just the opposite. Little wonder then that Roger Tubby used the term "surprise" to describe the reaction of the White House to news of the Chinese invasion. Even as late as November 20, just four days prior to MacArthur's planned offensive, the U.S. Embassy staffers in Seoul assessed that, unless the Chinese forces picked up the combat pace of the preceding two weeks, they would be fighting a delaying action rather than waging an all-out invasion.[8] Also of potential concern was the impending Korean winter—by mid-November, the relatively balmy 40° days had dropped to -20° Fahrenheit.[9]

Meanwhile, the 1st Marine Division (MARDIV) to the east was skittish, despite the optimism of MacArthur and Almond. The encounter at Unsan was still a mystery, as were the ever-increasing numbers of Chinese prisoners. Nevertheless, Almond proved relentless in his quest to make his commander's vision of a rapid advance to the Yalu a reality. He was later criticized by fellow U.S. Army officers for advancing without regard for either his flanks or the location of enemy forces. Historian Richard Stewart, who has studied the withdrawal of X Corps in the face of the Chinese assault, has pointed out that "as a commander of an independent corps, Almond should have been more vigilant and cautious." Almond was an officer who pushed his subordinates hard, perhaps none more so than 1st MARDIV commander Major General O. P. Smith. His caution, given his deployment in mountainous, enemy-occupied terrain far from maritime resupply, was palpable and resulted in several chiding visits from Almond. As another author concluded, "The underestimation of CCF [Chinese Communist Forces] strength and the rush to launch the X Corps offensive per schedule on 27 November had led to an ill-advised thinning out of American forces on the east side of the Chosin Reservoir." Perhaps no other single event provides more of a mirror into Almond's soul as a commander than the fateful statement he made to an isolated regimental combat team, Task Force MacLean, which would be decimated a few days later while trying to break out of a Chinese encirclement. To ease the jitters of the task force's officers, Almond told them, "The enemy who is delaying you for the moment is nothing more than remnants of Chinese divisions fleeing north … We're still attacking and we're going all the way to the Yalu. Don't let a bunch of Chinese laundrymen stop you!"[10] Willoughby also attempted to calm the jittery Leathernecks, flying over to Korea from Japan. After studying the tactical situation, he dismissed the Chinese presence as "no more than a battalion of troops from each of the [Chinese] units identified." Aware of lingering concern about the still-murky course of events at Unsan, Willoughby explained it away by saying that 8th Cavalry had allowed themselves to be overrun by a small, pointed surprise attack.[11]

Only later did American Intelligence learn the Chinese forces had begun filtering into North Korea on October 14. On the 29th, elements of X Corps, located approximately 30 miles northwest of Hamhung, reported they were being opposed by organized CCF units. Enemy prisoners of war reported their particular unit began crossing the Yalu at Manpojin on October 16, conducted a rapid night march, and then were directed to engage UN forces, wherever they were found.[12] This Chinese movement constituted their "First Phase Offensive" (October 25–November 6) and came as a shock to American/UN forces. For the Chinese, it served several purposes—it provided them with direct evidence of the American military's strengths and weaknesses; it shook Republic of Korea (ROK) troops out of their reverie; confused UN commanders; and likely enhanced the confidence of Chinese commanders in dealing with the American/UN offensive.[13] Though neither Willoughby nor MacArthur had any use for CIA analysis, Agency reporting from September 8 and October 12, as noted, indicated a Chinese military intervention was already underway, but stopped short of assessing that war between the People's Republic and American/UN forces was inevitable.[14]

The 8th Regiment, 1st Cavalry Division, had arrived at Unsan with what one observer referred to as a "cavalier frame of mind." Yet, I Corps' G-2 officer, Colonel Percy W. Thompson, told senior officers at the 8th that he assessed that CCF in Korea were massing for an attack against the Eighth Army; however, his misgivings were ignored, met with "indifference and disbelief." Early in the evening of November 1, a patrol from the 1st Battalion, 5th Cavalry Regiment, was surprised to find the road between the 8th and the 5th Cavalry Regiments had been cut—by the CCF's 347th Regiment. This shock to the reverie of the 1st Cavalry Division meant its subordinate 8th Cavalry Regiment was now surrounded to the north, south, and west.[15]

Earlier that day, 8th Cavalry Regiment Commander Colonel Hal Edson had noticed smoke from forest fires covering the area to his front. He assessed, correctly, these fires had been set to mask the movement of Chinese troops from UN ground and aerial observation. That afternoon, a spotter plane reported large numbers of unidentified troops advancing toward the Ch'ongch'on River, despite heavy American counterbattery fire. General Gay, Commander of the 1st Cavalry Division, requested permission from I Corps to withdraw the 8th Cavalry Regiment, currently exposed, to a more defensible position south of Unsan; his request was denied. The enemy units encountered—the 115th and 116th Divisions, 39th Chinese Field Army—would decimate 8th Cav later that same night.[16]

As the first day of November turned from day to night, Chinese troops poured out of the hills near Unsan, North Korea, blowing bugles, throwing grenades, and firing machine guns at the stunned troops of the 8th Cavalry Regiment, 1st Cavalry Division. The ensuing din of bugles,.whistles, drums, and gongs prompted one GI to respond, "My God ... A Chinese funeral!" Only after the melee was over did the American soldiers involved realize they and their scattered South Korean allies had been attacked simultaneously from the north, northwest, and west. This massive assault rendered the ROK 15th Regiment combat-ineffective, exposing the 8th Cav's right flank, and compelled the 1st and 2nd Battalions to pour pell-mell into the city of Unsan. The following morning, November 2, the remnants of 8th Cav attempted to withdraw, but a Chinese roadblock to the rear stymied that tactical maneuver, compelling them to take to the hills in small groups. Meanwhile, the only unscathed battalion of the 8th Cav, the 3rd—located some three miles southwest of Unsan on the tragic night of November 1—was having to deal with the bugle-blowing assault of the Chinese at the same time. In the predictable and ensuing confusion, a company-sized element of Chinese troops was mistaken for South Korean allies and allowed to cross a critical bridge near the battalion command post (CP)—the Chinese maximized the unexpected opportunity, unleashing satchel charges and grenades on the CP, overrunning it. As Lieutenant W. C. Hill, in charge of troops guarding the Nanmiyon River Bridge, explained, "I thought I was dreaming when I heard a bugle sounding taps and the beat of horses' hooves in the distance. Then, as though they came out of a burst of smoke, shadowy figures started shooting and bayoneting everybody they could find." A rescue attempt by fellow 1st Cavalry Division elements—the 5th and 7th Cavalry Battalions—was unsuccessful in dislodging the Chinese, primarily because 5th Cav was soon hit by an attack conducted by five companies of the CCF's 8th Route Army. At sundown on November 2, General Gay ordered 5th Cav to withdraw, leaving the 3rd Battalion, 8th Cav, on its own. In the process of trying to break out, 8th Cav lost 453 killed in action (KIA) and 410 wounded in action (WIA), nearly one-third of its total strength. When a GI was informed he was now a CCF prisoner, he blurted out, "For God's sake ... this isn't your war!";—in halting English, a CCF officer replied, "It is now." The cruel irony was that this extensive damage was inflicted by Chinese forces whose existence—until early November—had only been rumored. Other Eighth Army elements also faced Chinese attacks in early November, only to have the attackers melt away into the surrounding hills, leaving the area eerily quiet by November 6.[17]

As expected, the news of the mauling of 8th Cav at Unsan struck like lightning at 1st Cav Division, I Corps, Eighth Army Headquarters. There, G-2 Lieutenant Colonel Tarkenton assessed, based on the 17 prisoners in Eighth Army hands, that elements of at least six divisions from two armies (the 39th and the 40th) were in contact with Eighth Army. He also noted the enemy use of heavy mortars, multiple rocket launchers, and explosives to defeat Eighth Army tanks and added, ominously, "This enemy group displayed an unusual ability to fight at night." Eighth Army Commander Lieutenant General Walker meanwhile sent a message to MacArthur about the "ambush" in which his forces were routed by "fresh, well-organized, and well-trained units," some of which consisted of "Chinese Communist forces." Despite the rather cryptic nature of Walker's report, it should have been a clear indication to both MacArthur and Willoughby that there had been a dramatic shift in the nature of the Korean War—and that likely no one would be home by Christmas. On November 2, Willoughby met Walker at P'yŏngyang, where the latter told him, "Charles, we know the Chinese are here; you tell us what they are here for." [emphasis added].[18] In a later interview, Foreign Service officer and Korea desk officer Niles W. Bond recalled, "There was tremendous unhappiness when the Chinese attack came across the Yalu River. This was something Willoughby had said would not happen."[19]

Willoughby's next-day reports to Headquarters allowed for up to thirty-four thousand Chinese troops in North Korea, with the ability of the young People's Republic to commit up to four hundred fifteen thousand more at any time. The Far East Command G-2's report to the Army G-2 also noted, ominously, that a "considerable" number of enemy vehicles were moving across the Yalu River into North Korea. This information prompted MacArthur to ask, on November 3, for permission to use B-29 Superfortresses to bomb the bridges over the Yalu, which was approved on November 8, a week after the mauling of 8th Cav at Unsan. Four days after MacArthur's request, on November 7, Willoughby reported the volume of cross-border traffic was up sharply, which complemented U.S. Air Force reports of increasing encounters with MiG-15 fighters scurrying across the Yalu into the People's Republic of China (PRC). As American fighter pilots soon learned, the MiG-15 fighter could fly higher and faster than any aircraft in the UN inventory and though the F-86 Sabre proved its equal, there were few of the latter in theater as yet. The other disturbing aspect of the MiGs' appearance was the earlier intel assessment that neither North Korea nor China had a jet air force, leading to the troubling question, "Who's flying the MiGs?" Ironically, the November 12 CIA report listed "lack of air assets" as one of the reasons why the Chinese could not intervene in Korea.[20]

Grudging acceptance of the growing Chinese intervention pervaded the November 7 Daily Intelligence Summary (DIS), prepared by Willoughby's staff, which reiterated the capability of CCF to move 29 divisions from the Manchurian border into North Korea. "The Chinese have already displayed their ability," the DIS noted, "to infiltrate troops into Korea with comparative ease. Utilizing back roads and the cover of darkness, it is entirely possible that the CCF could secretly move all or a large portion of this readily available force into position south of the Yalu in preparation for a counteroffensive."[21]

***

By mid-month, a general consensus had developed that some type of major Chinese intervention was underway in Korea, though there was considerable wrangling among American officials as to the scope and purposes of such an intervention. By this date, Willoughby also admitted that Chinese forces appeared to be massing near the Chosin Reservoir, posing a major threat to X Corps. In a November 10 report, he recounted the story of a captured Chinese officer who explained a technique that had initially confused American commanders and intelligence analysts—he explained how the 38th Army had entered Korea on October 20 and then changed its true unit designator to the "54th Unit" as a security measure. Folding in such bits and pieces of enemy order-of-battle information prompted Willoughby to assess that, as of November 11, there were 76,800 Chinese troops in Korea, all that stood between MacArthur's forces and the Yalu River. While Willoughby was slowly warming to increasing and more accurate figures for Chinese troops committed in Korea, he still lowballed their numbers at the time and did not provide his commander with a "most probable enemy course of action," the most basic of requirements for even a junior intelligence officer.[22] Also on Armistice Day, the Eighth Army interrogated a new batch of Chinese prisoners, one of whom claimed there was "an entire Chinese Communist army in North Korea."[23] Yet the same day, a report compiled by Willoughby's staff indicated "some withdrawal by enemy forces in front of Eighth Army." The report postulated that the reasons for such a withdrawal could be: 1) high casualties incurred in the period November 1–5; 2) the regrouping of forces out of artillery range prior to the beginning of an offensive; or 3) a temporary defensive stance while awaiting the outcome of unspecified political developments. Interestingly, Willoughby's analysts assumed the most likely explanation was the second one—preparation for an offensive. The uncertainty concerning the most likely enemy course of action was reflected in a report a week later which noted that, while such lulls had preceded offensives in the past, "the sudden reversal ... may indicate a high level decision to defend from previously selected and prepared positions." In a telephone call to Washington the following day, Willoughby provided a detailed intelligence report on enemy rail and vehicle movements in the North Korean portion of the Manchurian–North Korean border area. He reported that, although there had been little rail movement between October 15 and November 5, there had been a high volume of vehicular traffic in the area—specifically, 1,287 vehicles and 66 tanks.[24]

However, on the 20th, MacArthur issued a directive still dismissive of the Chinese buildup in North Korea, reassuring the Joint Chiefs that UN airpower would be sufficient to blunt the threat of Chinese reinforcements. On Thursday, the 23rd—Thanksgiving Day—American troops feasted on holiday goodies, as their CCF counterparts made do with cabbage soup and rice. That night the temperature at Yudam-Ni fell to -4° Fahrenheit.[25]

On approximately November 16, MacArthur had told Ambassador Muccio, in regard to suspected Chinese movements into North Korea, "there are no organized enemy units in that area, it's merely a mop-up operation. My intelligence has established that there are some twenty-five to thirty thousand Chinese in that area, but not more than that could have crossed the Yalu or my intelligence would know about it."[26]

In mid-to-late November, signals intelligence—information that both MacArthur and Willoughby were cleared for and presumably would have seen—provided a key indicator of imminent Chinese military actions. A series of PRC civil communications revealed an order for 30,000 maps of Korea to be sent from Shanghai to Chinese forces in Manchuria. Army Intelligence analysts calculated that that many maps would supply 30 divisions—just the number that would attack American and UN forces in a matter of days.[27]

Willoughby's inaccurate assessment of his foe and his most likely courses of action was in evidence again on November 23 when he reported to the Department of the Army that the Chinese were having supply problems of their own, since they in some cases had deployed troops with only three days' rations and were being confronted daily by UN ground forces and, when the weather would cooperate, American aircraft. "Constant United Nations pressure along the entire line during the past few weeks," stated the G-2, "should make it perfectly clear to the Reds that this drain on fire power is certainly not apt to be decreased but increased." He also doubted the Chinese high command would replenish its troops, "... as the Chinese have always been, by Western standards, notoriously poor providers for their soldiers."[28]

On November 24, the Eighth Army began its push northward, the opening of MacArthur's campaign to drive to the Yalu and have his troops home for Christmas. Enemy resistance was initially light to moderate and some Eighth Army elements advanced 12 miles within 36 hours. But MacArthur had been informed the Chinese might have committed as many as twelve divisions to the fight in Korea and that day Willoughby surmised, "Even though Chinese Communist strategy may not favor an immediate full-scale war, preparations for such an eventuality appear to be in progress."[29]

The growing specter of Chinese intervention on the peninsula prompted the CIA on November 24 to publish NIE-2/1 (National Intelligence Estimate) given the need to "re-estimate the scale and purpose of Chinese Communist intervention in North Korea." Agency analysts predicted the Chinese would simultaneously maintain Chinese–North Korean holding operations in North Korea, maintain or increase military strength in Manchuria, and seek UN withdrawal from Korea by intimidation and diplomatic means. They added, notably, that should that initiative fail, "there will be increasing Chinese intervention in Korea," possibly involving "prolonged attrition against UN forces in Korea." Hedging their bets, the authors pointed out that "available evidence is not conclusive as to whether or not the Chinese Communists are as yet committed to a full-scale offensive effort," but hastily added, "There has been no suggestion in Chinese propaganda or official statements that the Chinese support of North Korea has a limited objective such as protecting power plants, establishing a buffer zone on the border, or forcing the UN forces back to the 38th Parallel."[30]

In the manuscript notes for his book *MacArthur, 1941–1951*, Willoughby claims MacArthur had become so concerned about the Chinese threat that, on November 24, he flew in an unarmed plane along the entire length of the Yalu River, in an application—or so his G-2 observed—of his commander's theory of "you can't fight 'em if you can't see 'em." Willoughby was part of the entourage that flew from Korea to Tokyo, to assess the damage situation. The group flew in MacArthur's new (and unarmed) VC-121A Constellation—the only one in the Far East, which MacArthur christened "Bataan"—and landed at Sinanju airstrip, near I Corps headquarters along the Ch'ongch'on River. On the return trip to Tokyo in mid-afternoon, MacArthur ordered his pilot, Lieutenant Colonel Anthony F. Story, to head for the mouth of the Yalu River, 60 miles behind enemy lines and just across the border from MiG fighters deployed in Manchuria. As Whitney outlined the itinerary, "We are going to reconnoitre [*sic*] the Yalu river and the Suiho dam and anything else that looks interesting." From his 5,000-foot vantage point, MacArthur described the scene below as "an endless expanse of utterly barren countryside, jagged hills, yawning crevices, and the black waters of the Yalu locked in the silent death grip of snow and ice. It was a merciless wasteland." Predictably, one newspaper account filed the day of the flight gushed, "He is the first Supreme Commander in history to calmly fly far into enemy territory and examine the objectives of the offensive." Almond described his boss's trip as "what I would call thumbing your nose at the Chinese." MacArthur apparently saw nothing, not surprising since the Chinese troops were moving exclusively at night, using the mountain passes for cover and concealment.[31]

But they were there—and in force. The Chinese had committed six armies (38th, 39th, 40th, 42d, 50th, and 66th) from the Thirteenth Army Group to the fight, 19 divisions of 57 regiments, including 150,000 light infantry. Willoughby sent information to Washington indicating American forces were facing 82,799 North Korean troops and 40,000 to 70,935 Chinese Communist troops, an estimate Korean War historian Lieutenant Colonel Roy Appleman assessed was "grossly in error," in part because, aside from a handful of lost North Korean soldiers, the assault was a completely CCF affair.[32]

By late November, Lieutenant General Walker's Eighth Army was deployed on the Ch'ongch'on River to the west, X Corps, commanded by Major General Almond, at the Chosin Reservoir, to the east. Edging ever closer to ground truth, on November 26 Willoughby unwittingly prophesied, "Should the enemy elect to fight in the interior valleys, a slowing down of the United Nations offensive may result."[33] Eerily, Almond had just reported that, as of the third week in November, successful completion of the X Corps mission was in sight "except for the foreboding cloud on the combat horizon of increasing Chinese Communist 'Volunteers' appearing

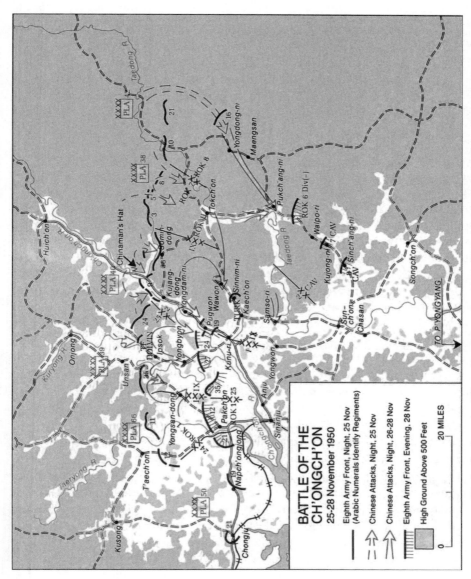

The battle along the Ch'ongch'on, November 1950. (U.S. Army Center of Military History)

on all fronts." When the Chinese attack came, it fell first on the Eighth Army, then on X Corps, followed in rapid succession by the Republic of Korea's II Corps (on the Eighth Army's right flank) and the American 2nd Infantry Division (2nd ID). On the bitterly cold evening of November 25, elements of the 2nd "Indianhead" Division, IX Corps, Eighth Army, moving through hills along the eastern bank of the Ch'ongch'on River near the small village of Kunu-ri, were overrun by Chinese troops, who by the following evening had compelled the UN forces to retreat two miles down the Ch'ongch'on. To its left, the 25th Infantry Division was also in full retreat. A private from the 35th Regiment noted, "There was a complete loss of leadership. It was a nightmare, really. Many times, I felt that we'd never really make it out of there, that to survive this would be a miracle. Those Chinese were just fanatics—they didn't place the value on life that we did." As one historian notes, "The miscalculation of Chinese Communist intentions was now painfully evident." Eyewitnesses commented that "bug-out fever raged everywhere" as American forces began what has been described as "the longest retreat in United States military history." On November 28, Walker reported to Tokyo that he was under attack by some two hundred thousand Chinese troops—he likely would have agreed with the same-day assessment by Ambassador Muccio that the CCF presence was "of such power and intensity as to constitute a general offensive." On the afternoon of November 30, General Keiser ordered the beleaguered 2nd ID to break out to the south; however, the lengthy resulting convoy found itself having to run a six-mile-long gauntlet of withering enemy fire, which decimated it. When night fell, Chinese troops crept down to finish their offensive. In one afternoon, the 2nd ID lost approximately one-third of its strength—1,193 KIA, 552 WIA, 24 percent of the division MIA and declared dead—and virtually all its equipment and transport, rendering the unit "combat ineffective" for several months. On the morning of the 30th, Captain Harris M. Pope, Commanding Officer, 1st Company, 3rd Battalion, 9th Infantry Regiment, 2nd ID, could only find 37 men from his battalion, compared to the average complement of 919.[34]

Several days before, on Monday, November 27, the number of disquieting dispatches reaching Tokyo from both Walker's Eighth Army and Almond's X Corps began steadily increasing. As one report put it, "it was evident that something had gone wrong"; another explained that "strong enemy counterattacks ... stalled yesterday the United Nations general offensive." Willoughby was frantically piecing together snippets of information until late that night, but the emerging picture was unmistakable—the Chinese had launched a massive invasion along a 300-mile-long front. MacArthur reported to Washington and Lake Success—the temporary home of the UN, from 1946 to 1951, in New York—that the Chinese sought the "complete destruction" of his army; the president told his staff, "The Chinese have come in with both feet."[35]

The bloodying of American and South Korean troops along the Ch'ongch'on River stunned many observers, both in theater and well beyond. One writer grandiloquently described it as "one of the major decisive battles of the present century" in which "a Chinese peasant army had put to flight a modern Western force commanded by a famous, and here-to-almost-ever victorious American general." Literally overnight, China had become a major player on the world stage. The Chinese press understated its pleasure at the development when it commented, "The gigantic counter-offensive launched by the Korean People's Army and the Chinese volunteers is developing victoriously."[36]

Over the centuries, Chinese armies had heartily adopted the idea that "ground is the handmaid of victory" and had repeatedly demonstrated their willingness to do whatever was necessary to control the ground. In terms of tactics, a hallmark of Chinese offensives was the extensive use of a sudden onslaught of horns, shouting, and trumpets to disorient the enemy from the get-go and thereby gain a tactical advantage. More specifically, a favorite maneuver technique used by Marshal Lin Pao was the so-called "one point, two sides" method, which called for a frontal fix at the base of a "V" and using a double-envelopment tactic. Such an assault was expressed in the Chinese term san-meng kung tso, translated as "the three fierce actions"—fierce fires, assault, and pursuit. A general ignorance of, or lack of respect for, Chinese military writings continued to plague American senior commanders; for example, had either Willoughby or MacArthur ever read Mao's *On Protracted War*, they might have taken notice of the following passage: "We should concentrate a big force under cover beforehand along the route which the enemy is sure to take, and while he is on the move, advance suddenly to encircle and attack him before he knows what is happening, and thus quickly conclude the battle." United Nations' forces were discovering, in dramatic and tragic fashion, that the Chinese were exacting military tutors.[37]

One of the unintended effects of the Chinese invasion was that it exposed members of the American press to some of the most bizarre briefings they had ever attended. In early December 1950, following the Chinese defeat of the 2nd Infantry Division near Kunu-ri, Joe Fromm, a reporter from *U.S. News and World Report*, attended a press briefing in Tokyo delivered by Willoughby. As Fromm recalled, Willoughby's words made it appear Far East Command (FECOM) had known all along about the Chinese presence and their numbers, that they had been tracking them since they entered North Korea from southern China, and that they knew all along what they were planning to do. Willoughby explained that when MacArthur made his unfortunate "home by Christmas" pledge, he knew there were Chinese troops from 30 divisions on both sides of the Chinese–North Korean border. When the question came as to why MacArthur conducted the offensive that he did, supposedly knowing he was outnumbered 3–1, Willoughby replied, "We couldn't just sit passively by. We had to attack and find out the enemy's profile." Reflecting years later on Willoughby's incoherent answer, Fromm commented, "It's madness, pure madness. Someone is crazy."[38]

***

Yet, as bad as events in the west were, the situation to the east bordered on critical. The first large-scale Chinese attack fell on the ROK's II Corps, several of whose regiments were destroyed. In full retreat, II Corps left a trail of scattered vehicles and equipment—and an 80-mile-wide gap in the Allied line between the Eighth Army in the west and X Corps in the east. Chinese leaders had committed Song Shi-Lun's Ninth Army Group, which had entered Korea on November 10, into combat in order to amputate MacArthur's right arm. Of the group's 12 divisions (120,000 troops), eight were specifically tasked with the destruction of the 1st MARDIV and the Army's 7th Infantry Division, both located near the Chosin Reservoir. Despite temperatures of -20° Fahrenheit, the beleaguered marines held off three nights' worth of attacks, leaving the Chinese attackers with the remnants of only two divisions. According to a prisoner of war formerly assigned to the medical unit of a regiment subordinate to the 59th Division, 70 percent of the CCF troops committed to the offensive suffered frostbite injuries, 5 percent of those requiring amputation. Of the 2,000 troops in his regiment, the prisoner claimed 1,000 had been lost in the fighting and that tetanus and night blindness—the direct result of a vitamin deficiency—were both common.[39]

In the later estimation of Medal of Honor winner General Raymond G. Davis, USMC (Ret.), the marines were outnumbered 10–1 at Chosin and suffered casualties accordingly. Of the three rifle companies in the 1st Battalion, 7th Marine Regiment, one (B Company) was reduced to 27 men out of its normal complement of over 300. In describing this carnage, Davis tellingly remarked, "They suffered casualties that proper preparation would have avoided." However, these units, particularly the 10,000 men of the 5th and 7th Marine Regiments, were able to wage a fighting retreat as they moved from the Chosin Reservoir down to the port city of Hamhung.[40]

On November 27, the Army's 31st Regimental Combat Team (31st RCT) was dispatched to relieve the beleaguered 1st MARDIV east of the Chosin Reservoir and then attack northward, toward the Yalu River. However, when the Chinese 80th Division and a regiment of the 81st Division waged a surprise attack, they expected to be facing the battle-hardened 5th Marine Regiment, 1st MARDIV; however, two days prior, the 31st RCT—also known as Task Force Faith—had relieved their USMC brothers, who had moved to Yudam-ni, on the other side of the reservoir. By the evening of the 27th, the American unit had elements widely dispersed along a 90-mile front, stretching from the port city of Hungnam in the south to forward positions to the east of the Chosin Reservoir. On the night of the 28th, MacArthur summoned Generals Walker and Almond from Korea, to meet with him and Willoughby, among others, in Tokyo at the theater commander's American Embassy residence. The meeting, which lasted from 9:50 pm until 1:30 am on November 29, examined possible countermoves to Chinese entry into the conflict. Driven to save his forces, MacArthur ordered Walker to withdraw as necessary to prevent the Chinese from outflanking him and Almond to maintain contact with the Chinese but to concentrate X Corps' forces into the Hamhung–Hungnam area. By the evening of December 1/2, aided by what one author referred to as "organizational leadership failures" at corps, division, team, and battalion level, the 31st RCT found it virtually impossible to break out of the ensuing Chinese encirclement and ceased to exist.[41] As one source described it, the 31st RCT put up an "unorganized, but fierce" fight, yet suffered numerous casualties—as did the CCF's 80th and 81st Divisions, which were both rendered combat ineffective due to UN airstrikes.[42]

As USMC General Holland "Howling Mad" Smith told war correspondents on December 4, "Gentlemen, we are not retreating. We are merely advancing in another direction." Even so, it was December 10 before advance marine units reached Hamhung—they had sustained 4,400 combat casualties and 7,300 non-combat casualties, mostly minor cases of frostbite. On Christmas Eve, X Corps and the remainder of the ROK forces—100,000 men total—were evacuated from Hamhung to Pusan.[43] The day after Smith's announcement, East German Ambassador to the PRC and "Communist of long standing" Johannes Koenig met in Peiping with Chinese Foreign Minister Zhou En-lai. Zhou told Koenig that unless either Chinese or United Nations troops were willing to leave Korea—and the Chinese weren't going anywhere—World War III was inevitable. "China has therefore made itself ready for World War III," Zhou announced matter-of-factly.[44]

To the east, X Corps had also bagged several Chinese prisoners early on. On October 25, both the 1st Marines and the 1st ROK Division had each taken their first Chinese Communist (CHICOM) prisoners. Three days later, subordinate ROK troops captured two more Chinese near Sudong, along the corps' avenue of approach to the Chosin Reservoir. On October 30, Almond personally went to see the ROK I Corps Commander at Hamhung, where he interviewed 16 Chinese prisoners, who thoughtfully provided detailed information on their units' movements into South Korea beginning October 14. Despite what has been described as his "fierce" loyalty to MacArthur, Almond immediately radioed him and informed him that there were "CCF units in North Korea and in contact with my forces." Almond added that his prisoners were healthy, well-clothed in new uniforms and boots; well-trained and alert; and most were 26–30 years old with an average of 2–3 years' military service. They apparently belonged to the 124th CCF Division and, although none of the 16 could provide the names of their immediate superiors, all knew the name of Lin Piao. They were assigned to a mortar company that moved its equipment using horses. They estimated there were some 10 thousand CCF troops in immediate contact with UN forces and added that their division, and others, were currently occupying Hamhung.[45]

By the second week of November, Willoughby had admitted Chinese forces were massing near the Chosin Reservoir and posed a significant threat to Almond's X Corps. Even considering this information and the mauling American and ROK forces had endured at Unsan just a few days prior, he only gradually acknowledged the presence of Chinese forces in North Korea in any sizable numbers. As of November 6, FECOM in Tokyo listed only 34,500 Chinese troops in theater, when in reality there were over three hundred thousand at that point, organized into 30 divisions.[46]

In his November 13 report to the Department of the Army, Willoughby was able to correctly identify elements of four Chinese armies committed in Korea—the 38th, the 39th, the 40th—all part of the Thirteenth Army Group—and the 42nd, a sub-element of the Fourteenth Army Group. Unknown to Willoughby was the fact that all these CCF units—as well as the 4th Field Army, considered the elite of the five field armies and commanded by Lin Piao—all held the honorary title of "Iron" troops. Unique among the CCF units wreaking havoc with American forces was the 50th Army, the former Nationalist 60th Army, a unit that had defected to the CCF *in toto* during the 1949 civil war. While Willoughby was unaware of the caliber of the Chinese forces he faced, he continued to characterize PLA elements in Korea as "composite units of token forces"—thus, if prisoners from one division of a PLA army of three divisions was identified, the other two divisions were not counted as committed and were therefore omitted from Willoughby's count. As a result, he was only accounting for *one-third* of the PLA troops inside North Korea at any given time.[47] Accordingly, Willoughby downgraded the Chinese intervention Priority Intelligence Requirement to third position—at least until Truman and several of his staffers directly asked for MacArthur's thoughts on the subject, after which it was returned to first position.[48]

While a growing body of evidence pointed to Chinese intervention in Korea on a grand scale, that evidence was less than clarifying when it came to estimating the numbers of Chinese troops believed to be in Korea. The CIA's October 30 *Daily Korea Summary* categorically denied Chinese units positively identified down to division-level were even *in* Korea. Such examples vividly demonstrated the often large gap that existed between field and headquarters units when it came to that most basic of tasks for military intelligence—estimating the strength of the enemy engaged in battle or waiting in reserve. Colonel Percy Thompson, I Corps G-2, Eighth Army, was convinced by late October that the PLA was present in North Korea. However, when he tried to warn Colonel Edson, Commander, 8th Cavalry Regiment, 1st Cav Division, Edson refused to believe him. Willoughby's October 31 report to the Department of the Army G-2 acknowledged there were 28 CHICOM soldiers in UN hands.[49]

After spotty reporting in its *Daily Summary* on the Korean situation throughout November, the CIA finally characterized CHICOM operations on the peninsula as an "offensive." The U.S. Embassy in Seoul provided its "ground truth" by describing the level of Chinese attacks at the time as "of such power and intensity as to constitute a general offensive rather than a series of counterattacks as first presumed."[50]

***

As initially concerning as they were, the Chinese offensives of late November did not dissuade MacArthur from submitting a "Plan for Victory" that proposed four specific strategies to defeat the Communist forces: first, a blockade of China's coast; second, approval to bomb Chinese military installations in Manchuria; third, the deployment of Chinese Nationalist forces in Korea; and fourth, that Jiang Jieshi—better known to Americans as Chiang Kai-Shek—launch an attack from Taiwan on the Chinese mainland. Until more optimistic reports came from the front lines, the U.S. Joint Chiefs of Staff were seriously considering these options. The fact that Truman was actively pondering the use of nuclear weapons in Korea was an indication of how shaken some American leaders were at the disaster unfolding on the peninsula.[51] In July, Truman had ordered Strategic Air Command (SAC) to send 10 atomic-capable B-29 bombers—with assembled bombs but without their plutonium cores—to Guam. But the Chinese offensive in November clearly indicated they were not intimidated by the threat to use nuclear weapons. At the end of that month, Truman upped the ante, announcing to reporters he would do whatever it took to win the war, including the use of nuclear weapons, with control delegated to military commanders in the field (in April 1951, after MacArthur's firing, President Truman ordered nine nuclear bombs *with* fissile cores delivered to Okinawa, along with 10 more B-29s to Guam, and the standup of a SAC control team in Tokyo. However, by June 1951, the B-29s deployed to Guam and Okinawa had flown back to the United States, their deterrent value in the Far East ended for the time).[52] Little wonder that some historians have posited the United States was closer to deploying nuclear weapons during the Truman administration than during that of his successor, Dwight Eisenhower.

As U.S. Army Intelligence and Security Command historian John Patrick Finnegan summarized the situation on the ground, "The strategic surprise that befell the United Nations command at the end of November was perhaps the most telegraphed surprise in the history of American arms … The massive intervention of thirty PLA divisions in the Second Phase offensive finally brought home the catastrophic failure of United Nations Command intelligence."[53] Predictably, it would also contribute to a long-running, at times acrimonious, debate about how well the profession of intelligence acquitted itself during the Korean War.

On December 1, Willoughby briefed a group of 68 war correspondents and fellow officers which, as such briefings often do, likely left them less than satisfied. Speaking of the Chinese, Willoughby noted that "the only way to find out whether they meant business is to go in and test …" The disjointed conversation continued:

> Q: General, last weekend we were told by the briefer an estimated 80,000 Chinese were in Korea. On Tuesday we were told (in the *Communique*) 200,000. Were the 200,000 there at the time of the attack?
> A: I do not recall. I told you those sightings are 24-hour-around-the-clock sightings …

Q: General, what is your intention of Chinese ultimate objective in Korea?

A: I don't like to stipulate what the other fellow is thinking. He has come with very considerable strength … For the present he is a potential of driving on Pyongyang or continuing south … If he goes south, we will attack. I am in no position to forecast [sic] movements of Eighth Army, and shall we say is an unofficial speculation.

Q: General, continuing on speculation, do you think they have sufficient forces to drive us out of Korea?

A: Come, come, come. You don't push Britishers and Americans like that. That may be their wishful thinking …[54]

That same day, MacArthur provided the UN with an update for the period from November 16–30. He wrote:

Beginning in October 1950, Chinese Communists started moving into Korea and attempted to cover their moves by statements that it was individual volunteer participation. It is perfectly clear that the Chinese started moving the mass of their forces to position for the invasion by the middle of September. The Chinese Communist forces are now invading Korea and attacking United Nations Forces in great and ever increasing strength … There is no alternative but to face this situation as a new war which poses new issues beyond the authority of the United Nations Military Command … On 24 November a general attack was launched by all available UN forces. The attack progressed satisfactorily for two days, at which time strong counterattacks … required readjustment of UN forces and resuming defensive operations. The UN offensive successfully developed and revealed the strength and intentions of the Chinese Communists. The enemy forces now opposing United Nations operations in Korea demonstrated considerable strategic and tactical skill.[55]

This clinically sterile report glossed over the actual situation on the ground and put a considerably better face on the job of MacArthur as commander and Willoughby as his chief intelligence officer than perhaps the facts warranted.

On December 2, the United Nations Command Public Information Office released the replies by MacArthur to press questions as of 4:00 pm that day. MacArthur explained that "a state of undeclared war between the Chinese Communists and the United Nations forces now exists." He estimated total enemy strength at 600,000, including approximately 100,000 to 150,000 North Korean troops, and stated that about half the 600,000 were engaged with United Nations forces, with rear echelon troops moving up rapidly from bases north of the Yalu River. He admitted the enemy troop totals outnumbered "overwhelmingly our forces, the exact strength of which I would not care to give." The FECOM commander also provided a frank assessment of the enemy troops encountered thus far, describing them as:

… thoroughly equipped with modern and efficient weapons. Man for man our fire power is probably slightly greater than his, but this is compensated for by his simpler and less complicated organization which puts a greater number relatively in the combat echelon. His is a modern ground force in every sense of the term and capable of comparison with that of any other nation.

The line of questioning then turned to the $64,000 question: "Could this have been avoided?" MacArthur replied, "I know of no way that this could have been avoided under the conditions which existed. The risk was inherent in the United Nations actions of June 27th." The question then came, "Could this risk have been avoided by any manipulations of your forces different from those which transpired?" MacArthur responded, "Not that I can see—the risk of attack from China was one which existed from the beginning and which the United Nations command itself had to accept from the start of operations. It was always inherent and always present but impossible to avoid by any field maneuver or generalship …"[56]

***

As December dawned, the good news for UN forces was in short supply—one historian has referred to these days as "one of the most inglorious episodes in American military history." On December 5, UN troops abandoned P'yŏngyang—the Eighth Army had suffered 11,000 casualties in the first few days following the Chinese intervention and was still fleeing south, literally for its life. The tenacity and fighting prowess of the 1st MARDIV and 7th Infantry Division around the 4,000-foot-high Chosin Reservoir, "a saga of epic heroism" written about by several participants, is a testament to their training and determination, in the face of daunting obstacles, not the least of which was the bitterly cold weather—temperatures fell to -35°F in the coldest winter in a decade. Survivors vividly remembered their Thanksgiving turkey freezing solid on its way from mess kit to mouth. As USMC Corporal Harley Trueblood, B Company, 1st Tank Battalion, 1st MARDIV, put it, "What you had was kind of a turkey popsicle." Mere hours later, Trueblood and his Marine comrades would be fighting for their lives from ditches in Yudam-ni, against CCF divisions that Eighth Army intelligence officers insisted either were not there at all or were present in such small numbers as to be inconsequential. When the beleaguered UN forces were finally able to link up with a relief force at Chinhung-Ni, approximately 35 miles south of Chosin, the 3rd and 7th Infantry Divisions had lost 460 KIA and 872 WIA, with 7,313 more lost to frostbite and intestinal ailments; the figures for the 1st MARDIV—13 members of which received the Medal of Honor for their heroism around Chosin—were 765 KIA and 3,508 WIA. Reeling from the Chinese onslaught, UN forces beat a hasty retreat, down both sides of the Korean Peninsula.[57]

By early December, the shock of what had occurred on the frozen battlefields of the Korean Peninsula had become common knowledge, not only at Eighth Army Headquarters in Tokyo but also—and far more importantly—at home. The reality of the unfolding disaster seemed to dawn on MacArthur only slowly—he was truly surprised the same tactics that had led to victory in the Pacific in World War II didn't work only five years later, with a similar enemy. Especially vexing to MacArthur was the indecisive role of airpower—as one historian noted, it had apparently escaped MacArthur's notice Korea was *not* an island. As he wrote later of the Chinese onslaught, "that there was some leak in intelligence was evident to everyone"—by which, of course, he meant that only espionage or other treachery could account for the disaster, certainly *not* inept intelligence analysis. While the theater commander may not have grasped the scope of the disaster just yet, the commander in chief and others 7,000 miles away certainly did—Truman described the CCF involvement as "in great force" and the battlefield situation as "uncertain."[58]

The one piece of good news was that Chinese troops had seemingly disappeared as rapidly as they had appeared, leaving the North Koreans to pursue a retreating Eighth Army. A grateful but perplexed Willoughby was compelled to explain this unexpected development to superiors in Washington. "Due to the depth of the withdrawal executed by Eighth Army," he wrote, "it is evident that the enemy, lacking any great degree of mobility has been unable to regain contact … There is little doubt but that he [the enemy] is now regrouping his forces under the screen of North Korean units preparatory to renewing the offensive at a time of his own choosing."[59]

In order to ameliorate a bad situation, in early December, U.S. Air Force Director of Intelligence General Charles P. Cabell and Army Chief of Staff General J. Lawton Collins made a brief visit to Japan, which included two conferences with FECOM leaders, the first with MacArthur alone, the second with MacArthur and Willoughby. In the course of the conversation, MacArthur told Collins that:

> … he recognized the importance of the mission of CIA and realized that in the discharge of its responsibility it was necessary for the CIA to do things that did not particularly appeal to him. He was prepared to be of assistance to the CIA, but he wanted to be certain that his staff was kept sufficiently acquainted with the activities of the CIA in order to provide him with the necessary degree of protection to his own position, especially in his role as Supreme Commander of the Allied Forces (SCAP).

In a private conversation which occurred the night prior to the last meeting with MacArthur, Cabell told Willoughby that Walter Bedell Smith's arrival as Director of Central Intelligence (DCI) "was welcomed by all in Washington and that relationships between CIA and the military establishment should improve as a result of this development." Willoughby simply responded that he was glad to hear of this news but made no further comment. During the final meeting with MacArthur, Willoughby made some positive comments concerning the advent of General Smith and MacArthur asked that Collins deliver to the new DCI "a most cordial invitation" to visit FECOM. MacArthur asked Collins to let Smith know he would receive a warm welcome and that "it should be possible to iron out any difficulties which might exist." Willoughby reiterated he did not seek to curtail CIA operations in any way but only wished to be kept aware of what the Agency was doing. After he later became Deputy Director of CIA, Cabell expressed his own thoughts about the FECOM–CIA relationship and stated that:

> … it would do not good whatever for us [CIA] to solicit any directives or instructions from the Joint Chiefs of Staff or other Defense Department officials to General MacArthur on the subject of the CIA relationship. The only way to get anything done would be for General Smith or a representative of very considerable stature to visit the theater in person.[60]

Following his visit, Cabell described MacArthur's intelligence construct in Japan as a "closed corporation" and when Cabell sought to meet with Willoughby one-on-one, the latter replied he was too busy and instead sent a bottle of whiskey to his hotel room. Cabell, however, had the last laugh, as he was staying in the same hotel as Willoughby's permanent quarters and was able to force a meeting between the two. However, Willoughby appeared in his bathrobe for the short, unproductive meeting. In the words of one historian, "This did not augur well for Western intelligence on the brink of a major war."[61]

As late as December 19, Willoughby was still puzzled as to the Chinese offensive—or lack thereof. As he informed Washington, "The whereabouts of the Chinese Communist forces and the reasons why these units have remained so long out of contact continue in the speculative realm." He did, however, doubt that another Chinese offensive was forthcoming in the near future, given the continuing absence of Chinese units and the relative leisurely pursuit of the Eighth Army by the North Koreans.[62]

Prosecution of the war effort was powerfully pre-empted in late December, when a tragic road accident brought a revolutionary change to the leadership of the Eighth Army. On December 23, General Walker was killed in a collision between his command car and a South Korean 2.5-ton truck. The new commander, General Matthew Ridgway, made it immediately clear that one thing the Eighth Army was now going to do was to know their enemy and dispel the previous racist views of inferior Oriental fighting prowess. Speaking of the enemy, the questions now became "How many miles can they move on a given night?", "How much ammo and food do they carry into each battle?", and "How fixed are their orders once a battle begins?" In sharp contrast to MacArthur, who never spent a night in Korea throughout his tenure, Ridgway was in Korea constantly, despite his headquarters being in Tokyo. As a former paratrooper, Ridgway recognized the significance of intelligence and the combat multiplier it could be. He was no doubt equally aware, however, that the Army of his day, as the late David Halberstam put it, approached the subject "somewhat casually." Furthermore, from the standpoint of 1950, men historically assigned to intelligence duty were generally not "fast-trackers" destined for command. In terms of the caliber of intelligence personnel Ridgway sought to surround himself with, one colleague commented that "Willoughby would have lasted about an hour on Ridgway's staff."[63] Ironic then, that the new Eighth Army commander not only retained Willoughby as his G-2 but was complimentary of his efforts. As D. Clayton James notes, "Easily the most astonishing holdover from MacArthur's inner circle was … Willoughby … [He] was colorful, arrogant, opinionated, hard to control, and a Mac adulator." Surprisingly, Ridgway regarded him as "a very fine Chief of Intelligence" and believed the intelligence he collected was quite accurate—Ridgway's problem with the intelligence was that the *evaluation* of the intelligence was flawed, as was the work accomplished by the rest of the intelligence community.[64]

On January 4, 1951, Chinese troops captured Seoul. It took the herculean efforts of Ridgway to finally bring the retreat to a halt, but not before his forces were deep inside South Korea. One historian has noted that the Armistice finally signed in Korea in July 1953 could easily have been signed before Christmas 1950 had MacArthur and the U.S. Government not dismissed the Chinese as a fighting force out-of-hand.[65] This assessment is an accurate one, but exonerates one individual who played a central and critical role in the tragic events which occurred on the Korean Peninsula in the fall and winter of 1950—MacArthur's G-2, Major General Charles A. Willoughby.

Recriminations aside, the more pressing matter, of course, was recovering from, and responding to, the Chinese onslaught. A *New York Times* article of December 4 breezily remarked, "It may safely be assumed that more than half a million troops are now committed against United Nations forces of less than a third that number."[66] A more sobering article written by noted political journalist brothers Joseph and Stewart Alsop, provocatively titled "Who Failed?", sought to address the question of responsibility for the unfolding disaster in Korea:

> Every American, in and out of public life, is asking who is responsible for the disastrous intelligence failure which has now led to military disaster in Korea. The answer is simple. The whole responsibility belongs to Gen. Douglas MacArthur's own intelligence organization, headed by one of the little circle of high staff officers who have been with MacArthur since Bataan, Maj. Gen. Charles A. Willoughby ... The horror that confronts us proves the converse of a rule already given. Just as a great commander can work miracles with good intelligence, so even the greatest commander cannot overcome bad intelligence. Since the bad intelligence emanated from Gen. MacArthur's own headquarters, this may displease those who like to believe that he has attained a sort of divine perfection. *But facts are facts, none the less, and they must be faced.*[67] [emphasis added]

Ironically, that very same month, an article appeared in the American press which expressed a diametrically opposed view of Willoughby. In this article, entitled "Life of the Soldier and the Airman," Willoughby was specifically cited as an example of the truism that America was the land of opportunity, where "ability, courage, initiative, and determination" enabled America's sons—whether native or, as Willoughby, adopted—could reach the top of their respective fields. The writer gushed:

> In the Korean conflict, as chief intel officer, General Willoughby approached his work with rolled-up sleeves ... The men who serve with General Willoughby call him a "soldier's general." They point with pride that he started as a private and soared to the star-crest heights of a general. With him to emulate, many of them are also working their way up the ladder of military achievement.[68]

However, no amount of praise could sweeten the taste of recent military disaster in the mouths of many observers of events on the peninsula. A fuller understanding of the impact of the Chinese assault prompted a January 15 tasking to determine if the Eighth Army could even remain in Korea. To answer that question, Willoughby, FECOM G-2, arrived at Taegu on January 17, along with DCI Walter Bedell Smith, and Army G-2 Major General Bolling. Following the lengthy meeting, the subsequent report to the Joint Chiefs assessed that the Eighth Army's condition on the peninsula had "improved" and that it likely could remain in Korea.[69]

In February, two writers for *Look* magazine penned a somber article, "The Tragedy of the US Army," which painted a similarly grim picture of the situation. They wrote: "The flight of our troops before Chinese peasant soldiers in Korea last November was the most shameful disgrace suffered by American arms since Northern troops cut and ran at the first Battle of Bull Run in 1861. The question we have been asking ourselves in an agony of bewilderment ever since is: 'How could it have happened?'"

The two journalists noted that $48 billion had been spent in the preceding four years and that technological superiority and the complete domination of land and sea "should have more than compensated for our inferiority in numbers." Looking beyond the immediate disaster, they posited that all armies—notably including the U.S. Army at the time—were affected by "military-mindedness," which they defined as "a kind of creeping paralysis that tends to make an army bureaucratic, inefficient, hidebound and introverted, absorbed in itself and forgetful of its only reason for existence—to prepare to fight its nation's enemies ..." They also pointed out the all too common but dangerous tendency to fight the last war rather than the next one and the "strange compulsion to prepare for battle with an enemy of its own invention, instead of a real one." In their article they quoted a U.S. Army officer who claimed he and his colleagues were being taught how to fight—*the U.S. Army*. In the assessment of the two journalists, the atomic bomb and long-range bombers had been the Maginot Line for the American military—the only flaw in this line of reasoning, they pointed out, was that "our leaders failed to ask the enemy if he would play the role they assigned him."[70]

In writing of the shock and surprise resulting from the Chinese assault, Willoughby considerably understated the situation facing his commander when he noted, "Red China would present for MacArthur new conditions and a totally new war." Although he succumbed to the popular idea that behind Red China stood, "of course," the Kremlin, Willoughby did correctly assess that the UN chose to ignore what he referred to as this "uncomfortable problem" and observed that "no means were ever furnished or even considered to meet it."[71] However, an author who has focused on the various intelligence "failures" in Korea lays the blame for the ignominious retreat of UN military forces in November 1950 squarely at the feet of MacArthur and Willoughby; the latter in particular is castigated for his "near-exclusive control over the enemy information to which MacArthur had access," a factor this author considers "key."[72]

CHAPTER EIGHT

"A Mishandling of Intelligence"

"Intelligence is like a mosaic in which many colored chips are fitted until suddenly
the pattern is revealed."
—MAJOR GENERAL CHARLES A. WILLOUGHBY, MANUSCRIPT NOTES TO THE CHAPTER
ENTITLED "CHINESE COMMUNIST WAR" IN *MACARTHUR, 1941–1951*

"The fact that military intelligence often becomes the convenient whipping boy of
politicians, governments, and the press is a condition to which intelligence staffs
throughout the world are probably resigned."
—MAJOR GENERAL CHARLES A. WILLOUGHBY, MANUSCRIPT NOTES TO
"THE CHARACTER OF MILITARY INTELLIGENCE"

The craft of intelligence suffers from a Walter Mitty complex—it cannot broadcast
its successes abroad, for legitimate reasons of security, and yet, when it faces failures,
whether of its own doing or not, no rational explanation can exonerate it from serving
as a scapegoat. As President John F. Kennedy commented on November 28, 1961—
the day prior to the firing of CIA Director Allen Dulles for the Bay of Pigs fiasco,
"Your successes are unheralded, your failures are trumpeted."[1] A student of military
intelligence concurred, noting "Much better known for its failures than its successes,
military intelligence is widely regarded as the quintessential oxymoron." This same
author also concluded that, during the Korean War, "military intelligence performed
the best that it could within prescribed geopolitical and military constraints."[2]

Taking this questionable conclusion as a point of departure, how should we,
after seven decades, assess the actions of Willoughby as an intelligence officer?
Regrettably, we sometimes recognize excellence only after witnessing mediocrity and
incompetence, an observation which may be relevant in examining Willoughby's
performance strictly as an intelligence officer, evaluating his actions in light of
what we have since defined as "performance objectives" for an intelligence officer,
regardless of rank, position, or era.

Willoughby and World War II Intelligence

A review of Willoughby's record as an intelligence officer reveals a mixed bag,
with some notable contributions to the field of military study in general and the

organization of an intelligence entity in particular, but with sometimes equally egregious failures. On the one hand, during World War II, he focused on the development of what one authority described as "an effective intelligence organization" in which the "centralization of intelligence" played a key role.[3] Similarly, shortly after he was promoted to lieutenant colonel in 1938, he correctly assessed that placing an embargo upon Japan at that time would prompt the Japanese military to seize the Dutch East Indies, Indochina, the Philippines, and Malaya in their quest for the oil, iron ore, tin, and rubber necessary to fuel their war machine. The realization of this assessment was clearly demonstrated when the United States implemented an embargo in 1941 and the Japanese responded just as Willoughby assessed they would. This uncommon incident indicates he was, at least at times, capable of crafting accurate strategic intelligence estimates.[4]

However, during the Philippines campaign, the new G-2 made several "mis-estimates," as one author has characterized them. He originally predicted the Japanese would land in the Philippines on or about December 28, 1941, but they actually appeared in Lingayen Gulf on the 22nd. Willoughby was also one of MacArthur's staffers who convinced the theater commander *not* to move large food stocks to the Bataan Peninsula once it became clear the Japanese had landed in force. As a result, American troops on the peninsula fought for five months on starvation rations. Yet, neither misstep prompted MacArthur to replace Willoughby as his G-2, then or ever.[5]

In April 1942, U.S. Navy Commander Edwin T. Layton, Admiral Nimitz's chief intelligence officer, predicted a Japanese offensive in New Guinea and posited an attack on Port Moresby, in order to cut off Australia from receiving American supplies. Willoughby received this same information but came to a different conclusion; initially believing the Japanese would occupy the northeastern coast of Australia, he soon reversed himself, predicting a Japanese landing at Port Moresby. As the Japanese Combined Fleet steamed toward that location in early May 1942, an American carrier task force intercepted it, a meeting that came to be known as the Battle of the Coral Sea. Though the conflict was actually a draw, it was the first time the U.S. Navy, still badly bruised from the Pearl Harbor attack, was able to meet a Japanese naval force in battle and acquit itself well. In July 1942, as MacArthur was in the midst of moving his headquarters from Melbourne to Brisbane, Willoughby predicted the Japanese would move a sizable body of troops to Buna or Milne Bay in New Guinea but again flip-flopped within three days, now assessing they were intent only upon reinforcing their troops in the area. On July 18, Willoughby reported to MacArthur that a convoy of Japanese ships was headed toward either Lae or Buna in New Guinea or possibly toward Guadalcanal, a rather imprecise bit of intelligence analysis. Meanwhile, U.S. Navy intelligence had deciphered a message which indicated the Japanese would land at Buna on July 21, intent upon crossing the formidable 13,000-foot-high peaks of the Owen Stanley mountain range, in order to attack Port Moresby, as an alternative to the forestalled Coral Sea invasion fleet strategy.

When Japanese troops indeed landed at Buna on the 22nd, Willoughby held firm to his belief they had seized Buna simply to establish an air base there and that they would be unable to traverse the deep jungle through the Owen Stanleys—not the first or last time his assumptions would be disproven. In response to these Japanese offensives, MacArthur planned to attack Buna and cut off the Japanese retreat, in collaboration with an Australian push against the Japanese forces. In preparation for his commander's offensive, Willoughby estimated the Japanese defenders at Buna numbered no more than fifteen hundred to two thousand troops, capable of doing little more than waging a defensive action. Willoughby assured MacArthur that their defeat was 'practically assured.' In reality, however, when Allied troops landed on Buna on November 19, they instead faced reinforcements of some thirty-five hundred rested Japanese troops, most from Rabaul or non-Kokoda Trail veterans, who had been ordered to fight to their deaths.[6] Though the difference in enemy strength may seem inconsequential in the normal scale of battle, Willoughby had underestimated his foe by at least fifty percent and miscategorized his morale and fighting zeal, an embarrassing gaffe for the senior intelligence officer in the theater and a man who consistently had the ear of his commander. It is dwelling upon such lapses in Willoughby's duty performance that has prompted one historian to describe his intelligence forecasts in the Southwest Pacific during World War II as "often inaccurate and invariably over-optimistic"; another concluded that he "had a remarkable propensity to be wrong in his analysis of enemy capabilities and intentions, a distressing characteristic for a high-level intelligence officer."[7]

During the August 1942–February 1943 campaign for Guadalcanal (codename *Cactus*) and Tulagi (codename *Ringbolt*), USMC General Alexander Vandegrift needed intelligence information on the streams near Lunga Point. He was displeased, however, to find the information he received was "dead wrong." In response, then-Colonel Willoughby promised aerial photos of the objectives. Willoughby's subordinates assembled a mosaic of pictures of *Cactus* and *Ringbolt*, but the photos were forwarded to the wrong address and Vandegrift never received the information he requested. Vandegrift charged Willoughby with misrouting the critical aerial photos, resulting in another dissatisfied customer.[8]

However, Willoughby also made an extremely accurate forecast that a significant Japanese convoy would reinforce units in New Guinea during the first week of March 1943, starting from the major Japanese base at Rabaul. In the resulting Battle of the Bismarck Sea, American and Australian aircraft attacked and heavily damaged the Japanese convoy en route.[9] Following the battle, Willoughby argued that the enemy casualty figures claimed and vigorously defended by MacArthur and Fifth Air Force chief General Kenney were in error—ironic, given Willoughby was the one often charged with wildly inaccurate estimates when it came to enemy battle strength. Both MacArthur and Kenney reported to Washington that they had sunk 22 Japanese ships, downed 102 enemy planes, and inflicted 15,000 KIAs on the foe.

In Washington, "Hap" Arnold's Air Corps staffers disputed such figures and, in August 1943, the pair was directed to submit revised reports. MacArthur angrily refused to alter figures that were correct, as far as he was concerned, and both he and Kenney stood by the original figures for the rest of their lives. Interestingly, Willoughby and Whitney did not; in *MacArthur, 1941–51*, the former excused the figures his boss had provided, describing them as estimates which "included duplication of eyewitness accounts that was inevitable in haze and rain." He also reported that Kenney's aircraft had sunk eight transports and four of eight destroyers, not the 22 ships MacArthur and Kenney had reported.[10]

Some observers have been sharply critical of Willoughby's performance as an intelligence officer in the New Guinea campaign in particular. One writer concluded that Willoughby made "several serious intelligence blunders," specifically:

- He did not make clear the fact that virtually none of the Japanese troops at Hollandia were combat troops;
- He misread enemy intentions while deciphering enemy troop movements around Sarmi;
- He was unable to discover the exact date of General Adachi's attack along the Driniumor River in time to be of use.

As this historian has charged, "These were certainly egregious errors, and a good number of GIs died as a result of them." Yet, in the interests of historical balance, he also notes that "... on the whole Willoughby's intelligence served MacArthur well." After all, it was Willoughby's intelligence that informed MacArthur of the identification and location of most enemy units in New Guinea; the fact that the Japanese were expecting an attack at Hansa Bay–Wewak, not Hollandia; that the Imperial Japanese Navy was marshaling its forces for the *Kon* operation (a reinforcing of Biak); that General Adachi's forces were deploying for an attack on Aitape; and, probably most importantly, that the Japanese had shifted emphasis from going on the offensive to creating a new defensive line in the western part of the island. As this writer noted, "This was much, and it enabled MacArthur to deploy his forces accordingly."[11]

In early 1944, during the amphibious assault on Hollandia, New Guinea—the largest Pacific war landing to that date—four infantry divisions were dispatched to deal with the "sizable" Japanese forces that Willoughby had identified there. Yet, when U.S. Marines stormed ashore, backed by virtually the entire Pacific fleet, they found only a force of some two thousand terrified Japanese warehouse and supply troops. The combination of wartime censorship and creative interpretation of this assessment of enemy strength as an example of MacArthur's "hitting them where they ain't" policy—a colorful way of referring to MacArthur's "island hopping" strategy to avoid Japanese strongpoints—ensured the intelligence gaffe was quickly forgotten. More serious was Willoughby's earlier miscalculation of the Japanese strength at Finschhafen. In early September 1943, he categorically stated the base was only lightly defended, protected by some three hundred fifty troops, an estimate which contributed to the optimism of both MacArthur and his Australian counterpart General Blamey. However, as of early October, General Eizo Yamada had some fifty-four hundred troops there, who doggedly fought the American invaders. An historian of the war in New Guinea noted, "How Willoughby arrived at the figure of only 350 men remains a mystery." Notably, in his biography of MacArthur, Willoughby simply ignored this off-the-mark assessment. Pacific war historian Walter Borneman notes, "This was not the first time that Willoughby had made a major blunder in numbers, and it would not be his last." His selective memory also played a part in his recounting of the campaign against Biak Island in late May 1944. In preparation for his commander's campaign, Willoughby estimated 5,000 to 7,000 Japanese personnel on the island, only 2,300 of whom were combat troops; signals intercepts pegged the number of effective combat troops at twice that figure. MacArthur expected "stubborn but not serious resistance." In reality, there were actually 12,350 Japanese personnel there, approximately four thousand of whom were combat troops and many of whom were effectively dug into the many caves on the island, making their neutralization that much more difficult. Other writers have pointed to this error—which Willoughby again left out of his 1954 MacArthur biography—as part of the reason MacArthur placed great pressure on USMC commanders General Krueger and Lieutenant General Eichelberger for a speedy conquest of the island.[12]

It was Willoughby's indirect encounter with a formidable Japanese commander in mid-1944 that demonstrated his being sucked into the same trap that has bedeviled every intelligence officer since that day—the tendency to "mirror image," to assume that, in any given situation, your foe will make the same decision you would, had the situation been reversed, discounting differences in history, culture, military education, and personal idiosyncrasies. In the wake of the Allied invasion of Hollandia, Lieutenant General Adachi Hatazō, Eighteenth Army commander, had moved to the vicinity of Aitape, in the Wewak region. Willoughby assumed Hatazō—likely leading an exhausted army, low on supplies, and moving through impenetrable jungle—would bypass Aitape in order to strike Hollandia instead, because this is what Willoughby himself would have done. Notably, the G-2's assessment was contradicted by signals intercepts, aerial reconnaissance information, and prisoner-of-war interrogation, all of which indicated Hatazō's intent to attack Aitape. By June, Willoughby had flip-flopped, now predicting the Japanese would attack Aitape in late June or early July. Willoughby knew from a decrypted Eighteenth Army message to Tokyo that Hatazō had requested a submarine be rushed to Wewak with supplies for an offensive targeting Aitape. On that basis, on July 10, Willoughby reported Hatazō had postponed his attack until he could be resupplied by submarine—however, that same night, 10,000 Japanese troops attacked the American stronghold at Aitape, unleashing a month-long campaign which resulted in some three thousand American casualties, including 400 killed in action. Willoughby did also learn, however, that the offensive was challenging for the Japanese as well; from other intercepted and decrypted Eighteenth Army messages, he learned the pace of the Japanese advance was initially 6–7 miles per day but that, within weeks, the speed of the advance had been cut in half. In terms of the sudden enemy offensive, Willoughby covered his wandering tracks by claiming after the fact that Hatazō's attack had actually not been a surprise—his *Daily Intelligence Summary* for July 12–13 included this statement with regard to the Aitape attack: "From the accumulated intelligence, it can be seen how logically the attack was built up and reported, giving us a very clear picture of the enemy's plan of attack prior to it actually being scheduled."[13]

Willoughby's estimates were also flawed when it came to surmising how many Japanese troops were defending Luzon during the late 1944 retaking of the Philippines. The extent of his misfiguring comes into clearer focus when his estimates are compared to those of his Sixth Army counterpart, Colonel Horton White. Like Willoughby, White was also a large man physically; unlike Willoughby, White was described as a "quiet and good-natured staff officer" with "a reputation for competence and ability." In sharp contrast to Willoughby's most "generous" estimate of 172,400 defenders, White assessed in early December that General Yamashita had 234,500 troops on Luzon, meaning Willoughby had only accounted for 63 percent of the enemy forces. White also estimated that nearly one hundred sixty thousand of Yamashita's troops were concentrated north of Manila, on the Americans' left flank, whereas Willoughby maintained there were "only" 110,000 deployed there. The numerical discrepancy between the two estimates was due to a different approach to the same data—Willoughby took the fragmented information he had at face value, not including service or unattached troops in his estimate, whereas White counted both, identifying more than two hundred thirty Imperial Japanese Army units that Willoughby missed.[14]

One author of an article called "Intelligence in the Philippines" cited Willoughby's flawed analyses and wondered if perhaps his loyalty to MacArthur may not have clouded his judgment. More specifically, this author charged that Willoughby "consistently underestimated Japanese strength," refused to let facts alter his pre-conceived opinions, and was seemingly incapable of creating a coherent "whole cloth" from fabric scraps of intelligence. Finally, the writer was also critical of the intelligence organization Willoughby had crafted, citing various systemic problems with the construct.[15]

The near-symbiotic relationship between MacArthur and Willoughby is one noted by virtually all who study the life and times of either man. For example, one intelligence historian particularly critical of the pair asserted MacArthur was "constitutionally incapable of working jointly with almost everybody," a man who "demanded total control of every outfit in his theater"; then, turning to Willoughby, he described him as an "intensely loyal intelligence officer" but castigated him for his reportedly custom-tailored uniforms and his reputed wearing of a monocle, an oft-repeated charge not confirmed by any extant photographic evidence. "As close[d]-minded to outsiders as MacArthur," writes this author, Willoughby vied "for the title of stupidest intelligence chief of World War II." This most-scathing assessment—overly critical, since Willoughby clearly sometimes got it right—is followed by the equally damning charge from an anonymous military historian that Willoughby "habitually" produced faulty reports on the nature of the beaches in the Southwest Pacific and underestimated the numbers of Japanese defenders.[16] The record suggests such "errors" were due more to inexperience than to willful intent to mislead his superiors in terms of military intelligence information. Another author described MacArthur as "an imaginative, bold, and determined general" but also "arrogant, ambitious, vain, and stubborn," adding that "his character and methods evoked in most of his immediate subordinates a blind, unreasoning, and ferocious loyalty," an assessment which accurately describes the relationship between Willoughby and his boss. Commenting further on that key relationship, David Halberstam has described Willoughby as "conspiratorial" and assessed "the key to the importance of Willoughby was not his own self-evident inadequacies; it was that he represented the deepest kind of psychological weakness in the talented, flawed man he served, the need to have someone who agreed with him at all times and flattered him constantly."[17] As early as 1945, this relationship was noticed even by those outside the American command structure—British counterparts were astounded by Willoughby's disinterest in any aspect of intelligence save tactical matters and his complete disregard for anything occurring outside his own sphere of influence, an attitude that would be demonstrated again with regard to Korea, which Willoughby regarded—rightly or wrongly—as "barely on the fringe of his responsibilities."[18]

Some have criticized Willoughby for equating the reading of History with consummate skill as an intelligence officer.

> Willoughby was flawed, as an intelligence officer by the conviction that his avid reading of military history had made him an authority on strategy. Worse than that, he was jealous in his own domain and resented excessively the intrusion of others. MacArthur, aware of this quirk, nevertheless protected him—of all "the gang" he was the only one to serve his master without a break from 1941 to 1951—and was prone to accept his appreciations as gospel, particularly as Willoughby produced the intelligence estimates which were most likely to be palatable.[19]

And yet, on several occasions during the Pacific war, Willoughby demonstrated his ability to correctly assess the information on the disposition and most likely course of action for the enemy. For example, on February 22, 1943, Allied aerial reconnaissance disclosed the presence of 59 Japanese merchant vessels anchored in the harbor at Rabaul, in the Solomon Islands. Willoughby, noting the inactivity of the Japanese in that area at the time, assessed they may have been planning to use these ships to reinforce their presence in New Guinea. Further sharpening his analytical pencil, Willoughby ultimately stated his educated opinion that the destination of this fleet of merchant ships was Lae. Armed with this information—and opportunity—Fifth Air Force commander General Kenney dispatched aircraft to attack the merchant ships, sinking seven of eight transports, killing an estimated three thousand enemy troops, and downing 25 Japanese planes, at a cost of only two American bombers and two fighters. Similarly, some six months later, during the assault on the Admiralties in late February 1944, Willoughby reported to MacArthur there were approximately four thousand Japanese troops in the area; General Kenney, however, steadfastly assessed there were actually only very few in the vicinity. Thanks to the imprecise information gathered by air intelligence, and the skill of the Japanese commander in hiding his troops, it was only later the actual number of Japanese troops was determined to be 3,646, an acceptable margin of error, considering.[20] Willoughby's correct reading of the tea leaves had provided the opportunity for a significant blow to the enemy.

Similarly, thanks to the efforts of Willoughby's creation, the Central Bureau, MacArthur was aware Hollandia was not adequately defended and that Japanese commanders believed an invasion in the Madang–Hansa Bay area was likely. With this critical intelligence in hand, Willoughby recommended the Allies strike Hollandia and bypass the Madang–Hansa Bay redoubt. Furthermore, Willoughby advised a series of deceptions to reinforce the incorrect Japanese conclusion, including strategically placing rubber boats on the beaches in the vicinity and increasing B-25 bombing of the area. As a partial result of Willoughby's intelligence analysis, the April 22, 1944, invasion of Hollandia was a complete surprise to the Japanese. Willoughby's assessment of Japanese troop strength at 22,000—when the actual figure was 16,000—was nevertheless acceptable, as he correctly concluded most were support troops rather than first-line combat troops. That same month, as part of his overall plan to return to the Philippines, MacArthur launched an assault on the Wakde–Sarmi region; Willoughby assessed enemy troop strength at approximately 6,500, of which only a portion were combat troops. Although the correct figure was some 11,000 total, the number of actual combat troops was virtually the same as Willoughby's estimate, vindication of sorts for his earlier assessment.[21]

Furthermore, in January–February 1944, as MacArthur feared the Joint Chiefs of Staff in Washington would side with Admiral Chester Nimitz in terms of an overall strategy for the remainder of the Pacific war vice MacArthur's ongoing plan, General Kenney brought him tantalizing news. Fifth Air Force pilots had been heavily bombing the Admiralty Islands, located northwest of the Japanese stronghold at Rabaul, but noticed minimal activity on the islands—they had not reported seeing any Japanese troops and the airfield was overgrown. Such news was puzzling; the Admiralty Islands constituted a fine anchorage strategically situated so the Japanese could control Allied access to New Guinea. Kenney especially wanted to use Los Negros as an airbase to target the major Japanese base at Rabaul. MacArthur queried whether the islands—already scheduled for attack in April—could be taken sooner; Kenney and his deputy, Major General Ennis C. Whitehead, assured him they could be. Whitehead estimated there were 400 Japanese on Los Negros, but Willoughby disagreed, estimating there were 4,050 Japanese defenders there, a stark difference. As it turns out, Willoughby was absolutely correct; according to captured documents found later, the Japanese commander, Colonel Ezaki Yoshio, had ordered his troops to keep out of sight and resist the natural urge to fire at American reconnaissance planes as they overflew the islands. The airstrip was overgrown simply because it had not been used in a while, not because it was uninhabited. Armed with this information, MacArthur set the invasion date as February 29 and landed 1,000 troops. Although the assault proved successful, it took longer than anticipated and the cost in casualties was higher than expected—the decision to set aside the order-of-battle data rather than alter existing plans had much to do with the result. Although MacArthur sided with Kenney and Whitehead, Willoughby had made the correct assessment and accordingly informed his commander, thus satisfying the most basic responsibility of an intelligence officer.[22] One World War II historian critical of Willoughby for the "maddening inconsistencies that characterized his intelligence summaries" and his flip-flopping on enemy strength figures also admits that Willoughby was sure the Japanese were in the islands in strength—and lots of signals intercepts backed him up in that belief—and they considered the islands too important to give up without a fight.[23]

One writer who has studied Willoughby in some detail concluded that, during the course of the Pacific war, he made only four key estimates that proved to be accurate; nine others, this author assesses, were "badly flawed" and ones which Willoughby sought to hide from view. This assessment prompts the immediate question as to why MacArthur would have retained someone on his staff whose job performance was at times so lacking. The answer is a three-part one: first, because of his own personality, MacArthur needed such adulators as Willoughby on his staff, regardless of their actual accomplishments; second, suitable intelligence officers were noticeably lacking at the time, leading to such strange circumstances as the appointing by General Dwight Eisenhower of a British officer—Major General Kenneth Strong—as his joint intelligence officer (J-2); and third, MacArthur may have concluded that, because of his vaunted "island hopping" campaign style, accurate intelligence assessments of Japanese troop strength were unusually difficult to make.[24] Nor should it be forgotten that Willoughby was one of MacArthur's "inner circle," a "Bataan boy," a personal friend of MacArthur's, untouchable as long as he never turned on MacArthur (and he never did). Willoughby was also one of the few who, looking at the Bataan campaign with the advantage of hindsight, viewed it as a positive. As he grandiloquently wrote, "The epic operation in Bataan and Corregidor became a decisive factor in the winning of the war," certainly a novel take on a near-disastrous event. The reasons, he explained, were because the campaign wreaked havoc with the Japanese invasion schedule for the East Indies and because it prevented the redeployment of sufficient numbers of men, planes, ships, and materiel to subdue Guadalcanal.[25]

A pair of leading historians of World War II have also expressed criticism of Willoughby's performance from the vantage point of 1943. They wrote, "Ill-served by his intelligence officer ... Charles Willoughby, MacArthur sent forces against numerically superior Japanese garrisons on several occasions and exposed his naval forces with objectives beyond land-based air cover." Their criticism became sharper when examining the intelligence background to the Luzon campaign of 1944. Speaking of Willoughby and Whitney, they sniped, "Like good court jesters, they fed their king's humor. Rational operational planning received secondary attention. They also continued the bad habit they had exhibited in the Southwest Pacific, which was to underestimate Japanese opposition and confuse press releases with the truth."[26]

General Thomas Handy, the soon-to-be named Army Deputy Chief of Staff, was more even-handed in his assessment of Willoughby's performance as an intelligence officer. He observed:

> He [Willoughby] was not as bad an intelligence officer as a lot of people will tell you. He was really not too bad. But they used to laugh at some of his estimates of enemy strength ... After we collected all the evidence and found out how many were buried, how many got away, and how many were killed in previous bombardments, counting one thing or another, it would add up pretty close to his estimate.[27]

***

In the midst of flinging rocks at Willoughby, it is worth noting he also deserves credit for a spirited defense of his oft-maligned occupation; in the manuscript "The Character of Military Intelligence," he opined:

> The present trend in Washington is against the military controlling intelligence. In my observation ... it is my belief that it has acquitted itself ably in every related activity, from fighting at the front to civil administration in the twilight ozone of military occupations. The record in the field of military intelligence is equally creditable [sic], especially under the handicap of limitations in money, personnel, and organization.[28]

It also comes as little surprise that, looking back on events, Willoughby was firmly of the persuasion that Southwest Pacific Area intelligence had contributed significantly to the victory in the Pacific Theater. After reviewing the challenges faced by his staff, he commented:

> The fact that they were solved successfully is evidenced by the historical achievements of the forces in the Southwest Pacific Area. An advance of some 2,500 miles from Papua to the Philippines was made with a minimum of means and tactical losses. Victories were forged at the end of the longest supply lines the world has ever seen and were made possible only by the most economical use of usually limited means. Not a single tactical setback occurred in a mostly

difficult, tropical theater against a competent enemy who fought tenaciously to the last ditch. The victories in the Southwest Pacific Area were substantially based on accurate intelligence information of every category. A mere trickle of enemy information, at the beginning of the war, became a flood of intelligence data on every phase of operation of the Japanese armed forces and the territory they occupied.

Willoughby also credited centralization of the intelligence effort for the successes he observed, though he admitted that was a problem he never completely solved. In the post-war period, he wrote:

> Whatever success G-2 was able to achieve can be attributed to a continuous, vigilant, uncompromising effort to establish and maintain centralized control of all intelligence agencies, affiliates, and subordinates, in spite of obviously adverse conditions, and to maintain the highest standards in G-2 publications which won final recognition by their intrinsic merit ... Experience gained in the war in the Southwest Pacific shows the absolute necessity for centralized intelligence control. Competitive, quasi-independent agencies must be eliminated, or ruthlessly subordinated as they tend to unduly assert their individuality and operate independently, causing friction, duplication of effort, loss of valuable time, general inefficiency, and unsatisfactory command relationships. Centralized control was found to be imperative if intelligence was to operate at peak efficiency; everything else was tried reluctantly, only to result in failure.[29]

Ironically, in what was to come in later years, at least one historian has posited that Willoughby was at his most fallible neither in World War II nor in Korea, but in post-war Japan. A MacArthur biographer wrote in 1952 that:

> Willoughby's poorest showing, I believe, was in Japan, where in opposition to the liberal current of the population, he showed his own inclination toward centralized, authoritarian control. He has been called the "Senator Joe McCarthy of the occupation." There is some justification in this characterization, for Willoughby countenanced, if he did not instigate, the persecution and blacklisting of good and hard-working American citizens whom he falsely suspected of Communistic tendencies; his suspicions even extended to men of highly conservative background who opposed him on some point of occupation policy.[30]

Willoughby and Korean War Intelligence

As noted, Willoughby is most often pilloried for his perceived "errors" during the Korean War, which, by the time the Armistice was signed on July 27, 1953, had partially accounted for more than 550,000 UN casualties; of this total, 33,686 American personnel were killed in action and 103,284 wounded. Estimated enemy casualties were more than 1.5 million, including 900,000 Chinese. Most casualties had occurred during the first year of combat.[31] Historians since 1950 have argued, to a greater or lesser degree, as to the nature and extent of, as well as responsibility for, what happened to American and UN forces in Korea during 1950. One has noted that the defeat of the Eighth Army was due in part to under-manning, a rickety logistics structure, and ineffective combat leadership. He adds, however, that "a failure of intelligence played an important role in the setbacks to UN forces and the prolongation of the war. The CIA and DoD intelligence organizations misgauged Chinese motivations for war and built their analysis on erroneous assumptions about the possibility of war. FEC[OM] ... failed in a more profound way to assess accurately Chinese military capabilities. It did not dismiss them, but neither did it adequately inform UN forces about the nature of the opposing forces," described as a "materially poor but doctrinally sophisticated opponent" and "well-disciplined foe" who "distorted and concealed" data to deceive the enemy.[32] Another observer has postulated that one reason American intelligence consistently underestimated Chinese combat capabilities was that the recent lessons of fighting a technologically-backward enemy—i.e., Japan—were unfortunately quickly forgotten and that, as a result, "the Americans did not respect the new enemy"—China.[33] General Ridgway agreed, noting, "[The] wholly human failing of discounting or ignoring all unwelcome facts seemed developed beyond average in MacArthur's nature."[34]

Others believed the intelligence failure was more widespread in nature—an October 18, 1950, postmortem on the North Korean assault, provided to the Army Chief of Staff, summarized CIA, FECOM, U.S. Embassy Seoul, Korean Military Advisory Group, and G-2 reporting and noted all were aware of the military buildup in North Korea and the DPRK's "capability" to invade the South. "At no time, however," the report observed, "did any of the reporting agencies give a definite date for the opening of hostilities, or state that an invasion was imminent." One author described the prognostications of the spring and summer of 1950 as "diffused, uncorroborated, and unconvincing reporting," adding "The body of evidence reaching national leadership was unconvincing," essentially because the "collection system had failed to deliver persuasive evidence." President Truman certainly agreed, commenting that he had received "no information to give any clue as to whether an attack was certain or when it was likely to come."[35] Historian Matthew Aid points to the "decrepit" state of the American intelligence community in the Far East at the outbreak of war as well as to the "inexcusably poor intelligence collection, processing, analysis and reporting practices and procedures" in both Tokyo and Washington.[36]

Both then and now, who was responsible for these losses depended upon who was asking and where they sat; however, even prior to the outbreak of war in Korea, Willoughby's name was frequently on the tongues of critics, many of whom noted over the years that he could be most unpleasant to be around. Sharing the assessment of others, Aid described Willoughby as "moody, prone to bouts of rage," a man who was "feared and loathed by many who worked directly for him, as well as by many officers on General MacArthur's staff."[37] More to the point, despite being MacArthur's primary intelligence officer, there were lingering questions about his most basic abilities in this role. Korean War veteran and military historian Michael Hickey has described his assessments at the time as "often inaccurate and invariably over-optimistic."[38] Intelligence author G. J. A. O'Toole concluded "the failure of the U.S./UN forces to detect the Chinese invasion force until they encountered it, and the vulnerable disposition of U.S./UN forces near the Yalu River, were undeniable field intelligence and command failures for which MacArthur and his staff must be held responsible."[38] Along with some of Willoughby's former colleagues, historian David Halberstam has charged that the intelligence provided to MacArthur during Korea was "deliberately prefabricated" so that "MacArthur's forces [could] get where they wanted to go militarily, to the banks of the Yalu." Such an accusation was a serious charge, but one easily forgiven in the minds of some given the ultimate victory.[39] Aid added that, while both MacArthur and Willoughby rightfully share a large part of the blame, there is plenty to go around, including within the departments of State and Defense and the CIA.[40]

Historian Bruce Riedel noted that the American intelligence community's first experience with North Korea and the People's Republic of China began with "a disaster, a catastrophic intelligence failure in 1950 that cost the lives of thousands of Americans. Worse, it was a self-imposed disaster—the result of terrible intelligence management, not the poor collection or analysis of information."[41] Also critical of Willoughby's performance in Korea is U.S. Army Major Justin Haynes, the author of a 2009 Master's thesis at the Army's Command and General Staff College (USACGSC), who discussed at length Willoughby's "flawed assessment," which was, according to Haynes, the result of "rampant mirror imaging, complicated by circular analysis." Like Riedel, Haynes concluded the strategic surprise of the Chinese assault in November 1950 was avoidable and that Willoughby was "the officer most responsible" for "one of the most glaring failures in U.S. military intelligence history." Willoughby provided MacArthur with an "inaccurate" intelligence picture, which contributed to MacArthur's flawed understanding of Chinese intent.[42]

While much of the criticism Willoughby faced was due to his myopia concerning the Chinese invasion in November, it is worth noting he also had a basic responsibility to assess the likelihood of a North Korean invasion of the South prior to June 1950. In that regard, Willoughby filed 1,195 reports, from June 1949 through June 1950, reporting that Chinese Communist troops of Korean descent had been entering North Korea in great numbers since the defeat of Nationalist Chinese leader Chiang Kai-Shek and there was a massive troop buildup underway in North Korea. As early as March 1950, Willoughby agreed with the CIA that war on the peninsula was likely by late spring/early summer.[43] A 1995 monograph on the ill-fated Task Force Smith assessed there was "adequate intelligence" available in June 1950 which indicated the likelihood of war on the Korean Peninsula and that the general failure to realize that strong possibility was due to "an untried intelligence system." In elaborating on that point, this historian commented, "Intelligence is of no value unless it gets into the hands of the commander. It must be pushed down to the decision maker, and if it is not, *the commander must become actively involved in the intelligence process and focus the intelligence effort*" (emphasis added). In light of the platitudes MacArthur continued to provide in response to the "nervous Nellies" who warned of the North's invasion of the South, the point made by author Richard Matthews is telling.[44]

Sharing this assessment is General Raymond C. Davis, USMC (Ret.), who earned the Medal of Honor in the fighting around the Chosin Reservoir. General Davis observed that, twice in 1950, the United States faced military catastrophe, which he assessed was due in both cases—the invasion of South Korea by North Korea and the invasion of Korea by China—to "errors of diplomacy and faulty intelligence" and concluded the American military was not prepared to deal with the enemy they had to face at the time. Major Charles Azotea assessed in his 2014 USACGSC monograph "Operational Intelligence Failures of the Korean War" that both the Air Force's Office of Special Investigation and Willoughby's Korean Liaison Office (KLO) had failed to "produce intelligence assessments of a looming North Korean invasion." He also noted Willoughby's staff shared a common belief in the flawed information provided by two key groups of informants, South Korean and Nationalist Chinese intelligence assets, whose products were described as "highly politicized, childish, and ultimately, prone to creating false alarms." Most Willoughby staffers would have agreed with the comment made by his executive officer, Colonel James H. Polk, who noted, "... no one trusted what they [Chinese Nationalists] produced because it was invariably biased or self-serving." Historian Eliot Cohen has noted the dual nature of Chinese Nationalist reporting; on the one hand, they provided "the best warnings of Chinese Communist intentions" and yet were considered suspect by Washington and FECOM analysts because the Nationalists had "interested motives" in convincing Americans of the Communist Chinese threat and because some of the information they provided seemed to be circular reporting.[45]

As a fellow Army officer, Azotea charged Willoughby with neglecting the most basic duty of an intelligence officer: "Willoughby's continued support of MacArthur's personal agenda, instead of performing his duties as his senior intelligence officer, only enabled MacArthur. Willoughby's reports assessed the possibility of the Chinese intervening, yet never addressed the probability or advised caution ... Willoughby failed to determine enemy capabilities and intentions, not just capabilities." In the conclusion of his 2014 monograph on Willoughby's flawed performance as an intelligence officer in Korea, Azotea wrote, "Willoughby's lack of appreciation of Chinese intentions and capabilities, combined with his unquestioning loyalty to MacArthur blinded him to possible alternatives. MacArthur's and Willoughby's long-standing relationship, as well as their personal and professional trait[s] perpetuated terrible consequences for MacArthur's forces."[46]

Peter Knight, author of a 2004 Master's thesis on the intelligence aspects of the 1950 to 1951 period in Korea, concluded Willoughby "vacillated on his assessment of North Korean intentions" in the period between March and June 1950. He notes that, on May 25, 1950, just a month prior to the actual North Korean invasion, Willoughby assessed the possibility of such in late spring or early summer that year, but even as late as June 19 was unwilling to commit to the certainty of an invasion. He adds that, by the end of October 1950, "Willoughby's military intelligence battlefield operating system had reached the limits of its capabilities" and that, by November, his greatest intelligence assets were aerial reconnaissance and ground patrolling.[47]

Willoughby also placed an inordinate amount of faith in traditional means of intelligence collection and had little use for the intelligence collection and analysis techniques developed during World War II. Compounding this error was his selective myopia when it came to the level of confusion and corruption within the South Korean Government—as a result, his reports misled MacArthur and the Joint Chiefs of Staff. As one historian concluded, speaking of Willoughby, "out of touch with what was happening, he appeared to have an unlimited series of excuses to explain away events as they occurred."[48] Indeed, a U.S. Army Center of Military History monograph cited as "principal difficulties" in the Korean conflict "failure to report unfavorable information because of face saving and failure to realize the importance of passing on information to higher headquarters."[49]

In this context, Justin Haynes, who regards Willoughby "most responsible" for this "most glaring" of failures, believes Willoughby "correctly identified the potential threat" but "failed to acknowledge the significance of China's strategic warnings, operational preparations for war and tactical confirmation of intentions."[50] He reminds us of the most critical duty for an intelligence officer: "*It is the intelligence professional's duty to analyze the information available to him and provide commanders with intelligence products that enable them to make sound decisions in combat*" (emphasis added).[51]

The late historian David Halberstam, author of *The Coldest Winter: America and the Korean War,* wrote a rich paragraph in that book which fully and accurately describes the job of an intelligence officer:

> The importance and value of a good, independent intelligence man in wartime can hardly be overemphasized. *A great intelligence officer* studies the unknown and works in darkness, trying to see the shape of future events. He covers the sensitive ground where prejudice, or instinctive cultural bias, often meet reality, and he *must stand for reality, even if it means standing virtually alone* [emphasis added]. Great intelligence officers often have the melancholy job of telling their superiors things they don't want to hear. A great intelligence officer tries to make the unknown at least partially knowable; he tries to think like his enemy, and he listens carefully to those with whom he disagrees, simply because he knows that he has to challenge his own value system in order to understand the nature and impulse of the other side. In all ways, Charles Willoughby not only failed to fit this role, he was the very opposite of it.[52]

Halberstam even impugned Willoughby's very motives and charged him with altering the facts. Referring to the Chinese onslaught in late November 1950:

> Willoughby did all he could to minimize the overwhelming evidence that the Chinese had been the ones who struck the ROKs and the Eighth Cavalry near Unsan. A good many men who

fought there came to believe that his refusal to act quickly on the evidence presented by the first captured Chinese prisoners and his unwillingness to add a serious note of caution to his intelligence briefings were directly responsible for the devastation inflicted on not just the Cav at Unsan but upon the Eighth Army soon after, for the loss of so many buddies, and, in some case, for their own long tours in Chinese and Korean prisons. To them, what he represented came perilously close to evil, someone who blustered about the dangers of Communism and the Chinese, but then ended up making their work so much easier by setting the U.N. forces up for that great ambush.[53]

Decades after the fact, Korean War historian John Finnegan summed up the intelligence picture in November 1950: "… it was clear that divided and over-extended U.N. forces were conducting aggressive military operations while lacking adequate intelligence collection mechanisms, appropriate linguistic skills to deal with contingencies, accurate maps, or any situational awareness of what was going on outside the Korean peninsula." Using a Japanese phrase, the United States was clearly suffering from "victory disease," the military equivalent of counting one's chickens before they were hatched.[54]

An article in the *New York Herald Tribune,* written after the Chinese invasion, was pointedly titled, "Why We Got Licked." In this undated article, correspondent Homer Bigart admitted that "in those victory-flushed days of early October, no one really believed the Chinese would strike." However, he coldly observed, "… a fine American Army, powerfully supported by the Air Force and Navy, was defeated by an enemy that had no navy, virtually no air force and scarcely any armor or artillery … At first, it was hard to believe that these great swarms of foot soldiers could perform so effectively without mountains of supplies and elaborate command posts." He also cited MacArthur's assessment—oft-repeated by correspondents in the wake of the Chinese intervention—that the enemy moved "surreptitiously," which prompted Bigart to add, "as though this were an unclean and indecent way of playing the game." He continued, "Unsound deployment of the United Nations forces and a momentous blunder by General MacArthur helped insure [*sic*] the success of the enemy's strategy … MacArthur *grossly miscalculated* [emphasis added] the intentions, strength and capabilities of the forces against him." However, since MacArthur obviously was not personally responsible for collecting and evaluating intelligence on Chinese tactical, operational, and strategic intentions, Bigart's assessment represents an indictment of Willoughby as MacArthur's G-2. A report by Willoughby was intended as a rebuttal to the article but was blocked, apparently by President Truman and Secretary of the Army Marshall. As an observer noted, "Willoughby's pedantry and tendency to pose and engage in diatribe has been his hallmark, and remained so."[55] Similarly, a study of the Chinese invasion of Korea written by the Foreign Denial and Deception Committee noted that, by 1950, Willoughby had been MacArthur's G-2 for eight years and during that period "had perfected a gift for interpreting intelligence information in ways that made his boss look infallible."

In his memoirs, then Secretary of State Dean Acheson, referring to MacArthur's disobedient push to the Chinese border that impelled Chinese intervention, put it more colorfully when he quipped, "We sat around like paralyzed rabbits while MacArthur carried out this nightmare."[56]

Ironically, in 1950 Willoughby had been described as "one of the most experienced intelligence officers the U.S. Army had to offer." He had the most robust intelligence system in the Far East at the time, was the most senior intelligence officer in the theater, had made the right call at Inchon, and was the right-hand man of a victorious general. Yet, U.S. Ambassador to South Korea John Muccio firmly believed Willoughby prevented MacArthur from receiving the information he needed, so that, by November 1950, MacArthur was "no longer in touch with the situation." Nor was the ambassador pleased with Willoughby's "major distraction" at the time—researching and penning *MacArthur, 1941–1951*. As far as Muccio was concerned, work on the book shunted Willoughby aside from his primary duties as an intelligence officer; as he once noted, the MacArthur biography was "dearer to his heart than keeping in touch with what was going on in Korea."[57] Predictably, Willoughby spent a good portion of the preface of the book explaining how critical not only the volume was and how every military headquarters compiles a history, but also how intently he labored on the project. After reciting all the various "MacArthur histories" written under his aegis in post-war Tokyo, Willoughby boasted, "As editor-in-chief (in addition to my other duties), I directed all of these projects, personally editing the more important works." He also felt obliged to address the way in which this book was a "headquarters story": "We have dealt in this book with a lesser-known field: the consideration of 'high command,' the analysis of the political, strategic, and economic factors that influenced General MacArthur's major decisions in the Pacific, in Japan, and in Korea during the period 1941 to 1951." The ambassador also faulted Willoughby for the latter's outdated knowledge of the Chinese, as he told an interviewer in 1971: "General Willoughby had a disdain of the capability of the Chinese, of all classes, and his appraisal of Chinese capabilities was based on the little that he knew about China years prior to the advent of the Communists."[58]

Several observers have noted the largely deleterious effect the close relationship between MacArthur and Willoughby had upon the conduct of intelligence collection and analysis during the Korean War. As historian D. Clayton James assessed the situation:

> Mac was shielded by his GHQ savior staff officers in unfortunate ways; this was part of the legacy of their adulation of him from World War II … Sadly, his [MacArthur's] trust in Willoughby was so deep by then that Mac's intel data came almost solely from his G-2, and Willoughby could be quite selective and sometimes erroneous in what he provided his commander.

James has described Willoughby as an "unstable personality, both hot-tempered and brooding," adding he was the sole member of the "Bataan Gang" to stay with

MacArthur until the end (1951).[59] One observer has commented that, for MacArthur, "loyalty was more important than proficiency," but that MacArthur paid a high price for that loyalty, prompting the former to observe that "such heart-felt loyalty would appear more admirable had not men's lives and national security also been at hazard."[60]

Assessments of Willoughby's performance were often witheringly candid; in 1950, Special Assistant to the President W. Averell Harriman remarked, "General MacArthur's intelligence was entirely different, or else—as I always thought—there was confusion in his own intelligence." The career diplomat also noted MacArthur had never witnessed the Chinese in combat and was not impressed with their fighting capabilities; Ambassador Muccio added that such an assessment "came to a great degree from Willoughby." Reflecting a desire to lay the ultimate blame at the Far East Commander's feet rather than that of his G-2, Harriman added that "Willoughby's intelligence may have been wrong, but General MacArthur's knowledge of the Chinese was obsolete." Echoing Harriman's doubts about Willoughby's capabilities was General Lawton J. Collins, the U.S. Army Chief of Staff in 1950, who observed, "Yes, Willoughby, his G-2, was wishy-washy—back and forth as to whether he thought that the Chinese were going to come in or not come in. There's no question about it; he gave MacArthur, in my judgment, poor G-2 intelligence."[61]

Collins' remark is one of the many made by Willoughby's enemies and critics over the years, assessing his desire to please MacArthur "often jeopardized the quality of the intelligence that Willoughby provided to MacArthur," according to one source.[62] Franz-Stefan Gady, Associate Editor of *The Diplomat*, a Washington, D.C.-based journal focusing on Asia–Pacific topics, wrote an article published in January 2019 which asked perhaps the most penetrating question concerning Willoughby's service as G-2 during the Korean War: "Is This the Worst Intelligence Chief in the U.S. Army's History?" Although he provides no comparisons to justify his selection of Willoughby as the "worst" in the past two centuries, and is prone to sweeping generalizations, he does cite assessments by several veterans and knowledgeable sources who point the finger at Willoughby. Provocatively, he includes the assessment of X Corps, Eighth Army operations chief Lieutenant Colonel John Chiles that "Anything MacArthur wanted, Willoughby produced intelligence for … In this case, Willoughby falsified the intelligence reports … He should have gone to jail."[63] His fraternity brother, USMC General Robert Eichelberger, described Willoughby as "a skilled shaper of data to various ends, good or ill. If Mac was brilliant and complex, with marked strengths and marked flaws, Willoughby mirrored him in all that."[64] On another occasion, Eichelberger commented, "I was always impressed with the intelligence from GHQ … He [Willoughby] was always very positive in his views … and usually wrong."[65]

Author Roger Beaumont concluded, "Willoughby, more than any other of Mac's lieutenants, typified the chauvinism, insularity, and xenophobia that characterized Mac's commands in the Pacific and Korea."[66] The editors of a volume on the clandestine cold war in Asia between 1945 and 1965 assessed that "from a regional perspective, American intelligence performed poorly during the early stages of the Korean War because of deficient leadership by the theater intelligence chief, General Willoughby. His intelligence organization, if it can be called such, was fragmented, uncoordinated, and its few resources misdirected," a reference to an overemphasis on the Soviet Union and an underemphasis on China and North Korea.[67]

Similarly, Carleton Swift, the CIA officer who was assigned to the U.S. Embassy in Seoul at the time of the initial invasion, castigated Willoughby for his arrogance:

> It was as if he was always right, had always been right. Certitude after certitude poured out of him. It was as if there was an exclamation point after all of his sentences … Worse, you couldn't challenge him. Because he always made it clear that he spoke for MacArthur and if you challenged him you were challenging MacArthur … So that made it very hard for intelligence in the field to filter up to higher headquarters on something that he has made up his mind on.

Reiterating a point made by others, Gady reminded his readers that a number of U.S. Army veterans despised the aristocratic G-2—as Chosin Reservoir veteran William J. McCaffrey, commander of the 31st Infantry Regiment, confessed, "I was always afraid he would be found murdered one day, because if he was, I was sure that they would come and arrest me, because I hated him so much …"[68]

Willoughby could also be faulted for the discrimination he practiced with regard to his sources of information. While he highly valued at least some human intelligence, he used only sparingly information from the other "ints," most notably signals intelligence (SIGINT). While access to signals intelligence information was highly restricted during World War II and the Korean War, Willoughby had access to and the "need to know" such information, by virtue of his position and responsibilities, yet placed little stock in it. In an October 1998 article in the National Security Agency key publication *Cryptologic Quarterly*, Guy Vanderpool asserted, "No one who received COMINT [communications intelligence, which includes signals intelligence] product, including MacArthur's own G-2 in Tokyo [Willoughby] should have been surprised by the PRC intervention in the Korean War."[69]

Assessments of Willoughby have prompted some creative looks at the G-2, including one by scholar Roger Beaumont, who used a sports analogy to evaluate the intelligence officer. Looking at Willoughby's intelligence assessments in the Southwest Pacific, the Philippines, and in Korea, Beaumont guesstimated he would have no better than a .500 "batting average," prompting the question, "What is a reasonable 'batting average' in intelligence estimating?" His follow-up question is a more penetrating one: "How much do loyalty, deference and compatibility weigh in the balance against competency in the selection of intelligence principals?"[70]

While the assertion of Korean War author and professor Paul Edwards that Willoughby "continually denied that the Chinese were involved" is unfounded, he is closer to the mark when he writes:

> Willoughby, who liked to call Mac a classic warrior, was ideal for his job; in many respects, Mac was his own intel officer. The brutal fact is that neither he nor any other responsible officers anticipated the early attack. Nor, once it happened, were they able to understand properly the lull that occurred in late October and early November of 1950. It was a period of miscalculation.

With regard to the lull, political science professor and PLA veteran Bin Yu claims the PLA *purposely* withdrew in order to entice United Nations troops into a trap. As Yu explained the ruse, the PLA released some 100 prisoners of war, 27 of whom were Americans, who returned to their own lines and related that their Chinese captors claimed they had to return to China because they were running low on supplies. While a plausible explanation, Yu pointed out that this technique was borrowed from the Chinese Civil War: "Lure the enemy deep, concentrate your forces under cover, attack suddenly while the enemy is moving, dispatch them with great speed."[71] An Army officer and student of Willoughby's intelligence campaign in Korea wrote in 2014 that Willoughby "downplayed or denied any intelligence analysis deemed too provocative or in conflict with MacArthur's views." He was also critical of the G-2's staff for its failure to "accurately estimate, or attempt to understand, the intentions and capabilities of the Chinese."[72]

In assessing responsibility for the perceived intelligence failure, one historian believes the blame lies at the feet of both MacArthur and Willoughby, the latter because of his "near-exclusive control over the enemy information to which MacArthur had access." Nor did the nature of MacArthur's command environment help as it "rewarded sycophants and isolated those who challenged the conventional wisdom." Willoughby has been described as the most important influence on FECOM intelligence assessments, the man who provided the "supporting intelligence" for MacArthur's "operational vision." One writer concluded Willoughby "defended MacArthur on every possible occasion" and once commented that MacArthur was not "surprised" by the Chinese attack, though he admitted his commander was "unaware of the actual size of the force and its intentions."[73] Another student of Willoughby and MacArthur and the relationship between them has assessed, "Their individual personality characteristics magnified their flaws," ultimately resulting in the tactical defeat of UN forces by Chinese troops. Given Willoughby was one of MacArthur's most experienced intelligence officers, how could such a disaster happen? As another historian noted, Willoughby's background and history "inculcated in him a devout affinity and intense loyalty for strong, authoritarian leaders"—such as Franco, Mussolini, and MacArthur—resulting in "significant flaws" in intelligence analysis.[74]

A student of the Chinese preparations for entry into the war on the Korean Peninsula concluded, with regard to the intelligence missteps of October and

November 1950 that "It would be a perversion of historical fact to assign *sole* [emphasis added] responsibility for this gross miscalculation to MacArthur or to Willoughby." However, as the overall commander and the ranking intelligence officer within FECOM, respectively, the conclusion that the primary responsibility was ultimately still theirs seems inescapable. This author continues by opining the consensus opinion that the Chinese would not intervene was "an emotional rather than an intellectual conclusion, an ascription to the enemy of *intentions* compatible with the desires of Washington and Tokyo." The rosy assessments in early- to mid-October 1950 were "subjective to a damaging degree" and demonstrated the fact that "the art of divination is not one which chiefs of state, their high advisers, and their field commanders can profitably practice."[75]

At the most generous end of the "blame spectrum" for the American intelligence "failures" in Korea in 1950 is the author of a 2004 Master's thesis who believes that, while neither MacArthur nor Willoughby are blameless in this scenario, it is a "historical travesty" that both have borne the brunt of criticism. Arguing the pair deserve "a more objective appraisal," Peter Knight writes, "More often than not, the roots of intelligence failure are a combination of errors at all echelons …"; while there is a kernel of truth in this assessment, the statement is overly glib and dismissive in a political and military structure characterized by a clear chain of command and clearly responsible parties. Knight's relook was driven by his opinion that "too many historians have limited their inspection of intelligence operations in the Korean War to the strategic level without exploring theater, operational and tactical level intelligence efforts of both friendly and enemy forces in Korea." To this end, he called for both "top down" and "bottom up" looks at the intelligence situation at the time, though acknowledging the "simple fact that the commander and his chief of intelligence drive the intelligence effort."[76]

Following up on the theme of broader responsibility for the failure to foresee the Chinese intervention, other observers have extended the blame to those in MacArthur's wider circle. As one observed, "The members of MacArthur's 'court' must bear much responsibility for the extent of the errors made, particularly over the likelihood of China entering into the war." One in particular cites Willoughby, to be certain, but also fellow "Bataan boy" Courtney Whitney, noting that both viewed their primary function as "to protect the great commander from those who would waste his time or upset him." Another close observer of events, Ambassador Muccio delicately commented he thought MacArthur had reached the point where he was "no longer fully conversant with all significant aspects of the situation." In his 1971 oral history interview, Muccio also addressed the ravages of time as a contributing factor:

> I think MacArthur is one of the biggest brains I've ever come in contact with, but he had gotten to the age where he was no longer in touch with the situation. And I think that was very, very

evident in the developments in November and December, in northern Korea. There was a failure
of intelligence more than anything else for the mess that we got into.

He added that a touch of the dramatic did not help. "MacArthur was a very theatrical personality. I think that John and Lionel Barrymore were theatrical amateurs
compared to MacArthur."[77]

Other observers have pointed out Willoughby was prejudiced against sources he
did not control—and sometimes even against those he did control. For example,
he not only refused to believe the accumulating evidence of North Korean pre-war
actions from external sources, but also from those of the KLO, whose standup he
had directed and which he did control.[78] While a healthy sense of skepticism can
be refreshing and even necessary, the intentional ignoring of numerous, confirmed
order-of-battle pre-conflict indicators is another thing entirely and is tragic in a
senior officer specifically trained to recognize and report such to his commander.

Willoughby's failure to accurately and completely predict the Chinese invasion of
North Korea also was not the first time he had been found wanting as an intelligence
officer. For example, several observers have detected a pattern of flawed analysis.
As Stanley Sandler notes, some elements of the embryonic American intelligence
community at the time had warned of the North Korean invasion of June 1950
and were at a loss to explain how and why their estimates just six months later
were so flawed.[79] As one writer has pointed out, "estimation" may well be "the most
important function of a military intelligence officer."[80]

Other students of Willoughby's career have detected evidence of a deep-seated
racial bias; one observer noted he had a persistent belief the Chinese were inferior
when it came to waging warfare, perhaps due to his study of the first Sino–Japanese
War (1894–95) and its lopsided results, and described this bias as one of Willoughby's
"most glaring faults." Ironically, observing the tactics used by the numerically inferior
Japanese forces against the larger number of Chinese troops led to the unfortunate
conclusion in Willoughby's mind that bold forms of maneuver would more than
compensate for numerical inferiority on the battlefield. This faulty conclusion would
powerfully influence his thinking in Korea.[81] Ambassador Muccio made a similar
observation when he was asked years later by an interviewer why Willoughby's
information was so incorrect. Muccio responded, "I think he just had a disdain of
Chinese generally. This was a factor, also he was working very assiduously on the
history of MacArthur in the Far East, the Pacific campaigns which was dearer to his
heart than in keeping in touch with what was going on in Korea."[82]

Willoughby has often been blamed for misreading the tea leaves with regard to
the Chinese invasion of North Korea; however, in doing so he was simply mirroring
the conclusions of his self-absorbed boss.[83] As one historian has noted, the Chinese
intervention was "an avoidable disaster" that completely changed the nature of the
war in Korea, which occurred as a result of both MacArthur and Willoughby ignoring

the evidence. Worse, Willoughby's miscalculations—the result of "informational, institutional, and personality factors" that distorted his judgment, in the words of another historian—had a significant ripple effect upon the Joint Chiefs of Staff, the CIA, and President Truman.[84] Perhaps most tragically, his miscalculations contributed to a three-year extension of the Korean War, which cost the lives of an estimated 34,000 American soldiers, sailors, marines, and airmen.[85] This charge that his incompetence had basically led to additional American casualties during the Korean War also stung Willoughby, who addressed such indictments in a January 1951 letter to media mogul William Randolph Hearst:

> As a historical comparison, our losses at Anzio [European Theater of Operations, World War II], Italy, an abortive, nonproductive operation were bigger, in a period of 4½ months than our aggregate losses in Korea, since the beginning of the war. Anzio was like Inchon—except that we broke up the North Korean Army and took 130,000 prisoners. But that is already forgotten under the impact of the Chinese coming in... *sic transit gloria mundi* [thus passes the glory of the world].[86]

Furthermore, the MacArthur magic crossed the many miles from Korea to Washington just as successfully—Secretary of the Army Frank Pace commented, "I do not believe at that time anyone seriously believed that the Red Chinese were going to enter the war." As some onlookers have noted, that comment accurately reflected the ability of MacArthur—and actually that of Willoughby—to powerfully shape opinion.[87]

Another historian recently noted MacArthur and his closest advisors "increasingly ignored opinions contrary to their own" and concluded "Willoughby and MacArthur ignored Mao's looming counteroffensive."[88] One of the most critical functions of an intelligence chief is that he consider and present to the commander all potential enemy courses of action in a given situation and then prioritize these possibilities from most likely to least likely, based upon a deep knowledge of the enemy and his particular characteristics. It was this critical function that Willoughby seemingly was either unable, or unwilling, to do.

In assessing the American response to the Chinese invasion, one historian penned these words: "It is difficult to see the American response to the situation as anything other than *a mishandling of intelligence* [emphasis added]. There had been several warnings ... In the field, the evidence of Chinese involvement was strong." As this author went on to observe, part of the problem was another aspect of the clash between Eastern and Western cultures on the field of battle; simply put, it was incomprehensible to American military officials that the average Chinese soldier knew more about the offensive than did their average American counterpart. Thus, when Chinese troops were captured, they freely identified themselves, their unit, and thoughtfully volunteered how and when their unit had arrived on the battlefield. As the author noted, "What was difficult to accept, apparently, was not that the

Chinese troops were gathering along the Yalu but that a Chinese private would have valid info concerning the proposed attack."[89]

Most observers of the intelligence report card in Korea have concluded the reportedly poor showing was not due to inadequate or incompetent analytical work. In 2001, a U.S. Army historian wrote, "The Intel failure of 1950 was not primarily due to poor assessments. It resulted from a combination of deficiencies: the exceedingly modest capabilities of a fledgling CIA; the general drawdown of military forces and their intel and recon assets before the war; and Mac's own overconfidence in the capabilities of his forces."[90] A CIA study of Agency reporting on the likelihood of Chinese intervention concluded "it seems clear from the public record that CIA, the several IAC [Intelligence Advisory Committee] agencies, and MacArthur's command were all in essential agreement … that intervention would not come."[91]

In his own defense, Willoughby—in the pages of *MacArthur, 1941–1951*— responded to criticism surrounding MacArthur's dismissal of the Chinese threat at the Wake Island Conference by explaining that at issue was a confusion of Chinese *capabilities* with Chinese *intentions*. However, such parsing of words given the gravity of the situation failed to exonerate Willoughby in the eyes of most observers; one historian says plainly that, in this instance in particular, Willoughby shirked his innate responsibility to "provide his commander with a prediction of potential enemy courses of action."[92] Furthermore, Willoughby so swayed his boss with his analysis that MacArthur repeated it to Truman, ironically just a few days prior to the Chinese invasion. As the journalist Alsop brothers put it in a December 1950 article, "The sudden appearance of Chinese troops in combat in October very evidently took our divisions in Korea wholly by surprise." They also concluded that "over 200,000 Chinese troops were somehow lost in the shuffle" and lamented that it was "a dreadful thing that General MacArthur thus walked into a huge, well-laid trap."[93]

In the wake of the Chinese intervention, and the relentless media criticism that followed, Willoughby responded in a newspaper article, which included his observation that "one can hardly blame the United Nations field command for the Chinese coming en masse at their own time and place. That monumental decision was beyond the local military intelligence surveillance; it lay behind the Iron Curtain and the secret councils of Peiping." MacArthur wanted to reply in kind to the barbs directed at his loyal G-2 but was prohibited from doing so by the Department of the Army, an indication of MacArthur's confidence in Willoughby. A key staffer also explained his assessment of the slings and arrows Willoughby has suffered historically. Philip B. Davidson, since 1948 and for the duration of the war the head of the Plans and Estimates section of the FECOM G-2, prepared the all-source daily intelligence estimates, the key vehicle used by Willoughby to disseminate intelligence analysis. Davidson briefed MacArthur every night at 6:00 pm to inform him of enemy activity and movements over the preceding 24 hours. As he recalled in a 1995 interview,

"He [MacArthur] wasn't interested particularly in our interpretation of intelligence, although he was quite willing to read it. Once you gave him the facts of the enemy situation, MacArthur was his own intelligence officer."[94] Despite that comment, Davidson believes Willoughby has been harshly judged by historians based solely on the *Daily Intelligence Summaries*, which Davidson characterized as "routine reports put out by junior officers to which Willoughby paid scant attention." Davidson claims Willoughby's "true voice" was embodied in the former's estimates, but because they "remain classified and thus unobtainable, historians have consistently garbled Willoughby's intelligence products and forecasts."[95]

In July 1950, Willoughby selected Davidson to head a new Special Intelligence Section (SIS), created to provide more usable SIGINT information to both Willoughby and MacArthur. Willoughby commented that the isolated COMINT indicators of enemy action were of little value and both he and MacArthur were dissatisfied with the quantity and quality of COMINT support in the first few months of the war. Joining them in their complaint was Eighth Army commander General Walton Walker, Jr. and his commanders—part of the explanation was the fact that U.S. Army regulations forbade the release of COMINT information to field commanders below Army level, meaning that Eighth Army corps and division commanders received no COMINT information during the critical first six months of the Korean conflict. Although Willoughby was one of the select few who had regular access to COMINT prior to the North Korean invasion—others included MacArthur's Chief of Staff Lieutenant General Almond, Deputy Chief of Staff Major General Doyle Hickey, and a few select G-2 staff officers—Willoughby nevertheless described the process of focusing COMINT collection and analysis as "extraordinarily complicated," leading him to stand up the SIS, with Davidson at the helm. The manpower consisted of the SIGINT analysts Willoughby had demanded from Army Security Agency Pacific. The SIS collated, analyzed, and disseminated all incoming COMINT traffic from other theater-level assets and from Armed Forces Security Agency finished intelligence reports.[96] One group of authorities has suggested that, given personnel and equipment shortages, dissemination restrictions, embryonic organizations, and a dearth of linguists, it is little wonder COMINT in general proved unable to provide pre-invasion warning information (in either June or November 1950), though the intelligence genre had proven its merits in the Pusan Perimeter breakout and during the Inchon amphibious assault.[97]

A student of Willoughby has caustically summarized his performance in Korea in these words: "Charles Willoughby's unique background as a German–American, combined with his extensive interaction and support for fascist leaders and virulent anti-Communist views had an incredible influence upon his performance as MacArthur's senior intelligence officer." The combination of these factors, continues this historian, with Willoughby's "unwavering support" for MacArthur and his Korea plans "directly led to the near destruction of the United Nations Command."[98]

A recent student of Willoughby's performance has concluded that, although he did recognize at least a potential Chinese threat, his assessment was ultimately undone by a host of factors: "rampant mirror imaging, circular analysis, and personal anti-Chinese bias."[99] This historian notes that even once Chinese forces clearly had been committed to the field of battle, Willoughby minimized their significance so as not to interfere with MacArthur's loudly trumpeted offensive to end the war. But this observer also reiterates a conclusion noted earlier that there was plenty of blame to go around—both MacArthur and Washington, D.C., were convinced the war was nearly over and that the numerous troops tied down on the Korean Peninsula were needed "more" in Europe. Other historians have pointed to the blurred lines of responsibility between Washington and the military hierarchy for the tragic results: "Because Washington permitted soldiers to make and act on decisions that were beyond the purview of the military ... the United States, intoxicated with the heady taste of triumph, was heading for disaster."[100] Also, MacArthur continued to trust more in technology than history, believing American airpower could ably defeat whatever Chinese forces appeared, in whatever numbers. This authority further charges that President Truman and the Eurocentric Joint Chiefs of Staff failed in their responsibility to provide guidance to a theater commander and in their reluctance to challenge MacArthur's offensive strategy; a similarly-minded author holds both the Joint Chiefs and political leaders in Washington responsible for not changing MacArthur's orders prior to the November 25 offensive, unwilling to challenge the Civil War precedent of considering the theater commander's prerogative as inviolate. Finally, neither Truman, as commander in chief, nor any of his senior policy advisors ever provided "clear objectives for the political end state for the war."[101]

Although the G-2 had both success and failure as an intelligence officer, the latter was in a most critical area—namely, in the estimation of enemy capabilities and intentions, arguably the most important responsibility of an intelligence officer to his commander.[102] "What is especially difficult to understand," wrote another historian, "is Willoughby's lack of intel data about the Chinese involvement—and his inability, even after they were involved, to get General MacArthur to take any action reflecting that knowledge." In this writer's estimation, as the consummate staff officer, Willoughby was "certainly prone to protect Mac, *even from knowledge that he should have had*" (emphasis added). Adding to Willoughby's ability to protect his chief was the clear impression he was not a man to be trifled with; "a powerful man, able to influence the intel picture," writes one authority, who also added the noteworthy postscript, "*A challenge to General Willoughby was the same as a challenge to MacArthur*" (emphasis added). However, the fact Willoughby consistently chose not to share disturbing news with MacArthur always caused his lenses to go rose-colored. As one writer put it, because MacArthur "did not want the Chinese to enter the war, Willoughby made it his job to convince everyone the Chinese were not involved.

His wishful thinking was the source of faulty reasoning ... Even in hindsight it is difficult to understand the intel chief and his 'strangely unfounded views.'"[103]

A MacArthur biographer noted, with regard to Chinese intervention, that:

> Willoughby's error lay in failing to anticipate the strength and direction of this blow. The Central Intelligence Agency made the same mistake. The CIA reported to Truman that there were "as many as 200,000 Chinese troops" in MacArthur's path, but as late as November 24 the agency assured the President that "there is no evidence that the Chinese Communists plan major offensive operations in Korea."[104]

Somewhat fittingly in light of his post-war activities, Willoughby has been charged by some with possibly engineering war between the People's Republic of China and the United Nations forces in Korea. Historian David Halberstam concluded that "Willoughby may have deliberately supported a MacArthur agenda to bring China into the Korean War." He supports his theory by pointing to SIGINT intercepts from the Spanish and Portuguese missions in Tokyo indicating MacArthur consciously planned to expand the Korean War, in order to draw in the Chinese, a fascinating but unproven assertion.[105] One writer has questioned whether or not Willoughby actually falsified intelligence reports in order to support his boss and to sway others; however, there is no evidence to support that incendiary charge either, with that writer postulating that perhaps Willoughby was just "too narrow-minded and incompetent to maintain a reliable intelligence network." Dithering between the two equally distasteful alternatives, this writer concluded about Willoughby, "Whichever was the case, he did not provide the supreme commander what he needed to fight the war and thus failed to do the job for which he had been selected."[106]

In his life, Willoughby had many detractors, but few supporters—save MacArthur and a handful of others. Frank Wisner, CIA Directorate of Plans Chief, characterized Willoughby as a man who was "all ideology and almost never any facts." Historian David Halberstam observed, "In no other American headquarters could Willoughby have reached so important a post, and the higher he rose, the more Prussian he became."[107] Director of the State Department's Policy Planning Staff Paul Nitze described Willoughby as "... a peculiar kind of Prussian, romantic, intelligence operator ... I just never had any confidence in his soundness." Yet some were impressed by his obvious native intelligence; Peter Knight writes that "Willoughby's keen intellect was a well-established fact" and assesses that "undoubt-edly Willoughby possessed the intellect and persuasive skills required of a theater level chief of military intelligence."[108] Most, however, freely admitted he was difficult to work with. X Corps Commander Major General Almond characterized Willoughby as "not receptive to alternative analysis or ideas."[109] And yet, no less a figure than Matthew Ridgway assessed him as a "very fine Chief of Intelligence" and described the intelligence he acquired as accurate, just rendered useless and even harmful due to flawed evaluation.[110] Despite some highly public and vocal arguments between the two men, Colonel Sidney Mashbir, Willoughby's chief linguist during World War II, once described his boss as MacArthur's "brilliant" G-2.[111]

Similarly, a pair of historians who wrote a biography of MacArthur in 1952 assessed that "Major General Willoughby was, for all his eccentricities, a good intelligence officer ... On the whole, Willoughby has made no grave intelligence mistakes and his work has been sound and thorough." They felt compelled to add, however, that "His personality works against him in many cases; his urbanity can change quickly to vindictive harshness. Many officers refuse to take him seriously and call him a 'librarian.'"[112]

Some observers have referred to "clear warnings" provided by the Chinese at the strategic, operational, and tactical levels alike well in advance of their ultimate decision to intervene. These observers refer to "multiple indicators" of Chinese intervention as early as November 7, more than two weeks prior to the assault, and conclude Willoughby "repeatedly missed opportunities to predict Chinese intervention" by ignoring the information routed to him by strategic, operational, and tactical sources, resulting in the mauling of the Eighth Army and X Corps and extending the war for another three years.[113] Proponents of the idea that early warnings abounded point to Chinese strategic-level diplomatic warnings (such as the message delivered by Dr. Pannikar), operational warnings (massive troop concentrations north of the Yalu River in Manchuria), and tactical warnings (the capture of Chinese soldiers by American and ROK troops in late October/early November). Willoughby was, of course, aware of all of this information but, according to some critics, did not fuse it all into a coherent threat assessment to alert MacArthur.[114]

Among Willoughby's supporters, or at least those who believed he was stuck playing the time-honored role of scapegoat, were a number who believed attacks on Willoughby were actually thinly disguised attacks on MacArthur himself. Scripps-Howard staff writer Jim Lucas expressed his opinion in a December 1950 article in which he characterized accusations of a breakdown in MacArthur's intelligence operations as "exaggerated." As Lucas wrote,

> Pillorying Gen. Willoughby is a popular past[time]. It involves almost no risk for the critics. To defend himself, Gen. Willoughby would be forced to reveal secret information. He has no political backing. Hence, the attack on him ... satisfied the homefront demand for a scapegoat. If someone's throat is to be cut, Gen. Willoughby's is the most exposed.[115]

Also subscribing to the "scapegoat" designation attached to Willoughby is Peter Knight, who throughout his 2004 thesis reiterated his conclusion that Willoughby got a raw deal in historiographic terms. Referring to historian Clay Blair's assertion—based on comments from X Corps G-3 John Chiles—that Willoughby falsified intelligence records and gave MacArthur doctored intel to suit his commander's wishes, Knight refers to such an assessment as just one of the "slanderous accusations of historians regarding Willoughby's professional integrity." To conclude, as other observers have done, that everyone was afraid to challenge Willoughby's and MacArthur's interpretations of intelligence reporting is "a drastic oversimplification," says Knight, who adds that it is "drastically unfair" to label Willoughby a "sycophantic moron," as William Stueck, Bruce Cummings, and other revisionist Cold War historians have done.[116]

Warming to his subject, Knight broadened his assessment of Willoughby's talents as an intelligence officer to the latter's entire tenure with MacArthur:

> In his ten years as MacArthur's G-2, Major General Charles Willoughby, much like the intelligence operations he managed in the Korean War, improved with time and experience. Perhaps his only real flaw, which was apparently shared with the rest of the intelligence community, was an over reliance on COMINT as a pre-eminent source of information that carried over from the campaigns of World War II.[117]

As noted, the occasions during World War II when Willoughby's assessments of the Japanese were inaccurate belie this point, as does his and MacArthur's preference for prisoner-of-war interrogations as a source of accurate intelligence, and spreading the blame around does nothing to exonerate Willoughby from blame. Knight also returns to his major argument that Willoughby was a man ahead of his time in establishing and operating a modern intelligence apparatus and earned the condemnation of those too ignorant to understand his status as a visionary. Speaking of the competition for running the intelligence show in the Far East before, during, and after the Korean War, Knight says "that competition ... vastly complicated efforts to perform the military intelligence mission. Willoughby, despite any personal and analytical faults, emerged as a champion of centralizing the intelligence efforts in the Far East under MacArthur's purview. He tenaciously and, at times, successfully fought the resistance he encountered to his great credit." Similar statements also suggest Knight expects the passage of time to alter the, in his view, skewed picture of Willoughby's competence as an intelligence officer. He writes, "That the Truman administration allowed the American press to blame Willoughby for poor intelligence was a travesty considering the CIA and State Department's concurrence with Willoughby's assessments." That oversimplification is even more egregious when paired with his declarative statement that, once the CIA and State Department records from 1950 are declassified, "we will likely see those two agencies as the larger culprits in the failure to provide early warning of both the North Korean and Chinese Communist attacks."[118] Since those words were penned 15 years ago, most of those records have been declassified, leading to no such rehabilitation of Willoughby's damaged reputation as an intelligence officer.

Other observers have pointed out Korea was not an *intelligence* failure but rather a *policymaker* failure, an assertion which, if accepted, could be interpreted as a partial exoneration of Willoughby and MacArthur. One proponent of this concept notes that, as early as March 1950, the CIA presciently postulated that an attack in Korea could occur in June and that, in the wake of that assessment, no less than

1,200 reports followed, which indicated a massive North Korean military buildup. Although American military commanders tended to believe that "geostrategic considerations" would prevent a North Korean attack, they were wrong, both in June and in November, with regard to the Chinese intervention. Another supporter of this idea, George Poteat, has argued Chinese involvement in the war equated to the failure of policymakers to attend to critical intelligence because of policy commitments. As he notes, even if intelligence provides warning signals, it is still policymakers who must act. Even as often as MacArthur acted like a head of state, in fact, he was not and his decisions, and those of Willoughby, were, at least theoretically, ultimately determined outside FECOM.[119]

Another writer who has considered responsibility for the failure to accurately and completely assess Chinese intentions with regard to the unfolding war in Korea has written this evaluation:

> Prior to MacArthur's final offensive in November 1950, he received *sufficient significant and credible intelligence to indicate a Chinese Communist intent to intervene in the war*. MacArthur knew of *key national intelligence indicators of Chinese national resolve*. He had *accurate information* about the relocation of large numbers of Chinese Communist combat forces in Manchuria and into North Korea. MacArthur also had the *battlefield intelligence that clearly indicated Chinese involvement* prior to their 25 November counteroffensive. *The Chinese Communist intent was clear* [emphasis added].

This author concludes by assessing that "General MacArthur is culpable for his failure or refusal to accept valid Chinese Communist warnings," a judgment that could be laid solely at the feet of MacArthur were it not for the assigned role of Willoughby as his chief intelligence officer, a position he had held for nearly a decade by the time of the Chinese invasion.[120] The two historians who wrote a biography of MacArthur shortly after his removal tend to agree: "As to Korea, he [Willoughby] did gather and present to MacArthur correct information on the presence of Red Chinese 'volunteers' before the Communists' full-scale intervention. What MacArthur did on the basis of that information is his responsibility, and not Willoughby's … the intelligence failures in this case are not attributable to Willoughby."[121]

Historian Max Hastings, in his 2016 book, *The Secret War: Spies, Ciphers, and Guerrillas 1939–1945*, sums up his thoughts on the subject of intelligence in war in these thought-provoking words: "The indispensable element in making all intelligence useful, in peace or war, is that it should pass into the hands of a wise and effective leader; if such a person is absent, whether general, admiral, or statesman, then even the most privileged information is worthless."[122] For the purposes of this book, the question then becomes, "Were either MacArthur or Willoughby the "wise and effective leader" necessary to make the most of the intelligence take during the Korean War? The evidence suggests both were lacking in this respect.

Perhaps what ultimately counted most for Willoughby, however, was the constant praise heaped on him by his superior, a pattern repeated many times during their more than a decade together. As early as the withdrawal from Corregidor, MacArthur was quick to recognize the accomplishments of his subordinates, including Willoughby. In November 1941, he commented, "My staff was unsurpassed in excellence, and comprised such outstanding figures as ... Willoughby in Intelligence ... No commander was better served."[123] Not only was Willoughby never reprimanded, or worse, for his failings as an intelligence officer, in honor of his accomplishments, he was inducted into the U.S. Army's Intelligence Corps as a recognized hero in the Intelligence Corps pantheon.[124]

CHAPTER NINE

Post-War Paranoia

"The mortal peril of the West today is traceable to Franklin D. Roosevelt, a dynastic
dreamer who had both the talent and the villainy of all the Caesars of history."
—"TWINING AND DE GAULLE: 1959" ARTICLE BY WILLOUGHBY, *AMERICAN MERCURY*,
MARCH 1960

During the post-war years, and for the rest of his life, Willoughby was able to
nurture and further develop his penchant for neo-conservative/fascist historical
figures, concomitant with an equal passion for identifying and vilifying "leftists,"
of whatever stripe. This mindset was aided immensely by what one student of
Willoughby has described as his "conspiratorial mind which intertwined with this
fanatical anti-communism."[1] In this regard, he got an early start; in 1946–47, as
Supreme Commander Allied Powers (SCAP) Intelligence Chief, Willoughby began
writing a report entitled, "The Leftist Infiltration of SCAP," which sought to identify
those he assessed could be a threat to himself, MacArthur, and the Allied occupation
of Japan. By 1949–50, he had larger fish to fry, and Japanese authorities had taken
up the gauntlet, purging the Japanese Communist Party and other leftists, and
rebuilding the reputations of those who earlier in the occupation had been vilified
as "ultranationalists" and "warmongers" but now venerated as anti-Communists.[2]

It took no convincing whatsoever of Willoughby to prove there was an extensive
witch hunt focused on MacArthur—and himself—in the post-war years. He was a
firm believer in the dictum that "movers and shakers" inevitably make enemies and
the post-war period confirmed his long-held paranoia in this regard. In December
1950, Willoughby shared his historical *Weltanschauung* (world view) and his phobias
with the Honorable Walter H. Judd, U.S. House of Representatives. In a letter to
the congressman, he wrote:

> The "smear" campaign against MacArthur (and myself) is linked with the hatred of Communism
> against the General. They have long wished to destroy him ... We were sent to Korea to fight,
> not to stack Arms [*sic*] waiting for the Chinese Communists, or walk into their troops or
> surrender to them. That was the reason why we went into action on November 24th ... We
> are fighting and now, for the first time, the Nation knows the full extent of the Communist
> Red Menace and will have to face it.[3]

Willoughby expressed a similar sentiment to others as well at the time, notably including like-minded Senator Joseph McCarthy (R-WI). Willoughby had already discovered in McCarthy a kindred spirit; in August 1950, he lauded the efforts of the senator: "You are to be complimented on your unabashed crusade against the Communist elements in our midst." In a letter to McCarthy dated January 28, 1951, Willoughby wrote:

> There is no doubt that the persistent attacks on MacArthur are Communist inspired. I happen to be in the line-of-sight of the sniping. However, I am also a marked man, in the sense that my anti-Communist stance has become well-known. It started with my reporting on Dr. Sorge and Agnes Smedley. This is a case of international espionage and subversion, with the overthrow of Chiang Kai-Shek as its objective.[4]

A former colleague expressed his appreciation to Willoughby for defending both himself and "the General"; Ned Almond, now a lieutenant general and Commandant, Army War College—wrote in a letter, "I am glad to know that you are contributing worthwhile factual information so that all who write and comment, mostly from a biased or ignorant viewpoint, may get the correct slant on many things now obscure, if they take the pains to do so, in the interest of truth and justice." Almond specifically thanked Willoughby for "taking on both your detractors and those of General MacArthur and I sincerely hope that it will be of some value to counteract the distorted impressions which these 'writers for profit' have created."[5]

Despite criticism, Willoughby remained dedicated to the Sorge project and sought to share his "lessons learned" with a new-found correspondent, fellow intelligence professional and CIA Deputy Director Allen Dulles. On January 22, 1951, Dulles had written to Willoughby to thank him for his courtesies during the former's hurried trip to Tokyo. He wrote:

> We had a very pleasant trip back, enlivened by the reading of the fascinating "Sorge Story." It seems to me we ought to find some way of getting broader publicity for this story, and if the occasion to do this is presented, I shall certainly get in touch with you ... Please let me hear from you from time to time and let me know if there are any matters which arise in your relationship with any of our people where you feel I can be of any assistance. *We are working for the same objectives* [emphasis added].[6]

In a letter to Willoughby a few months later, on the eve of MacArthur's dismissal by President Truman, Dulles gushed, "I wish to assure you how much the Director and I appreciate the cordial and effective cooperation we have been receiving from you and which I feel has been advancing our mutual interests."[7]

Willoughby also entrusted Dulles with material to address a sensitive subject—his disputed heritage. Though Willoughby told the same story throughout his life about his family background, he seemed to realize there might be questions, even controversies, that might arise in the coming years. To hopefully address such concerns, he wrote a letter, entitled "Biographical Data C. A. Willoughby," to Dulles in February 1951. In that letter he presciently noted that:

Since I may need a friend in court, and you will undoubtedly have run across all kinds of conflicting stories about me, I take the liberty of filing with you some biographical data of which there are many garbled versions, for your files in case the subject matter comes up and you will know exactly where I stand and all about me.[8]

In his testimony before the House Un-American Activities Committee in August 1951, Willoughby demonstrated his growing closeness with the CIA in the post-war period—as well as his selective memory. While discussing his obtaining and using the files of the Shanghai Municipal Police to attest to Sorge's Communist spying activities, he commented, "I was able to track down and obtain a substantial portion … of the Shanghai municipal police files,[9] with the assistance of British, French, and Chinese officials, and *the Central Intelligence Agency, with whom I had been on efficient and friendliest collaboration for a number of years*" (emphasis added).[10] In a September 1952 letter, Willoughby expressed to Dulles his "long-standing commitment to turn over to your instructional or training section several hundred copies of the 'Partial Documentation of the Sorge Espionage Case' which is more complete, juridically, than the popular, commercial version 'Shanghai Conspiracy.'"[11]

Colleagues of Willoughby also applauded his exposure of the spy ring. Fellow GHQ officer Lieutenant Colonel Bonner Fellers—who collaborated with Willoughby on the Sorge case and also on effective propaganda measures—expressed his thoughts in a June 26, 1950, letter to Willoughby: "The Willoughby technique, which in my mind approaches perfection, is evident in the way you are handling this very important and revealing Sorge case. You are making a distinct contribution." As an indication of their friendship, Fellers signed his letter, "With kind personal regards."[12]

***

On April 11, 1951, when MacArthur learned he had been relieved of command by President Truman, he turned to Willoughby and said, "You had better get out of here with me. Nobody will ever take you." In a statement subject to challenge, Peter Knight notes, "Mac was correct that no other commander would likely take Willoughby simply because he and Mac were both too much alike in their stubborn beliefs in intelligence centralization and in the correctness of their own assessments compared with those of everyone else."[13] While Willoughby took that advice from his long-time superior, he was intent on remaining loyal to the end. On April 17, Willoughby commented, in response to MacArthur's sudden retirement:

I have considered it a great privilege to have served with the General, and expect to join him to offer what modest services I can render … I leave a thoroughly integrated intelligence section with General Ridgway, whom I have known on friendliest terms for many years, whose talent and leadership is amply evident in the brilliant operations of the Eighth Army since his assumption of Command.

Overlooked in MacArthur's sudden departure was the emotional parting between Jean MacArthur and Willoughby, with whom he'd been every step of the way since

1941. Several months after MacArthur's forced retirement, and mimicking the actions of the man he had served faithfully—to a fault—for more than a decade, Major General Charles A. Willoughby returned to the United States of his own accord and retired from the U.S. Army, effective August of that year. In anticipation of such action, Willoughby wrote to the National Commander of the American Legion in May 1951, "In the meantime, the catastrophal [*sic*] exit of General MacArthur has taken place. I shall join him in 'exile,' whatever that is; with over forty years [*sic*] service, it seemed an appropriate gesture." His official retirement date was September 1, 1951, after which time he became increasingly caught up in the craze of the anti-Communist movements which stirred America in the 1950s.[14] He had served the Army for over four decades, at least one of which was unusually stressful, when he was no longer a young man.[15]

Predictably, Willoughby's somewhat abrupt departure from his employer of 40 years left him wistful. In an April 1951 letter he penned to U.S. Navy Captain John Ford—serving his military time as a director at Argosy Pictures—and speaking of MacArthur's dismissal, Willoughby wrote:

> This leaves me as the final remnant of the Bataan crowd, the "last of the Mohicans" and it gave me a chilled and lonesome feeling. I decided to execute that classical [*sic*] naval maneuver of getting the hell out of here. I have applied for retirement after forty years' service, the last thirteen of which were spent in the Pacific and on the staff of the General. I am too old of a dog to learn new tricks and sit on my haunches for a new master. Besides, I want some freedom to talk.[16]

Similarly, in a letter written a month later to Mr. Clark H. Getts, in New York, Willoughby further explained: "My own retirement from the service is for the expressed purpose of associating with the General in the future. Needless to say, I feel that I have most extensive material on the Far East and international communism which I feel would be of interest to the nation."[17]

By "associating with the General," Willoughby clearly meant corresponding with the general before writing any books or articles dealing with their time together, either in the Southwest Pacific or in Korea, and especially when it came to defending MacArthur from a bevy of hostile journalists and selectively informed members of the general public. For example, in April 1951, following MacArthur's sacking, Willoughby wrote an article that embodied his concerns. Entitled "Aid and Comfort to the Enemy: Trends of Korean Press Reports," he provided MacArthur with a copy, accompanied by a personal note:

> My dear General [Willoughby's standard address when writing MacArthur post-1951]: This is an advance copy of a semi-historical piece which I have been working on, as you know, for some time. I am sorry that I am late with it because it contains a lot of good material suitable for some of your speeches to come, and certain statistics that are self explanatory … We follow with delight the evidence of your popularity in the homecoming receptions, so far accorded you. It looks good from every angle … On the broader aspects of the betrayal of China in to the Hands of Communism, which is an interesting subject in itself, Courtney [Whitney] has a copy, in fact the only one of the Shanghai Police files and the Sorge case. It is worth reading.[18]

In a letter later that year, Willoughby reiterated MacArthur's domestic popularity:

> Needless to say, I have followed the triu,phal [sic] sweep of your return to the States, with joy and satisfaction. Congratulations. I tuned in on your Southern speeches. Your voice comes well over the air and is of a quality that will rival the famous "fire side chats" of the persuasive elder Roosevelt. From various cobtacs [sic], since my arrival in the California area, I feel that the Republic is behind you. I attended a Shrine luncheon, the other day; very heavy attendance; I made a few impromptu remarks; when I mention your name—prolonged applause.

Willoughby also made a point of informing MacArthur he had printed at personal expense ("since I do not trust the War Department at all") 1,000 copies each of "A Partial Documentation of the Sorge Espionage Case"; "Intelligence in War: Operations of McArthur's [sic] Intelligence Service 1941–1951"; and "Aid and Comfort to the Enemy."[19]

On May 3, 1951, the recently fired MacArthur appeared before a Senate hearing focused on the impact of the Chinese intervention, chaired by Senator Richard Russell. In the course of the hearing, Russell asked the now-retired five-star general, "Did your intelligence have any previous knowledge of … Chinese … crossing the boundaries in any considerable force prior to the attack and our reversals in North Korea last December?" MacArthur replied, "We had knowledge that the Chinese Communists had collected large forces along the Yalu River … The Red Chinese … were putting out, almost daily, statements that they were not intervening, that these were volunteers only." In his response, he also referred to Secretary of State Acheson's observation in September 1950 that he thought there was "little chance, and no logic, in Chinese intervention" and to the November 1950 assessment of the CIA that there was "little chance of any major intervention on the part of the Chinese forces."[20] Thus, as far as the theater commander was concerned, the Chinese intervention was a complete surprise.

However, in a June 1 press interview—after MacArthur's Congressional testimony—his G-2 specifically denied that the Chinese intervention in Korea had been a "monumental surprise." "That is not the case," asserted Willoughby, "Chinese troops were known to be along the Yalu River … Their build-up inside Korea was known, but not in detail." He added, significantly, that what *was* unknown was "whether or not the Chinese meant business—entry into the war on a large scale." As far as the G-2 was concerned, the "only way" to acquire such knowledge was via "reconnaissance in force," i.e., "take prisoners, capture maps and orders, and slice into the threatening Chinese mass and break it up."[21] Such a viewpoint clearly demonstrates Willoughby's marked lack of creativity and "Yankee ingenuity" regarding intelligence collection methods, forgivable in a layman, but inexcusable for a professional intelligence officer.

In a vivid demonstration of the length of the shadow cast by MacArthur and Willoughby, an historian familiar with the tortuous history of relations between the CIA and Far East Command (FECOM) assessed the impact of Willoughby:

188 • LOYALTY FIRST

"The active interference of the FEC[OM] G-2 under Willoughby and his successor stifled many Agency initiatives, and FEC[OM] antagonism toward outside civilian 'interlopers' remained strong even after Willoughby left with MacArthur." Congress was understandably concerned about the fractious Agency relationship with FECOM and, during MacArthur's May 1951 Senate hearing, Senator Wayne Morse (R-OR) asked MacArthur to comment on that relationship. The now septuagenarian denied any obstructionism on the part of FECOM, noting there should be "proper coordination" between MacArthur's intelligence personnel and the CIA. "The CIA out in my command," noted MacArthur, "has worked in complete unity and with my Chief of Intelligence, General Willoughby, G-2." He also commented, in reference to Director of Central Intelligence (DCI) Smith's trip to Japan in January 1951—widely believed to be a rebuke to MacArthur and Willoughby from President Truman, using the "good offices" of the DCI—was instead intended to "perfect and expand the CIA; it was not to iron out any friction, it was not because of any difficulties," certainly a different take on the situation. In a follow-up question from Senator Morse concerning internecine warfare, MacArthur responded, "Nothing that would not be normal and minor, nothing that ever reached me." Still not getting the answer he wanted, Morse pointedly asked if the CIA had ever been "denied access" to "whatever intelligence your [MacArthur's] system could supply." MacArthur replied, "That would be ridiculous."[22] In his recall of the visit, Smith remembered clearly conveying to MacArthur that the CIA and other national intelligence organizations would operate in Korea and throughout the Far East, period. He delivered the message to MacArthur and Willoughby that "their days of intelligence monopoly were over" and that MacArthur would be compelled to obey the same rules for intelligence operations in his area as any other commander. Chastened but unrepentant, MacArthur's continuing to treat FECOM as his private fiefdom would have much to do with his curtailed tenure.[23]

Predictably, Willoughby maintained a steady correspondence with MacArthur, especially during the rest of 1951, with many of the conversations revolving around Korea and the Sorge espionage case. In a late July letter, for example, Willoughby noted he was on the verge of obtaining his own radio outlet, in the form of a small contract with North American Newspaper Alliances (Bell Syndicate) for the writing of 20 to 35 compact articles on Korea and the Sorge case. Willoughby assured his former boss, "The Korean treatment will be exclusively in your behalf, or the Eighth Army behalf and the substance is contained in 'Aid and Comfort to the Enemy.'" He also reviewed with MacArthur his contacts with various publishers; "I have had bids," he wrote, "from several good publishers, Houghton-Mifflin, Dutton, Scribners, Doubleday Page. Apparently, I am better known than I though [sic], principally because of *Maneuver in War* and *The House of Bolivar*—which is old (1926) but evidently known. They are interested in (a) Sorge Espionage and (b) Intelligence."

He also shared his perpetual misgivings about the press, and their handling of the Sorge case with Military Aide to the President Major General Harry Vaughn in the summer of 1951. Referring to the subpoena he had received to appear before the House Un-American Activities Committee and the Senate Judiciary Sub-Committee on the Sorge Case and the Shanghai Police Files, Willoughby intoned, "The Press, as usual, has treated this matter in a wholly exaggerated manner. I am trying to tone them down, by making my own statements."[24] He also felt compelled to comment on a common characteristic of his letters during these years in particular, obvious to anyone who works in his archival materials, namely, numerous errors in his typewritten correspondence. He contritely wrote, "You must excuse my typin [*sic*] errors; I used to have two secretaries; now I type with four fingers and my correspondence [sic] has suffered." An additional personal note in this letter concerned his health: "The Medicoes have given me a 50% disability on spinal arthritis and related symptoms."[25] Actually, his orders of mid-August 1951 explained—in only the way coldly official departmental language can—that he was deemed "permanently unfit for duty by reason of physical disability of 40 percent incurred while entitled to receive basic pay is retired from active service 31 August 1951 with grade and retired pay of Major General."[26]

In his correspondence with MacArthur, Willoughby occasionally waxed maudlin in describing his own circumstances. He lamented:

> It is difficult to adjust to a new mode of life, on retirement [*sic*], when many of the facilities which the self-protective Army develops, are suddenly lacking. I have the benefit of staying temporarily with relatives in a very comfortable setting, nevertheless, I must plan to be on my own. I have found that living costs, since I was in the States, around 1939, have increased threefold. Naturally this is quite an impact on the shrinking retirement [*sic*] resources; savings and investments do not quite make up for it … I believe that I can yet be of service to you … I will certainly dispel any false public notions, *re* Korea.[27]

As this letter implies, Willoughby had a hard time finding an area of the country and climate that suited him upon his return to the United States, having spent the previous 15 years overseas. In June 1951 correspondence with fellow intelligence officer Major General Bolling, Willoughby discussed the physical symptoms he had suffered with spinal arthritis but also his tentative "living arrangements": "I find the East already difficult; the heat oppressive, though I am in the Country. I also find living complicated, especially as regards servants, etc. I may go toward California, in the end. Or perhaps Spain, where I have many friends."[28] In a September 1951 letter to Courtney Whitney, Willoughby expressed his dislike of New York City as well, complaining, "I do not like the place or its atmosphere anyway. I have already collided with some sharp practices, in what I consider a collection of crooks."[29] As noted, he had complained to Bedell Smith several months prior of his equal distaste for Washington, D.C., not only because of the physical climate but also the political one.

In August, Willoughby again wrote to MacArthur, explaining why his projected radio outlet and projected articles would not be happening after all. After further investigating the work done by Bell Syndicate and being disturbed by "an unmistakable trend of distortion," he had pulled out of the deal. He wrote:

> Since I will not lend myself to distortions of history, as known to me in an eyewitness capacity, or to innuendo derogatory of your position, I cancelled the contract (to a very substantial sum) and returned the down-payment check ... However, I have signed a contract with E. P. Dutton, who have a Centenary, next year, for two titles, one of "Soviet Espionage," the other on "Intelligence in War." This will keep me occupied for some time. My disillusionment about the East continues and after some preliminary work with the Publisher, I shall go away. I may return to Gettysburg, where I graduated 1914 and where I am well-established, or take a vacation cruise immediately after retirement, thru South America, where I am still known.
> With kind personal regards.
> Faithfully
>
> Charles Willoughby (signed original)[30]

Justifiably proud of his book contract, Willoughby wrote to Colonel Lawrence "Larry" Bunker that same month, telling him that "E. P. Dutton is launching the Sorge book with great seriousness. They consider it a public service, to unmask the ramifications of a Kremlin controlled conspiracy."[31]

In mid-September 1951, the retiree Willoughby again wrote MacArthur, telling him how much he had enjoyed his brief visit and added he had taken MacArthur's suggestion to retitle an article he had written to "The Truth About Korea" which he assured him "has a direct bearing on your *conflict* with Truman" (emphasis added). Aware neither he nor MacArthur had any love lost for President Harry Truman or his appointees, Willoughby wrote, "... the trend of these books and articles [that Willoughby was writing] are directly critical of the present administration 'leadership' by overwhelming evidence of material, and as such contribute toward the education of the reading electorate; they somehow accompany, in intervals, your own periodical appearances, as a reminder of things that must not be forgotten."[32]

By November 1951, the Sorge book was complete, and MacArthur had agreed to write a foreword to the volume. Willoughby turned his attentions to his next book, one on intelligence operations in Korea, which he said could be fashioned into "a deadly rebuttal to Truman." In a letter that month to MacArthur, he also openly shared some negative thoughts about his former subordinate Dr. Gordon Prange, chief of the Historical Division, G-2, FECOM, from 1949 to 1951. Prange had been granted a leave of absence from the University of Maryland to lend his talents to the recording and analysis of MacArthur's intelligence operations. Willoughby wrote:

> A propos of "history" desires, Dr. Prange resigned his position, left three months ago for Maryland and is reported on usually reliable source, to prepare a history of the South West Pacific Campaigns ... Prange's attitude has always worried me somewhat. He came in when the bulk of the work was done; the "collective effort" was made; all that remained was footnote edit, which I supervised personally for many months. Woody Wilson or Col. Ring and some

others could make equally valid claims to "participation," whatever that means, than Dr. Prange. I noted that he quit his job, after Orlando Ward was out there. I am now waiting to have him re-appear in the War Dept. set-up.[33]

His immediate post-retirement years also freed Willoughby up to take care of a personal matter—on November 15, 1951, he married the former Marie Antoinette Pratt (divorced from Thomas Pratt, in London) in a judge's chamber in Weehawken, New Jersey. He had been without steady female company since his first wife, Puerto Rican native Juana Manuela Rodriguez, had died in 1940. The lack of correspondence between Willoughby and either of his wives is a puzzling omission from his archives, whether intentional or accidental, yet another oddity of his personal life.[34]

***

Even after the retirement of both MacArthur and Willoughby, it was clear there was still education necessary in order for the military and civilian practitioners of intelligence—specifically, the Army and the CIA—to understand each other and work together cooperatively. As one Chief of Station in Korea put it, "When the military can be told to seize and hold, the case officer must tell his agent to probe [and be prepared] to withdraw." Yet, as time passed, the barriers slowly fell and the CIA and FECOM found themselves in a less combative relationship.[35]

During the 1950s, Willoughby maintained a steady and collegial correspondence with CIA seniors, not only with Dulles, who became DCI in February 1953, but also with clandestine operations chief Frank G. Wisner. In a letter to Willoughby dated August 30, 1951, Wisner lauded Willoughby for having "added a great deal of very important and valuable information to the store of public knowledge," a reference to Willoughby's testimony before Congress. Less than two weeks later, Dulles wrote Willoughby—then living in Bronxville, New York, following his retirement—thanking him for the personal copy of the Japanese edition of the Sorge case and the offer to make more copies available to the Agency. Dulles also added as a final sentence, "I trust we can get together in the not too distant future to discuss further your plans which we had a brief chance to talk over when you were here."[36] CIA correspondence dated September 28, 1951, noted the Deputy Director (Plans) had heard from Willoughby, in a letter to the DCI, that Willoughby was now ready to turn over to the Agency "any and all documentation, which he has, which has still some bearing on the situation in Japan and Korea, such as estimates, briefs, etc., as well as extra copies of the Sorge story." This CIA correspondence, sent to the Assistant Director for Special Operations and the Assistant Director for Collection and Dissemination, diplomatically requested a response as to which office should be "responsible for viewing this material to determine items of value to CIA as well as on what arrangements which should be made to pick up any material of value to CIA so that a reply may be dispatched to General Willoughby."[37]

And yet, when push came to shove, Willoughby never forgot that he wore a uniform, not a suit. In a letter to Major General A. C. Smith, Chief, Military History, Department of the Army, Willoughby wrote:

> I have made it a point to defend the capacity of Army intelligence to accomplish anything that OSS [Office of Strategic Services] or CIA could or did undertake; the record proves it—at least for [the] MacArthur theater. While I have maintained friendly relations with all CIA heads, from Hillenkoetter to Dulles, I have made a wager with my friend Bedell Smith, that I could do anything CIA ever did, at approximately 3 cents to the dollar.[38]

***

Willoughby spent much time in retirement engaged in correspondence and visits with acquaintances, but even while still in uniform he paid a visit to an old friend. He turned up in Spain, in January 1951, as the honored guest of Generalissimo Francisco Franco, no surprise to anyone who had spent any time at all in Willoughby's shadow. He had first met Franco in the early 1920s in Morocco, where the Spanish were fighting Berber guerrillas in the mountainous area of northern Morocco known as the Rif.[39] The appearance, however, as Elliott Thorpe noted, "created something of a stir in military circles." Journalist John Gunther remembered that, while he was gathering material for his book *The Riddle of MacArthur*, he was at a dinner with Willoughby one evening when the general suddenly proposed a toast to "the second greatest military commander in the world, Francisco Franco"— MacArthur of course being the greatest; Gunther's wife Jane refused to share such a toast. Willoughby told a Madrid audience that, in the lectures he delivered at the U.S. Army's Command and General Staff School, he had spoken in favor of Franco as early as 1936. Following an impassioned defense of the *Caudillo* at a Falangist luncheon in Madrid, Willoughby was toasted by Secretary General of the Falangist Party Fernandez Cuesta with the words, "I am happy to know a fellow Falangist and reactionary."[40]

By apparent coincidence, in early April 1951—the period of General MacArthur's forced retirement—an American military mission had arrived in Spain to broach with *El Caudillo* the subject of establishing air and naval bases in Spain. The American representatives were unaware of how their already challenging assignment would be complicated by the "assistance" provided by Willoughby, still in Spain as a guest of the generalissimo. Though Willoughby described his visit to Spain as "without official character," any confusion on that point was understandable, given his initial 1 hour, 45-minute visit with Franco, Willoughby's quarters at the Velasquez Hotel, and the hot-and-cold running Spanish Government limousines and other VIP trappings he enjoyed until he left Spain that July. In sharp contrast to Franco's belief that Spain had a lot to offer the United States—such as its anti-Communist stance, its Pyrenees Mountains as a natural, defensible boundary, and its 450,000-man army—the American military actually had only limited use for the Spanish strongman. The U.S. Navy was interested only in anchorages, not shore installations; the U.S. Air Force was not highly motivated to make Spain the cornerstone of its European footprint; and the U.S. Army was similarly disinclined to upgrade Spain's obsolescent military equipment while NATO allies languished in terms of military equipment. But Willoughby, a long-time admirer of the Spanish fascist, did all he could to encourage the misguided notions of Franco concerning the value of his nation to the United States. In sharp contrast to American negotiators, Franco also considered the $100 million that Congress had earmarked in August 1950 for Spain's economic development a mere token of his nation's value to the United States, a view enhanced by the efforts of Willoughby who, on one occasion, told his Spanish hosts, "You can count on the friendship of U.S. naval and air circles." And when asked at a press conference, "Do you think it is the military people of America who best understand Spain?", Willoughby replied, "Yes, especially the naval people who are very sensible."[41]

As Willoughby noted in a letter to Dulles:

> My return from Spain, coincided with a nicely timed "smear" piece by one Kluckhohn, in the Aug 19th "Reporter." The owner editor Max Ascoli is an Italian immigrant of 1931. He ought to be more tolerant with another immigrant? Anyway, I am always curious what these birds did during the war. I would bet that neither of them wore the uniform. They prefer "suckers" like myself to make the bistros of New York safe for them, to plan and write their "smear" pieces.

The "us versus them" mentality that characterized Willoughby in earlier years—and which he inherited from, or more likely shared with MacArthur—remained as central to his core as ever.[42] In notes that he wrote in response to the article by Kluckhohn, entitled "Heidelberg to Madrid—The Story of General Willoughby," he summarized his thoughts in a few brief sentences: "This article is a blend of malicious innuendo and some irrelevant facts. The total effect is one of 'smear.' I expected to become a target, sooner or later ..." He also excoriated both Kluckhohn and Ascoli as immigrants who "never served the United States, either in war or peace."[43]

In September 1952, Willoughby—from his doubtless palatial suite 1606 at New York City's Hotel Wyndham—again wrote to Dulles, this time referring to a "number of communications, from Germany, from individuals whom I do not know but who erroneously assumed that I was on some sort of confidential mission. Madrid is a great center for that sort of thing." Referring to two specific letters from German citizens eager to assist the United States Government, Willoughby added, "It occurred to me that your German section could utilize these men, for obvious reasons; men who have a 'grievance' are generally more intense in their work, if oriented in the proper direction ... I know that your facilities abroad are so flexible that some gesture of interest toward these men, might bring some dividends." After addressing a few other subjects, Willoughby closed the letter, "With kind personal regards, Fraternally, /s/ C. A. Willoughby."[44]

By the mid-1950s, the Willoughby–Dulles letters had become a recurring correspondence. In response to a November 20, 1955, letter from Dulles, Willoughby responded on December 3. In this missive, Willoughby offered, "I am moving to Washington, for no particular reason and I am building a house at 3602 Massachusetts Ave, next to the Sebalds primarily because I am suddenly tired of New York—ghetto of the gentiles [*sic*]!" Later in the letter, Willoughby confirmed the likely suspicions of others when he noted:

> I imagine that I am restless and seek outlets for my energies. Since my particular talents are not employable in your outfit (which I deplore and consider just a bit silly), I must do something else. I sometimes wonder, if this relationship is tracable [*sic*] to the hatreds or prejudice engendered by MacArthur, whom I naturally defended, as I would any man, whom I work for …[45]

On December 22, CIA Western Hemisphere Chief J. C. King wrote a memo to Deputy Director (Plans) Wisner in reference to Willoughby's letter earlier in the month. He wrote, "In his letter General Willoughby intimates that he would be of use to this Agency for two reasons. One would be his present contacts with Venezuelan officials, especially military leaders. The second reason is less clearly stated in General Willoughby's letter, but apparently he has excellent press contacts and good cover as a writer and publisher." He explained Willoughby had apparently received an invitation to visit Venezuela and publicly compare conditions there under the current regime with those he experienced two decades prior. King then cut to the chase by observing:

> … with regard to the General's possible use to CIA, I wish to note that the Caracas Station has what we consider to be adequate coverage of newspaper and publishing circles in Venezuela … All present indications are that the present regime in Venezuela is firmly entrenched and will remain in power indefinitely. There appears to be no need for the United States Government to endeavor covertly to support that regime in the manner suggested to General Willoughby. In view of the above, I find no justification for considering the employment of General Willoughby by this Agency for use in Venezuela.

On June 11, 1956, Wisner responded to King's recommendation:

> I have the impression that the Director is anxious to retain the good will of General Willoughby, but would not be in favor of going so far as to create a "make-work" job for him in Venezuela or elsewhere … it would be my conclusion that we renew the earlier advice to the Director and submit to him a draft of a proposed reply, expressing appreciation for the offer of his services and indicating that the Director will bear this in mind and would like to feel free to call upon General Willoughby at sometime in the future, etc., etc.[46]

In late June 1956, Dulles replied diplomatically, "I am particularly appreciative of your thoughts of further service to your country, but we have no specific tasks of such importance at this moment in Venezuela as to require your extraordinary talents. I shall continue to bear in mind your friendly offer and in the event that an interesting occasion should arise, I will call on you."[47] Thus, the Agency ultimately gave Willoughby a dignified bum's rush to the door.

Also in June, Willoughby again wrote a personal letter to Dulles, lauding him for his address to the assembled members of the University of Pennsylvania Law Review, as reported in the May 25 edition of *US News and World Report*. He gushed:

> Considering your rare appearance in print, this is an outstanding essay, in every respect, in literary style which is hard to maintain with such a subject and in power of thesis and argument. I agree with your ideas in every particular. This important article will not only contribute to the prestige of C.I.A. but it ought to clarify and balance the utter confusion of parallel articles now written, on the Soviet enigma, by every armchair strategist and dry-martini commentator in the country.

He added he had just received a "high level" invitation to visit Venezuela, noting that "while I am normally inclined to handle such matters on my own cognizance, I suggest that it might be developed as a project to our mutual advantage. I have current links with Venezuela, Colombia, and Ecuador, all dating back to my long service there, in the period 1921–1929.[47] Willoughby would continue to plaintively beg and plead to keep his hand in the intelligence pie throughout the decade, often and ironically by using the "good offices" of the CIA.

He also shared his invitation to Venezuela with Chairman, Joint Chiefs of Staff (JCS) General Maxwell Taylor. In a letter to the JCS chief in mid-October 1956, Willoughby explained his rationale for wanting to return to Venezuela was to "develop (possibly) a series of articles and collect material for a book that will trace the remarkable developments [of the current regime] from 1926 to 1956." He informed Taylor he had been invited to address the Venezuelan General Staff and historical conferences and was thinking of speaking on the subjects "The Great Decisions of Eisenhower"; "The Campaigns of MacArthur in the Pacific"; The Sino–Korean War 1950–1951"; and "Soviet Espionage in the Far East."[48] However, there is no indication that either the JCS or the CIA ever took him up on his offer or that he returned to the South American nation.

***

Perhaps surprisingly, given his status as a member of MacArthur's inner circle, Willoughby survived the departure of the "American Caesar" and retained his position as the FECOM G-2, at least for the time being. He left voluntarily in late summer 1951 and the final edition of the *Daily Intelligence Summary* during his tenure was dedicated to him. As the tribute gushed:

> In the service of his country for 40 years, General Willoughby has been unflagging in his efforts on behalf of the intelligence establishment; the most tangible evidence of his outstanding success in the field of military intelligence is recorded for history in the pages of the 3,175 editions of the *Daily Intelligence Summary* published continuously under his aegis since 7 December 1941. Through the bitter campaigns in the Southwest Pacific during World War II, through the eventful years of the Occupation of Japan, and continuing into the Korean War, General Willoughby has contributed brilliantly and unstintingly to the development of the Far East Command *Daily Intelligence Summary* as a model of intelligence publications. Always an inspiration to

those who worked under him in the preparation and production of this publication, General Willoughby has made a lasting imprint in the annals of military intelligence, and, as a leader and mentor through the years, on the hearts and minds of his subordinates and students. It is thus, both out of devotion and respect, that those who remain salute in these pages the one who soon departs.

Given the tenure of Willoughby's association with MacArthur, it might be understandable that, once the latter had been dismissed, the former would follow suit. While some measure of that sentiment likely played a role in motivating Willoughby to retire, a letter he wrote to DCI Bedell Smith on June 24, 1951, suggests there may have been other factors that played a role in that decision:

> Ridgway wanted me to stay and I still have a vague feeling that I should have seen the war out? However, the Medicoes gave me a bad jolt; I have a serious arthritis of the Spine, with all sorts of future complications. Rest is indicated—but I do not see it around here. I find the East [he was living in Washington, D.C., at the time] and the Climate most uncomfortable and depressing.

He added he was pending some significant decisions in the near future, including apparently where to live, commenting that while "I could remain here, in the shelter of my relatives" it was too easy to "overdo that sort of thing." He added, morosely, "I have seen the General briefly. He is on his own, in many ways, in a political program, in which I find no immediate place."[49]

His medical maladies were also briefly mentioned in the course of his August 23–24 testimony before the House Un-American Activities Committee; in his initial statement to the Committee members, he stated he was "awaiting retirement for partial disability and length of service, as a veteran of several wars, namely, World War I, 1917; World War II, 1941; the North Korean War, 1950; and the Chinese Communist War, 1951." The subject of his testimony was "American Aspects of the Richard Sorge Spy Case," on which topic the committee had first contacted Willoughby in 1949.[50]

Before his actual appearance, Willoughby sent a draft statement to DCI Bedell Smith, saying he was:

> ... confident that I can steer a middle course and not leave a bad taste, after all. Note draft of my statement (not for the Press whom I dislike thoroughly) on the occasion of first appearance. I do not think that anyone could consider this objectionable or an "attack" on anybody? Show it to Mr. Allen [Dulles, Director of Plans, CIA, shortly to become Deputy Director] and his Brother [John Foster Dulles, Secretary of State].[51]

Select portions of his draft address include these words:

> Recent newspaper reports have developed a tendency to attribute sensational qualities to my impending testimony before certain Congressional Committees. I am described as "threatening a brand new ruckus," as being "sore at the Pentagon," as "vowing to jar the Capital with Spy tales"; yet another enfant terrible of the Press charges me with "promises to redden faces and to set off explosions," as being "a thorn in the side of the Pentagon."

After denying any animosity toward either the Pentagon or the State Department—being a veteran of both organizations—he explained what he really would be testifying about:

> The real subject matter of my presentation is in a field of international danger, in which all political parties could meet amicably, on grounds of common interest.
>
> There are recognizable historical factors, the dangerous impact of which is only now beginning to be felt. The dead hand of the past rests heavily on a precarious present. We are still in the shadow of Cairo, Yalta, Teheran and Potsdam. Retribution has been swift and terrible. The victors of 1945 have created a Frankenstein that may yet slay them: the Red menace, international Communism ... It fell within the purview of MacArthur's intelligence section to confront this menace in the Far East, to unmask the grimacing face of the red Medusa. The story of Richard Sorge, Soviet master spy, became the vehicle of presentation ...
>
> My cumulative reports contain over 180 identities, surnames, aliases, and code-designations, derived from Court records authenticated by American lawyers ... The exact degree of relationship or association ranges from direct espionage by Comintern "agents" to the twilight zone of fellow-traveling dupes and befuddled liberals—apparently unaware that they have drifted into an international conspiracy for the sole benefit of an alien and hostile Government.
>
> I have filed detailed evidence with appropriate Federal agencies and certain Congressional Committees. (Let the chips fall where they may! As regards my personal fortune, it is supremely unimportant, and does not concern me; one of the Committees has already received letters threatening my life.) It is thus that I discharge my moral obligation toward the United States which has received me as an immigrant boy and given me shelter and citizenship as a man.[52]

While the focus was on the Sorge spy case and particularly its unique ramifications in the United States, Willoughby's testimony offered him the opportunity to express his clearly defined political views, in between fawning compliments directed to Committee members. When one member prompted Willoughby with the statement, "... you feel that we have to study the manipulations of the Communist Party and the international Comintern over the past quarter century in order to get a clear picture of what their present manipulation might be?", Willoughby replied, "I feel that strongly, and I agree entirely with your view on that particular subject." In the same vein, when Willoughby was questioned about the prospects for an armed Communist uprising in the United States, he responded, "I firmly believe that there is an international conspiracy; that there is a mechanism for its accomplishment; that these perhaps fragmentary disclosures here are the early glimpses of the framework of the conspiracy ... The perversion is in full swing. We are fortunate that it has not taken hold here as it has elsewhere."[53]

Finally, in a remarkable development which indicated the political affinity Willoughby shared with the committee members, he was asked by one member about any "remedial legislation" Congress might develop to help blunt the Communist threat in the United States. Missing the point of the question, Willoughby rattled off several suggestions, though none which involved legislation. "First," he intoned, "the Federal Government should give full and unqualified support to this committee ... Second, the FBI should be rigorously supported ... Third, their work should be made easier by the elimination of legalistic juridical objections." To explain more fully, Willoughby cited, as an example, restrictions on wiretapping, which he considered "in the same category as furnishing a pistol to a law enforcing agency combating crime." Untroubled by the possibility of denying criminals their legal rights, he added, "To be morally sensitive when you are dealing with a criminal strikes me as silly." He then added, "Fourth … I would recommend that each State legislature form and maintain such a committee [as the California State Committee on Un-American Activities]." When the member pointed out that none of these suggestions involved new legislation, Willoughby simply recommended the present committee be made a permanent entity.[54]

In the fall of 1951, not long after his retirement, Willoughby became the editor of *Foreign Intelligence Digest*, a publication which dated to 1938 (when it was the *Foreign Military News Digest*) and whose masthead portrayed it as "an impartial analysis of political, economic and military events in the critical areas of the world, derived from sources not normally available."[55] He would remain editor until 1961, also taking up common cause with "hill-billy evangelist" and professional anti-Communist Billy James Hargis, who operated the Christian Crusade organization from Tulsa, Oklahoma; Willoughby became the Washington representative of the Christian Crusade and in 1961 wrote a series of four articles for their paper, the *Weekly Crusader*. In a letter to DCI Allen Dulles, Willoughby freely shared his thoughts, opinions, and recommendations, including the observation that:

> … if you dabble in military operations, it would be desirable that your training courses involve some basic instruction in the "art of war," in the immutable principles, in the cultural approach to military history that is an element of all staff colleges of all armies. I recommended that, too, the insertion of the lectures of "Maneuver in War," which I conducted at Leavenworth …

Then, perhaps catching himself, he added, "Well—this is not intented [*sic*] to make recommendations where they are not wanted. I expect to go my own way, as usual, with or without help …" In conjunction with this letter, Willoughby sent previews of one article to Dulles and also pushed hard to get the CIA to pay $150 for each issue of the *Weekly Crusader*, with the Christian Crusade providing 1,000 copies for distribution throughout the Agency. When push came to shove, however, Dulles wrote Willoughby a few days later: "I am fully aware of your good intentions and of the practicality of your suggestion but I regret that CIA may not in any way participate in such a program. I am sure you understand why this must be so. Every good wish to you and the patriotic work you are doing."[56]

Besides fending off the Communists that skulked beneath every bed in America, Willoughby also felt compelled to take up pen to answer charges leveled at both himself and MacArthur for their misreading of the tea leaves in Korea, a crusade that would continue nearly to his dying day. In a *New York Times* story that ran on November 28, 1951, Willoughby charged the previous day that "biased, prejudiced and inaccurate" press coverage of the Korean War had contributed to MacArthur's very public dismissal. He specifically targeted six war correspondents and three news magazines for creating "an atmosphere of tension, uneasiness and distrust between Tokyo and Washington." The journalists signaled out for criticism included syndicated columnist Joseph Alsop; *New York Times* military correspondent Hanson W. Baldwin; the *New York Herald Tribune*'s Homer Bigart; *Associated Press* writer Hal Boyle; syndicated columnist Drew Pearson; and former *Herald Tribune* Far East staffer Christopher Rand. Willoughby identified the offending publications as *Time*, *Newsweek*, and *US News and World Report*, which "appeared to go out of their way to create defeatist-thought patterns and to belittle the country's armed forces." In topical terms, Willoughby was most irritated by the way the press had reported the pull-back of American forces following the Chinese offensive in late November 1950, and their characterization of that move as a "defeat," and by their assessment that MacArthur's headquarters had either received "faulty intelligence about the Chinese build-up or had improperly valued it."[57]

Predictably, several of the targeted journalists responded in kind to Willoughby through the vehicle of the *Times*. For example, Hanson Baldwin retorted, "As an intelligence officer, General Willoughby was widely and justly criticized by Pentagon officials as well as in the papers. His present article is as misleading and inaccurate as were some of his intelligence reports." Homer Bigart responded, "General MacArthur and his tight little circle of advisers have never been able to stomach criticism, whether from a war correspondent or the President of the United States. In an attempt to silence criticism, they have adopted the line that anyone who questions their judgment is 'inaccurate, biased and prejudiced' and that any criticism of them involves a slur on the whole army." In a fit of pique, Joseph Alsop observed that "men like Homer Bigart and Hal Boyle who were frontline correspondents right through the war knew a damn sight more of what was going on than General Willoughby, so far as I was able to observe." Two days after Willoughby's article appeared in the *Times*, a *Washington Post* article referred to his well-known animosity towards Korean War correspondents. "The list of newspapermen he ticks off is long," wrote the journalist, mentioning that he referred to them collectively as "careless chroniclers, ragpickers of modern literature, roughly between *belles-lettres* and the police blotter." The article also cited Willoughby's firm conviction that it was the correspondents who were responsible for the "atmosphere of tension, uneasiness and distrust between Tokyo and Washington," which was "the major cause of the MacArthur–Truman split." In a telling statement, the article concluded with this observation: "For our own part, we are inclined to think that the major cause of the split was an incurable tendency on the part of the Far East commander and his intelligence officer to refer to this relationship as 'MacArthur–Truman' instead of Truman–MacArthur. They never understood the importance of this priority."[58]

In December 1951, Willoughby scribed an article entitled "The Truth About Korea" for *Cosmopolitan* magazine. In it, he disputed the earlier testimony of his former boss to the United Nations and to a Senate committee concerning responsibility for the collection and processing of intelligence on Korea pre-war. Willoughby wrote that, while MacArthur was not responsible for intelligence collection or surveillance in Korea, FECOM's Tokyo headquarters did indeed have a reporting unit deployed to Korea; this unit had been sending information to Washington as early as March 1950, fully three months before war erupted on the peninsula, but had dismissed reports of buildups, saying they should not be taken seriously. In the course of the article, Willoughby also addressed the question of why Republicans in Congress did not press for an investigation into events leading up to the Korean War. Willoughby inadvertently disclosed that MacArthur had misled both the United Nations and the Senate Committee that investigated his dismissal. Had there been any such Congressional investigation, Willoughby pointed out, MacArthur would have had to make damaging admissions about the "quality of his intelligence staff and the honesty of his official reporting."[59]

Willoughby also repeated many of his accusations about the "defeatist" press at home. He wrote:

> With our nation confronted by the U.S.S.R., the most menacing and vicious military power in modern and ancient history, with jittery experts prattling about global psychological warfare against the enemy, and with public confidence in our armed forces absolutely essential, some of our reporters have, during the Korean war, appeared to go out of their way to create defeatist thought patterns in their readers, and to belittle the country's armed services ... It was a foregone conclusion that, as a corollary to this defeatist theme, military intelligence would be pilloried. When things go sour, intelligence becomes a convenient whipping boy.[60]

He then reminded readers yet again of how deleterious an effect leftist journalists had had on the war's conduct. Focusing on Pearson, Boyle, Bigart, Alsop, and Baldwin, Willoughby inveighed, "During the most difficult days of Korea, these men were often inaccurate, biased, prejudiced, petulant; they confused an unhappy public. The corrosive effect of their irresponsible reporting was equal to that of calculated defeatism, even if such was not intended. Their reporting furnished aid and comfort to the enemy." He then turned to military decision making in Korea, in a continuing attempt to exonerate MacArthur from charges of at least incompetence, if not dereliction of duty. He explained that the disposition of American troops in Korea in November 1950 was based on the defeated North Korean Army, "not on the concept that at the end of the trail the full force of Communist China would be met ... Higher authority could have issued orders to the United Nations forces to stop at any time at any line in Korea—but no such orders were issued ... The ultimate decision was up to the United Nations ..." He bristled at the use by MacArthur of what proved to be a cruel joke, "getting the boys home by Christmas." He told readers that that very slogan had been approved in Washington and the intended psychological effect was to persuade China to stay out of Korean affairs; that effort failed only "when Red China became an open aggressor." Warming to his subject, Willoughby went on to make a sweeping generalization:

> From 1941 to 1945, from Australia to the Philippines, MacArthur's intelligence made no serious errors ... The entry of Communist China into the war was a piece of political intelligence; it became military only at the point of collision ... The criticism of the intelligence job done before the Chinese Reds crossed the Yalu must be viewed against geographical distances.

To refute press reporting, the Intelligence Section in Tokyo called a press conference and released the complete Chinese and North Korean order of battle.[61]

On several occasions during the post-war period, Willoughby compared American casualties in select battles and campaigns of the WWII European Theater of Operations with those in Korea. He did so not only to blunt criticism of the allegedly high casualty count in Korea but also to highlight the difference in reporting by the press on the conflicts between 1941 and 1945 and those in 1950. Willoughby reported that, between July 1 and December 1, 1950, there were 46,000 casualties overall:

> ... a little more than the expensive price that was paid at Anzio. But no one shouted from the housetops that Anzio was the greatest disaster in the history of American arms. The press exercised delicate restraint regarding the European show, while a cataract of venom was incessantly poured on Pacific operations from 1941 to 1951 ... The reporting of the Korean war consistently belittling the efforts of our men on the battlefield was not a matter of isolated or freak instances; it took on the design of a calculated system.[62]

He admitted:

> To some extent we can understand the daily confetti of banalities that is turned out, with practically no research, under the impact of the editorial deadline. It must be hell to turn out a doctoral dissertation every twenty-four hours. However, war is hell, too—a different and more convincing kind of hell. The typewriter attack from the rear can sometimes be worse than the enemy. In the case of Korea, I am convinced the nuance of defeat created an atmosphere of tension, uneasiness, and distrust between Tokyo and Washington. This is believed to have been the major cause of the MacArthur–Truman split.[63]

In 1952, Willoughby again sought to answer those who were sharply critical of the course of events in Korea, from the perspective of military intelligence in wartime. In his notes, he wrote:

> Korea: I stand on my article in the December issue of *Cosmopolitan*. The Eighth U.S. Army was accused of panic and disaster in November 1950. It is this same Army that took 130,000 prisoners of war in September and October. Their November losses were normal and actually less than the defense period around Pusan ... Had they [Washington and the United Nations] been worried, they could have given orders to stop our further advance into North Korea.

He rationalized, "... in the cacophony of frenzied accustaions [sic], I am reminded of an ancient saying: It is better to fail in a cause that might ultimately succeed—than to succeed in a cause that will ultimately fail."[64]

202 • LOYALTY FIRST

Nevertheless, the sting of the critics lingered and, in correspondence of August 1952, Willoughby responded in kind, hissing:

> ... the reds and the pinks have their sights ranged in; essentially, I don't give a damn. If 30/40 [years'] military service is not enough for an entrée [sic], vis-avis-vis [sic] these damned draft evaders—I am going to be the sucker like several million others, who were at the front so that bastards like these hackwriters can be safe to turn out these smear pieces.[65]

Two years later, in 1954, Willoughby published *MacArthur, 1941–1951*, though the volume was largely ghost-written by John Chamberlain; an early 1955 review of the book in *Foreign Affairs* magazine described it as "an admiring, partisan and comprehensive account of General MacArthur's role in the Pacific war, the occupation of Japan and the Korean war, by his former Chief of Intelligence."[66] Colonel Laurence Bunker, who served as an aide to MacArthur from April 1946 to November 1952, explained how the volume that emerged was not what was originally intended. Bunker detailed that Willoughby had been working on a book previously, with the intended title of *MacArthur's Intelligence, 1941–1951*—essentially a history of the staff section for which Willoughby was responsible. However, according to Bunker, the McGraw-Hill publishing firm wanted to take full advantage of public interest in MacArthur by publishing a biography and pressured Willoughby into converting his volume into a biographical history of that part of the FECOM commander's life. The way in which the story was presented to the press made it appear the volume was MacArthur's story, edited by Willoughby. No one explained this situation to MacArthur, who became rather irate when he found out about the subterfuge; as Bunker recalled, MacArthur wrote a letter to McGraw-Hill refusing to accept that as the basis for publication. The book, of course, was published regardless, with Willoughby gathering material from other staff officers to provide the "padding" the publisher sought and lending the volume the appearance of being a general history of the period. Despite the criticism from other staff officers that Willoughby had published a volume giving the impression he won the war almost single handedly, Bunker explained this was due to the G-2's "conforming, shall we say, to the minimum extent practicable for what McGraw-Hill was asking." He did note, however, that "the report in that book of those war years, I feel, is probably as sound and reliable as anything that has come out."[67]

In the book, Willoughby and Chamberlain concluded that what "undoubtedly tipped the scales in Red China's future decisions [i.e., the Korean intervention], was the amazing order from Washington, issued to the Seventh Fleet in June [1950] to 'neutralize Formosa,'" which they claimed meant the freeing up of two Chinese armies for deployment to Manchuria. They also pointed to MacArthur's intelligence summaries of August 27, 1950, which "contained a miscellany of highly suggestive and completely ominous reports from Chinese Nationalist channels," according to Willoughby's 1954 recollection. The G-2 also recalled a specific "high level meeting" in Peking, of which he became aware, regarding the appointment of a Chinese commander for Korea, and the movement of various Chinese units.[68]

That same year, on Friday, June 4, 1954, Willoughby was featured at the 40th anniversary of his graduation from Gettysburg College; at the Alumni Council Dinner held that evening, the last two items on the agenda were "Introduction of Major General Charles A. Willoughby '14" and "Address by General Willoughby." At 9:00 that Sunday morning, June 6, Willoughby commissioned the College's Reserve Officers' Training Corps graduates at a ceremony held in Christ Chapel on the campus—of note, the commencement speaker who mounted the podium at 2:30 that afternoon was, somewhat ironically, "Mr. William L. Shirer," the noted journalist who penned one of the best-known popular histories of pre-war and wartime Germany, *The Rise and Fall of the Third Reich: A History of Nazi Germany*, which would not be published for another six years.[69]

In the post-war period, another blindly loyal follower of MacArthur came to his defense and, indirectly, that of Willoughby: former Chief of Staff Courtney Whitney, a fellow "Bataan Gang" member and MacArthur admirer. Like Willoughby, Whitney had also taken pen in hand to defend MacArthur's staffers, in a book grandiosely entitled *MacArthur's Rendezvous with History*, which was serialized in *Life* magazine in August and September 1955. Readers who had missed earlier such hints of the author's leanings were directly confronted with them in Whitney's fourth chapter, "The War MacArthur Was Not Allowed to Win." In this chapter, he boiled down the tangled web of conflicting evidence to one specific point:

> There can be only one circumstance under which the Chinese did finally decide to enter the Korean War: Someone must have told them what no one told MacArthur. Someone must have told them that even if the Red Chinese swarmed across the Yalu into North Korea in overwhelming hordes, even if they slaughtered U.N. soldiers by the thousands on the battlefield and in the prisoner of war camps, the U.S. Government would meekly decline to retaliate and the Reds' staging and supply area in Manchuria would remain a sanctuary. Despite false charges to the contrary, Mac did not predict unequivocally that the Chinese would not enter the Korean War. It was only later, when Mr. Truman made his amazing charge that MacArthur had misinformed him on the possibility of Red Chinese intervention, that MacArthur understood what the Wake Island meeting actually was: a sly political ambush.[70]

For all his detractors, there were certainly those who remembered Willoughby, if not fondly, at least in terms of appreciation. In January 1956, Lieutenant General Clark L. Ruffner—then the commander of the 2nd Armored Division—wrote Willoughby to thank him for his support during the 1950 chaos in Tokyo:

> I never see your name that I don't think of the hectic three weeks I had around Tokyo while I was Chief of Staff of the X Corps, trying to pull that headquarters together, and all the wonderful support and encouragement you gave me. I am forced to admit that there were periods when I almost felt that the sponge had to be thrown in, but somehow or other you were able to impart to me the necessary determination on my part to stay with it. Your wise counsel and advice helped me over many rough spots.[71]

The following month, Willoughby received a similar letter from Major General G. B. Barth, acting commander of the First Army, praising him for actions two decades prior: "I will always remember," wrote Barth, "the superb instruction you gave our class at Leavenworth. I was in the last two-year class (1934–36) and your instruction … was something I'll never forget."[72] Willoughby also volunteered his services in order to encourage more young American men to consider a stint in the Armed Forces, specifically the Army. In a letter from July 1956, General Maxwell D. Taylor, Chief of Staff, U.S. Army, thanked Willoughby for his offer to help tell the Army story to the American public. Taylor wrote, "I agree that you are in a position to contribute to our public relations program" and added he was sending Willoughby material "to acquaint you with the present Army positions on certain matters."[73]

CHAPTER TEN

Watchman of the Republic

"Son of Man, I have made thee a watchman unto the house of Israel ..."
—EZEKIEL 3:17 NKJV

Following the forced retirement of his beloved MacArthur, Willoughby became increasingly involved in right-wing politics, including involvement with the John Birch Society, and embraced a number of conspiracy theories. Willoughby's book, *Shanghai Conspiracy*, originally published in 1952, was reprinted in paperback as part of the One Dozen Candles series of history and opinion books published by Western Islands, the publishing arm of the John Birch Society. As one student of Willoughby observed, he "consistently displayed right-wing political views throughout his career," to which he could turn his full attention in retirement. In the opinion of this student, Willoughby's fondness for right-wing, authoritarian governments "sowed the seeds of failure in Willoughby's leadership as an intelligence officer."[1]

His strident anti-Communist views had developed over many years. As early as the late 1930s, when he was writing *Maneuver in War* (published in 1939), he let his inner feelings slip out through his pen in the chapter on the Sino–Japanese War and the influence of Communism. In that chapter, Willoughby predicted "a sentimental world may eventually have to choose between the rising sun and the red sickle";—ironically, just two years later, he found himself fighting the Japanese in the Philippines. Shortly after the war, while writing *Shanghai Conspiracy*, Willoughby described the activities of Richard Sorge, the German Communist who was actually a Russian spy. When Willoughby returned to the States in 1951, shortly after his mentor, he testified before Congress about the American members of the Sorge spy ring. It is telling that the two documents key to the case against Sorge were prepared under Willoughby's aegis: "A Partial Documentation of the Sorge Espionage Case"; and "Extracts From an Authentic Translation of Foreign Affairs Yearbook, 1943, Criminal Affairs Bureau, Ministry of Justice, Tokyo, Japan." As further indication of his obsession and the popularity of the topic at the time, another G-2 product "The Sorge Spy Ring—A Case Study in International Espionage in the Far East" was reproduced in the *Congressional Record*. Nor was his prejudice contained when assessing the Korean War and its unfolding; he described the Chinese threat to North Korea in these words: "Behind the Red Chinese, of course, stood the Kremlin, ever alive to its chances of pushing to the warm waters of the Pacific."[2] Similar thoughts were clearly in the mind of the man Willoughby asked to write the foreword to *Shanghai Conspiracy*—his newly retired former boss, Douglas MacArthur. As an introduction to Willoughby's monograph, MacArthur wrote that the book "presents a clear delineation of a worldwide pattern of Communist sabotage and betrayal which is still being practiced today."[3]

Nor did Willoughby's obsession with Communists within and without the government fade throughout the 1950s—and he sought every means possible to ensure his adopted nation did not forget the imminent threat either. He was no doubt encouraged by many Americans during those years of paranoia, such as U.S. House of Representatives member Harold O. Lovre (R-SD), who penned the following note to Willoughby on February 20, 1950:

> I believe your idea of subjecting the tactics of the Communists to public ridicule on every occasion is the most effective way you can assist in waging the cold war. You are to be congratulated on the pamphlet [on the Sorge spy case], which I would like to see read by every American interested in preserving the world from Communist domination.[4]

Willoughby also lent his talents to the American Security Council (ASC), established by notable acquaintance, and former general, Robert Wood, the Sears Roebuck chairman, and Robert R. McCormick of the *Chicago Tribune*. The two had established the ASC in 1955 in response to what they considered the influence of Communist infiltrators, whom they believed had brought defeat to the United States in the Korean War. The ASC banner explained, "The American Security Council is operated by business for the improvement of business and public understanding of the Cold War and how to meet the Communist challenge." Notably, two other influential persons in Willoughby's orbit were members of the ASC's inner circle—Henry and Clare Booth Luce. Willoughby and Henry Luce were both listed as members of the ASC's Cold War Victory Advisory Committee and Willoughby may also have been a member of the organization's Citizen Foreign Relations Committee.[5]

In a 1958 letter to Senate Foreign Relations Committee chairman Theodore Francis Green (D-RI), Willoughby wrote:

> The Communist scheme for world conquest has not been abandoned merely because many Americans have become tired of hearing about it. We can accept that the "cold war" (i.e., the brutal intransigeance [*sic*] of Communist Russia in its dealing with the West) is the historical continuity of "Mongoloid-Panslavism," as practiced by the Czars and that the Russian menace, then and now, is primarily military.[6]

During the post-war years, Willoughby published the *Foreign Intelligence Digest* newsletter and worked closely with Texas oil tycoon H. L. Hunt on the International Committee for the Defense of Christian Culture, an extreme right-wing group with connections to anti-Communist groups. A 1966 membership list identified Willoughby as the National Executive Secretary for the organization.[7]

CIA documents declassified in 2005 and publicized by the National Archives in 2007 also implicated Willoughby in a potential *coup d'etat* during the post-war period in Japan. A group of Japanese right-wing politicians and unreconstructed militarists was actively plotting to overthrow the Japanese Government and assassinate pro-American prime minister Shigeru Yoshida, hoping to replace him with the more right-wing Takushiro Hattori, the former private secretary to wartime prime minister Hideki Tojo, who had been hanged for war crimes in 1948. As the documents attested, this right-wing, anti-Communist conspiracy had worked in close coordination with Army intelligence (G-2) during the American occupation of the late 1940s and early 1950s. More specifically, Hattori had worked under the oversight of Willoughby, described in the documentation as being the second most-powerful American on-scene—after MacArthur, of course. However, the departure of Willoughby—described as the group's "patron and paymaster" in 1951, after his boss had been sacked by President Truman, helped defuse the plot, as did the overall incompetence of the plot, characterized by leaks, bumbling agents, and internal fractures. A CIA document of April 18, 1952, noted, "The government attitude toward the Hattori group has been increasingly antagonistic, and the group has lost influence since the departure of General Willoughby."[8]

As a right-wing observer of world events and a former practitioner of Intelligence, Willoughby predictably paid close attention to the shocking news in May 1954 of the French defeat by the Viet Cong in Vietnam. For many observers, certainly including Willoughby, this disastrous defeat of a European military power by an Asian nation—eerily reminiscent of the Japanese defeat of the Russian fleet in the Tsushima Strait in 1905—called for drastic action. In May, Joint Chiefs chairman Admiral Arthur W. Radford sent a memo to Defense Secretary Charles Wilson which stated that "the employment of atomic weapons is contemplated in the event that such course appears militarily advantageous." Willoughby concurred with such advice, advocating the use of such weapons to create, as he put it in his inimitable fashion, "a belt of scorched earth across the avenues of communism to block the Asiatic hordes."[9]

Despite strident criticism of his work as an intelligence officer, Willoughby was among an illustrious group of individuals who were consulted and acknowledged during the compilation of the report of The Commission on Organization of the Executive Branch of Government in June 1955. The organization, better known as the Clark Committee—named for its head, General Mark Clark, then President of The Citadel—provided its Report on Intelligence Activities to the Congress. Due to the rising Soviet threat, the existence of nuclear weapons, and the desire to establish a "baseline" for the embryonic American intelligence community (IC), this select group was tasked with conducting a thorough examination of the intelligence enterprise, with an emphasis on "correcting the weaknesses, improving the quality, and increasing the efficiency" of the IC. When the final report was submitted, a concluding note read: "The task force further wishes to express its deep gratitude for the valuable aid of those public-spirited individuals who gave freely of their time, and who by their objective approach to the problem and their government experience materially enlightened our members." Cited by name were former Office of Strategic Services Director Donovan, FBI Director J. Edgar Hoover, former CIA seniors Bedell Smith and William H. Jackson and—the last to be mentioned by name—"Major General Charles A. Willoughby, former Assistant Chief of Staff, G-2, Far East Command."[10]

Willoughby's right-of-center message found a ready audience in 1950s America and he proved to be a popular speaker in retirement, at least to politically conservative organizations. At the March 19, 1956, meeting of the Veterans of Strategic Services organization, held at the Columbia University Club in New York City, Willoughby was the guest speaker. Organization president Henry S. Prescott noted in his announcement to members of the event that "we have been fortunate in obtaining the services of one of the world's foremost authorities on Intelligence Operations and Soviet Espionage in the Far East." Prescott went on to explain that no one had been closer to MacArthur or was more qualified to speak to the subjects on the agenda: "Soviet Espionage in the Far East" and "Intelligence Highlights of America's Wars in the Far East." He noted Willoughby would "also treat with particular emphasis … the world-famous SORGE case which he exposed and its current ramifications in the Communist conspiracy in the United States." Interestingly, the attendance card sent to Director Central Intelligence (DCI) Allen Dulles was returned, indicating the DCI would *not* be attending.[11]

Nevertheless, Willoughby maintained connections with the CIA in the post-war period. The Agency's October 23, 1957, *Weekly Activities Report* noted in passing that a CIA office, its identity redacted, "has secured the consent of Major General Charles A. Willoughby, USA Retired, General MacArthur's wartime Intelligence Chief, to lecture on the Pacific war in the Regional Survey-East Asia."[12]

In the February 2, 1957, issue of the *National Review*, edited and published by conservative icon William F. Buckley, Jr., Willoughby was listed as a contributor and a March 1958 article from the Gettysburg College publication *The Phi Gamma Delta* referred to their illustrious alumnus as Xi Chapter officer, "Major-General Charles A. Willoughby, 1914, whose hazardous journey from Corregidor has become a national legend."[13]

When the Eisenhower White House announced in 1959 that Premier Khrushchev and his wife would be paying a lengthy visit to the United States, Willoughby and other like-minded individuals—coalesced into the "Committee Against Summit Entanglements"—picked up their pens in anger and disgust, trying to organize last-minute conservative opposition to such a travesty. In a *Christian Crusade* article,

Willoughby referred to Khrushchev as "the butcher of Hungary and the Ukraine," but, when asked to co-sign a petition of protest to the invitation, declined, noting that public opinion should have been rallied in 1917, 1933, or 1941, not now. In his jeremiad, Willoughby stated, "There was a reason for Eisenhower's acquiescence in Khrushchev's visit. The same reason prevails today: A sobering realization that the West is deteriorating."[14]

Another way for Willoughby to help save democracy, at least to his way of thinking, was to provide a necessary "boost" to the fledgling CIA. In May 1960, Dulles responded to a letter from Willoughby in which the latter apparently volunteered his services to "improve" the training of CIA officers. Dulles wrote:

> It was good seeing you and I enjoyed very much our talk. I might say that I appreciate your interest in our organization and I am now looking into the possibility of our taking advantage of your offer to be of assistance in our training activities. You will hear further from me on this when we have completed exploring the situation.[15]

Just five days later, Willoughby responded:

> Hold your views in abeyance until you have received a copy of my "Maneuver in War," i.e., my course in Leavenworth, 1930–1935 ... Personnel in the C.I.A. (with limited military strategic experience) can be fully oriented, in this course to thereafter be on familiar, intellectual ground, in dealing with military Staffs and Headquarters, in a planning or liaison basis. It may bridge the gap between C.I.A. and the intelligence sections of the Services.

He continued his tutelage of Dulles by chiding him, "In general terms, I have felt that you (and other Federal enterprises) do not make sufficient use of retired specialists. On the other hand, time is fleeting—and I have built my own European contacts, for my own amusement."[16] In short, if the CIA would not take advantage of Willoughby's generous offer to "straighten out" the wayward national intelligence entity, he would simply take his ball and go home.

Meanwhile, Willoughby continued to write about the Agency, regardless of Dulles' perceived coolness. In 1961, he proposed to write four articles in the *Weekly Crusader* on the CIA. Dulles responded, "Your letter of 2 June 1961 was most interesting. It was thoughtful of you to let me know your opinion on several matters discussed and also to give me the program for the four articles by you that will appear in the *Weekly Crusader*. Every good wish to you and the patriotic work you are doing."[17] And, Dulles reciprocated—in a March 1963 letter, written some 18 months after he had been removed as DCI by President John F. Kennedy, by sending Willoughby an advance proof of his *Encyclopedia Britannica* article on "The Craft of Intelligence." He explained he planned to expand it and bring it out as a book in the fall and invited Willoughby's comments and criticisms.[18]

Willoughby also addressed perceptions he was an inveterate critic of Langley. In the wake of the Chinese intervention, for which many blamed the CIA as much as MacArthur's command, he came to the Agency's rescue, in a fashion:

You speak of "Willoughby and C.I.A. blaming each other." There was no element of "blame." We soberly appraised and jointly faced the Chinese "potential menace along the Yalu" ... When the North Korean invasion and the customary search for a "scape-goat" fell on C.I.A., I immediately and publicly ranged myself with that organization. Washington, of course, had known all about the North Korean potential.

In response, Dulles' replacement as DCI, Admiral Roscoe Hillenkoetter wired:

Greatly appreciate your fine message. I want particularly at this time to express special appreciation of the help and co-operation you have extended to our people in your area. Your understanding of the mutuality of interest of our organizations has served to mutually advance the interest and aims of U.S. intelligence. The only "frictional area," if that term is really applicable, was in our pioneering to define the role of C.I.A. within the framework of a theater commander. This problem was amicably and profitably solved.[19]

In a 1967 *Foreign Intelligence Digest* article, Willoughby pointedly wrote, in an eyebrow-raising statement, "I am not critical of the C.I.A. I understand it far better than the average citizen. I gave it wide scope in Japan (1945–1951) and had occasion to support it publicly ..." He also felt compelled to add that MacArthur had operated in the intelligence arena without either the Office of Strategic Services or the CIA, noting that his intelligence systems were "adequate in war and peace" and that "the occupation of Japan (80 million people) was a real test of security."[20]

Willoughby also found a receptive audience in Congress when he had the opportunity to share his perspective on the creeping global threat of Communism in the post-war years. In a letter to DCI Dulles in January 1958, House Un-American Activities Committee Chairman Francis E. Walter of Pennsylvania mentioned the committee "will soon release a consultation with General Charles A. Willoughby on the Communist penetration of Indonesia."[21] The result of that "consultation" was Willoughby's pointed warning that "Communist encroachment in Indonesia, actively abetted by President Sukarno, now threatens the entire United States defense line in the Pacific." He pointed to Communist subversion in Washington as the root cause of the problem, "which induced the United States government to champion Sukarno in his efforts to 'liberate' the former Dutch Republic, despite his previous role as one of Japan's chief wartime collaborators." And, as he usually did, Willoughby saw in all of this the black hand of the USSR:

The links with Communism and the Kremlin are demonstrably present; indeed, the so-called nationalist movements contain elements of Communist agitation and guidance, in every known instance. Russia is exploiting the traditional American predilection for "freedom" and "anticolonialism" as a smokescreen for the Czarist-Communist colonial expansion from Tashkent to Mongolia. The "nationalist" leaders are frequently Communist stooges or Socialists en route to Marxism.[22]

When asked if he had informed the government of his concerns about the fate of the Southeast Asian nation, Willoughby complained:

The eclipse of MacArthur affected his immediate staff—*sic transit gloria mundi* [thus passes the glory of the world]. They do not enjoy the confidence or favor of the Pentagon. They have not asked my views, and I assume that they do not want them. I have offered my services, and they were declined. However, I have written extensively for publication; books and magazine articles have appeared in *Reader's Digest, Cosmopolitan, National Review*, and elsewhere. Some of these articles have found their way into the *Congressional Record*. My purpose of course, was not capricious criticism, but an effort to offset the leftist trends in some quarters and the obviously calculated attempts to brainwash an uninformed public by certain tax-exempt foundation[s] …

In one such *Congressional Record* entry in 1964, Willoughby boldly declared to members of the House that:

1. The Indochina situation in (1954 and again in 1964) is a repetition of the worldwide Communist conspiracy—as in Korea, in Greece and in Spain.
2. The strategic impact is more important than Korea, which was bloodletting without recompense; the stakes in southeast Asia are bigger, higher, better.
3. The stakes are access to and control of enormous strategic raw materials: rubber, manganese, oil, tungsten, tin and rice.
4. In 1941–45 the Japanese made a major bid for these stakes. The Communist general staff follows the Japanese blueprint.[23]

Willoughby also appealed directly to the White House in his attempt to save Indonesia from Communist encroachment. In mid-March 1958, he wrote a letter to General Wilton B. Persons, the Deputy Assistant to the President. Referring to a congressional hearing on the Southeast Asian nation, Willoughby observed, "It is a case-history of why and how the U.S. is losing the cold war and one of the most important strategic areas in the Far East. The current Indonesian embroglio has a direct bearing on our Pacific frontier."[24]

***

Whenever he found an organization whose views and actions matched his own, Willoughby proved an inveterate "joiner." One of his more curious involvements was with the Order of Saint John of Jerusalem, Knights of Malta. Though finding non-sensational information about the order is a challenge, it appears it traces its origins to a dispute while the order was in Russia during the days of Czar Paul (ruled 1796–1801), after it had fled Malta. A 1970 document from the order listed Willoughby and Brigadier General Bonner Fellers as members of its Military Affairs Committee. The order achieved some moments of fame in the early 1980s when it officially recognized the claims of Russian defector Michael Goleniewski as Aleksei Romanoff, heir to the Russian Imperial House of Romanov—another supporter of the Goleniewski claim was former CIA Counterintelligence Chief James J. Angleton.[25]

In September 1959, Willoughby received an invitation from the Convent of the Order in Shickshinny (the oddly named Pennsylvania town where it is headquartered). The invitation read, "Permit us to congratulate you upon your personal merit and patriotic career in being selected by our Board of Directors as one of 500 eminent Christian laymen in the U.S. best qualified to be considered a prospective Knight of our Order." An accompanying postcard illustrated the symbol of the order—a white cross with four arms and eight points. It explained that the white cross stood for "Purity" and the four arms represented "Prudence, Justice, Fortitude, and Temperance." The eight points were:

> Spiritual joy
> To live without malice
> To weep over thy sins
> To humble thyself to those who injure thee
> To love justice
> To be merciful
> To be sincere and pure of heart
> To suffer persecution

Not only accepted as a Knight of the Order, Willoughby was also listed as a "specially qualified Knight selected by the Supreme Council to serve on the Armed Services Committee of the Sovereign Order of Saint John of Jerusalem." A statement describing the mission of the Committee explained that those selected "have been singled out for their brilliant and outstanding careers as Soldiers of Christ and Advocates of a Free World to petition governments, senates, and legislatures to cooperate with, recognize and respect the work program of the Order." In a note dated September 1963, Willoughby was listed as the "Security General" for the group, which also counted General Albert C. Wedemeyer as a member.[26]

Little wonder, then, that Willoughby was not a fan of the speech presented by President Dwight "Ike" Eisenhower to the United Nations General Assembly on December 8, 1953, the former's so-called "Atoms for Peace" speech. Seeking to reassure a jittery United States and world press in the aftermath of the Hiroshima and Nagasaki atomic bombings of 1945, Ike's speech was part of Operation *Candor*, intended in part to educate America about a nuclear future and stressing a balance between nuclear armament efforts on one hand and peaceful uses of atomic energy on the other. Also directed at a European audience, the speech was intended to encourage continental allies to cooperate in the shift in NATO strategy from large standing armies and conventional weapons to cheaper nuclear weapons. Willoughby, an inveterate critic of European nations who were not making their fair share contribution to NATO's ground forces—the key element in a nation's defense, in Willoughby's mind—was predictably opposed to any effort to expand the nuclear weapons base at the expense of ground forces; given Willoughby's four decades in the U.S. Army, such a stance was predictable.[27]

When Willoughby took pen in hand in the post-war years, he found a press—or at least a portion of the media—that eagerly welcomed his thoughts and writings. An article in the January 1959 issue of H. L. Mencken's *American Mercury* provided a vehicle for Willoughby's conservative opinions. In addressing the topic of "Espionage and the American Communist Party," he described the Potsdam Declaration as "as much an instrument of evil as the Yalta Conferences which shocked the world," prior to turning to a discussion of a topic near and dear to his heart, the Sorge case. Noting that "the virus of Communism works slowly," Willoughby referred to Agnes Smedley as a writer of Communist literature and an "intimate" of Chinese General Chu-Teh, whom she accompanied in his retreat from Chiang Kai-Shek in the 1930s. Willoughby delighted in the discovery that the book Smedley wrote about this trek was dedicated, "To my blood brothers of the Ninth Red Army." He also charged that Smedley was an associate of former Secretary of the Interior Harold Ickes and praised the Congressional committees for "exposing the Communists, the local fellow travelers and the gullible 'liberal' stooges." Putting the struggle in apocalyptic terms yet again, Willoughby wrote, "Hang one spy and another steps into his shoes, one more proof that international Communism relentlessly wages war against Western civilization."[28]

In the early 1960s, Willoughby was named one of America's prominent conservatives while working as a faculty member at the Christian Crusade Anti-Communist school in Tulsa, Oklahoma.[29] Furthermore, he soon joined the staff of *American Mercury*, whose forward-leaning masthead read, "To Bear Witness to the Truth." Willoughby, introduced as the man with a "distinguished, world-wide military career," served as the magazine's military editor and, in the March 1960 issue, he wrote what initially appears to be a blasé article entitled "Twining and De Gaulle." However, the article proved to be a strident attack upon NATO and American military weakness in the face of the "armed to the teeth" USSR and a vigorous defense of the morals and capabilities of the soldier as compared to the statesman. In introducing his subject—basically the response of Joint Chiefs of Staff head U.S. Air Force General Nathan Twining to President Charles de Gaulle's refusal to approve the stockpiling of nuclear weapons on American bases in France unless France shared control of those weapons—Willoughby gave vent to his ultra-conservative views. He vilified Harry Hopkins, praised the 11-division military contribution of Spain to NATO (not surprising given his near-deification of Franco), and characterized NATO, a favorite "whipping boy" of neo-conservatives, as "moribund" and "a cellophane façade of the West." He made a sharp distinction between military intelligence and the "laggard or prudently silent intelligence services," which suffered from "a persistent failure to recognize and admit the steadily growing Soviet menace in every military category." As he viewed the current situation, the balance of power had shifted which, he claimed, should have come as no surprise, given the fact "the Communists took over with a fanatical energy, a diplomatic brilliance and a brutality of force, never conceived of by the Czars."[30]

Demonstrating a less-than-solid grasp of history, he asserted the United States had "rescued" Denmark and Norway in World War II—a statement that likely came as a surprise to the Danes and the Norwegians. He further exhibited his belief in the reality of the United States–USSR "missile gap," which he concluded made the maintenance of large standing armies that much more important, and castigated the British for the paltry size of their defense budget (about four billion dollars, about 10 percent of the American figure), noting their contribution was more than offset by "calculated welfare spending in the same amount. *Free glasses and dentures will not stop the Cossacks on the move!*" As did others in the post-war period, Willoughby considered the international diplomatic agreements that resulted from the Yalta, Teheran, and Potsdam conferences as "suicidal 'give aways'" resulting from the misguided efforts of "megalomaniac politicians like Roosevelt and Churchill" who "wandered off into a surrealist dreamland of coexistence with Stalin." Since this is the case, "the moral responsibility for national, military guidance rests almost exclusively with the JCS [Joint Chiefs of Staff] in Washington, the custodian of Armies, the august keepers of war and peace"—clearly, Willoughby had a unique understanding of American democracy, chain of command, and civilian control of the military. In his diatribe, Willoughby also took a swipe at organized labor (charging that the Pentagon switchboards were controlled by "a communist-infested union"), the Air Force ("which generally has not the slightest conception of the battlefield but thinks largely in terms of strategic attrition"), civilians in the defense sector ("strictly amateurs as compared with the hard-bitten professionals of the Soviet armies"), and, predictably, the "humiliating dismissal of MacArthur." He concluded his article by acting as secretary of state without portfolio, opining that the USSR was most vulnerable in the Far East and that "it should have been challenged and fought there" and assessing that there was only one solution to the nuclear imbalance: "… the rapid build-up of equivalent nuclear weapons capacity to equate Soviet blackmail. Indeed, all the reliable forces of the West (France, Germany, Italy, Spain, Turkey) should have these weapons in hand, in one form or another and without diplomatic quibbling. We have the know-how; they have the manpower." Willoughby was also suspected of helping establish the politically conservative youth activism organization Young Americans for Freedom (YAF), founded in 1960 and still extant, headquartered in Herndon, Virginia. However, in 1960, he was 68 years old and YAF membership is limited to those 39 years of age and younger. As fellow Gettysburg alumnus (Class of 2018) Jeff Lauck has discovered, while Willoughby was not involved in the birth of YAF, he did serve on the National Advisory Board, though, according to YAF historian Wayne Thorburn, likely played only a ceremonial role in the organization. Nevertheless, even this indirect connection was enough to sweep up Willoughby's name into the endless, pointless John F. Kennedy conspiracy theory.[31]

Several months after "Twining and De Gaulle" appeared on the pages of *American Mercury*, Willoughby had another opportunity to excoriate the insidious Soviets, in an article entitled, "Khrushchev and the Flight to Sverdlovsk," about the furor resulting from the May 1960 shootdown of the U-2 reconnaissance aircraft piloted by Francis Gary Powers. In this article, Willoughby expressed surprise at the visceral response to the shootdown, given the "nature" of the Soviet bear; as he queried in the article, "Why is one U-2 spy plane a shock to the world, but not 35 years of intense world-wide Soviet espionage?" As he pointed out to readers:

> The Bolshevik successors to the Czars have seen fit to carry lethal measures into every category of human relations: for them it is war, cold and hot, savage, relentless, merciless war, since the commies sneaked into power. Shooting down unarmed planes is a war measure. The reconnaissance flight that culminated in this shooting is also a war measure. That was all the explanation or philosophizing that officially was required of that situation.[32]

In June 1960, Willoughby appeared before the Senate Appropriations Committee to express his informed opinion on the subject of "mutual security." After reviewing his background and experience for the committee members, he explained, "I represent the 'American Coalition,' a nationwide network of conservative, patriotic organizations." In his remarks, he addressed familiar ground—the European allies were not carrying their fair share of the NATO load and were no deterrent to the USSR, intoning:

> The United States has neither the capacity nor the obligation to posture as a "world leader." It has only one principal obligation and that is to its own security, welfare and solvency … Communist Russia and her satellites have armed remorselessly … Conversely, Western Europe failed to arm proportionately … The burden of international armament endangers U.S. fiscal solvency … To maintain its military posture at home and abroad, the U.S. must reappraise its Mutual-aid system … There is no longer room for "butter and guns."[33]

At 2:30 in the afternoon of March 30, 1962, Willoughby—one of the invited guest speakers at the American Strategy Seminar, held on the campus of the University of Buffalo and sponsored by the Buffalo (NY) Junior Chamber of Commerce—spoke on the topic, "Kremlin-Directed Espionage, in the International Field." In the biographic sketches of the speakers that accompany the program, Willoughby's *Foreign Intelligence Digest* was eloquently—if not dispassionately—described as "an impartial analysis of political, economic and military events in the critical areas of the world." This sketch also identified Willoughby as:

> … instrumental in exposing the top-leadership of the American Communist Party, notably by way of the Sorge Spy Ring. This documented exposé contains all details on Russian techniques as they are practiced throughout the world and in the U.S. This Spy case will be discussed during the Seminar. The story is of direct personal experience. It is part of the MacArthur saga and an important element of his intelligence system.

If those words did not disclose the nature and message of the event, a paragraph from the "Purpose" paragraph of the program made clear the intent: "A recent Gallop poll established that 81% of the American people would rather fight a nuclear war rather than live under Communist rule and die in a concentration camp—*Come on Americans Let's Win the Cold War*. [emphasis in the original].[34]

For a man such as Willoughby, the increasingly serious situation in post-Dien Bien Phu Vietnam was further confirmation of the long, cold grasp of the Soviet Union and a tocsin for the United States and other world democracies. To Willoughby, the situation in Southeast Asia and what occurred in Korea were eerily similar. In April 1964, Congressman Daniel J. Flood (D-PA) described Willoughby as a "competent authority" and quoted extensively from the latter's article in the February–March 1964 issue of the Tulsa, Oklahoma-based *Christian Crusade* magazine. Entitled "American Dilemma: From Laos to South Vietnam," the article expressed opposition to a ground war in Southeast Asia which would "pit the limited and educated youth of the United States against the inexhaustible and expendable, illiterate manpower of distant Asia, armed with Czech or Soviet machineguns or other lethal weapons and practicing all the barbaric atrocities typical of Communist revolutionaries." Willoughby advocated the learning of a lesson from the French debacle of ground combat in Vietnam and argued for a "new strategic policy: the calculated employment of nuclear mass-destruction weapons to offset the inexhaustible manpower of Asia. The use of these modern weapons (and the air delivery system) imposes no more moral strain than when Truman unleashed the first atomic bomb on Hiroshima—indeed, the provocation was far less."[35] In late 1965, after Willoughby's advice had been ignored and American troops had been committed to Vietnam, he wrote a letter to the *New York Times*, urging America's allies to help in Vietnam, suggesting an American "foreign legion … international brigade."[36]

In 1966, Willoughby wrote an article for *Argosy* magazine expanding on the unconventional idea he had first proposed in the letter to the *Times*—the creation of an American foreign legion. He wrote:

> Today, there are tens of thousands of young men all over the world who would jump at the opportunity to join an American fighting force, patterned after the "international brigades" formed by the Russians to fight in the Spanish Civil War in the late thirties. These are men conceivably from all walks of life, from all parts of the world, representing all races and religions … Events have forced the United States to bear the major share of defense of the free world. Despite the threat of nuclear warfare, strength is still measured in terms of military divisions of which the Communist nations have many more than the rest of the free world. Unfortunately, as in the case of Western Europe, these Allies in the past have fielded vast armies, but today they plead inability to afford the same number of divisions they had in times of peace prior to World Wars I and II … The potential of a blitzkrieg Soviet invasion of central Europe cannot be shrugged off … Apparently Europe lacks the will to fight …

He estimated that if the United States offered to enlist men into an "international brigade," 100,000 would do so. "Now the United States has reached a point in history and development which demands that its armed forces be bolstered by contributions of manpower from other areas of the world. Specifically, by a relatively small force composed of international brigades constituting part of the Regular Army." Willoughby closed his article with an accusatory question: "Throughout the world there are men eager to enlist in just such a 'foreign legion.' They are ready to fight fire with fire. Is this country?"[37]

***

By the late 1960s, the Willoughbys were looking for new pastures and, on April Fool's Day, 1968, Willoughby and his second wife Marie Antoinette (nee DeBecker) Willoughby—a civilian internee at the Japanese-run Santo Tomas Internment Camp in Manila during World War II—left Washington, D.C., for the sunny climes of Naples, Florida, where the general would spend his remaining years.[38] As expected, they settled in a well-to-do neighborhood, but a neighbor and committeeman pointed out not all their neighbors were as convinced as they should be of the Communist menace. As a letter from 5th District Committeeman Durward Packer put it, speaking of the neighborhood, "There are quite a few well to do residents there, many of whom as you stated, are still not impressed with the dangerous trends in our affairs. However, we have had a great many additions to the Republican registration list, and I feel, as far as this precinct is concerned, that is a very good indication."[39]

Correspondence from these years indicates Willoughby became very involved in the local community. In May 1970, he received a letter from Naples Mayor Lloyd M. Easterling: "Naples is indeed fortunate to have both you and Mr. Sebald [Willoughby's brother-in-law and a former American ambassador] as residents. I know of no other city which would have two people who had been so closely associated with General MacArthur."[40] Five months later, Willoughby received a letter from the president of the local Chamber of Commerce welcoming him as a new member. He was also in close touch with state legislators, political figures, and the Rotary Club. A member of the private Gulfshore Club, he also wrote defending Lieutenant Calley and other soldiers charged with murder in Vietnam, decrying the fact that a soldier could no longer simply do his duty without engendering criticism—or worse.[41]

Even as late as 1970, Willoughby was still refighting the Korean War; in May of that year, House member John R. Rarick (D-LA) addressed what he viewed as the fear mongering concerning the possible entry of China into the Vietnam–Indochina war, a la "the alleged surprise [of] Red Chinese involvement in Korea because of under evaluation from our military intelligence and commanders at that time." He reminded his fellow legislators that three years prior he had quoted from Willoughby a communication which refuted such charges. Despite that fact, Rarick noted "the military political apologist" General James M. Gavin continued to hold MacArthur and Willoughby responsible for being unprepared when the Chinese armies appeared on the battlefield. Rarick had decided to contact Willoughby at his retirement home in Florida for his response. Willoughby sent a telegram, select portions of which read:

> Reference General Gavin's remarks the whole trend is to warn against the intervention of Red China and thus disparage Nixon's current strategy including the maneuver in Cambodia which is approved of by many professional soldiers I know of … In quoting me as believing that the Chinese would not enter, he [Gavin] also revives the old Truman hoax that MacArthur misled him at Wake Island. The President had daily reports for months that the Chinese were massing along the Yalu.
>
> So had Gavin as a member of J.C.S … We reported 24 Red divisions along the Yalu as of October 15th, 1950 ready and able to cross the river. Washington's guess was as good as Tokyo's if they would dare to cross … Why browbeat Nixon on what is still a speculative potential.

Or browbeat him to learn from the Sino–Korean War 1951 with allegations that long have been disproved. This whole gambit is a repetition of the Wake Island hoax. It still crops up from time to time.

Rarick added, "General Willoughby's telegram as well as his written reports should convince objective scholars that General Gavin's recent testimony is unsubstantiated, in fact denied, by the G-2 for General Douglas MacArthur." Rarick and Willoughby were also sharply critical of a 1967 *Washington Post* article by Marquis Childs, entitled "The Vietnam War: Will China Enter?" which sought to draw parallels between the situation in 1950 and that in 1967. Childs wrote:

> The tune is somewhat different but the words are the same: China, it is being said by men of authority, cannot or will not enter the war in Vietnam. These comfortable words are strikingly like the repeated assurances of 17 years ago when the United States was deeply committed in Korea and preparing to advance to the Yalu River, the boundary between North Korea and China. Moreover, certain of the same men then in authority have responsibility today for Asian policy ...
>
> Had American leaders been familiar with the classic works which have governed the Chinese conduct of war they might not have fallen into such a fog of self-deception as in Korea when the massive Chinese invasion sent American armies reeling with heavy losses.

Willoughby rehearsed all the particulars of events in November 1950, noting that "recent isolated editorials and fragments of daily columns unwittingly perpetuate a 'malicious hoax' which is damaging to General MacArthur and the Eighth U.S. Army and represent a complete historical falsehood."[42] Whatever else could be said about Willoughby, he remained fanatically loyal to MacArthur and his beloved Army decades after the Korean War truce was signed.

Whatever name Willoughby had made for himself in the decades since he retired from the U.S. Army, he continued to have value in the eyes of his long-time employer. In a March 1971 letter from Third Army commander Lieutenant General A. C. Connor to Willoughby, the commander explained his letter was being sent to retired Army officers to:

> ... improve service attractiveness in an effort to increase the retention rate of trained personnel and induce more men and women to select the Army as a career ... As a retired member of the Army, you are a valuable link between the active Army and the general public, as well as an ambassador of good-will to our younger enlisted men and officers, and their dependents.[43]

But despite the crying need to support the military in the throes of the Vietnam War, Willoughby was now 79 years old and in declining health, unable to participate in publicizing the numerous benefits of an Army career.

CHAPTER ELEVEN

To the Grave ... and Beyond

On January 24, 1972, Hamilton Fish, the former ranking Republican member of the House Foreign Affairs Committee from 1933 to 1943 and at the time the President Emeritus of The Order of Lafayette, wrote Willoughby concerning the former's 50-page article entitled "The Unwanted and Unnecessary War with Japan." Fish asked Willoughby to review the article and, if he agreed with the premise, write a foreword. Fish clearly described the premise of his article:

> President Roosevelt was determined to get into war with Japan by the backdoor to get into the war with Germany and Italy. I use throughout my article, the word trickery. Clare Booth Luce was far more emphatic when she said Roosevelt lied us into war through the backdoor ... I believe you were the right arm of MacArthur and that he relied on you more than anyone else ...

Despite this flattering offer, and the likelihood that Willoughby agreed with such an assessment, there is no indication he ever responded, likely due to his worsening health.[1]

At the end of June 1972, William Sebald wrote to a mutual friend and member of Willoughby's close-knit group of friends, Captain Miles P. DuVal, Jr. USN (Ret.). Sebald informed the captain that Charles Willoughby had been hospitalized on June 8 and was seriously ill. He spent 10 days in the hospital before returning home. Sebald explained that, since he and Willoughby had married sisters, he was taking care of Willoughby's personal business during the latter's recovery. Willoughby had told his brother-in-law he would continue to write articles for the *Foreign Intelligence Digest*—whose initial issue had appeared in 1938—as long as he could.[2]

That period proved to be short—Major General (Ret.) Charles Andrew Willoughby passed away on Wednesday, October 25, 1972, at the age of 80, dying in his sleep after a four-month illness.[3] The *New York Times* ran a brief special the following day highlighting his military career and his life. The article noted the retired general left as survivors his wife, Marie, and a daughter, Mrs. Olga McKeever, of McAllen, Texas, and that he would be honored with a military funeral at Arlington National Cemetery on Thursday, November 2.[4] Looking back on events, retired Ambassador William Sebald—the executor of Willoughby's estate—responded to a query from a Military District of Washington official concerning photographs of Willoughby's service at Arlington. Although an official photographer had been assigned to take pictures of the service and interment, a political demonstration that could have posed a threat to the Asian photographer assigned prompted the cancellation of that scheduled event; thus, no photographs were actually taken of Willoughby's service and interment.[5]

In another letter from Sebald to DuVal, several weeks after Willoughby's passing, he indicated the *Foreign Intelligence Digest* would be allowed to die, in accordance with Willoughby's wishes. As he explained to DuVal, Willoughby had always viewed the *Digest* as a personal undertaking and "would rather have it simply die out."[6]

DuVal presented a eulogy for Willoughby before the House of Representatives, in which he referred to his friend as a "Great Military Thinker." He continued:

> Mr. Speaker, the Armed Forces of the United States have produced many eminent soldiers but few have left for future generations a legacy of authoritative professional writings in the field of military affairs and foreign military intelligence of the magnitude and quality of those by Maj. Gen. Charles A. Willoughby ... Knowledgeable, realistic, and courageous, General Willoughby throughout his writings had one prime objective—the defense of Western Civilization now under violent and subversive attack in various parts of the world, including the U.S.

DuVal also included obituaries from the *Washington Post* and the capital's other major daily, the *Evening Star*, though he was irritated the *Post* linked MacArthur's firing to his dependence on Willoughby's intelligence reports concerning the Chinese intervention.[7]

At Willoughby's passing, the *Gettysburg Times* was effusive in its praise of a man counted as a native son, despite his having spent only one year at Gettysburg College. Nevertheless, to the local populace, he had acquitted himself well since his graduation—shortly after the conclusion of World War II, the paper already characterized him as "perhaps the best known among the many sons of Gettysburg who ably served their nation in the recent conflict" and referred to him as the "loyal Gettysburg alumnus-general." The writer noted Willoughby was "Gettysburg's highest-ranking army officer," a man who at that time had spent all but two years since his graduation from the College in the American military. This same article added, "His brilliant record is a fitting symbol of Gettysburg's ability and willingness to serve its nation in time of peril."[8] Willoughby had also endeared himself to the citizens of the historic town by donating 300 personal items, the First Edition of *MacArthur, 1941–1951*, and a copy of the Japanese surrender documents from September 1945.[9]

Perhaps it is fitting that, even after his passing, Charles Willoughby continues to be in the public eye, in one way or another. The fact that he had been the *major domo* to one of the prominent figures of the century undoubtedly helps, as does his own controversial nature and much-debated place in history, and the developing scholarship surrounding the Korean War. Readers of any of the more than 50 novels in the seven series written by William Edward Butterworth III—better-known by the most familiar of his 13 pen names, W. E. B. Griffin—have encountered the name of Willoughby in the pages of several volumes, especially in the series entitled *The Corps*. Interestingly, whenever Willoughby makes an appearance, he is usually portrayed in a negative light. For example, in one volume of that fictional series, he is portrayed presenting an intelligence briefing to MacArthur and his fellow staffers on the Pacific Theater Battle of Midway in June 1942. Described by Griffin as a "portly U.S. Army officer in tropical worsted blouse and trousers standing almost at attention beside a lectern," Willoughby begins the briefing by stating, "The intelligence that we have developed indicates that Admiral Yamamoto, commanding the entire Japanese fleet, is aboard the battleship *Yamoto* [sic] somewhere in this general area," pointing to an area roughly equidistant between Midway and the Aleutian Islands." Upon hearing such a claim, U.S. Naval Reserve Captain Pickering mentally responds with a profane tirade: "You phony sonofabitch. 'Intelligence we have developed' my ass. You didn't develop a goddamn bit of that. It came from the Navy. After the fact, of course, much later than they should have told us, but they came up with it."[10] Even in death, Willoughby's name was connected with claiming accomplishments that were not his own, in whole or in part.

The life and career of Charles Willoughby can provide valuable lessons to present and future generations, if we are attuned to them—about loyalty to one's superior and organization, about the ability to tell truth to power, about the training of current and future intelligence analysts and their unique profession, about our own human thought processes and, on a larger scale, about the true meaning of honor and virtue. The continuing historical need for a military force ensures such issues of command and control as MacArthur and Willoughby faced—such as the critical skill of relaying bad news from subordinate to superior both accurately and completely—will always be with us and behooves us to learn from past examples of such, both good and bad. The question also arises, how do we ensure no one ever again has "undue influence over intelligence analysis"? One authority on Willoughby believes such tactics as collaborative analytical tools, web-based information sharing, and improved interagency cooperation might keep any one individual, such as Willoughby, from exercising such unchecked power.[11] Another student of the career intelligence officer points out the importance of ensuring individuals are actually *qualified* for their positions—this author notes that "during his whole career, Willoughby was often placed by circumstances in areas for which he was no [sic] remotely prepared" and makes the point that the best military intelligence chiefs—he cites Admiral Bobby Ray Inman, Major General Kenneth Strong, and Lieutenant General Daniel Graham—had deep experience prior to their assumption of major positions in the field. He advises:

> The failures of General Willoughby, in contrast to the successful performance of the latter [the officers named above] suggests that general and flag officers should not be placed as heads of intelligence agencies on the basis of their administrative abilities, mastery of military history, or strategic vision with the comfortable assurance that they will do a good job in intelligence work. Before an officer is posted in this sensitive post, he should have learned this complicated art from the bottom up through the decision-making level.[12]

Finally, those who returned from the Korean War broken or who did not return at all—in part as a direct or indirect result of the decisions made by men such as Charles Willoughby—demand we recognize and internalize sober lessons from his life and times.

APPENDIX I

Dramatis Personae

Major General Edward Mallory "Ned" Almond, USA—Placed in charge of Inchon amphibious landing at Wonsan, September 1950; had a poor working relationship with Major General O. P. Smith, 1st Marine Division Commander, and General Walker, Eighth Army Commander; underestimated strength and skill of Chinese; Ridgway retains him as Commander, X Corps, participated in the Eighth Army's counteroffensive, Operation *Killer*, against Chinese offensives of February–March 1951; promoted to lieutenant general February 1951; became head of U.S. Army War College, July 1951; retired 1953, worked in insurance industry until his death in 1979.

General Omar Bradley, USA—Immediately following World War II, chosen by President Harry Truman to head and modernize Veterans Administration; 1948, selected as Army Chief of Staff; 1949, selected as first Chairman, Joint Chiefs of Staff, followed by selection as first Chairman of the Military Committee of NATO; 1950, promoted to General of the Army (five-star) rank; left active-duty service in 1953, consultant to industry and business, advocate of U.S. Army issues; died 1981.

John Chamberlain—Writer, journalist, literary critic; Co-author, with Willoughby, of *MacArthur, 1941–1951*, published in 1954; editorial writer for *Wall Street Journal*, 1950–60; long-time contributor to *National Review;* died 1995.

William Costello—Hard-hitting Columbia Broadcasting System (CBS) reporter and constant critic of Willoughby's during post-war occupation in Tokyo; often accused by Willoughby and "fellow travelers" of being a Communist; Willoughby's secretary able to smooth his ruffled feathers by inviting him to a stag dinner hosted by Willoughby; later sportswriter for Baltimore *Evening Sun, Life* magazine writer, and advertising manager for National Brewing Company; died 2016.

Miles P. DuVal, Jr.—1918 U.S. Naval Academy graduate, received M.A. degree in Foreign Studies from Georgetown University in 1937; close friend of Willoughby, delivered his obituary before Congress; before his death in 1989, endowed Collection on Inter-Oceanic Canal and Naval History at Georgetown University; papers in archives of Naval History and Heritage Command, Washington, D.C.

General Robert Eichelberger, USMC—Commandant, U.S. Military Academy, West Point, NY; Commander, 77th Infantry Division, then I Corps; led campaign at Buna, Hollandia, Biak, Luzon; retired as Lieutenant General, 1948, headed U.S. Eighth Army occupation of Japan; published his memoirs, *Our Jungle Road to Tokyo* in 1950; promoted to General by Congress, 1954; died of pneumonia1961, but humorous memoir of his life in Pacific war, *Dear Miss Em: General Eichelberger's War in the Pacific, 1942–1945,* published in 1972; buried in Arlington National Cemetery.

Enlai, Chou—Politician who served as Chinese premier from 1949–76 and foreign minister from 1949–58; described as "affable, pragmatic, and persuasive," survived series of purges of government officials; considered one of great negotiators of 20th century; 1950, signed a 30-year treaty of alliance with USSR; 1956–64, traveled widely through Asia, Africa, and Europe; traveled to USSR in 1964, but unable to bridge gap that had developed between PRC and USSR; historic meeting in 1972 between President Nixon and Chinese leader Mao Zedong largely result of Chou's efforts; regarded as most important stabilizing influence during Cultural Revolution; died in 1976.

Generalissimo Francisco Franco—Spanish general of right-wing persuasion living under leftist Spanish Republic; selected as Army Chief of Staff in 1935, begins purge of leftists from the Army; joins rebels during Spanish Civil War (1936–39), allies with Mussolini's Italy and Hitler's Nazi Germany; known as "El Caudillo" ("The Leader"); becomes leader of military dictatorship for rest of his life; died in 1975.

Major General Hobart "Hap" Gay, USA—1st Cavalry Division Commander in Korea, then Deputy Commander, Fourth Army; Commander, VI Corps, 1952; Fifth Army Commander 1954; retired in 1955 as lieutenant general, Commander of Antiaircraft and Guided Missile Center, Fort Bliss, Texas; earned two Distinguished Service Crosses, two Distinguished Service Medals, two Legions of Merit, three Silver Stars, two Bronze Stars; died 1983, El Paso, Texas.

General Torashiro Kawabe—served in Imperial Japanese Army, 1912–45; became lieutenant general in 1941, specialized in field artillery; 1943, 2nd Air Force Commander, Imperial Japanese Army, but returned to staff, 1944; April 1945, Vice Chief, Imperial Japanese Army General Staff, headed Japanese delegation to Manila for Japanese surrender; died 1960.

Major General Laurence "Dutch" Keiser, USA—Commander of 2nd Infantry Division, first Stateside unit deployed to peninsula following Korean War outbreak; unit suffered 4,000 casualties in Ch'ongch'on River assault; relieved of command, ostensibly for medical reasons, though he believes he is made a scapegoat for UN reverses following Chinese invasion; retired from Army, 1953; died 1969.

General Douglas MacArthur, USA—West Point graduate and World War I veteran; Superintendent of West Point; Army Chief of Staff; Field Marshal of the Philippines; serves as Southwest Pacific Area (SWPA) commander during World War II; post-war administrator of Japan; commander, UN Forces in Korea; died 1964.

Olga (Tonie) McKeever—Only child of Charles A. Willoughby and Juana Manuela Rodriguez; born December 25, 1925, in Caracas, Venezuela, passed away July 23, 2012, in San Antonio, Texas; lifelong volunteer, extensive traveler who loved "good food and a stiff Scotch Old Fashion," owner of La Petite Maison, a jewelry store in McAllen, Texas; preceded in death by her husband of 37 years, Lieutenant Colonel Eugene C. McKeever; survived by four children, eight grandchildren.

John Muccio—First United States Ambassador to South Korea, appointed 1949; had held previous diplomatic posts in Germany, Far East, Central America; January 1950, negotiated first Republic of Korea (ROK) agreement on American military aid, worth $10 million; when ROK invaded, relocated with South Korean government to Taegu, Pusan; received two medals from ROK for his actions; retired from Foreign Service in 1961 with career minister rank, highest possible; died at age 89, of heart failure, in Washington, D.C.

Paul Nitze—Director of Policy Planning, U.S. Department of State, in 1950; 1953, appointed Assistant Secretary of Defense for Intelligence Security Affairs, resigned to become president of fundraising arm of School of Advanced International Studies (SAIS), Johns Hopkins University; served as national security advisor for Kennedy campaign, then Assistant Secretary of Defense, Secretary of the Navy (1963), later Deputy Secretary of Defense; negotiated SALT I antiballistic missile treaty, 1972; resigned as part of Watergate scandal, 1974; presented with Medal of Freedom by President Reagan; 1989, SAIS renamed Paul Nitze School of International Studies; died at age 97 in 2004, funeral at Washington National Cathedral, pallbearers crewmen from USS *Nitze*.

K. M. Pannikar—Kavalam Mahava Pannikar; Indian scholar, journalist, historian, administrator, diplomat (in China until 1952); Ambassador to Egypt, 1952–53, France, 1956–59; severe stroke prompts return to India; returned to college teaching/administration; died 1963.

Marshal Lin Piao, People's Liberation Army—One of Chinese Communist Party's (CCP) most brilliant generals, youngest of "Ten Marshals," named in 1955; suffered from debilitating mental, physical health problems after 1938 injury, becomes increasingly detached, paranoid; despite private criticisms of Chairman Mao, has leading role in 1966 Cultural Revolution; died September 13, 1971, suspicious plane crash in Mongolia, may have been part of failed plot to oust Mao; post-death, condemned as traitor by CCP.

Manuel Quezon—First President of Philippine Republic, 1935; re-elected, 1941; formed government-in-exile in United States when Japanese invaded, 1942; died August 1, 1944, of tuberculosis, in exile, Lake Saranac, New York.

Dr. Synghman Rhee—First President, Republic of Korea, 1948–60; first Korean to earn PhD at an American university, Princeton, 1910; forced to resign, 1960; died, 1965, Honolulu, Hawaii.

Major General Matthew Ridgway, USA—Appointed Deputy Chief of Staff, 1949; goes to Korea December 1950 to replace deceased General Walton W. Walker as Eighth Army Commander; defeats Chinese at Chipyong-Ni, Wonju, February 1951; replaces MacArthur following latter's dismissal by President Truman; promoted to general, becomes military governor of Japan; succeeded Dwight Eisenhower as Supreme Allied Commander Europe for NATO; U.S. Army Chief of Staff, August 1953; quarreled with Eisenhower about Vietnam involvement and cutting of Army strength in face of USSR threat; retired June 1955; died 1993, age 98, buried in Arlington National Cemetery.

Juana Manuela Rodriguez—Peruvian-born wife of Charles A. Willoughby, mother of Olga (Tonie) McKeever.

William Sebald—Career Foreign Service officer who had come to Japan in 1925 as a Navy language officer, attached to the American Embassy Tokyo; 1933–39, worked as an international lawyer in Kobe, Japan; with outbreak of World War II, returned to the Navy, in charge of Combat Intelligence Division for Pacific Area, Headquarters, U.S. Navy Commander in Chief; MacArthur's political advisor from September 1947 until MacArthur relieved; Ambassador to Burma, Deputy Assistant Secretary of State for Far Eastern Affairs, Ambassador to Australia from 1957 to 1961; Willoughby's brother-in-law, executor of his estate.

Colonel Van S. Merle-Smith, USA—Executive Intelligence Officer to MacArthur during World War II; suffered mental breakdown due to South Pacific workload, 1943; died three months later, November 1943.

Richard Sorge—Soviet military intelligence officer working undercover as a German journalist in Germany and Japan; leader of an extensive spy network, his espionage outed in part due to Willoughby's investigation; imprisoned in Japan 1944, repudiated by both Soviets and German military intelligence (*Abwehr*), tried, tortured, and hanged by the Japanese in November 1944.

General Andres Soriano—Spanish Filipino industrialist who served as influential cabinet member in administration of Filipino president Manuel Quezon; later a colonel on MacArthur's staff, granted United States citizenship in return for his services; died 1964.

General Carl "Tooey" Spaatz, U.S. Army Air Forces—West Point graduate 1914, then serves as officer in charge at Issodoun, France, while Willoughby is in the unit; shot down three enemy aircraft in three-week period near end of conflict; Commander, Strategic Air Forces, World War II; only general officer present for German surrender to American forces, German surrender to Russian forces, Japanese surrender to American forces; first Chief of Staff of the U.S. Air Force, 1947; retired as general, 1948; served as military affairs editor for *Newsweek* until 1961; died 1974.

Sung, Kim Il—Premier and president of North Korea from 1948 until 1974; known as the "Great Leader," creates a cult of personality; authorized North Korean invasion of South Korea in 1950; third longest-serving non-royal head of state in the 20th century; birthday celebrated as a public holiday, "Day of the Sun"; died 1994, succeeded as national leader by son Kim Jong-Il.

Marshal Peng Dehuai, PLA—Professional soldier at age 16, originally fought with Chiang Kai-Shek and Nationalists, but turns to Communists; "Long March" veteran and supporter of Mao Zedong; early supporter of Chinese entry into Korean War, serves as commander of Chinese People's Volunteer Army during early war years; Defense Minister, People's Republic of China, 1954–59; falling out with Mao, 1959, sentenced to life in prison, dies in prison, 1974; reputation restored after Mao's death in 1976 by former colleague Deng Xiaopeng.

Colonel Percy Thompson, USA—Serves as I Corps G-2, considered one of the most able intelligence officers in Korea; warned of Chinese entry into war, but reports widely dismissed; daughter married John Eisenhower, son of Dwight D. Eisenhower, 1947; died 1974.

Harry Truman—Missouri senator, vice-president, 33rd President of the United States, 1945–53; following death of President Roosevelt, authorized dropping of atomic bombs on Hiroshima and Nagasaki to end World War II in the Pacific;

pursues policy of defeating North Korea, but rejects MacArthur's call to widen the war; survives 1950 assassination attempt by two Puerto Rican nationalists; in wake of MacArthur's insubordination, illicitly releasing White House plans to press, relieves MacArthur of command in Korea, April 1951; died 1972.

Pancho Villa—Mexican revolutionary leader and general during the Mexican Revolution; led 1916 raid against town of Columbus, New Mexico, U.S. Army under John J. Pershing responds, nine-month-long unsuccessful pursuit of Villa ends with American entry into World War I; Willoughby part of the pursuit force.

Lieutenant Colonel Russ Volckmann, USA—1934 West Point graduate, U.S. Army infantry officer, leader of anti-Japanese resistance forces in the Philippines; post-war, tasked by General Eisenhower with writing Army's first counterinsurgency doctrine, released in September 1950; considered one of co-founders of Green Berets Special Forces unit; retired from Army as brigadier general, 1956; died 1982.

Lieutenant General Walton W. Walker, USA—Member of a military family, graduated from West Point, 1912; heroically serves as commander in World War I, World War II, and in Korea, where he serves as commander of 8th Infantry Division, American occupation force in Japan; in response to North Korean invasion, compelled to retreat to "Pusan Perimeter"; with reinforcements, leads new offensive into North Korea but compelled to retreat again with Chinese entry into war; died December 23, 1950, in jeep accident, posthumously promoted to general.

Major General Courtney Whitney, USA—World War I veteran who became a lawyer in Philippines, then intelligence officer in China until MacArthur requests him for service in SWPA; close to MacArthur, resigns in 1951 after MacArthur fired; 1956, published *MacArthur: His Rendezvous with Destiny*; fellow "Bataan Boy," like Willoughby, with whom he crosses swords in post-war Japan; died 1969.

Frank Wisner—An Office of Strategic Services veteran, Wisner headed the CIA's Office of Policy Coordination (OPC) from 1948 to 1950, when OPC became Directorate of Plans, Wisner served as deputy director until 1958 breakdown; retired from Agency in 1962, committed suicide in 1965; target of Willoughby's opposition to the CIA in Far East Command.

Zedong, Mao—Chinese Communist revolutionary and founder of the People's Republic of China; Chairman of the Communist Party of China, 1949–76, authorizes Chinese entry into Korean War; as leader of Communist forces, defeats Chiang Kai-Shek's Nationalist forces to emerge victor in Chinese Civil War; died 1976.

Dates of Rank and Military Awards— Charles A. Willoughby

Dates of Rank

—Private, United States Army, October 10, 1910; Discharged as Sergeant, October 9, 1913
—Second Lieutenant, United States Army, November 27, 1916
—First Lieutenant, United States Army, November 27, 1916
—Captain, United States Army, June 30, 1917
—Major, United States Army, March 6, 1928
—Lieutenant Colonel, United States Army, June 1, 1938
—Colonel, Army of the United States*, October 14, 1941
—Brigadier General, Army of the United States*, June 20, 1942
—Major General, Army of the United States*, March 17, 1945; Terminated May 31, 1946
—Colonel, United States Army, September 1, 1945
—Brigadier General, Army of the United States*, May 31, 1946 (Date of rank June 20, 1942)
—Brigadier General, United States Army, January 24, 1948
—Major General, Army of the United States, January 24, 1948

*During the interwar years (1920s and 1930s), the Regular Army (RA) was ranked 16th in the world—promotions were extremely slow and it was not uncommon for officers to spend 10 to 15 years in junior grades and for enlisted to never rise above the rank of private. During World War II, the Regular Army/U.S. Army served as the professional core of the Army of the United States (AUS). Regular Army officers typically held two ranks—permanent rank in the Regular Army and temporary rank in the AUS; AUS rank could be revoked, meaning reversion to RA rank, an effective demotion. Enlisted personnel were either RA (enlistees) or AUS (draftees), distinguished by the letters "RA" or "AUS," respectively, before their service numbers. The AUS was demobilized in 1946 and the U.S. Army was divided into RA and U.S. Army Reserve components. During the Korean War, the AUS was revived, but only for enlisted draftees.

Military Awards (American and foreign)

Distinguished Service Cross	Army Distinguished Service Medal (two Oak Leaf Clusters)		
Silver Star	Legion of Merit	World War I Victory Medal	American Defense Service Medal
Asiatic Pacific Campaign Medal (seven service stars)	World War II Victory Medal	Army of Occupation Medal	National Defense Service Medal
Korean Service Medal (one service star)	United Nations Medal for Korea	Grand Officer of the Order of Orange-Nassau (Netherlands)	Commander of the Order of Saints Maurice and Lazarus (Italy)
Distinguished Service Star (Philippines)	Philippine Defense Medal	Philippine Liberation Medal (two bronze stars)	Order of Abdon Calderon (Ecuador)

The Grand Officer of the Order of Orange-Nassau (Netherlands) is a chivalric order open to "everyone who has earned special merits for society," i.e., those who "deserve appreciation and recognition from society for the special way in which they have carried out their activities." The Commander of the Order of Saints Maurice and Lazarus (Italy) is a dynastic order of knighthood that has been awarded by the House of Savoy since the 16th century. Although there are an estimated 2,000 individuals worldwide who have received this award, it has not been recognized by Italy since 1951. There are six classes of the award for men, three for women. Other notable World War II American recipients of this award include General Mark Clark, General Ira Eaker, and General George Marshall. The Order of Abdon Calderon (Ecuador) has been awarded since 1904 for "extraordinary military service."

Endnotes

Chapter 1: Of Uncertain Origins: The Early Years of "Sir Charles"

1. Russell Spur, *Enter the Dragon: China's Undeclared War Against the U.S. in Korea, 1950–51* (New York: Newmarket Press, 1988), 161; David Halberstam, *The Coldest Winter: America and the Korean War* (New York: Hyperion Books, 2007), 373, 375; William Manchester, *American Caesar: Douglas MacArthur, 1880–1964* (New York: Dell Publishing Co., Inc., 1978), 467; Michael C. Hickey, *The Korean War: The West Confronts Communism* (Woodstock, NY: Overlook Press, 1999), 24; "Charles A. Willoughby," accessed September 10, 2019, www.thefullwiki.org/Charles.A.Willoughby.

2. Frank Kluckhohn, "Heidelberg to Madrid—The Story of General Willoughby," *The Reporter* (New York Journal), August 19, 1952, 3.

3. Ibid.

4. Jon Halliday and Bruce Cummings, *Korea: The Unknown War* (New York: Pantheon Books, 1988), 152.

5. Paul M. Edwards, *To Acknowledge a War: The Korean War in American Memory* (Westport, CT: Greenwood Press, 2000), 80; Dennis D. Wainstock, *Truman, MacArthur and the Korean War* (Westport, CT: Greenwood Press, 1999), 9.

6. Michael E. Haas, Col., USAF (ret.), *In the Devil's Shadow: UN Special Operations During the Korean War* (Annapolis, MD: Naval Institute Press, 2000), 178.

7. Blaine Harden, *King of Spies: The Dark Reign of America's Spymaster in Korea* (New York: Viking, 2017), 52; Franz-Stefan Gady, "Is This the Worst Intelligence Chief in the U.S. Army's History?", *The Diplomat*, January 27, 2019, 2.

8. Eric Larrabee, *Commander in Chief: Franklin Delano Roosevelt, His Lieutenants and Their War* (New York: Harper and Row, 1987), 333.

9. Letter to Willoughby from Mrs. Austin F. Prescott, dated January 21, 1952, Box 8-24, MS-024, Special Collections/Musselman Library, Gettysburg College, Gettysburg, PA.

10. Hickey, *The Korean War*, 24; Willoughby biographic data sheet, Willoughby personal papers, Box 1-1, MS-024, Special Collections/Musselman Library, Gettysburg College, Gettysburg, PA; Kluckhohn, 3; Bio sheet, Charles Andre Willoughby, War Department, Public Information Office, undated, in Box 1-1, MS-024, Special Collections/Musselman Library, Gettysburg College, Gettysburg, PA; Obituary, *Gettysburg Times*, Thursday, October 26, 1972.

11. These scandalous charges—the first possibly true, the second undoubtedly so, given Willoughby's heritage—appear to have no other documentation supporting them than a Wikipedia article.

12. Willoughby biographic data sheet, Special Collections/Musselman Library; Article in *Flying* magazine, Vol. VII, No. 8, September 1918, 740, accessed online, September 28, 2010; Kenneth J. Campbell, "Major General Charles A. Willoughby: General MacArthur's G-2—A Biographic Sketch," *American Intelligence Journal* 18, no. 1/2 (1998), 87–91. As Campbell points out, there is conflicting information concerning Willoughby's college education—according to records of

the Public Information Press Branch, Department of Defense, Willoughby had taken courses at Heidelberg University in Germany and at the Sorbonne in Paris prior to his coming to the United States. However, most Germans are 19 years of age when they pass the *Abitur* examination, a prerequisite for entering a German university. The only possibilities are that either Willoughby demonstrated a gifted nature at 17 years of age that proved temporary, or the record is flawed. Philology was an area of expertise for the young Willoughby, who became fluent in English, Spanish, French, German, and, later, Japanese.

13. Obituary, *Gettysburg Times*, Thursday, October 26, 1972; Halberstam, *The Coldest Winter*, 375.

14. Ibid.; Bob Brent, "On the Cover: Brig-General C. A. Willoughby," *Gettysburg College Bulletin*, Vol. XXXIII, No. 2, February 1943, 3.

15. Andrew J. Birtle, *U.S. Army Counterinsurgency and Contingency Operations Doctrine 1860–1941* (Washington, D.C.: Center of Military History, United State Army, 2009), 245.

16. Halberstam, *The Coldest Winter*, 374.

17. Roger A. Beaumont, "The Flawed Soothsayer: Willoughby, General MacArthur's G-2," *Espionage*, August 1985, 23.

18. www.spartacus.schoolnet.co.uk/JFKwilloughbyC.htm, accessed May 19, 2010, Beaumont, "The Flawed Soothsayer," 23.

19. Mae Brussell, "The Nazi Connection to the John F. Kennedy Assassination," accessed September 16, 2010, www.maebrussell.com. Brussell is a Carmel, CA-based private researcher whose work needs to be approached with caution. This medal is awarded for chivalry by Italy's House of Savoy, which dates to the 16th century. There are six classes of the award for men, three for women. Other notable Word War II American recipients include General Mark Clark, General Ira Eaker, and General George Marshall.

20. Halberstam, *The Coldest Winter*, 375; www.spartacus.schoolnet.co.uk/JFKwilloughbyC. htm, accessed May 19, 2010; Charles Andre Willoughby bio sheet, War Department, Public Information Office, in Willoughby personal papers, Box 1-1, MS-024, Special Collections/ Musselman Library, Gettysburg College, Gettysburg, PA; "World War II Intelligence in the Pacific Theater: Charles Willoughby," Fort Huachuca, accessed June 14, 2012, www.huachuca. army.mil/sites/History/PDFS/MWILLOU.pdf; Kluckhohn, "Heidelberg to Madrid," 3.

21. Beaumont, "The Flawed Soothsayer," 20.

22. Col. Forrest R. Blackburn, USAR, "Military Review, 1922–1972", *Military Review*, February 1972, 55, 61; Letter to the Editor, *Military Review*, Vol. 77, No. 2, March/April 1997, n.p.

23. Oral Reminiscences of Major General Charles A. Willoughby, Naples, Florida, interview with D. Clayton James, July 30, 1971, RG 23, Box 12, Folder 12, MMA, Norfolk, VA, 3.

24. Halberstam, *The Coldest Winter*, 375; Kluckhohn, "Heidelberg to Madrid," 3; Willoughby manuscript, "The Character of Military Intelligence," Box 11-1, MS-024, Willoughby papers, Special Collections/Musselman Library, Gettysburg College, Gettysburg, PA, 1, 4; Beaumont, "The Flawed Soothsayer," 24; Interview with D. Clayton James, July 30, 1971.

25. Arthur Herman, *Douglas MacArthur, American Warrior*, 299; Beaumont, "The Flawed Soothsayer," 20.

26. Douglas MacArthur, *Reminiscences*, as cited in *Reader's Digest Illustrated Story of World War II* (Pleasantville, NY: 1969), 161.

27. Clark Lee and Richard Henschel, *Douglas MacArthur* (New York: Henry Holt and Company, 1952), 182–83.

28. Spur, *Enter the Dragon*, 161; Harden, *King of Spies*, 52.

29. Harden, *King of Spies*, 52.

30. Gady, "Is This the Worst Intelligence Chief," 2.

31. Kenneth J. Campbell, "Major General Charles A. Willoughby: A Mixed Performance," text of an unpublished paper, edited version published as "Major General Charles A. Willoughby: General MacArthur's G-2—A Biographic Sketch," *American Intelligence Journal* 18 no. 1 (1998), 2.
32. Kluckhohn, "Heidelberg to Madrid," 3–4.
33. Ibid., 5.
34. Halberstam, *The Coldest Winter*, 375; Kluckhohn, "Heidelberg to Madrid" 3; "The Character of Military Intelligence," 1, 4; General Orders No. 26, November 12, 1941, RG 23, Box 12, Folder 14, MMA, Norfolk, VA.
35. Colonel Alison Ind, *Allied Intelligence Bureau: Our Secret Weapon in the War Against Japan* (New York: David McKay Company, Inc., 1958), 7–9.
36. Lee and Henschel, *Douglas MacArthur*, 166.
37. Clarke Newlon, *The Fighting Douglas MacArthur* (New York: Dodd, Mead and Co., 1965), 3.
38. Herman, *Douglas MacArthur*, 395, 435.
39. Campbell, "Major General Charles A. Willoughby," 87–91; "World War II Intelligence in the Pacific Theater: Charles Willoughby," Fort Huachuca, 4.

Chapter 2: "Sir Charles" in the Pacific, 1942–45

1. Eric Larrabee, *Commander in Chief: Franklin Delano Roosevelt, His Lieutenants and Their War* (New York: Harper and Row, 1987), 321.
2. "Charles Andre Willoughby (04615)," CADRE biographic data sheet, document number CO2131052, February 1951 (?), CIA archives; www.spartacus.schoolnet.co.uk/JFKwilloughbyC.htm., accessed May 19, 2010.
3. Larrabee, *Commander in Chief*, 25–26.
4. William Manchester, *American Caesar: Douglas MacArthur, 1880–1964* (New York: Dell Publishing Co., Inc., 1978), 320–21.
5. Ibid., 296.
6. Ibid., 480; Kenneth J. Campbell, "Major General Charles A. Willoughby: A Mixed Performance," text of an unpublished paper, edited version published as "Major General Charles A. Willoughby: General MacArthur's G-2—A Biographic Sketch," *American Intelligence Journal* 18 no. 1 (1998), 3.
7. Douglas MacArthur, *Reminiscences*, as cited in *Reader's Digest Illustrated Story of World War II* (Pleasantville, NY: 1969), 113.
8. Bob Brent, "On the Cover: Brig-General C. A. Willoughby," *Gettysburg (PA) College Bulletin*, Vol. XXXIII, No. 2, Feb 1943, 3.
9. William B. Breuer, *MacArthur's Undercover War: Spies, Saboteurs, Guerrillas, and Secret Missions* (Edison, NJ: Castle Books, 2005, 36–37.
10. Carol Morriss Petillo, *Douglas MacArthur: The Philippine Years* (Bloomington, Indiana: Indiana University Press, 1981), 198.
11. Arthur Herman, *Douglas MacArthur: American Warrior* (New York: Random House, 2016), 299.
12. Stephen R. Taafe, *MacArthur's Jungle War: The 1944 New Guinea Campaign* (Lawrence, KS: University Press of Kansas, 1998), 41.
13. Brigadier General Elliott R. Thorpe, *East Wind, Rain: The Intimate Account of an Intelligence Officer in the Pacific, 1939–1949* (Boston Gambit Inc., 1969), 95–96.
14. Herman, *Douglas MacArthur*, 435–36.
15. "Charles Andre Willoughby (04615), CADRE biographic data sheet, CIA archives; Charles Andre Willoughby bio sheet, War Department, Public Information Office, in Willoughby

personal papers, Box 1-1, MS-024, Special Collections/Musselman Library, Gettysburg College, Gettysburg, PA. An interesting note in his official biographic data sheet indicated that he "brilliantly developed" the CGSC School Quarterly. Kenneth J. Campbell, "Major General Charles A. Willoughby: General MacArthur's G-2—A Biographic Sketch," *American Intelligence Journal* 18, no. 1/2 (1998), 87–91; "World War II Intelligence in the Pacific Theater: Charles Willoughby," Fort Huachuca, accessed June 14, 2012, www.huachuca.army.mil/sites/History/PDFS/MWILLOU.pdf, 4.

16. Colonel Alison Ind, *Allied Intelligence Bureau: Our Secret Weapon in the War Against Japan* (New York: David McKay Company, Inc., 1958), 118; Joseph R. McMicking biography, accessed February 13, 2020, bataanlegacy.org/uploads/3/4/7/6/34760003/joseph_mcmicking_8.5x11_on11x17_reduced.pdf.

17. Herman, *Douglas MacArthur*, 343.

18. Petillo, *Douglas MacArthur*, 203.

19. Herman, *Douglas MacArthur*, 383.

20. Douglas MacArthur, *Reminiscences*, 161; John Toland, *But Not in Shame: The Six Months After Pearl Harbor* (New York: Random House, 1961), 186–87.

21. Breuer, *MacArthur's Undercover War*, 122–25, 129–30; Michael Schaller, *Douglas MacArthur: The Far Eastern General* (New York: Oxford University Press, 1989), 101.

22. Schaller, *Douglas MacArthur*, 78; Manchester, *American Caesar*, 498; David Halberstam, *The Coldest Winter: America and the Korean War* (New York: Hyperion Books, 2007), 129.

23. Clark Lee and Richard Henschel, *Douglas MacArthur* (New York: Henry Holt and Company, 1952), 137, 181–82.

24. Douglas Ford, "Dismantling the 'Lesser Men' and 'Supermen' Myths: U.S. Intelligence on the Imperial Japanese Army after the Fall of the Philippines, Winter 1942 to Spring 1943," *Intelligence and National Security*, Vol. 24, No. 4, August 2009, 544.

25. Ibid., 548–62.

26. Ind, *Allied Intelligence Bureau*, 7–8.

27. Clayton Laurie, "General MacArthur and the OSS, 1942–1945," *Studies in Intelligence*, Vol. 45, No. 1, 2001, accessed May 23, 2014, https://www.csi.cia.ic.gov/studies/vol45no1/article7.htm, 12–13.

28. Brown, *The Last Hero*, 515.

29. Stanley Sandler, "Secret Operations of the Central Intelligence Agency During the Korean War," unpublished manuscript, n.d., Center for the Study of Intelligence, Central Intelligence Agency, 7; Douglas Waller, *Wild Bill Donovan: The Spymaster Who Created the OSS and Modern American Espionage* (New York: Free Press, 2011), 232.

30. Laurie, "General MacArthur and the OSS," 12–13.

31. Ibid., 48.

32. John F. Kreis, general editor, *Piercing the Fog: Intelligence and Army Air Force Operations in World War II* (Washington, D.C.: Air Force History and Museums Program, Bolling Air Force Base, 1996), 253.

33. Laurie, "General MacArthur and the OSS," 48.

34. Campbell, "Major General Charles A. Willoughby," 87–91; Breuer, *MacArthur's Undercover War*, 56.

35. Michael E. Bigelow, "Allied Intelligence Bureau Plays Role in World War II," https://www.army.mil/article/174480/allied_intelligence_bureau_plays-role_in_world_war_ii, 1–3.

36. Edward J. Drea, *MacArthur's ULTRA* (Lawrence, KS: University of Kansas Press, 1992), 22; Ronald H. Spector, *Eagle Against the Sun: The American War with Japan* (New York: Vintage Books, 1985), 458.

37. John Prados, *Combined Fleet Decoded: The Secret History of American Intelligence and the Japanese Navy in World War II* (New York: Random House, 1995), 417.

38. "Battle of Sio," *Wikipedia*, accessed January 10, 2018, https://en.wikipedia.org/wiki/Battle_of_Sio, 3, 7, 9.
39. Herman, *Douglas MacArthur*, 311–12.
40. Laurie, "General MacArthur and the OSS," 49.
41. Kreis, *Piercing the Fog*, 253.
42. Bradley F. Smith, *The ULTRA-MAGIC Deals and the Most Secret Special Relationship, 1940–1946*, 107–08; James C. McNaughton, *Nisei Linguists: Japanese Americans in the Military Intelligence Service during World War II* (Washington, DC: Department of the Army, 2007), 184.
43. Sandler, "Secret Operations of the Central Intelligence Agency During the Korean War," 23–24.
44. Larrabee, *Commander in Chief*, 321.
45. Thorpe, *East Wind, Rain*, 95; Larrabee, *Commander in Chief*, 324.
46. Prados, *Combined Fleet Decoded*, 417.
47. Ed Drea, "A Very Savage Operation," *World War II* magazine, accessed December 9, 2004, http://www.thehistorynet.com/wwii/blsavageoperation/, 1, 5.
48. Memo to Chief of Staff, G-3, 21 April 1942, Subject: Japanese Offensive Expected End of April/Early May, RG 23C, Box 1, Folder 4, MMA, Norfolk, VA; GHQ, SWPA, MIS, G-2 Info Bulletin, May 5, 1942, Subject: General Review of Probable Enemy Plans, RG 23C, Box 1, Folder 4, MMA, Norfolk, VA; Walter R. Borneman, *MacArthur at War: World War II in the Pacific* (New York: Little, Brown and Co., 2016), 199; John C. McManus, *Fire and Fortitude: The U.S. Army in the Pacific War, 1941–1943* (New York: Caliber, 2019), p. 303.
49. Herman, *Douglas MacArthur*, 442; Roger A. Beaumont, "The Flawed Soothsayer: Willoughby, General MacArthur's G-2," *Espionage*, August 1985, p. 26; Borneman, *MacArthur at War*, 220, 228; Larrabee, *Commander in Chief*, 324.
50. Larrabee, *Commander in Chief*, 325; McManus, *Fire and Fortitude*, 296.
51. Brent, "On the Cover," 3.
52. Michael E. Bigelow, "Intelligence in the Philippines," *U.S. Army Intelligence History: A Sourcebook*, James P. Finley, ed., U.S. Army Intelligence Center and Fort Huachuca, Fort Huachuca, Arizona, 1995, 196–201.
53. Kreis, *Piercing the Fog*, 109; "Battle of Sio," *Wikipedia*.
54. Ibid., 257; "Army Intelligence in WW II: The Pacific," *Military Intellligence*, July–September 2012, 45–50; McNaughton, *Nisei Linguists*, 184.
55. Drea, "A Very Savage Operation," 1, 5.
56. Entry on "John Fugio Aiso '31," in *Brown Alumni Magazine*, November/December 2000, 2–3.
57. Memo from C. A. Willoughby, Brigadier General, U.S. Army, A.C. of S., G-2, March 15, 1943, Subject: Estimate Enemy Casualties in Philippines and Southwest Pacific Area since December 7th, 1941, RG 23C, Box 1, no folder number, MMA, Norfolk, VA; Summary Review of Enemy Losses in S.W.P.A., April 21, 1942–April 10, 1943, dated April 13, 1943, RG 23C, Box 1, no folder number, MMA, Norfolk, VA.
58. Dr. Greg Bradsher, "From Rabaul to Stack 190: The Travels of a Famous Japanese Army Publication," National Archives blog post, August 10, 2012, http://blogs.archives.gov/TextMessage/2012/08/10from-rabaul-to-stack-190-the-travels...
59. Schaller, *Douglas MacArthur*, 101–02; "Guerrilla Resistance Movement in Central Luzon," *G-2 Information Bulletin*, October 26, 1944, RG 30 Box 24, Folder 15, MMA, Norfolk, VA.
60. Schaller, *Douglas MacArthur*, 102.
61. Ibid.; Spector, *Eagle Against the Sun*, 459; McNaughton, *Nisei Linguists*, 183–84; David W. Hogan, Jr., *U.S. Army Special Operations in World War II* (Washington, D.C.; Center of Military History, Department of the Army, 1992), 79.
62. Kreis, *Piercing the Fog*, 277–79; James P. Duffy, *War at the End of the World: Douglas MacArthur and the Forgotten Fight for New Guinea, 1942–1945* (New York: NAL Caliber, 2016), 283–84.
63. "Army Intelligence in WW II: The Pacific," 47.

64. Greg Bradsher, "The Z Plan Story: Japan's 1944 Naval Battle Strategy Drifts Into U.S. Hands," Pt. 1, *Prologue Magazine*, https://www.archives.gov/publications/prologue/2005/fall/z-plan-1.html, 1–2.

65. Bradsher, "The Z-Plan Story," 2–5.

66. Ibid., 5–6.

67. Ibid., 7–8.

68. Bradsher, "The Z Plan Story," Pt. 2, 1.

69. Ibid., 2.

70. Ibid.

71. Ibid.

72. Campbell, "Major General Charles A. Willoughby," 87–91.

73. "Daily Summary of Enemy Intelligence," November 12, 1944, General Headquarters Southwest Pacific Area, Military Intelligence Section, General Staff, Philippine Islands, RG 30, Box 24, Folder 15, MMA, Norfolk, VA.

74. Bigelow, "Intelligence in the Philippines," 196–201.

75. MacArthur, *Reminiscences*, 165.

76. Bio sheet, Charles Andre Willoughby, Public Information Office, War Department, in Box 1-2, MS-024, Willoughby papers, Special Collections/Musselman Library, Gettysburg College, Gettysburg, PA; Campbell, "Major General Charles A. Willoughby," 87–91; "Charles Andre Willoughby (04615)," CADRE biographic data sheet, CIA archives.

77. Breuer, *MacArthur's Undercover War*, 158; "Charles A. Willoughby: The Most Prominent American Intelligence Officer of World War II," Fort Huachuca, accessed June 4, 2012, www.huachuca.army.mil/sites/History/PDFS/MWILLOU.pdf, 5.

78. Campbell, "Major General Charles A. Willoughby: A Mixed Performance," 6.

79. "Army Intelligence in World War II: The Pacific," in "A Short History of Army Intelligence," by LTC (Ret.) Michael E. Bigelow, in *Military Intelligence Professional Bulletin*, July–September 2012, Vol. 38, No. 3, 48.

80. John F. Shortal, *Forged by Fire: General Robert L. Eichelberger and the Pacific War* (Columbia, S.C.: University of South Carolina Press, 1987), 83.

81. Laurie, "General MacArthur and the OSS," 53–54.

82. Ibid., 55; Brown, *The Last Hero*, 517.

83. Willoughby's comments to "Allied Air Countermeasures and Factors in the Event of a Japanese Fleet Sortie Against our Biak Seizure," RG 30, Box 6, Folder 2, MMA, Norfolk, VA; Campbell, "Major General Charles A. Willoughby: A Mixed Performance," 6.

84. Duffy, *War at the End of the World*, 330; Campbell, "Major General Charles A. Willoughby: A Mixed Performance," 5–6.

85. Shortal, *Forged by Fire*, 85; Beaumont, "The Flawed Soothsayer," 27.

86. Herman, *Douglas MacArthur*, 569.

87. Undated article from *Gettysburgian* newspaper, Box 1-2, Willoughby papers, MMA, Norfolk, VA.

88. Bigelow, "Intelligence in the Philippines," 198; Shortal, *Forged By Fire*, 103.

89. Breuer, *MacArthur's Undercover War*, 196; Larrabee, *Commander in Chief*, 348; Williamson Murray and Allan R. Millett, *A War to be Won: Fighting the Second World War* (Cambridge, MA: The Belknap Press of Harvard University Press, 2000), 495.

90. Haile H. Jaekel, "The End of World War II," 1996, 2. "Jake" Jaekel, a veteran of USS *Salt Lake City* during World War II, wrote this article for his granddaughter after he learned what her university textbook said about the dropping of the atomic bombs on Japan.

91. D. M. Giangreco, "Casualty Projections for the U.S. Invasions of Japan, 1945–1946: Planning and Policy Implications," *Journal of Military History*, 61 (July 1997), 533, 536.

92. Jaekel, "The End of World War II," 2; Giangreco, "Casualty Projections for the U.S. Invasions of Japan," 12, 15.
93. Douglas J. MacEachin, *The Final Months of the War With Japan: Signals Intelligence, U.S. Invasion Planning, and the A-Bomb Decision*, Center for the Study of Intelligence, Central Intelligence Agency, December 1998, 6, 9, 19, 21–23; Kreis, *Piercing the Fog*, 384.
94. McNaughton, *Nisei Linguists*, 327, 373.
95. Ibid., 373.
96. Ibid., 375.

Chapter 3: Victory and the Occupation of Japan

1. James C. McNaughton, *Nisei Linguists: Japanese Americans in the Military Intelligence Service during World War II* (Washington, D.C.: Department of the Army, 2007), 381.
2. Ibid., 390–91.
3. Willoughby memo to CinC, DC/S, G-3, August 12, 1945, RG 30, Box 24, Folder 15, MMA, Norfolk, VA.
4. Willoughby memo to Chief of Staff, August 27, 1945, Subject: Punitive Features of Annexes to Operations Instructions, RG 30, Box 24, Folder 15, MMA, Norfolk, VA.
5. William Manchester, *American Caesar: Douglas MacArthur, 1880–1964* (New York: Dell Publishing Co., Inc., 1978), 441, 516–17; Walter R. Borneman, *MacArthur at War: World War II in the Pacific* (New York: Little, Brown and Co., 2016), 497;Reports of General MacArthur, *The Campaigns of MacArthur in the Pacific*, Vol. I and Supplement (Washington, D.C.: U.S. Government Printing Office, 1966), fn. 50; McNaughton, *Nisei Linguists*, 386–87.
6. Oral Reminiscences of Major General Charles A. Willoughby, Naples, Florida, interview with D. Clayton James, July 30, 1971, RG 23, Box 12, Folder 12, MMA, Norfolk, VA, 9.
7. Mayumi Itoh, "U.S. Occupation and Hotoyama Ichiro's Purge," *Asian Studies on the Pacific Coast* electronic journal, Vol. 1, 2001–2002, 2.
8. "Edward M. Almond," Veteran Tributes: Honoring Those Who Served, accessed November 12, 2019, www.veteranstribute.org/TributeDetail.php?recordID=745.
9. Interview with D. Clayton James, July 30, 1971, 9.
10. Brigadier General Elliott R. Thorpe, *East Wind, Rain: The Intimate Account of an Intelligence Officer in the Pacific, 1939–1949* (Boston Gambit Inc., 1969), 95–96.
11. McNaughton, *Nisei Linguists*, 430.
12. Frank Kluckhohn, "Heidelberg to Madrid—The Story of General Willoughby," *The Reporter* (New York Journal), August 19, 1952, 5–6.
13. Ibid. To date, there is no further evidence to indicate the fate of the four volumes, the disposition of which was presumably known only to Generals MacArthur and Willoughby.
14. Jerome Forrest and Clark H. Kawakami, "General MacArthur and His Vanishing War History," *The Reporter*, October 14, 1952, Box 18, Folder 4, MMA, Norfolk, VA, 20–25.
15. "Southwest Pacific Historical Series," Box 1, Folder 9, MMA, Norfolk, VA.
16. Forrest and Kawakami, "General MacArthur and His Vanishing War History," 20–25.
17. "Charles Andrew Willoughby", Arlington National Cemetery website article, accessed January 21, 2014, http://www.arlingtoncemetery.net/cawilloughby.htm, used with permission, 5.
18. Foreword, The Intelligence Series, G-2 USAFE-SWPA-AFPAC-FEC-SCAP, Editor-in-Chief Major General Charles A. Willoughby, GSC.; Forrest and Kawakami, "General MacArthur and His Vanishing War History," 20–25. Two successive chiefs of the Army's Historical Division attempted to retrieve the volumes but both were thwarted. Willoughby told the second, General Harry J. Malony, that the "history" was actually "a personal memoir and therefore not subject

to Army jurisdiction." In a final bid to free the captive volumes, the Adjutant General's Office, Department of the Army, sent a letter to MacArthur indicating the Army did indeed consider the volumes an official "history" and U.S. Government property and requested that MacArthur make the volumes available to the Army—as of 1952, there had been no reply from MacArthur. As later events made clear, in 1953, MacArthur turned over the volumes and his notes, but under duress—Willoughby characterized the mandated turnover as a "confiscation" by President Truman. More than a decade later, the public learned MacArthur had been opposed to the publication of the volumes because he believed they needed further editing and contained some inaccuracies. In a 1961 letter to Willoughby, MacArthur complained, "I have always regarded the action of the Department of the Army as one of the most prejudiced and unprecedented in American history." The more blasé aspects of this saga were described in the Foreword to the two volumes (four books total, as published) by Army Chief of Staff General Harold Johnson in January 1966. The first of the four books was offered for sale by the Government Printing Office in April 1966, with the others due to appear by October. Predictably, the course of developments left Willoughby bitter as well: "On reflection, this is a miniature example of the growing parasitic influence of civil elements in the military establishments, suffocating the professionals—a reminder for the uniformed armed services, in every category, to resist this creeping menace, this evisceration of the esprit de corps!—an intangible thing that separates them from the proletarian mob!—that sustains them in battle and may save them at home." Forrest and Kawakami, "General MacArthur and His Vanishing War History," 20–25; "The Intel Series," Box 19, Folder 3, MMA, Norfolk, VA.

19. McNaughton, *Nisei Linguists*, 454–55. When MacArthur was recalled by President Truman in 1951, work on these volumes stopped although, as McNaughton notes, Willoughby used some of the material for *MacArthur, 1941–1951.*

20. Peter Lowe, *The Origins of the Korean War*, Second Edition (London: Longman, 1986), 87.

21. James M. Scott, "The Doolittle Raid Generated More Ripples Than Once Thought," *Military Times*, April 18, 2018, www.militarytimes.com/off-duty/military-culture/2018/04/18/the-doolittle-raid-generated-more-ripples-than-once-thought/.

22. McNaughton, *Nisei Linguists*, 459–60.

23. Ibid., 430.

24. Kenneth J. Campbell, "Major General Charles A. Willoughby: A Mixed Performance," text of an unpublished paper, edited version published as "Major General Charles A. Willoughby: General MacArthur's G-2—A Biographic Sketch," *American Intelligence Journal* 18 no. 1 (1998), 8; Chapman Pincher, *Too Secret Too Long* (New York: St. Martin's Press, 1984), 10; Charles A. Willoughby, *Shanghai Conspiracy: The Sorge Spy Ring* (New York: E.P. Dutton & Co., Inc, 1952), 15.

25. F. W. Deakin and G. R. Storry, *The Case of Richard Sorge* (New York: Harper & Rowe Publishers, 1966), 337, 340.

26. George Constantinides, *Intelligence and Espionage: An Analytical Bibliography* (Boulder, CO: Westview Press, 1983), n.p.

27. Michael Schaller, *Douglas MacArthur: The Far Eastern General* (New York: Oxford University Press, 1989), 122, 156. The article on Willoughby on the Arlington National Cemetery Website notes that when FBI Director J. Edgar Hoover read Willoughby's 64-page report on the Sorge espionage ring in general and Agnes Smedley in particular, he caustically noted, "It is readily apparent that the author of the report was involved with motives to the detriment of facts regarding the operations of the Sorge group"—in other words, the evidence Willoughby provided was not legally actionable for the purposes of prosecution.

28. Ibid., 8–9, 12; "Charles Andrew Willoughby, Major General, United States Army," Arlington National Cemetery website, p. 4 (http://arlingtoncemetery.net/cawilloughby.htm). Used with permission.

29. Kluckhohn, "Heidelberg to Madrid," 7. The Communist International (Comintern) existed from 1919 to 1943 and was succeeded by the Communist Information Bureau (Cominform), which dissolved in 1956.

30. Schaller, *Douglas MacArthur*, 170, 174.

31. Memo, GHQ FEC, Mil. Intel Section, General Staff, Subj: Foreign Elements Employed in General Headquarters, January 28, 1947, Box 18, Folder 4, MMA, Norfolk, VA.

32. "Leftist Infiltration into SCAP," Civil Intelligence Section Special Reports, March 5, 1947, Box 18, Folder 12, MMA, Norfolk, VA.

33. Michael E. Haas, Col, USAF (ret.), *In the Devil's Shadow: UN Special Operations During the Korean War* (Annapolis, MD: Naval Institute Press, 2000), 70; SGM (Ret.) Herbert A. Friedman, "The American PSYOP Organization During the Korean War," accessed December 2, 2019, www.psywarrior.com/KoreaPSYOPHist.html.

34. Stanley Sandler, "Secret Operations of the Central Intelligence Agency During the Korean War," unpublished manuscript, n.d., Center for the Study of Intelligence, Central Intelligence Agency, 33.

35. Ibid., 23–24.

36. Ibid., 26–27.

37. Letter, Willoughby to Herbert Hoover, October 21, 1948, Box 7-16, MS-024, Willoughby papers, Special Collections/Musselman Library, Gettysburg College, Gettysburg, PA; letter, Willoughby to MG Harry H. Vaughn, Military Aide to the President, The White House, June 7, 1949, Box 9-26, MS-024, Willoughby papers, Special Collections/Musselman Library, Gettysburg College, Gettysburg, PA.

38. Sandler, "Secret Operations of the Central Intelligence Agency During the Korean War," 24.

39. Richard Aldrich, *The Hidden Hand: Britain, America and Cold War Secret Intelligence* (New York: Overlook Press, 2001), 275.

40. Sandler, "Secret Operations of the Central Intelligence Agency During the Korean War," 27.

41. Ronald Lewin, *ULTRA Goes to War* (New York: Pocket Books, 1980), 302; Meirion and Susie Harries, *Soldiers of the Sun: The Rise and Fall of the Imperial Japanese Army* (New York: Random House, 1991), 486–87.

42. Charles Andrew Willoughby," Arlington National Cemetery Website, 4.

43. Ibid.

44. Schaller, *Douglas MacArthur*, 170, 174.

45. Peter Lowe, *The Origins of the Korean War*, 132.

46. "New Evidence of Japan's Germ Warfare in WWII Found," *China* View, accessed June 14, 2012, www.chinaview.cn; Mae Brussell, "The Nazi Connection to the John F. Kennedy Assassination," accessed September 16, 2010, www.maebrussell.com.

47. Letter, Willoughby to Herbert Hoover, October 21, 1948; Letter, Willoughby to MG Harry H. Vaughn, June 7, 1949.

48. Thaddeus Holt, *The Deceivers: Allied Military Deception in the Second World War* (New York: Scribner, 2004), 779–80.

49. Ibid.

50. Kluckhohn, "Heidelberg to Madrid," 7.

51. Borneman, *MacArthur at War*, 386; Roger A. Beaumont, "The Flawed Soothsayer: Willoughby, General MacArthur's G-2," *Espionage*, August 1985, 28; Richard M. Connaughton, *MacArthur*

and Defeat in the Philippines (Woodstock, N.Y.: Overlook Press, 2001), 122. Connaughton includes information in his book from Geoffrey Perett and the Luce Papers in the Library of Congress which indicate Willoughby "actually bedded the beautiful Mrs. Luce. She said he was the only man she might have run away with." While Luce's papers describe Willoughby as "besotted" with her, "it was a fling which Mrs. Luce took in her stride without further thought or interest."

52. Manchester, *American Caesar*, 414.
53. Ed Ivanhoe, *Dark Moon: Eighth Army Special Operations in the Korean War* (Annapolis, MD: Naval Institute Press, 1995), 7; Sandler, "Secret Operations of the Central Intelligence Agency During the Korean War," 29.
54. G. J. A. O'Toole, *The Encyclopedia of American Intelligence and Espionage: From the Revolutionary War to the Present* (New York: Facts on File, 1988), 267, 494–95.
55. Sandler, "Secret Operations of the Central Intelligence Agency During the Korean War," 29.
56. Kluckhohn, "Heidelberg to Madrid," 5.
57. Beaumont, "The Flawed Soothsayer," 29–30.
58. Bertrand M. Roehner, "Relations Between Allied Forces and the Population of Japan, 15 August 1945–31 December 1960," *Occupation of Japan*, 2009.

Chapter 4: The Korean War: The Curtain Rises

1. In Confucian society, there are five key relationships: 1) Ruler to ruled; 2) Father to son; 3) Husband to wife; 4) Elder brother to younger brother; and 5) Friend to friend. Of these five relationships, that between father and son, especially son, was most important. Confucius, the 5th century BC Chinese philosopher, noted the relationship between father and eldest son was the "hinge of civilization"—the father was obligated to love and care for his son and provide for his welfare, while the son was to obey his father.
2. John Toland, *In Mortal Combat: Korea, 1950–1953* (New York: William Morrow & Co., 1991), 15.
3. Ibid.; John A. Barnet, Jr., Captain, Infantry, *Soviet Propaganda and the Korean War*, U.S. Army Field Detachment "R" (8582), Office of the Assistant Chief of Staff, Intelligence, U.S. Army, June 1, 1957, CIA archives, 1.
4. Toland, *In Mortal Combat*, 16–17; Barnet, *Soviet Propaganda and the Korean War*, 2–3.
5. Foreign Denial and Deception Committee, "The Chinese Invasion of Korea, October 1950 (A): An Intelligence Community Case Study," 2.
6. Toland, *In Mortal Combat*, 17.
7. *Foreign Relations of the United States, 1949*, Vol. III, The Far East and Australasia, Pt. 2 (Washington, D.C.: Government Printing Office, 1976), 975, 987.
8. Barnet, *Soviet Propaganda and the Korean War*, 2–3.
9. *Foreign Relations of the United States, 1949*, Vol. III, 1041, 1043, 1056; William B. Breuer, *Shadow Warriors: The Covert War in Korea* (New York: John Wiley & Sons, Inc., 1996), 19.
10. Stephen C. Mercado, reviewer, *KLO ui Hangukchon Pisa (Secret History of the KLO in the Korean War)* (Seoul: Jisungsa, 2005) by Yi Chang-gon, in *"Studies in Intelligence,"* Vol. 56, No. 1 (March 2012), 63; P. K. Rose, "Two Strategic Intelligence Mistakes in Korea, 1950," *Studies in Intelligence*, Central Intelligence Agency, Fall/Winter 2001, http://www.odci.gov/csi/studies/fall_winter_2001/article06.html, 2; Michael Schaller, *Douglas MacArthur: The Far Eastern General* (New York: Oxford University Press, 1989), 163.
11. Aldrich *et al.*, eds., *The Clandestine Cold War in Asia, 1945–65: Western Intelligence, Propaganda and Special Operations*, Center for the Study of Intelligence, Central Intelligence Agency, 33–35.

12. Foreign Denial and Deception Committee, "The Chinese Invasion of Korea, October 1950," 6; John Patrick Finnegan, *The U.S. Army in the Korean War, 1950–1953: Operations and Intelligence Support* (Ft. Belvoir, VA: History Office, Office of the Chief of Staff, U.S. Army Intelligence and Security Command, May 2001), 61.

13. Richard A. Mobley, "North Korea's Surprise Attack: Weak U.S. Analysis?," *International Journal of Intelligence and Counterintelligence*, Vol. 13, No. 4, Winter 2000, 491.

14. James P. Finley, "The Uncertain Oracle: Some Intelligence Failures Revisited," at www.au.af.mil/au/awc/awcgate/army/uncertain.pdf; Foreign Denial and Deception Committee, "The Chinese Invasion of Korea," 6; James F. Schnabel, *Policy and Direction: The First Year* (Washington, D.C.: U.S. Army Center of Military History, 1992), 62.

15. Richard Whelan, *Drawing the Line: The Korean War, 1950–1953* (Boston: Little, Brown and Co., 1990), 103.

16. Breuer, *Shadow Warriors*, 19–21.

17. Ibid., 56–57; Herbert A. Friedman, SGM (Ret.), "The American PSYOP Organization During the Korean War," accessed December 2, 2019, www.psywarrior.com/KoreaPSYOPHist.html.

18. *Foreign Relations of the United States, 1949*, Vol. III, 987.

19. Mobley, "North Korea's Surprise Attack," 500; Whelan, *Drawing the* Line, 104.

20. Oral History Interview with Ambassador John J. Muccio, Washington, D.C., Harry S. Truman Library and Museum, February 10, 1971, Part 1, 8–9.

21. Beaumont, "The Flawed Soothsayer," 30.

22. Mobley, "North Korea's Surprise Attack," 498.

23. Ibid., 501–04.

24. Ed Evanhoe, *Dark Moon: Eighth Army Special Operations in the Korean War* (Annapolis, MD: Naval Institute Press, 1995), 18.

25. Finnegan, *The U.S. Army in the Korean War*, 63.

26. *The Korean War in History*, edited by James Cotton and Ian Neary, (Atlantic Highlands, New Jersey: Humanities Press International, Inc., 1989), 126.

27. Michael Warner, "From Good to Mediocre: Intelligence in the Korean War," in James I. Matray, ed., *Northeast Asia and the Legacy of Harry S. Truman: Japan, China, and the Two Koreas* (Kirksville, MO: Truman State University Press, 2012), 281–85.

28. John P. Finnegan, "The Evolution of US Army HUMINT: Intelligence Operations in the Korean War," *Studies in Intelligence*, Vol. 55, No. 2 (Extracts, June 2011), 58; David A. Hatch with Robert Louis Benson, *The Korean War: The SIGINT Background*, Center for Cryptologic History, National Security Agency, 2000, 8.

29. Finnegan, *The U.S. Army in the Korean War*, 62.

30. Maj. Charles M. Azotea, United States Army, "Operational Intelligence Failures of the Korean War," monograph for School of Advanced Military Studies, United States Army Command and General Staff College, Fort Leavenworth, Kansas, 2014, 14, 52.

31. Bruce Riedel, "Catastrophe on the Yalu: America's Intelligence Failure in Korea," Brookings Institute article excerpted and adapted from *JFK's Forgotten Crisis: Tibet, the CIA and Sino-Indian War* (Washington, D.C.: Brookings Institution Press, 2015), 3.

32. Justin M. Haynes, "Intelligence Failure in Korea: Major General Charles A. Willoughby's Role in the United Nations' Command's Defeat in November, 1950," U.S. Army Command and General Staff College M.A. thesis, June 2009, 71.

33. Blaine Harden, *King of Spies: The Dark Reign of America's Spymaster in Korea* (New York: Viking, 2017), 53.

34. Rose, "Two Strategic Intelligence Mistakes," 2; Stanley Sandler, "Secret Operations of the Central Intelligence Agency During the Korean War," unpublished manuscript, n.d., Center for the Study of Intelligence, Central Intelligence Agency, 33.

35. Rose, "Two Strategic Intelligence Mistakes in Korea," 3–4; G. J. A. O'Toole, *The Encyclopedia of American Intelligence and Espionage: From the Revolutionary War to the Present* (New York: Facts on File, 1988), 264.

36. Sandler, "Secret Operations of the Central Intelligence Agency During the Korean War," 33–35.

37. Aldrich, *The Clandestine Cold War in Asia*, 55–56.

38. Ibid., 9, 13, 15; "Fact Sheet: An Overview of the U.S. Army in the Korean War, 1950–1953," *State of New Jersey, Department of Military and Veterans Affairs*, accessed February 18, 2016, http://www.nj.gov/military/korea/factsheets/army.html, 1.

39. Saul David, *Military Blunders: The How and Why of Military Failure* (New York: Carroll & Graf Publishers, 1998), 269–70; William J. Webb, *The Korean War: The Outbreak, 27 June–15 September 1950* (pamphlet) (Washington, D.C.: The U.S. Army Center of Military History), September 13, 2006, 9; Joseph C. Goulden, *Korea: The Untold Story of the War* (New York: Times Books, 1982), 58; Foreign Denial and Deception Committee, "The Chinese Invasion of Korea," 7; Schnabel, *Policy and Direction*, 40.

40. Query from Department of the Army, December 8, 1949, RG 23, Box 14, Folder 4, MMA, Norfolk, VA.

41. Samuel B. Griffiths, *The Chinese People's Liberation Army* (New York: McGraw-Hill Book Company, 1967), 104–05; Rose, "Two Strategic Intelligence Mistakes," 3; Schnabel, *Policy and Direction*, 3; O'Toole, *The Encyclopedia of American Intelligence and Espionage*, 265.

42. Schnabel, *Policy and Direction*, 2; Harden, *King of Spies*, 54.

43. Goulden, *Korea*, 40.

44. Ibid.

45. Ibid., 279.

46. Manuscript notes to "Chinese Communist War" chapter, *MacArthur, 1941–1951*, Box 10-12, MS-024, Special Collections/Musselman Library, Gettysburg College, Gettysburg, PA.

47. O'Toole, *The Encyclopedia of American Intelligence and Espionage*, 264.

48. Stanley Weintraub, *MacArthur's War: Korea and the Undoing of an American Hero* (New York: The Free Press, 2000), 53; Whelan, *Drawing the Line*, 159.

49. Matthew Aid, "U.S. HUMINT and COMINT in the Korean War: From the Approach of War to the Chinese Intervention," in Aldrich, Rawnsley, Rawnsley, eds., *The Clandestine Cold War in Asia*, 17.

50. GHQ, FEC, G-2, "North Korean Pre-Invasion Build-up," RG 23, Box 14, Folder 4, MMA, Norfolk, VA.

51. "Statistical Data on Strength and Casualties for Korean War and Vietnam," accessed April 12, 2011, http://www.history.army.mil/documents/237ADM.htm.

52. Ibid.; Foreign Denial and Deception Committee, "The Chinese Invasion of Korea," 8.

53. D. Clayton James, with Anne Sharp Wells, *Refighting the Last War: Command and Crisis in Korea, 1950–1953* (New York: Free Press, 1993), 43.

54. Ibid.

55. Michael C. Hickey, *The Korean War: The West Confronts Communism* (Woodstock, NY: Overlook Press, 1999), 31–32.

56. Message, USMILAT at Seoul, Korea, June 23, 1950, RG 23, Box 14, Folder 4, MMA, Norfolk, VA.

57. David, *Military Blunders*, 270–71; Robert F. Futrell, *The United States Air Force in Korea, 1950–1953* (Washington, D.C.: Office of Air Force History, 1981), 52–54; Dr. Clayton Laurie, "The Korean War and the Central Intelligence Agency: CIA Reporting on Korea, 1948–1950," in *Baptism by Fire: CIA Analysis of the Korean War*, CIA, 2010, 10.

58. Sandler, "Secret Operations of the Central Intelligence Agency During the Korean War," 37, 40.

59. Mercado, "Studies in Intelligence," 63–64. The flag that MacArthur presented to Choe at Inchon is on permanent exhibit at the MacArthur Memorial in Norfolk, Virginia. Next to the lighthouse at Palmi-do is a plaque commemorating the memory of the KLO.

60. Memo, GHQ, FEC, Military Intelligence Section, General Staff, Subject: "Chinese Communist Assistance to North Korea," July 6, 1950, RG 23, Box 14, Folder 1, MMA, Norfolk, VA.

61. Goulden, *Korea*, 278–79; Finnegan, *The U.S. Army in the Korean War*, 79; Intel Memo No. 324, September 8, 1950, "Subject: Probability of Direct Chinese Communist Intervention in Korea," in *Study of CIA Reporting on Chinese Communist Intervention in the Korean War*, 2. Of note, this memo was prepared at the behest of the USAF Director of Intelligence but was not coordinated with State, the Army, the Navy, or the rest of the Air Force.

62. James I. Matray, "Revisiting Korea: Exposing Myths of the Forgotten War, Part 2," *Prologue*, Summer 2002, Vol. 34, No. 2, 1, accessed November 1, 2014, http://www.archives.gov/publications/prologue/2002/summer/korean-myths-2.html.

63. GHQ, FEC, G-2, *Daily Intelligence Summary*, August 27, 1950, RG 23, Box 14, Folder 1, MMA, Norfolk, VA.

64. Peter G. Knight, abstract of M.A. thesis, "MacArthur's Eyes: Reassessing Military Intelligence Operations in the Forgotten War, June 1950–April 1951," Ohio State University, 2004, 100, 102.

65. Knight, "MacArthur's Eyes," 113–14. Despite Willoughby's objections, Quinn remained as the X Corps G-2 and his career continued to flourish. Soon promoted to colonel, Quinn became the commander of the 17th Infantry Regiment, known as the "Buffaloes" because of their call sign, a name which stuck to the unit and explained Quinn's new nickname of "Buffalo Bill." In 1961, Quinn became the first Deputy Director of the new Defense Intelligence Agency, and in 1964 became the commander of the Seventh Army in Germany. He retired from the Army in 1966 as a lieutenant general and died in 2000 at age 92. He is interred at Arlington National Cemetery. https://army.togetherweserved.com/army/.

66. Schnabel, *Policy and Direction*, 2.

67. Ibid.; Haynes, "Intelligence Failure in Korea," 76; Paul M. Edwards, *To Acknowledge a War: The Korean War in American Memory* (Westport, CT: Greenwood Press, 2000), 61; Schnabel, *Policy and Direction*, 159.

68. Eliot Cohen, "The Chinese Intervention in Korea, 1950," approved for release, CIA Historical Review Program, September 22, 1993, https://www.cia.gov/library/readingroom/docs/1998-11-01.pdf, 50.

69. Foreign Denial and Deception Committee, "The Chinese Invasion of Korea," 11–12.

70. MacArthur, SCAP Intel Series document, Box 1-1, MS-024, Willoughby papers, Special Collections/Musselman Library, Gettysburg College, Gettysburg, PA.

71. Haynes, "Intelligence Failure in Korea," 5.

72. Goulden, *Korea*, 39–41.

73. Richard Thornton, *Odd Man Out: Truman, Stalin, Mao, and the Origins of the Cold War* (Washington, D.C.: Brassey's, 2000), 175.

74. Willoughby papers, Box 2-1, MS-024, Special Collections/Musselman Library, Gettysburg College, Gettysburg, PA.

75. Col. Michael E. Haas (USAF, Ret.), "The Clandestine Services in Korea," *Intelligence: Journal of U.S. Intelligence Studies*, Winter/Spring 2005, 97.

76. Interview with Carleton Swift, September 20, 1999, in Oral History collection of Center for the Study of Intelligence (CSI), Central Intelligence Agency.

77. Letter, DCI Hillenkoetter to Willoughby, July 7, 1950, RG 23, Box 5, Folder 3, MMA, Norfolk, VA.

78. Sandler, "Secret Operations of the Central Intelligence Agency During the Korean War," 37n, 42.

79. Rose, "Two Strategic Intelligence Mistakes," 4–5.

80. Ibid., 5.

81. Ibid., 6.

82. Breuer, *Shadow Warriors*, 87.

83. William Manchester, *American Caesar: Douglas MacArthur, 1880–1964* (Boston: Little, Brown and Company, 1978), 581.

84. David, *Military Blunders*, 271–72; Rose, "Two Strategic Intelligence Mistakes," 6.

85. Schnabel, *Policy and Direction*, 200.

86. "The Public Controversy in April–June 1951 as to the Adequacy of U.S. Intelligence Estimating, July–December 1950, with respect to Chinese Communist Intervention in Korea," CIA Historical Staff, October 1955, 4; Richard Aldrich, *The Hidden Hand: Britain, America and Cold War Secret Intelligence* (New York: Overlook Press, 2001), 274.

87. T. R. Fehrenbach, *This Kind of War: A Study in Unpreparedness* (New York: The MacMillan Co., 1963), 288.

88. David, *Military Blunders*, 271–72; Griffiths, *The Chinese People's Liberation Army*, 122; Muccio interview, February 18, 1971, Part II, 9.

89. Encl A, CIA TS memo of October 12, 1950, in Finnegan, *The U.S. Army in the Korean War*, 61.

90. "The Public Controversy in April–June 1951," 16–18.

91. Griffiths, *The Chinese People's Liberation Army*, 124–25.

92. Haynes, "Intelligence Failure in Korea," 85.

93. Ibid., 272–73.

Chapter 5: "A Period of Miscalculations"

1. Justin M. Haynes, "Intelligence Failure in Korea: Major General Charles A. Willoughby's Role in the United Nations' Command's Defeat in November, 1950," U.S. Army Command and General Staff College M.A. thesis, June, 2009, 79; *Daily Intelligence Summary*, 2937, September 24, 1950, RG 23, Box 14, Folder 1, MMA, Norfolk, VA; D. Clayton James, *Refighting the Last War: Command and Crisis in Korea, 1950–1953* (New York: The Free Press, 1993), 185.

2. GHQ, FEC, G-2 *Daily Intelligence Summary* 2943, September 30, 1950 and DIS 2948, October 5, 1950, RG 23, Box 14, Folder 1, MMA, Norfolk, VA.

3. Haynes, "Intelligence Failure in Korea," 85; Saul David, *Military Blunders: The How and Why of Military Failure* (New York: Carroll & Graf Publishers, 1998), 273.

4. Michael Hickey, *The Korean War: The West Confronts Communism* (Woodstock, NY: Overlook Press, 1999), 88–89.

5. Robert F. Futrell, *The United States Air Force in Korea, 1950–1953* (Washington, D.C.: Office of Air Force History, 1981), 201.

6. Samuel B. Griffiths, *The Chinese People's Liberation Army* (New York: McGraw-Hill Book Company, 1967), 126–27.

7. James F. Schnabel, *Policy and Direction: The First Year* (Washington, D.C.: U.S. Army Center of Military History, 1992), 199.

8. William Stueck, *The Korean War: An International History* (Princeton, NJ: Princeton University Press, 1995), 97.

9. David, *Military Blunders*, 45–46.

10. Ibid., 79; Griffiths, *The Chinese People's Liberation Army*, 202.

11. Joseph C. Goulden, *Korea: The Untold Story of the War* (New York: Times Books, 1982), 280.

12. Wake Island conference notes, compiled by General Omar Bradley, Chairman, Joint Chiefs of Staff, RG 5, Box 86, Folder 5, MMA, Norfolk, VA.

13. Ibid.

14. Ed Evanhoe, *Dark Moon: Eighth Army Special Operations in the Korean War* (Annapolis, MD: Naval Institute Press, 1995), 14.

15. David, *Military Blunders*, 47, 81–82, 84–86; Griffiths, *The Chinese People's Liberation Army*, 202.

16. Goulden, *Korea*, 279.

17. Matthew M. Aid, "American COMINT in the Korean War (Part II): From the Chinese Intervention to the Armistice," 14.

18. Ibid., 284; Stanley Weintraub, *MacArthur's War: Korea and the Undoing of an American Hero* (New York: The Free Press, 2000), 196–97.

19. Weintraub, *MacArthur's War*, 185; Obituary, CDR Eugene Franklin Clark (1911–1998), accessed November 11, 2013, http://www.findagrave.com.

20. "Indications of Chicom Intervention in Korea, October 1950–December 1950," as reported and evaluated in CIA *Daily Summary*, n.p.

21. Hickey, *The Korean War*, 89.

22. Stanley Sandler, *The Korean War: No Victors, No Vanquished* (Lexington, KY: The University Press of Kentucky, 1999), 112.

23. Haynes, "Intelligence Failure in Korea," 48.

24. James, *Refighting the Last War*, 185.

25. Peter G. Knight, abstract of M.A. thesis, "MacArthur's Eyes: Reassessing Military Intelligence Operations in the Forgotten War, June 1950–April 1951," Ohio State University, 2004, 75.

26. Haynes, "Intelligence Failure in Korea," 30, 32; David, *Military Blunders*, 275; Griffiths, *The Chinese People's Liberation Army*, 132; Russell Spur, *Enter the Dragon: China's Undeclared War Against the U.S. in Korea, 1950–51* (New York: Newmarket Press, 1988), 161; Bruce Riedel, "Catastrophe on the Yalu: America's Intelligence Failure in Korea," Brookings Institute article excerpted and adapted from *JFK's Forgotten Crisis: Tibet, the CIA and Sino-Indian War* (Washington, D.C.: Brookings Institution Press, 2015), 4; Maj. Charles M. Azotea, United States Army, "Operational Intelligence Failures of the Korean War," monograph for School of Advanced Military Studies, United States Army Command and General Staff College, Fort Leavenworth, Kansas, 2014, 49.

27. David Halberstam, *The Coldest Winter: America and the Korean War* (New York: Hyperion Books, 2007), 15.

28. Ibid., 380–81.

29. GHQ, FEC, G-2, *Daily Intelligence Summary* 2971, October 28, 1950, RG 23, Box 14, Folder 1, MMA, Norfolk, VA.

30. Weintraub, *MacArthur's War*, 211.

31. Spur, *Enter the Dragon*, 161.

32. James P. Finley, *The Uncertain Oracle: Some Intelligence Failures Revisited*, www.au.af.mil/au/awc/awcgate/army/uncertain.pdf.

33. Griffiths, *The Chinese People's Liberation Army*, 132; Riedel, "Catastrophe on the Yalu", 4.

34. Jon Halliday and Bruce Cummings, *Korea: The Unknown War* (New York: Pantheon Books, 1988), 130.

35. Griffiths, *The Chinese People's Liberation Army*, 128.

36. Haynes, "Intelligence Failure in Korea," 36, 48. In *MacArthur, 1941–1951*, Willoughby claims that in the October 28 DIS, he assessed there were 300,000 Chinese troops in Manchuria at the time but he omitted that analysis from the summary. Willoughby's critics have pointed to

this single incident as one of several attempts by Willoughby to "rewrite history"; Griffiths, *The Chinese People's Liberation Army*, 128–29; Knight, "MacArthur's Eyes," 165; Stanley Sandler, "The CIA, Willoughby, and Military Intelligence in East Asia, 1946–1950," in James I. Matray, ed., *Northeast Asia and the Legacy of Harry S. Truman: Japan, China, and the Two Koreas* (Kirksville, MO: Truman State University Press, 2012), 306.

37. Haynes, "Intelligence Failure in Korea," 1; Halliday and Cummings, *Korea*, 114.

38. Haynes, "Intelligence Failure in Korea," 41; Knight, "MacArthur's Eyes," 165. As Army historian Dr. James Schnabel has noted, "Chosin Reservoir" was the Japanese—and adopted UN name—for the Changjin Reservoir.

39. Haynes, "Intelligence Failure in Korea," 26.

40. Ibid., 23–24; David, *Military Blunders*, 275.

41. Haynes, "Intelligence Failure in Korea," 33.

42. U.S. Army Center for Military History, "Intelligence and Counterintelligence Problems During the Korean Conflict: Chapter V, Theater Level Collection Problems", accessed October 10, 2012, www.history.army.mil/documents/Korea/intkor/intkor5.htm.

43. Goulden, *Korea*, 288–89.

44. Ibid., 289. Interestingly, Willoughby later told Paul Nitze of the State Department that he had "correctly estimated" the extent of Chinese intervention at the time but had been unable to convince MacArthur to take the threat seriously. In his discussion with Nitze, Willoughby claimed he even knew the size of the Chinese force. These incredulous statements are not part of Willoughby's memoirs, which were published while MacArthur was still alive. Goulden, *Korea*, 289.

45. Knight, "MacArthur's Eyes," 156.

46. Goulden, *Korea*, 26; D. Clayton James, *The Years of MacArthur, 1954–64* (New York: Houghton Mifflin, 1985), 519; Sandler, "The CIA, Willoughby, and Military Intelligence in East Asia," 307.

47. Goulden, *Korea*, 297.

48. GHQ, FEC, G-2, *Daily Intelligence Summary* 2976, November 2, 1950, RG 23, Box 14, Folder 1, MMA, Norfolk, VA.

49. Haynes, "Intelligence Failure in Korea," 33.

50. Goulden, *Korea*, 297; Manuscript notes to *MacArthur, 1941–1951*, chapter on "Chinese Communist War," Box 10-12, MS-024, Special Collections/Musselman Library, Gettysburg College, Gettysburg, PA, 2.

51. Griffiths, 134.

52. GHQ, FEC, G-2, *Daily Intelligence Summary* 2979, November 5, 1950, RG 23, Box 14, Folder 1, MMA, Norfolk, VA.

53. Haynes, "Intelligence Failure in Korea," 27; David, *Military Blunders*, 275; "Chinese Communist Intervention in Korea," National Intelligence Estimate Number 2, November 8, 1950, CIA archives, 1.

54. Haynes, "Intelligence Failure in Korea," 34–35, 41.

55. Robert Leckie, *Conflict: The History of the Korean War, 1950–1953* (New York: G.P. Putnam's Sons, 1962), 194–95.

56. GHQ, FEC, G-2, *Daily Intelligence Summary* 2981, November 7, 1950, RG 23, Box 14, Folder 1, MMA, Norfolk, VA.

57. Schnabel, *Policy and Direction*, 241, 263; Goulden, *Korea*, 327.

58. Haynes, "Intelligence Failure in Korea," 42.

59. General Carl A. Spaatz, USAF (Ret.), "Enter the Chinese Communists," *Newsweek*, November 13, 1950, n.p., RG 23, Box 14, Folder 2, MMA, Norfolk, VA.

60. Sandler, "The CIA, Willoughby, and Military Intelligence in East Asia," 112.

61. William M. Leary, *Perilous Missions: Civil Air Transport and CIA Covert Operations in Asia* (University of Alabama Press, 2005), 121.

62. Richard W. Stewart, *The Korean War: The Chinese Intervention, 3 November 1950–24 January 1951* (Washington, DC; U.S. Army Center of Military History, n.d.), 5.

63. Finley, *The Uncertain Oracle*, n.p.

64. Callum A. MacDonald, *Korea: The War Before Vietnam* (New York: Free Press, 1986), 213.

65. Stewart, *The Korean War*, 5.

66. Haynes, "Intelligence Failure in Korea," 71; Sandler, "The CIA, Willoughby, and Military Intelligence in East Asia," 308.

67. Griffiths, *The Chinese People's Liberation Army*, 136; Haynes, "Intelligence Failure in Korea," 71. The "Chinese People's Volunteers" were actually part of the People's Liberation Army—the name was an intentional grammatical misdirection to preserve the fiction that China was not formally at war with the United States.

68. Halberstam, *The Coldest Winter*, 15.

69. "Progressive Identification of Chinese Communist Forces in North Korea as Reported in Daily Intelligence Summary and Washington Teleconference," October to December 1950, Box 2-1, MS-024, Special Collections/Musselman Library, Gettysburg College, Gettysburg, PA.

70. Roy E. Appleman, LTC USA (Ret.), *Disaster in Korea: The Chinese Confront MacArthur* (College Station, Texas: Texas A&M Press, 1989), 61–62.

71. Weintraub, *MacArthur's War*, 278.

72. Knight, "MacArthur's Eyes," 247; John Toland, *In Mortal Combat: Korea, 1950–1953* (New York: William Morrow & Co., 1991), 364–65.

Chapter 6: The Dragon Sharpens its Claws

1. *Study of CIA Reporting on Chinese Communist Intervention in the Korean War, September–December 1950*, prepared by the CIA Historical Staff, October 1955, previously Top Secret, approved for release June 2001, 4.

2. Dr. Qiang Zhai, "China and the Korean War," in *Understanding & Remembering, A Compendium of the 50th Anniversary Korean War International Historical Symposium*, June 26–27, 2002, Old Dominion University, Norfolk, VA (Norfolk, VA: General Douglas MacArthur Foundation, 2003), 57; Samuel B. Griffiths, *The Chinese People's Liberation Army* (New York: McGraw-Hill Book Company, 1967), 78.

3. Zhai, "China and the Korean War," 58; Griffiths, *The Chinese People's Liberation Army*, 116; Michael H. Hunt, "Beijing and the Korean Crisis, June 1950–June 1951," *Political Science Quarterly*, Vol. 107, No. 3 (Autumn 1992), 458.

4. "Formosa Policy and the Korean War," CQ Researcher Plus archive, August 29, 1950, 1.

5. Ibid., 1–2; "Danger Zones: Reconnaissance in Formosa," *Time*, Monday, August 14, 1950, 1; "General MacArthur's Statement on His Trip to Formosa, August 1, 1950," *The New York Times*, August 1, 1950.

6. "Formosa Policy and the Korean War," 2.

7. Foreign Denial and Deception Committee, "The Chinese Invasion of Korea," 14.

8. Zhai, "China and the Korean War," 58.

9. Foreign Denial and Deception Committee, "The Chinese Invasion of Korea," 15.

10. Wanli Hu, abstract of dissertation "Mao's American Strategy and the Korean War," University of Massachusetts Amherst, 2004.

11. James I. Matray, "Revisiting Korea: Exposing Myths of the Forgotten War, Part 2," *Prologue*, Summer 2002, Vol. 34, No. 2, accessed November 1, 2014, http://www.archives.gov/publications/prologue/2002/summer/korean-myths-2.html, 1.

12. Jon Halliday and Bruce Cummings, *Korea: The Unknown War* (New York: Pantheon Books, 1988), 112; Hunt, "Beijing and the Korean Crisis," 458.

13. Griffiths, *The Chinese People's Liberation Army*, 117–18.

14. Zhai, "China and the Korean War," 59.

15. Hunt, "Beijing and the Korean Crisis," 459.

16. Griffiths, *The Chinese People's Liberation Army*, 120.

17. Bruce Riedel, "Catastrophe on the Yalu: America's Intelligence Failure in Korea," Brookings Institute article excerpted and adapted from *JFK's Forgotten Crisis: Tibet, the CIA and Sino-Indian War* (Washington, D.C.: Brookings Institution Press, 2015), 8.

18. Michael Hickey, *The Korean War: The West Confronts Communism* (Woodstock, NY: Overlook Press, 2000), 89.

19. Hunt, "Beijing and the Korean Crisis," 460–61.

20. Ibid., 89–90. However, in his 1967 book, historian Samuel B. Griffiths reiterates the fact Mao had an onerous burden in trying to decide whether to intervene militarily or not but concludes the potential use of atomic weapons by the United States should the Chinese intervene was *not* a decisive factor in making the ultimate decision. See Griffiths, *The Chinese People's Liberation Army*, 123.

21. Griffiths, *The Chinese People's Liberation Army*, 121.

22. William Stueck, *The Korean War: An International History* (Princeton, NJ: Princeton University Press, 1995), 112; James P. Finley, "The Uncertain Oracle: Some Intelligence Failures Revisited," www.au.afmil/au/awc/awcgate/army/uncertain.pdf.

23. Zhai, "China and the Korean War," 59–60.

24. Eliot Cohen, "The Chinese Intervention in Korea, 1950,", approved for release, CIA Historical Review Program, September 22, 1993, https://www.cia.gov/library/readingroom/docs/1998-11-01.pdf, 58.

25. Ibid.

26. Adam Cathcart and Charles Kraus, "The Bonds of Brotherhood: New Evidence on Sino-North Korean Exchanges, 1950–1954," *Journal of Cold War Studies*, Vol. 13, No. 3, Summer 2011, 29.

27. Hunt, "Beijing and the Korean Crisis," 462.

28. Zhai, "China and the Korean War," 59–60; Joseph C. Goulden, *Korea: The Untold Story of the War* (New York: Times Books, 1982), 285; Hunt, "Beijing and the Korean Crisis," 460.

29. Hunt, "Beijing and the Korean Crisis," 463.

30. Goulden, *Korea*, 60, 118; Hunt, "Beijing and the Korean Crisis," 463.

31. Hunt, "Beijing and the Korean Crisis," 464–65.

32. Richard Stewart, *The Korean War: The Chinese Intervention, 3 November 1950–24 January 1951*, U.S. Army Center for Military History brochure, n.d., http://www.history.army.mil/brochures/kw-chinter/chinter.htm, 5–6.

33. Manuscript notes to *MacArthur, 1941–1951*, Box 10-12, MS-024, Special Collections/Musselman Library, Gettysburg College, Gettysburg, PA, 24.

34. Ibid., 5.

35. P. K. Rose, "Two Strategic Intelligence Mistakes in Korea, 1950," *Studies in Intelligence,* Central Intelligence Agency, Fall/Winter 2001, http://www.odci.gov/csi/studies/fall_winter_2001/article06.html, 8.

36. Manuscript notes to *MacArthur, 1941–1951*, 24; Callum A. MacDonald, *Korea: The War Before Vietnam* (New York: The Free Press, 1986), 211; Griffiths, *The Chinese People's Liberation Army*, 103.

37. Oral History interview with Col. Paul W. Steinbeck, USA Retired, November 15, 1985, U.S. Army Military History Institute, Carlisle Barracks, Pennsylvania, 19.
38. Griffiths, *The Chinese People's Liberation Army*, 138.
39. Alexander L. George, *The Chinese Communist Army in Action: The Korean War and its Aftermath* (New York: Columbia University Press, 1967), 3.
40. Manuscript notes to chapter on "Chinese Communist War" of *MacArthur, 1941–1951*, Box 10-12, MS-024, Special Collections/Musselman Library, Gettysburg College, Gettysburg, PA.
41. Justin M. Haynes, "Intelligence Failure in Korea: Major General Charles A. Willoughby's Role in the United Nations' Command's Defeat in November, 1950," U.S. Army Command and General Staff College M.A. thesis, June 2009, 77. While some have interpreted Secretary Pace's comment as indicative of the murky situation in Korea at the time, others have pointed to his statement as an example of how successfully MacArthur—actually Willoughby—could influence public opinion, especially at senior military and political levels.
42. *Study of CIA Reporting on Chinese Communist Intervention in the Korean War*, 6–7.
43. "Review of the World Situation As It Relates to the Security of the United States," CIA 10-50, October 18, 1950, in *Study of CIA Reporting on Chinese Communist Intervention in the Korean War*, 1, 3; Memo for the President from DCI Smith, Subject: "Chinese Communist Intervention in Korea," November 1, 1950, in *Study of CIA Reporting on Chinese Communist Intervention in the Korean War*, n.p.; Foreign Denial and Deception Committee, "The Chinese Invasion of Korea," 16.
44. Halliday and Cummings, *Korea*, 113.
45. Haynes, "Intelligence Failure in Korea," 130.

Chapter 7: "Don't Let a Bunch of Chinese Laundrymen Stop You!"

1. Russell Spur, *Enter the Dragon: China's Undeclared War Against the U.S. in Korea, 1950–51* (New York: Newmarket Press, 1988), 161; Jon Halliday and Bruce Cummings, *Korea: The Unknown War* (New York: Pantheon Books, 1988), 112.
2. Curtis Peebles, *Twilight Warriors: Covert Air Operations Against the USSR* (Annapolis, MD: Naval Institute Press, 2005), 71–72.
3. Justin M. Haynes, "Intelligence Failure in Korea: Major General Charles A. Willoughby's Role in the United Nations' Command's Defeat in November, 1950," U.S. Army Command and General Staff College M.A. thesis, June 2009, 49.
4. Halliday and Cummings, *Korea*, 112.
5. Ibid., 162.
6. Sheila Miyoshi Jager, *Brothers at War: The Unending Conflict in Korea* (New York: W. W. Norton & Co., 2013), 124–25.
7. Halliday and Cummings, *Korea*, 162.
8. Ibid., 71.
9. Ibid., 164.
10. Richard W. Stewart, *Staff Operations: The X Corps in Korea, December 1950* (Ft. Leavenworth, KS: Combat Studies Institute, U.S. Army Command and General Staff College, 1991), 3–4.
11. Halliday and Cummings, *Korea*, 165.
12. Manuscript notes from chapter of *MacArthur, 1941–1951*, Box 10-11, MS-024, Willoughby papers, Special Collections/Musselman Library, Gettysburg College, Gettysburg, PA, 6.
13. Eliot Cohen, "The Chinese Intervention in Korea, 1950," approved for release, CIA Historical Review Program, September 22, 1993, https://www.cia.gov/library/readingroom/docs/1998-11-01.pdf, 50, 55.

14. Halliday and Cummings, *Korea*, 19.
15. Richard Kolb, editor, *Battles of the Korean War: Americans Engage in Deadly Combat, 1950–1953*. Kansas City, Missouri: Veterans of Foreign Wars, 2003, 29.
16. Haynes, "Intelligence Failure in Korea," 36–37.
17. Richard W. Stewart, *The Korean War: The Chinese Intervention, 3 November 1950–24 January 1951*, U.S. Army Center of Military History brochure, accessed April 12, 2011, http://www.history.army.mil/brochures/kw-chinter/chinter.htm, 2, 4; Kolb, *Battles of the Korean War*, 29.
18. Haynes, "Intelligence Failure in Korea," 38.
19. Maj. Charles M. Azotea, United States Army, "Operational Intelligence Failures of the Korean War," monograph for School of Advanced Military Studies, United States Army Command and General Staff College, Fort Leavenworth, Kansas, 2014, 57.
20. Ibid., 50; John Patrick Finnegan, *The U.S. Army in the Korean War, 1950–1953: Operations and Intelligence Support* (Ft. Belvoir, VA: History Office, Office of the Chief of Staff, U.S. Army Intelligence and Security Command, May 2001), 65.
21. Peter G. Knight, abstract of M.A. thesis, "MacArthur's Eyes: Reassessing Military Intelligence Operations in the Forgotten War, June 1950–April 1951," Ohio State University, 2004, 202.
22. Haynes, "Intelligence Failure in Korea," 49.
23. "Treatment of Chinese Communist Intervention Issue in CIA's "Daily Korean Summary," July–November 1950, CIA Historical Staff, October 1955, 4.
24. Cohen, "The Chinese Intervention in Korea," 59; Knight, "MacArthur's Eyes," 204, 208.
25. Samuel B. Griffiths, *The Chinese People's Liberation Army* (New York: McGraw-Hill Book Company, 1967), 140; Knight, "MacArthur's Eyes," 203.
26. Oral History Interview with Ambassador John J. Muccio, Washington, D.C., Harry S. Truman Library and Museum, February 18, 1971, Part II, 9.
27. David A. Hatch with Robert Louis Benson, *The Korean War: The SIGINT Background*, Center for Cryptologic History, National Security Agency, 2000, 10.
28. James F. Schnabel, *Policy and Direction: The First Year* (Washington, D.C.: U.S. Army Center of Military History, 1992), 272–73.
29. Ibid., 274, 276.
30. *Chinese Communist Intervention in Korea*, NIE-2/1, November 24, 1950, 1.
31. Notes to chapter on "Chinese Communist War," in *MacArthur, 1941–1951*, Box 10-12, MS-024, Willoughby papers, Special Collections/Musselman Library, Gettysburg College, Gettysburg, PA, 15; Relman Moran, "MacArthur's Bold Flight to Korean Warfront Signals U.N. Offense," *The Register-News*, Mt. Vernon, Illinois, November 24, 1950; Roy E. Appleman, LTC USA (Ret.), *Disaster in Korea: The Chinese Confront MacArthur* (College Station, Texas: Texas A&M Press, 1989), 44–45. MacArthur would use "Bataan" to fly to Wake Island for his meeting with Truman, on 17 missions over the Korean battlefield, and on his last flight on the aircraft, to San Francisco following his firing by the president. The aircraft was then used by his successors, Ridgway and Clark. It was retired from the U.S. Air Force in 1966, then sold to NASA for use in conjunction with the Apollo space program. It now resides at the Planes of Fame Air Museum in Chino, California, awaiting a full restoration. (https://planesoffame.org/aircraft/plane-VC121A).
32. Appleman, *Disaster in Korea*, 56.
33. Schnabel, *Policy and Direction*, 274.
34. Saul David, *Military Blunders: The How and Why of Military Failure* (New York: Carroll & Graf Publishers, 1998), 277; Kolb, *Battles of the Korean War*, 33; Manuscript notes from chapter of *MacArthur, 1941–1951*, Box 10-11, MS-024, Willoughby papers, Special Collections/Musselman Library, Gettysburg College, Gettysburg, PA, 6; Alexander L. George, *The Chinese Communist*

Army in Action: The Korean War and its Aftermath (New York: Columbia University Press, 1967), 2; Haynes, "Intelligence Failure in Korea," 7; Stanley Sandler, "The CIA, Willoughby, and Military Intelligence in East Asia, 1946–1950," in James I. Matray, ed., *Northeast Asia and the Legacy of Harry S. Truman: Japan, China, and the Two Koreas* (Kirksville, MO: Truman State University Press, 2012), 308.

35. William Manchester, *American Caesar: Douglas MacArthur, 1880–1964* (New York: Dell Publishing Co., Inc., 1978), 608.

36. Griffiths, *The Chinese People's Liberation Army*, 146–47.

37. Ibid., 145; "Chinese People's Volunteer Army order of battle," *Wikipedia*, accessed March 5, 2015, http://en.wikipedia.org/wiki/Chinese_People%27s_Volunteer_Army_order_of_battle.

38. David Halberstam, *The Coldest Winter: America and the Korean War* (New York: Hyperion Books, 2007), 476–77.

39. Griffiths, *The Chinese People's Liberation Army*, 142–43, 146; Cohen, "The Chinese Intervention in Korea," 58.

40. Joseph R. Owen, *Colder Than Hell: A Marine Rifle Company at Chosin Reservoir* (Annapolis, MD: Bluejacket Books, 1996), foreword.

41. Paul T. Berquist, "Organizational Leadership in Crisis: The 31st Regimental Combat Team at Chosin Reservoir, Korea, 24 November–2 December 1950," Master's Thesis, U.S. Army Command and General Staff College, Ft. Leavenworth, KS, June 16, 2007, abstract; Schnabel, *Policy and Direction*, 278–79.

42. Schnabel, *Policy and Direction*, 278–79.

43. Mark E. Bennett, Jr., "Perceptions of Victory: Differing Views of Success by Nations and Echelons at the Chosin Reservoir," accessed April 8, 2015, www.militaryhistoryonline.com.

44. David, *Military Blunders*, 7, 276–78; Owen, *Colder Than Hell*, 37.

45. Central Intelligence Agency Information Report, number redacted, November 23, 1949, declassified May 31, 1978, CIA archives.

46. David, *Military Blunders*, 40; Manuscript notes from chapter of *MacArthur, 1941–1951*, Box 10-11, MS-024, Willoughby papers, Special Collections/Musselman Library, Gettysburg College, Gettysburg, PA, 7; Haynes, "Intelligence Failure in Korea," 40.

47. David, *Military Blunders*, 50; Stewart, *The Korean War*, 5.

48. Haynes, "Intelligence Failure in Korea," 50; George, *The Chinese Communist Army in Action*, 5.

49. Haynes, "Intelligence Failure in Korea," 45.

50. Ibid., 35–36.

51. James I. Matray, "Revisiting Korea: Exposing Myths of the Forgotten War," *Prologue*, Summer 2002, Vol. 34, No. 2 (https://www.archives.gov/publications/prologue/2002/summer/Korean-Myths-1, 7.

52. Carl A. Posey, "How the Korean War Almost Went Nuclear," *Air and Space Magazine*, July 2015, 3–4.

53. Matray, "Revisiting Korea," 1; Posey, "How the Korean War Almost Went Nuclear," 3–4.

54. Finnegan, *The U.S. Army in the Korean War*, 66.

55. Willoughby press briefing, December 1, 1950, RG 23, Box 6, Folder 6, MMA, Norfolk, VA.

56. CINCUNC Report No. 10 to the United Nations, December 1, 1950 (for the period November 16–30), RG 23, Box 14, Folder 2, MMA, Norfolk, VA.

57. Public Information Office, United Nations Command, December 2, 1950, RG 23, Box 6, Folder 6, MMA, Norfolk, VA.

58. Kolb, *Battles of the Korean War*, 32.

59. Griffiths, *The Chinese People's Liberation Army*, 146, 148.

60. Schnabel, *Policy and Direction*, 304.

61. Memorandum for Mr. Allen W. Dulles, Office of the DCI, Subject: Developments in the Willoughby Situation and Certain Recommendations, December 15, 1950, original CIA Top Secret memo, approved for release May 8, 2003.

62. Richard Aldrich, *The Hidden Hand: Britain, America and Cold War Secret Intelligence* (New York: Overlook Press, 2001), 275–76.

63. Schnabel, *Policy and Direction*, 304.

64. Halberstam, *The Coldest Winter*, 486, 499–500.

65. D. Clayton James, with Anne Sharp Wells, *Refighting the Last War: Command and Crisis in Korea, 1950–1953* (New York: Free Press, 1993), 70–71.

66. David, *Military Blunders*, 278.

67. "Retreat in Korea," *New York Times*, December 4, 1950, Box 2-1, MS-024, Willoughby papers, Special Collections/Musselman Library, Gettysburg College, Gettysburg, PA.

68. Undated letter (likely December 1950) from Joseph and Stewart Alsop, Box 2-1, MS-024, Willoughby papers, Special Collections/Musselman Library, Gettysburg College, Gettysburg, PA.

69. Excerpts from article, "Life of the Soldier and the Airman," December 1950, Box 9-28, MS-024, Willoughby papers, Special Collections/Musselman Library, Gettysburg College, Gettysburg, PA.

70. Roy Appleman, LTC, USA (Ret.), *Ridgway Duels for Korea* (College Station, Texas: Texas A&M Press, 1990), 155.

71. Manuscript notes to chapter on "Chinese Communist War," in *MacArthur, 1941–1951*, Box 10-12, MS-024, Willoughby papers, Special Collections/Musselman Library, Gettysburg College, Gettysburg, PA, 2.

72. Haynes, "Intelligence Failure in Korea," 8.

Chapter 8: "A Mishandling of Intelligence"

1. "Allen Carves Out Prominent Intelligence Role for DHS," *Federal Times*, September 4, 2006, www.federaltimes.com.

2. Peter G. Knight, abstract of M.A. thesis, "MacArthur's Eyes: Reassessing Military Intelligence Operations in the Forgotten War, June 1950–April 1951," Ohio State University, 2004.

3. August W. Bremer, Jr., "United Nations' Command's Defeat in November, 1950," U.S. Army Command and General Staff College M.A. thesis, June 2009, 98–99.

4. Kenneth J. Campbell, "Major General Charles A. Willoughby: General MacArthur's G-2—A Biographic Sketch," *American Intelligence Journal* 18, no. 1/2 (1998), 87–91.

5. Roger A. Beaumont, "The Flawed Soothsayer: Willoughby, General MacArthur's G-2," *Espionage*, August 1985, 26.

6. Campbell, "Major General Charles A. Willoughby," 87–91; Ronald H. Spector, *Eagle Against the Sun: The American War with Japan* (New York: Vintage Books, 1985), 189; John C. McManus, *Fire and Fortitude: The U.S. Army in the Pacific War, 1941–1943* (New York: Caliber, 2019), p. 293.

7. Michael C. Hickey, *The Korean War: The West Confronts Communism* (Woodstock, NY: Overlook Press, 1999), 24; McManus, *Fire and Fortitude*, p. 293.

8. John Prados, *Combined Fleet Decoded: The Secret History of American Intelligence and the Japanese Navy in World War II* (New York: Random House, 1995), 359.

9. Beaumont, "The Flawed Soothsayer," 27.

10. Walter R. Borneman, *MacArthur at War: World War II in the Pacific* (New York: Little, Brown and Co., 2016), 279.

11. Stephen R. Taafe, *MacArthur's Jungle War: The 1944 New Guinea Campaign* (Lawrence, KS: University Press of Kansas, 1998), 230.

12. Frank Kluckhohn, "Heidelberg to Madrid—The Story of General Willoughby," *The Reporter* (New York Journal), August 19, 1952, 5; Campbell, "Major General Charles A. Willoughby," 87–91; Borneman, *MacArthur at War*, 310; Harry A. Gaily, *MacArthur's Victory: The War in New Guinea, 1943–1944* (New York: Presidio Press, 2004), 76, 208–09.

13. Campbell, "Major General Charles A. Willoughby," 87–91; James P. Duffy, *War at the End of the World: Douglas MacArthur and the Forgotten Fight for New Guinea, 1942–1945* (New York: NAL Caliber, 2016), 363.

14. Michael E. Bigelow, "Intelligence in the Philippines," *U.S. Army Intelligence History: A Sourcebook*, James P. Finley, ed., U.S. Army Intelligence Center and Fort Huachuca, Fort Huachuca, Arizona, 1995, 196, 198.

15. Ibid., 200.

16. Douglas Waller, *Wild Bill Donovan: The Spymaster Who Created the OSS and Modern American Espionage* (New York: Free Press, 2011), 232.

17. Samuel B. Griffiths, *The Chinese People's Liberation Army* (New York: McGraw-Hill Book Company, 1967), 115; David Halberstam, *The Coldest Winter: America and the Korean War* (New York: Hyperion Books, 2007), 377.

18. Richard Aldrich, *The Hidden Hand: Britain, America and Cold War Secret Intelligence* (New York: Overlook Press, 2001), 274.

19. Ronald Lewin, *The Other Ultra: Codes, Ciphers, and the Defeat of Japan* (London: Hutchinson and Co., 1982), 180.

20. Campbell, "Major General Charles A. Willoughby," 87–91.

21. Ibid.

22. Spector, *Eagle Against the Sun*, 280–81; John F. Kreis, general editor, *Piercing the Fog: Intelligence and Army Air Force Operations in World War II* (Washington, D.C.: Air Force History and Museums Program, Bolling Air Force Base, 1996), 277–79.

23. Taafe, *MacArthur's Jungle War*, 58–59.

24. Campbell, "Major General Charles A. Willoughby," 87–91.

25. Borneman, *MacArthur at War*, 181.

26. Williamson Murray and Allan R. Millett, *A War to Be Won: Fighting the Second World War* (Cambridge, MA: The Belknap Press of Harvard University Press, 2000), 208, 495.

27. Taafe, *MacArthur's Jungle War*, 41.

28. Willoughby manuscript, "The Character of Military Intelligence," Box 11-1, MS-024, Special Collections/Musselman Library, Gettysburg College, Gettysburg, PA.

29. "World War II Intelligence in the Pacific Theater: Charles Willoughby," Fort Huachuca, accessed June 14, 2012, www.huachuca.army.mil/sites/History/PDFS/MWILLOU.pdf, 6–7.

30. Clark Lee and Richard Henschel, *Douglas MacArthur* (New York: Henry Holt and Company, 1952), 181–82.

31. "Fact Sheet: An Overview of the U.S. Army in the Korean War, 1950–1953," State of New Jersey, Department of Military and Veterans Affairs, accessed February 18, 2016 (http:www.nj.gov/military/korea/factsheets/army.html), 5.

32. Eliot Cohen, "The Chinese Intervention in Korea, 1950," approved for release, CIA Historical Review Program, September 22, 1993, https://www.cia.gov/library/readingroom/docs/1998-11-01.pdf, 61–62.

33. Griffiths, *The Chinese People's Liberation Army*, 138.

34. G. J. A. O'Toole, *The Encyclopedia of American Intelligence and Espionage: From the Revolutionary War to the Present* (New York: Facts on File, 1988), 266.

35. Richard A. Mobley, "North Korea's Surprise Attack: Weak U.S. Analysis?", *International Journal of Intelligence and Counterintelligence*, Vol. 13, No. 4, Winter 2000, 508–10.

36. Matthew Aid, "U.S. HUMINT and COMINT in the Korean War: From the Approach of War to the Chinese Intervention," in Aldrich, Rawnsley, Rawnsley, eds., *The Clandestine Cold War in Asia*, 17.

37. Ibid., 18.

38. Hickey, *The Korean War*, 292.

39. O'Toole, *The Encyclopedia of Intelligence and Espionage*, 266; Halberstam, *The Coldest Winter*, 374.

40. Aid, "U.S. HUMINT and COMINT in the Korean War," 18.

41. Bruce Riedel, "Catastrophe on the Yalu: America's Intelligence Failure in Korea," Brookings Institute article excerpted and adapted from *JFK's Forgotten Crisis: Tibet, the CIA and Sino-Indian War* (Washington, D.C.: Brookings Institution Press, 2015), 1.

42. Justin M. Haynes, "Intelligence Failure in Korea: Major General Charles A. Willoughby's Role in the United Nations' Command's Defeat in November, 1950," U.S. Army Command and General Staff College M.A. thesis, June 2009, abstract, iv.

43. William Manchester, *American Caesar: Douglas MacArthur, 1880–1964* (New York: Dell Publishing Co., Inc., 1978), 543.

44. Richard E. Matthews, "Task Force Smith: An Intelligence Failure," U.S. Army Command and General Staff monograph, December 14, 1995, abstract.

45. Cohen, "The Chinese Intervention in Korea," 52; Maj. Charles M. Azotea, United States Army, "Operational Intelligence Failures of the Korean War," monograph for School of Advanced Military Studies, United States Army Command and General Staff College, Fort Leavenworth, Kansas, 2014, 18–19, 48.

46. Azotea, "Operational Intelligence Failures of the Korean War," 58–59.

47. Knight, "MacArthur's Eyes," 41–42, 180, 196.

48. Joseph R. Owen, *Colder Than Hell: A Marine Rifle Company at Chosin Reservoir* (New York: Bluejacket Books, 1996), foreword; Paul M. Edwards, *To Acknowledge a War: The Korean War in American Memory* (Westport, CT: Greenwood Press, 2000), 81.

49. U.S. Army Center of Military History, Intelligence and Counterintelligence Problems During the Korean Conflict: "Chapter II, Army-Level Intelligence Production," accessed on October 10, 2012, www.history.army.mil/documents/Korea/inkor/intkor2.htm.

50. Haynes, "Intelligence Failure in Korea," abstract, iv.

51. Ibid., 14.

52. Halberstam, *The Coldest Winter*, 378.

53. Ibid.

54. John Patrick Finnegan, *The U.S. Army in the Korean War, 1950–1953: Operations and Intelligence Support* (Ft. Belvoir, VA: History Office, Office of the Chief of Staff, U.S. Army Intelligence and Security Command, May 2001), 65.

55. Homer Bigart, "Why We Got Licked," *New York Herald Tribune* article, n.d., in Box 2-1, Willoughby materials, Special Collections/Musselman Library, Gettysburg College, Gettysburg, PA.

56. Foreign Denial and Deception Committee, "The Chinese Invasion of Korea, October 1950 (A)," November 2007, 17.

57. Oral History Interview with Ambassador John J. Muccio, Washington, D.C., Harry S. Truman Library and Museum, February 18, 1971, Part II, 4, 9–10; Beaumont, "Flawed Soothsayer," 33.

58. Muccio interview, Part II, 18 February 1971, 10.

59. D. Clayton James, with Anne Sharp Wells, *Refighting the Last War: Command and Crisis in Korea, 1950–1953* (New York: Free Press, 1993), 43.

60. Ibid., 34. Beaumont, "Flawed Soothsayer," 34.

61. Francis H. Heller, ed., *The Korean War: A 25-Year Perspective* (Lawrence, Kansas: Regents Press of Kansas, 1977), 29–33.

62. *Military History, Vol. II*, edited by Spencer C. Tucker (Santa Barbara, CA: ABC-CLIO, 2000), 739–40.

63. Franz-Stefan Gady, "Is This the Worst Intelligence Chief in the U.S. Army's History?", *The Diplomat*, January 27, 2019, 1–3.

64. Beaumont, "Flawed Soothsayer," 36.

65. Taafe, *MacArthur's Jungle War*, 41.

66. Beaumont, *Flawed Soothsayer*, 36.

67. Aldrich, *The Clandestine Cold War in Asia*, 55.

68. Gady, "Is This the Worst Intelligence Chief in the U.S. Army's History?", 3. McCaffrey would ultimately fight in three wars and would retire as a lieutenant general. He was the father of U.S. Army General Barry McCaffrey.

69. Azotea, "Operational Intelligence Failures of the Korean War," 51; Stanley Sandler, *The Korean War: No Victors, No Vanquished* (Lexington, KY: The University Press of Kentucky, 1999), 113; Haynes, "Intelligence Failure in Korea," 107–09; Russell Spur, *Enter the Dragon: China's Undeclared War Against the U.S. in Korea, 1950–51* (New York: Newmarket Press, 1988), 161; Haynes, "Intelligence Failure in Korea," 2, 10, 77, 75, 84, 76.

70. Beaumont, "Flawed Soothsayer," 24.

71. Paul M. Edwards, *To Acknowledge a War: The Korean War in American Memory*, Contributions in Military Studies No. 193 (Westport, Connecticut: Greenwood Press, 2000), 63.

72. Azotea, "Operational Intelligence Failures of the Korean War," 55.

73. Edwards, *To Acknowledge a War*, 61; Haynes, "Intelligence Failure in Korea," 94.

74. Haynes, "Intelligence Failure in Korea," 93–94.

75. Griffiths, *The Chinese People's Liberation Army*, 202.

76. Knight, "MacArthur's Eyes," 5, 9, 11.

77. Muccio interview, Part II, 18 February 1971, 4, 11; Peter Lowe, *The Origins of the Korean War*, Second Ed., (London: Longman, 1986), 202.

78. Blaine Harden, *King of Spies: The Dark Reign of America's Spymaster in Korea* (New York: Viking, 2017), 53.

79. Sandler, *The Korean War*, 113.

80. Campbell, "Major General Charles A. Willoughby," 87–91.

81. Haynes, "Intelligence Failure in Korea," 107–09.

82. Muccio interview, Part II, 18 February 1971, 10.

83. Spur, *Enter the Dragon*, 161.

84. Haynes, "Intelligence Failure in Korea," 2.

85. Ibid., 10. The total American casualty figure for the United States during the Korean War has been subject to much dispute since the war itself. However, the most current figures (last revised in 1994) used by the Pentagon are that American combat deaths in Korea numbered 33,652, not including 3,262 "other deaths," for a total of 36,914.

86. Letter from Willoughby to William Randolph Hearst, January 28, 1951, Willoughby documents, Box 7-8, Special Collections/Musselman Library, Gettysburg College, Gettysburg, PA.

87. Haynes, "Intelligence Failure in Korea," 77.

88. Ibid., 75.

89. Edwards, *To Acknowledge a War*, 81.

90. Finnegan, *The U.S. Army in the Korean War*, 73.

91. *Study of CIA Reporting on Chinese Communist Intervention in the Korean War, September–December 1950*, CIA Historical Staff, October 1955, CIA archives, pp. 14–15.

92. Haynes, "Intelligence Failure in Korea," 84.

93. Joseph and Stewart Alsop article, "Who Failed?" in Willoughby papers, Special Collections/Musselman Library, Gettysburg College, Gettysburg, PA.

94. Ruth Quinn, "LTG Philip Davidson Presides Over First MI Officer Advanced Course Graduation at USAICS," March 24, 2014, https://www.army.mil/article/122431/LTG_Philip_Davidson_presides_over_first_MI_Officer_Advanced_Course_Graduation_at_USAICS, n.p.

95. "World War II Intelligence in the Pacific Theater: Charles Willoughby," Ft. Huachuca, AZ (www.huachuca.army.mil/sites/History/PDFS/MWILLOU.pdf), p. 8.

96. Knight, "MacArthur's Eyes," 53, 72; Aldrich, *The Clandestine Cold War in Asia, 1945–1965*, 48, 51.

97. Aldrich, *The Clandestine Cold War in Asia*, 56.

98. Hickey, *The Korean War*, 25.; Haynes, "Intelligence Failure in Korea," 113.

99. Halberstam, *The Coldest Winter*, 373; Hickey, *The Korean War*, 25.; Haynes, "Intelligence Failure in Korea," 113. "Mirror imaging" refers to the tendency of analysts to base enemy courses of action on what the analysts *themselves* would do in the given situation, rather than taking into account what the enemy may have done in similar circumstances in the past. As one historian has defined it, "Information about the enemy is interpreted in a way that conforms to the personal beliefs and hypotheses of the analyst who will then resist and dismiss any information that contradicts his beliefs." In more recent years, the American intelligence community has adopted a set of Analytic Integrity Standards (AIS) to help guard against this tendency and at least one observer has pointed out that the routine use of collaborative analytical tools, web-based information sharing, and improved interagency cooperation might prevent individuals such as Willoughby from again having "undue influence over intelligence analysis."

100. T. R. Fehrenbach, *This Kind of War: A Study in Unpreparedness* (New York: The MacMillan Co., 1963), 283.

101. Haynes, "Intelligence Failure in Korea," 118–21. In assessing the *denouement* of the Korean War, this same author has opined that "The U.S. repeatedly demonstrates a tendency to prematurely assume that its conflicts are complete before achieving decisive victory."; Knight, "MacArthur's Eyes," 198.

102. Campbell, "Major General Charles A. Willoughby," 87–91.

103. Ibid.; Edwards, *To Acknowledge a War*, 81.

104. Manchester, *American Caesar*, 604.

105. Haynes, "Intelligence Failure in Korea," 121, 124.

106. Edwards, *To Acknowledge a War*, 81.

107. Halberstam, *The Coldest Winter*, 374.

108. Paul H. Nitze Oral History Interview, June 11, 1975, Harry S. Truman Library and Museum, Independence, MO; Knight, "MacArthur's Eyes," 25–26.

109. Haynes, "Intelligence Failure in Korea," 99.

110. James, *Refighting the Last War*, 70.

111. Colonel Sidney F. Mashbir, as told to Jim Aswell, "I Was an American Spy," *Saturday Evening Post*, March 27, 1948, CIA archives. Mashbir's autobiography, with the same title, appeared in hardcover in 1953.

112. Lee and Henschel, *Douglas MacArthur*, 166, 181–82.

113. Haynes, "Intelligence Failure in Korea," 12.

114. Ibid., 15.

115. Jim Lucas, "Intelligence Slur Called Slap at MacArthur," Willoughby papers, Box 2-1, Special Collections/Musselman Library, Gettysburg College, Gettysburg, PA.

116. Knight, "MacArthur's Eyes," 208–09.

117. Ibid., 245.
118. Ibid., 260, 263.
119. Stephen Marrin, "Preventing Intelligence Failures by Learning From the Past," *International Journal of Intelligence and Counterintelligence*, Vol. 17, No. 4, Winter 2004–2005, 660.
120. Major August W. Bremer, Jr., USA, "Chinese Communist Intervention in the Korean War: Miscalculation or Provocation? A Study of the Failure to Predict the Chinese Communist Intervention in the Korean War, November 1950," U.S. Army Command and General Staff College M.A. thesis abstract, 1987.
121. Lee and Henschel, *Douglas MacArthur*, 181–82.
122. Max Hastings, *The Secret War: Spies, Ciphers and Guerrillas, 1939–1945* (New York: HarperCollins Publishers, 2016), 552.
123. Douglas MacArthur, *Reminiscences* (New York: McGraw-Hill Book Co., 1964), 113.
124. Gady, "Is This the Worst Intelligence Chief in the U.S. Army's History?", 3.

Chapter 9: Post-War Paranoia

1. Franz-Stefan Gady, "Is This the Worst Intelligence Chief in the U.S. Army's History?", *The Diplomat*, January 27, 2019, 2.
2. Bruce H. Siemon, "The Army's Historical Coverage of Operation JOINT ENDEAVOR," *Army History*, PB-20-97-2 (No. 41), Washington, D.C., Spring 1997, 17.
3. Letter from Willoughby to Honorable Walter H. Judd, U.S. House of Representatives, December 19, 1950, Willoughby documents, Box 7-22, Special Collections/Musselman Library, Gettysburg College, Gettysburg, PA.
4. Letter, Willoughby to Senator Joseph McCarthy, January 28, 1951, in Box 8-10, MS-024, Willoughby papers, Special Collections/Musselman Library, Gettysburg College, Gettysburg, PA; Letter from Ned Almond, LTG, Commandant, Army War College, to Willoughby, May 5, 1952, RG 23, Box 5, Folder 3, MMA, Norfolk, VA.
5. Letter from CIA Deputy Director Allen Dulles to Major General Charles A. Willoughby, AC of S, G-2, Headquarters, Far East Command, January 22, 1951, in CADRE (CIA Automated Declassification and Release Environment), Ref ID C03103521, accessed September 14, 2016.
6. Letter from CIA Deputy Director Allen W. Dulles to Major General Charles A. Willoughby, Acting Chief of Staff, G-2, Headquarters, Far East Command, April 14, 1951, in CADRE (CIA Automated Declassification and Release Environment, Ref ID C03103513, accessed September 14, 2016; Letter from Major General Charles A. Willoughby to Allen Dulles, September 1, 1952, in CADRE (CIA Automated Declassification and Release Environment), Ref ID C05963470, accessed September 14, 2016.
7. "Hearings on American Aspects of the Richard Sorge Spy Case," Hearings Before the Committee on Un-American Activities, House of Representatives, Eighty-Second Congress, First Session, August 9, 22, and 23, 1951, Harvard College Library, accessed January 29, 2020, https://archive.org/stream/hearingsonameric00unit/hearingsonamericunit_dvju.txt, n.p.
8. Letter from Willoughby to Allen Dulles, dated February 2, 1951, CIA archives.
9. "Hearings on American Aspects of the Richard Sorge Spy Case," Hearings Before the House Un-American Activities Committee, n.p.
10. Peter G. Knight, abstract of M.A. thesis, "MacArthur's Eyes: Reassessing Military Intelligence Operations in the Forgotten War, June 1950–April 1951," Ohio State University, 2004, 242, 245. In January 1979, the CIA transferred 55 cubic feet of Shanghai Municipal Police (SMP) files—dating primarily from 1929 to 1944 and which Willoughby used in part to conduct his research and writing—to the National Archives. Also included in this transfer were bound

volumes containing copies of SMP documents selected and bound by Far East Command at Willoughby's direction. These files had been seized by the Japanese during World War II, then were transferred to the custody of the Chinese Nationalists until February 1949, when the CIA assumed control of them, to prevent their falling into the hands of the Chinese Communists.

11. Letter from Willoughby to Dulles, September 1, 1952, CIA archives.

12. Letter, Bonner Fellers to Willoughby, June 26, 1950, RG 30, Box 5, Folder 14, MMA, Norfolk, Virginia.

13. Knight, "MacArthur's Eyes," 242, 245.

14. GHQ, UN & FEC, Military Intelligence Section, General Staff, Major General C. A. Willoughby document, Box 1-1 (Biography), MS-024, Willoughby papers, Special Collections/Musselman Library, Gettysburg College, Gettysburg, PA; Letter, Willoughby to Eric Cocke, Jr., National Commander, the American Legion, Indianapolis 6, Indiana, May 8, 1951, Willoughby documents, Box 6-34, Special Collections/Musselman Library, Gettysburg College, Gettysburg, PA; Arthur Herman, *Douglas MacArthur: American Warrior* (New York: Random House, 2016), 814.

15. "Charles Andrew Willoughby, Major General, United States Army," Arlington National Cemetery website (http://arlingtoncemetery.net/cawilloughby.htm), p. 6. Used with permission.

16. Letter from Willoughby to Capt. John Ford USN, Argosy Pictures, April 27, 1951, Willoughby documents, Box 6-32, Special Collections/Musselman Library, Gettysburg College, Gettysburg, PA.

17. Letter from Willoughby to Mr. Clark H. Getts, New York, May 8, 1951, Willoughby documents, Box 7-2, Special Collections/Musselman Library, Gettysburg College, Gettysburg, PA.

18. Cover note to MacArthur from Willoughby, to accompany a copy of the Willoughby article, "Aid and Comfort to the Enemy: Trends of Korean Press Reports," April 18, 1951, RG 5, Box 61, Folder 2, MMA, Norfolk, VA.

19. Willoughby letter to MacArthur, April? 1951, RG 5, Box 61, Folder 2, MMA, Norfolk, VA. The question mark in the date appears in the original and the context of the letter suggests it was written somewhat later that year.

20. "The Public Controversy in April–June 1951 as to the Adequacy of U.S. Intelligence Estimating, July–December 1950, with respect to Chinese Communist Intervention in Korea," CIA Historical Staff, October 1955, 7.

21. Ibid., 11.

22. Ibid., 12.

23. William R. Corson, *The Armies of Ignorance: The Rise of the American Intelligence Empire* (New York: Dial Press, 1977), 320.

24. Letter from Willoughby to MG Harry Vaughn, White House, July 30, 1951, RG 23, Box 5, Folder 3, MMA, Norfolk, VA.

25. Letter from Willoughby to MacArthur, July 26, 1951, RG 5, Box 61, Folder 2, MMA, Norfolk, VA.

26. Special Orders No. 163, Department of the Army, August 14, 1951, RG 23, Box 12, Folder 14, MMA, Norfolk, VA.

27. Letter from Willoughby to MacArthur, June/July 1951, RG 5, Box 61, Folder 2, MMA, Norfolk, VA.

28. Letter from Willoughby to MG A. R. Bolling, June 24, 1951, RG 23, Box 5, Folder 3, MMA, Norfolk, VA.

29. Letter from Willoughby to Courtney Whitney, September 1951, RG 5, Box 61, Folder 2, MMA, Norfolk, VA

30. Letter from Willoughby to MacArthur, August 1951, RG 5, Box 61, Folder 2, MMA, Norfolk, VA.

31. Letter from Willoughby to Lawrence (Larry) Bunker, August 1951, RG 5, Box 61, Folder 2, MMA, Norfolk, VA.

32. Letter from Willoughby to MacArthur, September 15, 1951, RG 5, Box 61, Folder 2, MMA, Norfolk, VA.

33. Letter from Willoughby to MacArthur, November 22, 1951, RG 5, Box 61, Folder 2, MMA, Norfolk, VA.; List of Chiefs, Historical Division, G-2, FEC, undated, RG 23, Box 12, Folder 1, MMA, Norfolk, VA.

34. Letter from attorney E. F. Wildermuth, to unknown recipient, August 5, 1972, RG 23, Box 12, Folder 1, MMA, Norfolk, VA.

35. Stanley Sandler, "Secret Operations of the Central Intelligence Agency During the Korean War," unpublished manuscript, n.d., Center for the Study of Intelligence, Central Intelligence Agency, 53, 80.

36. Letter, Frank G. Wisner to Major General Charles A. Willoughby, dated August 30, 1951, CIA archives; Letter, Allen W. Dulles to Major General Charles A. Willoughby, September 10, 1951, CIA archives.

37. CIA memorandum, "Subject: General Charles A. Willoughby," dated September 28, 1951, CIA archives, approved for release January 29, 2001.

38. Letter from Willoughby to MG A. C. Smith, Chief, Military History, Department of the Army, October 30, 1954, RG 23, Box 5, Folder 3, MMA, Norfolk, VA.

39. John Prados, *Combined Fleet Decoded: The Secret History of American Intelligence and the Japanese Navy in World War II* (New York: Random House, 1995), 415.

40. Frank Kluckhohn, "Heidelberg to Madrid—The Story of General Willoughby," *The Reporter* (New York Journal), August 19, 1952, 1–2; Brigadier General Elliott R. Thorpe, *East Wind, Rain: The Intimate Account of an Intelligence Officer in the Pacific, 1939–1949* (Boston Gambit Inc., 1969), 96; Eric Larrabee, *Commander in Chief: Franklin Delano Roosevelt, His Lieutenants and Their War* (New York: Harper and Row, 1987), 333.

41. Kluckhohn, "Heidelberg to Madrid," 1–2.

42. Letter from Willoughby to Dulles, September 1, 1952, CIA archives.

43. Notes written by Willoughby in response to Kluckhohn article, "From Heidelberg to Madrid," RG 30, Box 5, Folder 14, MMA, Norfolk, VA.

44. Letter from Willoughby to Dulles, September 1, 1952, CIA archives.

45. Letter from Willoughby to Dulles, December 3, 1955, CIA archives.

46. Letter from Chief, WH (Western Hemisphere) J. C. King to Deputy Director (Plans) Frank Wisner, December 22, 1955, CIA archives; Letter from Wisner to King, June 11, 1956, CIA archives.

47. Letter from Willoughby to Dulles, June 6, 1956, CIA archives.

48. Letter from Willoughby to General Maxwell Taylor October 15, 1956, CIA archives.

49. Letter ER-1-9184 from Willoughby to Bedell Smith, June 24, 1951, CIA archives, approved for release September 2, 2003.

50. Willoughby testimony before the Committee on Un-American Activities, House of Representatives, Eighty-Second Congress, First Session, August 22, 1951, Harvard College Library.

51. Letter from Willoughby to Bedell Smith, 24 June 1951, CIA archive.

52. Undated statement from Willoughby, Box 1-2, MS-024, Willoughby papers, Special Collections/Musselman Library, Gettysburg College, Gettysburg, PA; "A Statement by Major General Charles A. Willoughby—MacArthur's Chief of Intelligence: 1941–1951," CIA archives, approved for release September 2, 2003, n.p.

53. "Hearings on American Aspects of the Richard Sorge Spy Case," Hearings Before the House Un-American Activities Committee, n.p.

54. Ibid.
55. *Foreign Intelligence Digest* masthead, RG 23, Box 15, Folder 5, MMA, Norfolk, VA.
56. FOIA request to FBI from Mr. Ernie Lazar, March 24, 2006, accessed October 15, 2019, https://archive.org/details/HARGISBillyJamesChristianCrusadeHQ973475181; Correspondence between DCI Allen W. Dulles and Major General (Ret.) Charles A. Willoughby, June 1961, CIA archives.
57. "Willoughby Hits Korea News 'Bias'," The *New York Times*, November 28, 1951, CIA archives, approved for release, January 29, 2003.
58. Ibid.; "Ragpicker," *Washington Post*, November 30, 1951, CIA archives, n.p.
59. I. F. Stone, *The Hidden History of the Korean War, 1950–1951* (Boston: Little, Brown & Co., 1952), 57–58.
60. Major General Charles A. Willoughby, "The Truth About Korea," *Cosmopolitan*, December 1951, 35, RG 23, Box 20, Folder 16, MMA, Norfolk, VA.
61. Ibid., 37, 134, 137.
62. Ibid., 138.
63. Ibid., 139.
64. Notes on Kluckhohn article, "From Heidelberg to Madrid," RG 30, Box 5, Folder 14, MMA, Norfolk, VA.
65. Letter from Willoughby to Bonner Fellers, August 31, 1952, RG 30, Box 5, Folder 14, MMA, Norfolk, VA.
66. Stanley Weintraub, *MacArthur's War: Korea and the Undoing of an American Hero* (New York: The Free Press, 2000), 357; Undated tribute, accompanied by photo of "Major General Charles A. Willoughby, Assistant Chief of Staff, G-2, General Headquarters, Far East Command," Box 1-1, MS-024, Willoughby papers, Special Collections/Musselman Library, Gettysburg College, Gettysburg, PA; Stone, *The Hidden History of the Korean War*, 58–59; Capsule review, *Foreign Affairs*, accessed October 22, 2013, www.foreignaffairs.com/articles/126540/major-general-charles-a-willoughy-and-john-chamberlain.com.
67. Oral History Interview with Colonel Laurence H. Bunker, by Benedict K. Zobrist, Truman Presidential Museum & Library, Independence, Missouri, December 14, 1976, 2–3.
68. "The Public Controversy in April–June 1951," 15.
69. Gettysburg College Alumni Council Dinner program, Friday, June 4, 1954, Box 1-3, MS-024, Willoughby papers, Special Collections/Musselman Library, Gettysburg College, Gettysburg, PA.
70. "The Public Controversy in April–June 1951," 20, 22.
71. Letter, MG Clark L. Ruffner, CDR, 2d Armored Division, to Willoughby, January 25, 1956, RG 234, Box 1, MMA, Norfolk, VA.
72. Letter, MG G. B. Barth, acting commander, 1st Army, February 28, 1956, to Willoughby, RG 23, Box 1, MMA, Norfolk, VA.
73. Letter, General Maxwell D. Taylor, Chief of Staff, U.S. Army, to Willoughby, July 2, 1956, RG 23, Box 1, MMA, Norfolk, VA.

Chapter 10: Watchman of the Republic

1. Justin M. Haynes, "Intelligence Failure in Korea: Major General Charles A. Willoughby's Role in the United Nations' Command's Defeat in November, 1950," U.S. Army Command and General Staff College M.A. thesis, June 2009, 101, 105; Michael Hickey, *The Korean War: The West Confronts Communism* (Woodstock, NY: Overlook Press, 2000), 24; "One Dozen Candles," *Wikipedia*, https://en.wikipedia.org/wiki/One_Dozen_Candles, n.p.

2.   Gordon W. Prange, *Target Tokyo: The Story of the Sorge Spy Ring* (New York: McGraw-Hill Book Co., 1984), xi.

3.   Foreword to *The Shanghai Conspiracy*, written by General (Ret.) Douglas MacArthur, November 1, 1951, from 90 Church St., New York City, New York. Copy in Box 1-1 (Biography), MS-024, Willoughby papers, Special Collections/Musselman Library, Gettysburg College, Gettysburg, PA.

4.   Letter from the Honorable Harold O. Lovre, U.S. House of Representatives, to Willoughby, dated February 20, 1950, Box 7-38, MS-024, Willoughby papers, Special Collections/Musselman Library, Gettysburg College, Gettysburg, PA.

5.   American Security Council information sheet, CIA archives.

6.   Letter from Willoughby to Chairman, Senate Foreign Relations Committee, April 30, 1958, in Box 1-10, MS-024, Willoughby papers, Special Collections/Musselman Library, Gettysburg College, Gettysburg, PA.

7.   "Major General Charles A. Willoughby," *The Education Forum*, accessed online September 29, 2008, 3; Membership List, January 15, 1966, Pennsylvania Membership of the International Committee for the Defense of Christian Culture, RG 23, Box 5, Folder 6, MMA, Norfolk, VA.

8.   "CIA Papers Reveal Japan Coup Plot," *Military.com*, accessed January 23, 2016, www.http://www.military.com/NewsContent/0,13319,126978,00.html.

9.   *The Times (London)*, June 2, 1954, quoting from an undated, untitled article by Charles Willoughby.

10. Commission on Organization of the Executive Branch of the Government, Commission Report on Intelligence Activities (aka The Clark Committee Report), ii.

11. Veterans of Strategic Services announcement, undated, CIA CADRE document CIA-RDP80B01676R002600080020-6, approved for release January 29, 2003, CIA archives.

12. Office Memorandum, United States Government, To AC/PPS From AC/LAS, Subject: Weekly Activities Report #43, October 23, 1957, CIA archives, approved for release July 30, 2001.

13. Extracts from *National Review*, February 2, 1957, CIA archives; M. P. Hartzell (Gettysburg 1939), "Xi Chapter at Gettysburg Reaches 100," reprinted from *The Phi Gamma Delta*, Volume 80, Number 4, March 1958, accessed December 9, 2004, http://www.phigam.org/history/Magazine/XiHistory.htm, 5.

14. Charles A. Willoughby, "The Summit and the Pit," *Christian Crusade*, undated, RG 23, Box 20, Folder 16, MMA, Norfolk, VA.

15. Letter from DCI Allen Dulles to Willoughby, May 18, 1960, RG 23, Box 2, Folder 4, MMA, Norfolk, VA.

16. Letter from Willoughby to DCI Dulles, May 23, 1960, RG 23, Box 2, Folder 4, MMA, Norfolk, VA.

17. Letter from DCI Dulles to Willoughby, June 14, 1961, RG 23, Box 2, Folder 4, MMA, Norfolk, VA.

18. Letter from Dulles to Willoughby, March 18, 1963, RG 23, Box 2, Folder 4, MMA, Norfolk, VA.

19. Willoughby notes on Sokolsky editorial, August 12 (no year, NFI), RG 23, Box 2, Folder 4, MMA, Norfolk, VA.

20. Charles Willoughby, *Foreign Intelligence Digest* article, February 26, 1967, RG 23, Box 2, Folder 4, MMA, Norfolk, VA.

21. Letter from Francis E. Walter, Chairman, House Un-American Activities Committee, Congress of the United States, to Honorable Allen W. Dulles, Director, Central Intelligence Agency, January 8, 1958, CIA archives, approved for release August 21, 2002, 1.

22. Committee on Un-American Activities, House of Representatives, Eighty-Fifth Congress, First Session, Staff Consultation with Gen. Charles A. Willoughby, Former Chief of Intelligence,

Far Eastern Command, Under General Douglas MacArthur, "International Communism" (Communist Designs on Indonesia and the Pacific Frontier), December 16, 1957, 1–2.

23. Ibid., 7; *Congressional Record*—House, April 7, 1964, CIA archives, 6953.

24. Letter from Willoughby to General Wilton B. Persons, The Deputy Assistant to the President, March 15, 1958, RG 23, Box 1, MMA, Norfolk, VA.

25. "The 'Other' Orders of the Knights of Malta," *Covert Action*, Number 25 (Winter 1986), 36.

26. Invitation to Willoughby to join Sovereign Order of Saint John of Jerusalem, Knights of Malta, September 11, 1959, Box 8, Folder 10, MMA, Norfolk, VA; List of officers, Sovereign Order of Saint John of Jerusalem, Knights of Malta, September 17, 1963, Box 8, Folder 10, MMA, Norfolk, VA.

27. "Atoms for Peace" materials, Eisenhower Library, Abilene, Kansas, accessed March 10, 2020, https://www.eisenhowerlibrary.gov/research/online-documents/atoms-peace.

28. Charles A. Willoughby, "Espionage and the American Communist Party," *American Mercury*, January 1959, 1–7, RG 23, Box 15, Folder 2, MMA, Norfolk, VA.

29. Roger A. Beaumont, "The Flawed Soothsayer: Willoughby, General MacArthur's G-2," Espionage, August 1985, p. 36.

30. Major General Charles A. Willoughby, "Twining and De Gaulle, 1959," *American Mercury*, March 1960, 3–6, 15.

31. Jeffrey L. Lauck, "The Missing Link: The Search for the Connection Between Young Americans for Freedom and Charles Willoughby," *The Gettysburg Compiler: On the Front Lines of History*, January 8, 2016, 128. The "conspiracy connection" concerned an intercepted phone call which seemed to implicate Fidel Castro in the assassination of John F. Kennedy and the future targeting of his brother, Bobby Kennedy. The phone call reportedly was traced to Emilio Nunez Portuondo, the Latin American Affairs editor on the staff of *the Foreign Intelligence Digest* newspaper, created and managed by Willoughby.

32. Maj. Gen. Charles A. Willoughby, "Khrushchev and the Flight to Sverdlovsk," *American Mercury*, August 1960, 35.

33. Statement of Major General Charles A. Willoughby, U.S.A. Ret. on behalf of the American Coalition of Patriotic Societies before the Committee on Appropriations, United States Senate June 1960 on Appropriations for Mutual Security for the Fiscal Year ending June 30, 1961, RG 23, Box 12, Folder 17, p. 10, MMA, Norfolk, VA.

34. Program, "American Strategy Seminar, March 30th–31st, 1962, Kleinhans Music Hall, University of Buffalo," Buffalo, New York, Box-1-2, MS-024, Willoughby papers, Special Collections/ Musselman Library, Gettysburg College, Gettysburg, PA.

35. Congressional Record, U.S. House of Representatives, April 7, 1964, 6952.

36. Beaumont, "The Flawed Soothsayer," 36.

37. "America Needs a Foreign Legion," by Major General Charles A. Willoughby (Ret.), with Edward Hymoff, *Argosy*, January 1966, Vol. 362, No. 1, 22–23, 106–07, RG 23, Box 13, Folder 2, MMA, Norfolk, VA.

38. Obituary, *Gettysburg Times*, Thursday, October 26, 1972; Haynes, "Intelligence Failure in Korea", 100–01. Marie Antoinette DeBecker had married Willoughby following World War II—his first wife, Juana Manuela Rodriguez, the mother of their only child Olga, had died in 1940, when Olga was 15 years old.

39. Letter to Willoughby from Durward Packer, n.d., Box 8, Folder 2, MMA, Norfolk, VA. Marie had been born in Kamakura, Japan, in 1901 and was living in Manila when World War II broke out; she was then captured by the invading Japanese and interned in the Santo Tomas Internment Camp in Manila. See www.findagrave.com/memorial/61216273/marie-antoinette-willoughby and www.findagrave.com/memorial/78317225/joseph-ernest-de_becker.

40. Letter from Naples, Florida Mayor Lloyd M. Easterling to Willoughby, May 19, 1970, Box 8, Folder 2, MMA, Norfolk, VA.
41. Letter from Naples Chamber of Commerce President Walter R. Rogers to Willoughby, October 5, 1970, Box 8, Folder 2, MMA, Norfolk, VA.
42. Congressional Record—House, May 21, 1970, pp. H4713–4715, CIA archives.
43. Letter from LTG A.C. Connor, USA, Commanding, Third Army, Ft. McPherson, GA, to Willoughby, March 19, 1971, RG 23, Box 1, MMA, Norfolk, VA.

Chapter 11: To the Grave ... and Beyond

1. Letter, Hamilton Fish, President Emeritus, The Order of Lafayette, Inc., to Willoughby, January 24, 1972, RG 23, Box 3, Folder 10, MMA, Norfolk, VA.
2. Letter, Ambassador William Sebald to Captain Miles P. Duval, USN (Ret.), Cosmos Club, 2121 Massachusetts Avenue, Washington, DC, June 29, 1972, Box 3, Folder 1, MMA, Norfolk, VA.
3. Obituary, *Gettysburg Times*, Thursday, October 26, 1972, Box 1-1 (Biography), MS-024, Willoughby papers, Special Collections/Musselman Library, Gettysburg College, Gettysburg, PA; Letter, Ambassador William Sebald to Captain Miles P. Duval, USN (Ret.), October 26, 1972, Box 3, Folder 1, MMA, Norfolk, VA.
4. "Maj. Gen. Charles Willoughby, Intelligence Aide in Pacific, Dies," obituary in the *New York Times*, October 26, 1972.
5. Letter from Ambassador William Sebald to unidentified Military District of Washington official, 1972, Box 3, Folder 1, MMA, Norfolk, VA.
6. Letter from William Sebald to Miles Duval, November 15, 1972, Box 3, Folder 1, MMA, Norfolk, VA.
7. Eulogy for Maj. Gen. Charles A. Willoughby, as presented by Captain Duval to the U.S. House of Representatives, n.d., Box 3, Folder 1, MMA, Norfolk, VA.
8. *Gettysburg Times* article, November 27, 1945, Box 1-1, MS-024.
9. Obituary, *Gettysburg Times*, Thursday, October 26, 1972.
10. W. E. B. Griffin, *Battleground*, Book IV of *The Corps* series (New York: G.P. Putnam's Sons, 2008), 4.
11. Haynes, "Intelligence Failure in Korea," 124.
12. Kenneth J. Campbell, "Major General Charles A. Willoughby: A Mixed Performance," text of an unpublished paper, edited version published as "Major General Charles A. Willoughby: General MacArthur's G-2—A Biographic Sketch," *American Intelligence Journal* 18 no. 1 (1998), 14–15.

Bibliography

Primary Sources

Correspondence between CIA Deputy Director Allen Dulles and Major General Charles A. Willoughby, 1951–1952, Central Intelligence Agency online archives, Langley, VA.

John J. Muccio Oral History Interview, February 18, 1971, Harry S. Truman Library, National Archives and Records Administration, Washington, D.C.

Reports of General MacArthur: The Campaigns of MacArthur in the Pacific, two volumes (Washington, D.C.: U.S. Government Printing Office, 1966).

Carleton Swift interview, September 20, 1999, in Oral History Collection, Center for the Study of Intelligence, Central Intelligence Agency, Langley, VA.

Willoughby Papers, MacArthur Memorial Archives, Norfolk, Virginia.

Willoughby papers, MS-024, Special Collections/Musselman Library, Gettysburg College, Gettysburg, PA.

Secondary Sources

William H. Bartsch, *December 8, 1941: MacArthur's Pearl Harbor*. College Station, TX: Texas A&M University Press, 2012 (second printing).

Michael E. Bigelow, "Intelligence in the Philippines," in James P. Finley, ed., *U.S. Army Intelligence History: A Sourcebook*. Arizona: U.S. Army Intelligence Center and Fort Huachuca, Fort Huachuca, 1995; 196, 198.

Andrew J. Birtle, *U.S. Army Counterinsurgency and Contingency Operations Doctrine 1860–1941*. Washington, D.C.: Center of Military History, United State Army, 2009.

William B. Breuer, MacArthur's Undercover War: Spies, Saboteurs, Guerillas, and Secret Missions. Edison, NJ: Castle Books, 2005.

William B. Breuer, *Shadow Warriors: The Covert War in Korea*. New York: John Wiley & Sons, Inc., 1996.

Anthony Cave Brown, *The Last Hero: Wild Bill Donovan*. New York: Times Books, 1982.

Kenneth J. Campbell, "Major General Charles A. Willoughby: A Mixed Performance," text of an unpublished paper, accessed June 14, 2012.

George Constantinides, *Intelligence and Espionage: An Analytical Bibliography*. Boulder, CO: Westview Press, 1983.

Saul David, *Military Blunders: The How and Why of Military Failure*. New York: Carroll & Graf Publishers, 1998.

James P. Duffy, War at the End of the World: Douglas MacArthur and the Forgotten Fight for New Guinea, 1942–1945. New York: NAL Caliber, 2016.

Paul M. Edwards, To Acknowledge a War: The Korean War in American Memory. Westport, CT: Greenwood Press, 2000.

T. R. Fehrenbach, *This Kind of War: A Study in Unpreparedness*. New York: The MacMillan Co., 1963.

James P. Finley, "The Uncertain Oracle: Some Intelligence Failures Revisited," in James P. Finley, ed., *U.S. Army Military Intelligence History: A Sourcebook*. Arizona: U.S. Army Intelligence Centre and Fort Huachuca, 1995.

Robert F. Futrell, *The United States Air Force in Korea, 1950–1953*. Washington, D.C.: Office of Air Force History, 1981.

Harry A. Gaily, *MacArthur's Victory: The War in New Guinea, 1943–1944*. New York: Presidio Press, 2004.

Alexander L. George, *The Chinese Communist Army in Action: The Korean War and Its Aftermath*. New York: Columbia University Press, 1967.

Bryan R. Gibby, *The Will to Win: American Military Advisors in Korea, 1946–1953*. Tuscaloosa, AL: The University of Alabama Press, 2012.

Bryan R. Gibby, *Korean Showdown: National Policy and Military Strategy in a Limited War, 1951–1952*. Tuscaloosa, AL: The University of Alabama Press, 2021.

Joseph C. Goulden, *Korea: The Untold Story of the War*. New York: Times Books, 1982.

Samuel B. Griffiths, *The Chinese People's Liberation Army*. New York: McGraw-Hill Book Company, 1967.

Michael E. Haas, Colonel U.S. Air Force (Ret.), *In the Devil's Shadow: UN Special Operations During the Korean War*. Annapolis, MD: Naval Institute Press, 2000.

David Halberstam, *The Coldest Winter: America and the Korean War*. New York: Hyperion Books, 2007.

Jon Halliday and Bruce Cummings, *Korea: The Unknown War*. New York: Pantheon Books, 1988.

Blaine Harden, *King of Spies: The Dark Reign of America's Spymaster in Korea*. New York: Viking, 2017.

Meirion and Susie Harries, *Soldiers of the Sun: The Rise and Fall of the Imperial Japanese Army*. New York: Random House, 1991.

Francis H. Heller, ed., *The Korean War: A 25-Year Perspective*. Lawrence, Kansas: Regent's Press of Kansas, 1977.

Arthur Herman, *Douglas MacArthur: American Warrior*. New York: Random House, 2016.

Michael C. Hickey, *The Korean War: The West Confronts Communism*. Woodstock, NY: Overlook Press, 1999.

David W. Hogan, Jr., *U.S. Army Special Operations in World War II*. Washington, D.C.: Center for Military History, Department of the Army, 1992.

Thaddeus Holt, *The Deceivers: Allied Military Deception in the Second World War*. New York: Scribner, 2004.

Colonel Alison Ind, Allied Intelligence Bureau: Our Secret Weapon in the War Against Japan. New York: David McKay Company, Inc., 1958.

D. Clayton James, with Anne Sharp Wells, *Refighting the Last War: Command and Crisis in Korea, 1950–1953*. New York: The Free Press, 1993.

Richard Kolb, editor. *Battles of the Korean War: Americans Engage in Deadly Combat, 1950–1953*. Kansas City, Missouri: Veterans of Foreign Wars, 2003.

John F. Kreis, general editor, *Piercing the Fog: Intelligence and Army Air Forces Operations in World War II*. Washington, D.C.: Air Force History and Museums Program, Bolling Air Force Base, 1996.

Robert Leckie, *Conflict: The History of the Korean War, 1950–1953*. New York: G.P. Putnam's Sons, 1962.

Clark Lee and Richard Henschel, *Douglas MacArthur*. New York: Henry Holt and Company, 1952.

Ronald Lewin, *ULTRA Goes to War*. New York: Pocket Books, 1980.

Ronald Lewin, *The Other Ultra: Codes, Ciphers, and the Defeat of Japan*. London: Hutchinson and Co., 1982.

Peter Lowe, *The Origins of the Korean War*, Second Edition. London: Longman, 1986.

Douglas MacArthur, *Reminiscences*. New York: McGraw-Hill Book Co., 1964.

Callum A. MacDonald, *Korea: The War Before Vietnam*. New York: The Free Press, 1986.

John C. McManus, *Fire and Fortitude: The U.S. Army in the Pacific War, 1941–1943*. New York: Caliber, 2019.

James C. McNaughton, *Nisei Linguists: Japanese Americans in the Military Intelligence Service during World War II*. Washington, D.C.: Department of the Army, 2007.

William Manchester, *American Caesar: Douglas MacArthur, 1880–1964*. New York: Dell Publishing Co., Inc., 1978.

Richard E. Matthews, "Task Force Smith: An Intelligence Failure," U.S. Army Command and General Staff monograph, December 14, 1995, abstract.

Williamson Murray and Allan R. Millett, *A War to Be Won: Fighting the Second World War*. Cambridge, MA: The Belknap Press of Harvard University Press, 2000.

Clarke Newlon, *The Fighting Douglas MacArthur*. New York: Dodd, Mead and Co., 1965.

Joseph R. Owen, *Colder Than Hell: A Marine Rifle Company at Chosin Reservoir*. Bluejacket Books: Naval Institute Press, Annapolis, MD, 2000.

Curtis Peebles, *Twilight Warriors: Covert Air Operations Against the USSR*. Annapolis, MD: Naval Institute Press, 2005.

Carol Morriss Petillo, *Douglas MacArthur: The Philippine Years*. Bloomington, Indiana: Indiana University Press, 1981.

Chapman Pincher, *Too Secret Too Long*. New York: St. Martin's Press, 1984.

John Prados, *Combined Fleet Decoded: The Secret History of American Intelligence and the Japanese Navy in World War II*. New York: Random House, 1995.

Gordon Prange, *Target Tokyo: The Story of the Sorge Spy Ring*. New York: McGraw-Hill Book Co., 1984.

Reader's Digest Illustrated Story of World War II (Pleasantville, NY: 1969).

Stanley Sandler, "Select Operations of the Central Intelligence Agency During the Korean War," unpublished manuscript, n.d.

Stanley Sandler, *The Korean War: No Victors, No Vanquished*. Lexington, KY: The University Press of Kentucky, 1999.

Michael Schaller, *Douglas MacArthur: The Far Eastern General*. New York: Oxford University Press, 1989.

James F. Schnabel, "Policy and Direction: The First Year," Vol. III of *United States Army in the Korean War*. Washington, D.C.: U.S. Army Center of Military History, 1992.

John F. Shortal, *Forged by Fire: General Robert L. Eichelberger and the Pacific War*. Columbia, S.C.: University of South Carolina Press, 1987.

Bradley F. Smith, *The ULTRA-MAGIC Deals and the Most Secret Special Relationship, 1940–1946*. Novato, CA: Presidio Press, 1992.

Ronald H. Spector, *Eagle Against the Sun: The American War with Japan*. New York: Vintage Books, 1985.

Russell Spur, *Enter the Dragon: China's Undeclared War Against the U.S. in Korea, 1950–51*. New York: Newmarket Press, 1988.

Richard W. Stewart, *The Korean War: The Chinese Intervention, 3 November 1950–24 January 1951*. Washington, D.C.: U.S. Army Center of Military History, n.d.

I. F. Stone, *The Hidden History of the Korean War*. New York: Monthly Review Press, 1952.

William Stueck, *The Korean War: An International History*. Princeton, NJ: Princeton University Press, 1995.

Stephen R. Taafe, *MacArthur's Jungle War: The 1944 New Guinea Campaign*. Lawrence, KS: University Press of Kansas, 1998.

Richard Thornton, *Odd Man Out: Truman, Stalin, Mao, and the Origins of the Cold War*. Washington, D.C.: Brassey's, 2000.

Elliott R. Thorpe, Brigadier General, USA (ret.), *East Wind, Rain: The Intimate Account of an Intelligence Officer in the Pacific, 1939–1949*. Boston: Gambit Incorporated, 1969.

John Toland, *But Not in Shame: The Six Months After Pearl Harbor*. New York: Random House, 1961.

John Toland, *In Mortal Combat: Korea, 1950–1953*. New York: William Morrow & Co., 1991.

Spencer C. Tucker, ed., *Encyclopedia of the Korean War: A Political, Social, and Military History, Vol. II*. Santa Barbara, CA: ABC-Clio, 2000.

Dennis D. Wainstock, *Truman, MacArthur and the Korean War*. Westport, CT: Greenwood Press, 1999.

Douglas Waller, *Wild Bill Donovan: The Spymaster Who Created the OSS and Modern American Espionage*. New York: Free Press, 2011.

William J. Webb, *The Korean War: The Outbreak, 27 June–15 September 1950* (pamphlet). Washington, D.C.: The U.S. Army Center of Military History, n.d.

Stanley Weintraub, *MacArthur's War: Korea and the Undoing of an American Hero*. New York: The Free Press, 2000.

Richard Whelan, *Drawing the Line: The Korean War, 1950–1953*. Boston: Little, Brown and Co., 1990.

Maochun Yu, *OSS in China: Prelude to Cold War*. New Haven: Yale University Press, 1996.

Articles, Case Studies, and Online Materials

"Atoms for Peace" materials, Eisenhower Library, Abilene, Kansas, available at https://www.eisenhowerlibrary.gov/research/online-documents/atoms-peace.

Matthew Aid, "American COMINT in the Korean War (Part II): From the Chinese Intervention to the Armistice," 14–49.

Mark E. Bennett, Jr., "Perceptions of Victory: Differing Views of Success by Nations and Echelons at the Chosin Reservoir," www.militaryhistoryonline.com.

Dr. Greg Bradsher, "From Rabaul to Stack 190: The Travels of a Famous Japanese Army Publication," August 10, 2012, available at https://text-message.blogs.archives.gov/2012/08/10/from-rabaul-to-stack-190-the-travels-of-a-famous-japanese-army-publication/.

Bob Brent, "On the Cover: Brig-General C. A. Willoughby," *Gettysburg College Bulletin*, Vol. XXXIII, No. 2, February 1943.

Kenneth J. Campbell, "Major General Charles A. Willoughby: General MacArthur's G-2—A Biographic Sketch," *American Intelligence Journal 18*, no. 1/2 (1998).

Adam Cathcart and Charles Kraus, "The Bonds of Brotherhood: New Evidence on Sino-North Korean Exchanges, 1950–1954," *Journal of Cold War Studies*, Vol. 13, No. 3, Summer 2011.

Ed Drea, "A Very Savage Operation," *World War II*, September 2002.

Douglas Ford, "Dismantling the 'Lesser Men' and 'Supermen' Myths: U.S. Intelligence on the Imperial Japanese Army after the Fall of the Philippines, Winter 1942 to Spring 1943," *Intelligence and National Security*, Vol. 24, No. 4, August 2009, 542–573.

Federal Times, "Allen Carves Out Prominent Intelligence Role for DHS," *federaltimes.com*, September 4, 2006.

Foreign Denial and Deception Committee, "The Chinese Invasion of Korea, October 1950 (A): An Intelligence Community Case Study."

Herbert A. Friedman, SGM (Ret.), "The American PSYOP Organization During the Korean War," 2006. www.psywarrior.com/KoreaPSYOPHist.html.

D. M. Giangreco, "Casualty Projections for the U.S. Invasions of Japan, 1945–1946: Planning and Policy Implications," *Journal of Military History*, 61 (July 1997), 521–582.

M. P. Hartzell, "Xi Chapter at Gettysburg Reaches 100," reprinted from *The Phi Gamma Delta*, Volume 80, Number 4, March 1958, 226–234.

Michael H. Hunt, "Beijing and the Korean Crisis, June 1950–June 1951," *Political Science Quarterly*, Vol. 107, No. 3 (Autumn 1992), 453–478.

Mayumi Itoh, "U.S. Occupation and Hatoyama Ichiro's Purge," *Asian Studies on the Pacific Coast* electronic journal, Vol. 1 (2001–2002).

Haile H. Jaekel, "The End of WWII," 1996, unpublished article available at https://ussslcca25.com/jaekel03.htm.

Frank Kluckhohn, "Heidelberg to Madrid—The Story of General Willoughby," *The Reporter* (New York Journal), August 19, 1952.

Stephen Marrin, "Preventing Intelligence Failures by Learning from the Past," *International Journal of Intelligence and Counterintelligence*, Vol. 17, No. 4, Winter 2004–2005.

James I. Matray, "Revisiting Korea: Exposing Myths of the Forgotten War, Part 2," *Prologue*, Summer 2002, Vol. 34, No. 2.

Stephen C. Mercado, reviewer, *KLO ui Hangukchon Pisa (Secret History of the KLO in the Korean War)* (Seoul: Jisungsa, 2005) by Yi Chang-gon, in *"Studies in Intelligence,"* Vol. 56, No. 1 (March 2012).

Relman Moran, "MacArthur's Bold Flight to Korean Warfront Signals U.N. Offense," *The Register-News*, Mt. Vernon, Illinois, November 24, 1950.

"New Evidence of Japan's Germ Warfare in WWII Found," China View, accessed 2012, www. chinaview.cn.

Carl A. Posey, "How the Korean War Almost Went Nuclear,*" Air and Space Magazine*, July 2015, 1–6.

Bertrand M. Roehner, "Relations Between Allied Forces and the Population of Japan," *Occupation of Japan*, 2009.

P. K. Rose, "Two Strategic Intelligence Mistakes in Korea, 1950, *Studies in Intelligence*, Central Intelligence Agency, Fall/Winter 2001.

Bruce H. Siemon, "The Army's Historical Coverage of Operation JOINT ENDEAVOR," *Army History*, PB-20-97-2 (No. 41), Washington, D.C., Spring 1997.

Garrett Underhill and Ronald Schiller, "The Tragedy of the U.S. Army," *Look* magazine, Vol. 15, No. 4, February 13, 1951.

Willoughby obituary, *Gettysburg Times*, Thursday, October 26, 1972.

Dr. Qiang Zhai, "China and the Korean War," in *Understanding & Remembering, A Compendium of the 50th Anniversary Korean War International Historical Symposium,* June 26–27 2002, Old Dominion University, Norfolk, VA (Norfolk, VA: General Douglas MacArthur Foundation, 2003).

U.S. Army Center for Military History, "Intelligence and Counterintelligence Problems During the Korean Conflict: Chapter V, Theater Level Collection Problems," available at https://history.army. mil/documents/Korea/intkor/intkor.htm.

U.S. Army Center for Military History, "Statistical Data on Strength and Casualties for Korean War and Vietnam" (Historical Manuscripts Collection (HMC), Office of the Chief of Military History, November 17, 1965) available at https://www.army.mil/cmh-pg/documents/237ADN.htm.

Theses and Dissertations

Paul T. Berquist, "Organizational Leadership in Crisis: The 31st Regimental Combat Team at Chosin Reservoir, Korea, 24 November–2 December 1950," Master's Thesis, U.S. Army Command and General Staff College, Ft. Leavenworth, KS, June 16, 2007, abstract.

August W. Bremer, Jr., USA, "Chinese Communist Intervention in the Korean War: Miscalculation or Provocation? A Study of the Failure to Predict the Chinese Communist Intervention in the Korean War, November 1950," U.S. Army Command and General Staff College, Master's thesis, 1987, abstract.

Justin M. Haynes, "Intelligence Failure in Korea: Major General Charles A. Willoughby's Role in the United Nations' Command's Defeat in November, 1950," Master's thesis, U.S. Army Command and General Staff College, June, 2009, abstract.

Peter G. Knight, "MacArthur's Eyes: Reassessing Military Intelligence Operations in the Forgotten War, June 1950–April 1951," Master's thesis, Ohio State University, 2004, abstract.

Wanli Hu, "Mao's American Strategy and the Korean War," University of Massachusetts Amherst, 2004, dissertation abstract.

Index